This Orient Isle

JERRY BROTTON

This Orient Isle

*Elizabethan England and
the Islamic World*

ALLEN LANE
an imprint of
PENGUIN BOOKS

ALLEN LANE

UK | USA | Canada | Ireland | Australia
India | New Zealand | South Africa

Allen Lane is part of the Penguin Random House group of companies
whose addresses can be found at global.penguinrandomhouse.com.

Penguin
Random House
UK

First published 2016
001

Copyright © Jerry Brotton, 2016

The moral right of the author has been asserted

Set in 10.5/14 pt Sabon LT Std
Typeset by Jouve (UK), Milton Keynes
Printed in Great Britain by Clays Ltd, St Ives plc

A CIP catalogue record for this book is available from the British Library

ISBN: 978-0-241-00402-9

MIX
Paper from
responsible sources
FSC   FSC® C018179
www.fsc.org

Penguin Random House is committed to a
sustainable future for our business, our readers
and our planet. This book is made from Forest
Stewardship Council® certified paper.

For my wife, Charlotte

This royal throne of kings, this sceptred isle,
This earth of majesty, this seat of Mars,
This other Eden, demi-paradise,
This fortress built by Nature for herself
Against infection and the hand of war,
This happy breed of men, this little world,
This precious stone set in the silver sea,
Which serves it in the office of a wall,
Or as a moat defensive to a house
Against the envy of less happier lands;
This blessèd plot, this earth, this realm, this England

Shakespeare, Richard II, 2.1.40–50

Contents

List of Illustrations

Elizabethan England and the Islamic world *c.* 1570–1603

N

ATLANTIC
OCEAN

NORWAY

SWEDEN

North Sea

ENGLAND

DENMARK

Lübeck

POLAND-
LITHUANIA

Hardwick

Great Yarmouth

Winchester

London

Antwerp

Wittenberg

Lvov•

Plymouth

Southampton

Brussels

HOLY ROMAN

•Prague

Paris•

EMPIRE

Vienna•

FRANCE

Orléans•

Augsburg•

Basel•

Milan•

Venice•

WALL

Ferrara•

Belgrade•

Florence•

O T T

PORTUGAL

Lisbon•

Madrid•

Rome•

Naples•

SPAIN

•Seville

Lepanto•

Cadiz•

•Granada

Zante•

Tangier•

Gibraltar

Algiers•

Sicily

El Ksar el-Kebir•

Arzila•

Tunis•

Casablanca•

•Fez

Malta•

Marrakesh•

•Agadir

MOROCCAN
SULTANATE

O T T O M A N   E M

Tripoli•

Mediterranean

Introduction

The Ambassador Arrives

It is midday on Yawm al-Jum'a, Jumada 'l-Ula. According to the Muslim lunar calendar it is 1009 years since the Hijra, the emigration of the Prophet Muhammad from Mecca to Medina. In the tiltyard of London's Whitehall Palace, on the site of today's Horse Guards Parade, stands a tall, dark, bearded man. He is instantly distinguished from the crowd by his long black robe (or *thawb*), bright white linen turban and the huge, richly decorated steel scimitar, a Maghreb *nimcha*, which hangs from his waist. His appearance and demeanour mark him out as a traveller of obvious stature, but also as an exotic and extravagant stranger regarded with awe by many of those around him. Abd al-Wahid bin Masoud bin Muhammad al-Annuri, the forty-two-year-old Moroccan envoy to the court of Queen Elizabeth I, is halfway through his six-month stay in London. He is there as ambassador of the Moroccan ruler, Mulay Ahmed al-Mansur, with orders to conclude an Anglo-Moroccan alliance that would unite English Protestants and Moroccan Muslims against their common enemy: Catholic Spain.

Al-Annuri takes his place beneath a canopy specially constructed for him at one end of the yard, along with his Moroccan retinue. They are watching a jousting match between some of England's most famous lords and knights, who enter the lists in pairs on horseback or pageant cars to the blare of trumpets. Some are dressed in armour, others in elaborate disguises, accompanied by attendants reciting songs and verse. Al-Annuri and his entourage are surrounded by thousands of Londoners, 'so great an assembly of people', wrote the London chronicler John Stow, 'as the like hath not been seen in that place before'.[1] Each has paid twelve pence to witness one of the great

I

occasions in the Elizabethan calendar, the Accession Day Tilts, the annual celebration commemorating the day on which Queen Elizabeth I succeeded her Catholic sister, Mary Tudor, to the English throne. If he looks up, al-Annuri can glimpse the queen and her ladies watching the entertainment from the windows of one of the palace's galleries. From this distance he cannot discern her blackened teeth which the German traveller Paul Hentzner had observed two years earlier, 'a defect', he wrote, which 'the English seem subject to, from their great use of sugar', a condiment that the queen had been importing from Morocco since the beginning of her reign.[2] But he probably can see the French ambassador, Monsieur de Boissie, and his Russian counterpart, Grigorii Mikulin, both honoured with seats next to Elizabeth. In contrast to their elevated position, al-Annuri and his followers are standing among the queen's subjects. We know what al-Annuri looked like, because in the autumn of 1600 the Moroccan ambassador sat for his portrait somewhere in London. Who commissioned and painted the picture remains a mystery, but it offers a tantalizing glimpse of its subject and his presence in the city. It is remarkable not only as the earliest surviving portrait of a Muslim painted from life in England, but also – considering the religion's official injunction against figurative images – simply because it depicts a Sunni Muslim.

Elizabeth's loyal subjects could have told al-Annuri that according to their Julian Christian calendar the date was 17 November 1600, exactly forty-two years since Elizabeth came to the throne in 1558, the year in which the Moroccan ambassador was born, and which he would have known as 966–967 AH in the Islamic calendar. Each year Elizabeth celebrated 17 November with a carefully staged ceremonial entrance into London, returning from her summer residence at Windsor, Richmond or Hampton Court. On this occasion she had arrived outside Chelsea on 14 November, where she was met by the lord mayor and 500 aldermen and citizens on horseback, wearing velvet coats and gold chains, each one attended by two retainers carrying torches as they led the queen towards her palace in Westminster. Across the kingdom the day was marked as a national festival of sermons, public feasts, bell ringing, prayers and bonfires designed to celebrate the rule of the Virgin Queen. The celebrations replaced the Catholic feast day of St Hugh of Lincoln with the Protestant cult of Elizabeth.

The plans for the Tilts in 1600 were more ambitious than ever. Intended to show a kingdom at domestic peace, they were meant to be admired by Elizabeth's powerful French, Russian and Moroccan allies. The queen had outlived her adversary, the Spanish king Philip II, who had died two years earlier, and although England was still officially at war with Spain, the threat of invasion had receded. But behind the tiltyard's glittering façade and noisy display, the seemingly unalterable edifice of more than four decades of Elizabethan rule was starting to crumble. Elizabeth was growing old. Her refusal to marry or nominate a male heir left the kingdom confronting an imminent crisis of political succession. Even worse, the queen was facing a political challenge from a virile young male pretender to her throne, her recently disaffected favourite, Robert Devereux, 2nd Earl of Essex. Handsome, charismatic, politically ambitious and a champion of militant Protestantism, Essex was a strong advocate of war against Spain, a policy to which the naturally cautious Elizabeth did not want to commit herself. He had fallen from favour after leading a disastrous military campaign to try to crush Catholic rebellion in Ireland in the summer of 1599. Returning to London without permission in September of that year, he was put on trial the following June for dereliction of duty, found guilty and placed under house arrest. Although he had appeared for years at the Accession Day Tilts as the queen's champion, in November 1600 he was noticeably absent from the festivities, and was in fact fortifying Essex House on the Strand, just a few hundred yards from the celebrations in Whitehall, preparing to lead an uprising against his sovereign.

Even as rumours of a coup swept London, Elizabeth and her advisers were busy hosting al-Annuri in readiness for an alliance with Morocco that promised to cast the upstart earl into political oblivion. The Moroccan ambassador's arrival had been anticipated throughout the spring of 1600, as English and Moroccan diplomats negotiated the terms of his mission. In late June that year a sixteen-man Moroccan delegation, together with a group of Dutch prisoners that Elizabeth had requested be released as a precondition for talks, left Morocco on board the English ship the *Eagle*. As they sailed northwards, English spies were writing to Queen Elizabeth's secretary of state Robert Cecil updating him on the news that a Spanish warship had tried to intercept the *Eagle*, and adding that 'the Spaniards here reported that our queen (whom the Lord long preserve!) was dead'.[3] On 8 August the *Eagle* docked in Dover where representatives of the Barbary Company trading in Morocco met al-Annuri and conveyed his party to London. Once there Essex's great political rival, Robert Cecil, entrusted the Moroccan's care to Thomas Gerard, a prominent Staffordshire landowner and member of Parliament. It was a shrewd move on Cecil's part. Gerard had been a close friend and supporter of Essex, but following the earl's return from Ireland had seen that Essex's star was on the wane and switched his political allegiance. Acting as al-Annuri's escort seemed like an effective way to integrate himself into Cecil's faction. On 11 August Gerard wrote to Cecil to confirm that he had met al-Annuri and had arranged for him and his embassy to stay in Alderman Anthony Radcliffe's house on the Strand near the Royal Exchange. As a former London sheriff and master of the Guild of Merchant Taylors, Radcliffe was a good choice to host the Moroccan delegation and keep them in touch with London's merchant community. On 15 August the Moroccans landed at Tower Wharf and were taken in four coaches to Radcliffe's house. However, Gerard reported that not everyone seemed pleased with the embassy's arrival. Some observers worried that 'they are very strangely attired and behavioured'.[4] Gerard had approached London's Barbary merchants to pay 'for the ambassador's diet, but they all plead poverty, and except her majesty discharge it, it will rest upon himself'. In an attempt to avoid drawing undue attention to their presence, the delegation were to be accommodated 'without scandal, and for that purpose they are lodged in a house apart, where they feed alone'.[5] Five days later they rode through Cheapside to Westminster, crossed over to Lambeth by boat, then took the 10-mile coach ride to Nonsuch Palace in Surrey, and an audience with the queen.

One eyewitness account of al-Annuri's reception described the elaborate 'royal preparation, in the manner of his receiving'. The court prepared 'rich hangings and furniture sent for from Hampton Court; the guard very strong, in their rich coats; the pensioners [royal bodyguards] with their axes; the lords of the Order [of the Garter] with their collars; a full court of lords and ladies'. Al-Annuri 'passed through a guard of halberds to the council chamber, where he rested;

he was brought to the presence, so to the privy chamber, and so to the gallery; where her Majesty sat at the further end in very great state, and gave them audience'.[6] The formalities dispensed with, the Moroccan and English delegations began discussing the business in hand. One wonders what the handsome Moroccan diplomat made of the sixty-seven-year-old English monarch – very old by the standards of the age – during their audience. If part of his mission was to assess the commercial impact of Moroccan sugar on the English economy, he would see it plainly enough if Elizabeth smiled.

Their conversation, held in Spanish, translated for the queen by the diplomat and courtier Sir Lewis Lewkenor, ostensibly dealt with commercial relations between the two crowns, but as one of the English courtiers reported, 'ere they departed, the interpreter of the embassy spoke Italian, and desired to deliver some thing in private, which her majesty granted'.[7] No definitive record remains of what they discussed, but one of the English diplomats present wrote that at the end of al-Annuri's reception 'her majesty for a further grace to the [Dutch] States Agent, caused him to be present, and so she received [the nine Dutch prisoners] of the barbarian with one hand, she gave them to him with another'.[8] Elizabeth was using the captives' release to show off to the watching Dutch her power over Morocco and her largesse in releasing fellow Protestants into the hands of her grateful Protestant allies. Another observer, the English merchant Rowland Whyte, offered a different interpretation of the meeting. Whyte noted, 'It is given out that they come for her majesty's letters to the Turk, to whom a brother of this king of Barbary is fled, to complain against him.'[9] One perspective stressed England's anti-Catholic alliance with the Dutch and the Moors; the other emphasized Elizabeth's alliance with the Muslim Turks. Whatever was actually said in whichever tongue at the appropriately named Nonsuch, many present would have understood this as a meeting of three of Catholic Spain's greatest political and theological enemies, and that the real agenda went far beyond trade agreements or diplomatic complaints.

Following the audience at Nonsuch the Moroccan delegation returned to their central London lodgings without any clear resolution to their mission. But over the next few months many at Elizabeth's court believed that what at first appeared to be just another trade delegation – though from an exotic part of the world – was actually a secret attempt to initiate both an Anglo-Moroccan military alliance with plans to invade Spain and a concerted attack on al-Mansur's other great enemy in North Africa, the Ottomans. If concluded, such an alliance would set Christian against Christian, and Muslim against Muslim, based on a Sunni–Protestant pact.

On 10 September a second audience was arranged, this time at Oatlands Palace in Surrey. Elizabeth's official Rowland Whyte wrote of this meeting that what al-Annuri 'delivered was in private to the queen; his business hath been very secretly handled, which is not yet come to light; it is supposed that he makes good offers to her majesty, if she will be pleased to aid him with shipping, fit for his ports, to conduct in safety some treasure he hath by mines in part of the Indies conquered by him'.[10] There was no truth whatsoever in Whyte's claims that the Moroccans were trying to use Elizabeth to smuggle New World treasure across the Atlantic, but his garbled report bore some relationship to what transpired.

The proposal that al-Annuri had been ordered by al-Mansur to submit to Elizabeth at Oatlands was in fact one of the most audacious in the history of Anglo-Islamic relations. In a memorandum dated 13 September al-Annuri explained that he was offering a formal military alliance that would involve the English and Moroccan fleets combining to attack Spain. Having come to London 'to speak in secret to her serene majesty' about the 'the King of Spain's perfidious ways and dealings, and his incessant treachery', al-Annuri argued that it would 'be an act of compassion and humanity for the benefit of all mankind if her serene majesty should embrace the perpetual friendship between her and the serene emperor his master [al-Mansur] and join forces against the King of Spain, their common foe and enemy'. Together Elizabeth and al-Mansur would invade Spain as part of the Moroccans' dream of a Muslim reconquest of Al-Andalus (the mainland of Spain that had been under Muslim rule for so many centuries): 'he will take the war to Spain', wrote al-Annuri,

> since our land is closer. Moreover, we have a large cavalry and infantry and all manner of munitions, as well as gunpowder and everything else needed to wage war, and plenty of wheat and other provisions. We

also have forests with trees for shipbuilding, and iron to fit them, pursuant to the art of war. And should Her Serene Majesty capture any strongholds or cities in Spain that are close to us and which she wishes to supply with soldiers, munitions or money, the Emperor his master shall see to all this, because the Emperor will accede with great love to whatever Her Serene Majesty should ask of him, bound by the ancient friendship between them.[11]

But an attack on Spain was not all that al-Mansur proposed. Al-Annuri was instructed also to suggest an even more audacious joint campaign against Spain's colonies in the Americas to the west and in the Far East:

> If the two Serene Majesties should forge this alliance, they could also wrest the East and West Indies from the Spanish, thus strengthening both Her Serene Majesty and the Emperor and weakening the King of Spain, because his strength as King of Spain comes solely from his control of the Indies.
>
> The Emperor would meet the needs of Her Serene Majesty's fleet in terms of wheat, munitions, gunpowder and provisions, as well as infantry and money. He would be best placed to supply the infantry because his people would be better accustomed to the heat of the Indies. Indeed, His Majesty the Emperor has conquered a very powerful kingdom on the River Niger in Guinea in which he has won land spanning ninety days' march and taken eighty-six thousand towns and cities and supplied them with all they need, as well as soldiers and munitions; and his people have borne the great heat of the hot climate there.[12]

Al-Mansur's relations with Elizabeth now led him to believe he could rid the world of Catholic Spain altogether. It seems ridiculously far-fetched, but the response of Elizabeth's advisers suggests that any proposal from a Muslim ruler that threatened to open up a new front against the Spanish was given serious consideration.

What motivated these proposals, and how Elizabethan England had become so close in its diplomatic, commercial and military policies to the Moroccan Sa'adian dynasty and many other Muslim powers, is the subject of this book. For reasons that were unique to

Elizabeth's forty-five-year reign, including her dramatic excommunication from the Roman Catholic Church by Pope Pius V in 1570, Protestant England established a relationship with a variety of Islamic kingdoms that played a crucial role in how English men and women came to understand their place in the sixteenth-century world. These connections affected how Elizabethans travelled and conducted business, what they ate, how they dressed and furnished their homes, how they understood religion, and how they acted on a stage that was graced with some of the world's finest playwrights, including Shakespeare and Marlowe.

Tudor fascination with the Islamic world went back at least as far as the reign of Elizabeth's father, Henry VIII. He and his court enjoyed wearing Ottoman clothing, with the king often described as appearing at festivities 'appareled after Turkey fashion', dressed in silk and velvet, and sporting a turban and a scimitar, adopting an Ottoman style that is now regarded as characteristically 'Tudor'.[13] As well as rich silk, velvet and other fabrics, Tudor merchants imported exotic commodities from Islamic lands that included cotton, rhubarb, currants, sweet wines and intricate textiles, as well as the Moroccan sugar that Elizabeth consumed in such copious quantities. As early as the 1550s Englishmen were doing business in Muslim countries as far apart as Morocco and Syria, travelling by land and sea, exchanging ideas and beliefs with Muslims from different social groups and religious denominations. By the end of Elizabeth's reign thousands of her subjects were to be found in the Islamic world, some working in trade and diplomacy, others as pirates, and many forced to convert and live as slaves throughout North Africa and the eastern Mediterranean. As Elizabethans left England to travel in the east, they soon returned with new commodities and experiences from encounters with Muslims. Few prosperous Elizabethan homes were without 'Turkey carpets', elaborately knotted floor and wall coverings with Islamic motifs made by Anatolian, Egyptian, Syrian or Persian weavers, not to mention rugs, silken quilts and embroidered tapestries. Even the language of sixteenth-century England was replete with neologisms drawn from commercial exchanges with Islamic countries. 'Sugar', 'candy', 'crimson' (from the Turkish *kirmiz*), 'turquoise' (or 'Turkey stone'), 'indigo' and 'tulip' (from the Turkish pronunciation of Persian *dulband*, or 'turban'), even 'zero' all entered the language and took on their modern associations during this period, primarily thanks to the effects of Anglo-Islamic trade.[14]

Despite the extensive nature of such exchanges, Shakespeare, his contemporaries and their queen would not even have recognized the term 'Muslim'. It was first used in English in 1615, defined as 'one that is instructed in the belief of the Mohammetanes'.[15] The first mention in English of 'Islam' as a religious belief system appears in 1625 when the travel writer Samuel Purchas quoted a Javanese prince saying that the 'religion of Islam doth not agree with the Christian Religion'.[16] In sixteenth-century England, when understanding of the theological dimension of Islam was sketchy and contradictory, various terms were used to describe its followers: 'Mahometans', 'Ottomites', 'Saracens', 'Persians', 'Moors', 'Pagans' or 'Turks' – the latter often used as a catch-all term for anyone who would be recognized today as a Muslim. Such terms embraced a range of beliefs and assumptions, from horror and disgust to wonder and curiosity. At virtually no point was there an attempt to understand Islam on its own theological terms; instead throughout the Tudor period a powerful set of misrepresentations, misconceptions and misunderstandings developed which defined relations between the two faiths. The amicable relationship that prospered briefly under Elizabeth arose not from natural amity and tolerance, but from expediency and *realpolitik*; yet it gave rise to a variety of unintended consequences, encounters and transactions between Muslims and English Protestants that have been largely ignored in most histories of the Elizabethan era.

Such relations, as we shall see, drew the interest of writers, from theologians and politicians to travellers and dramatists. On the same day that al-Annuri watched Elizabeth's Accession Day festivities, the Queen's printers published *A Geographical Historie of Africa, written in Arabicke and Italian by Iohn Leo a More, borne in Granada, and brought vp in Barbarie*, by the traveller and periodical writer John Pory. The 'More', or Moroccan, of Pory's title was better known to his Christian readership as Leo Africanus, though his given name was al-Hasan ibn Muhammad ibn Ahmad al-Wazzan, a Muslim born in Granada who grew up in Fez before being captured by

Christian forces while crossing the Mediterranean in 1518. Al-Wazzan converted to Catholicism and wrote his description of Africa in Rome in the 1520s; it was subsequently published in Latin, Italian and French before Pory translated it into English. Dedicating the book to Robert Cecil, Pory felt that his effort was particularly timely, 'in that the Moroccan ambassador (whose king's dominions are here most amply and particularly described) hath so lately treated with your honour concerning matters of state'.[17] Pory's book was a celebration of Elizabeth's Accession Day, but it also provided the queen's ministers with crucial information on an African Muslim ally with which they might be about to ratify a formal alliance.

Just three years later, Richard Knolles, a grammar school teacher from Kent, published a monumental, 1,200-page survey, *The General Historie of the Turkes, from the first beginning of that Nation to the rising of the Othoman Familie*, the first chronicle of the Ottoman Empire written in English. Drawing on generations of continental European books describing the rise of the Turks in minute detail, Knolles's book became the standard authority on the Ottomans, whom he described as 'the glorious empire of the Turks, the present terror of the world'.[18] A few months before he died in Greece in 1824 while fighting the Turks, Lord Byron claimed that Knolles's 'Turkish history was one of the first books that gave me pleasure when I was a child; and I believe it had much influence on my subsequent wishes to visit the Levant and gave, perhaps, the oriental colouring which is observed in my poetry'.[19] It even impressed Samuel Johnson 150 years after its publication. Writing in the *Rambler* in 1751 on the subject of English historians, Johnson claimed that 'none of our writers can, in my opinion, justly contest the superiority of Knolles, who, in his history of the Turks, has displayed all the excellencies that narration can admit'. But although he admired Knolles's style, Johnson displayed typical Georgian indifference to the Islamic world by ascribing Knolles's relative obscurity to his subject matter. 'Nothing could have sunk this author in obscurity', he argued,

> but the remoteness and barbarity of the people, whose story he relates . . . The nation which produced this great historian, has the grief of seeing his genius employed upon a foreign and uninteresting subject;

and that writer who might have secured perpetuity to his name, by a history of his own country, has exposed himself to the danger of oblivion, by recounting enterprises and revolutions, of which none desire to be informed.[20]

By the eighteenth century the Muslim world may have become remote and fantastical even to someone as informed as Johnson, but this was not how many Elizabethans saw it. Alongside the appetite for books describing the North African Muslim world of al-Annuri and the Ottoman Empire, London's dramatists also saw the potential of putting Moors, Turks and Persians on to the Elizabethan stage. In early August 1601, six months after al-Annuri's departure from London, the great theatrical impresario Philip Henslowe, founder of some of the city's most popular open-air theatres, recorded in his diary that he had paid ten shillings and four pence for a new play (or possibly an old revival) about the Prophet Muhammad that included 'apparel for Mahewmet [Muhammad]', and 'the making of crowns and other things for Mahewmet'. Three weeks later he paid forty shillings to the actor Edward Alleyn for 'the book of Mahemett' (a reference to the Muhammad play, since lost, rather than to the Qur'an). Alleyn was one of the Elizabethan stage's greatest actors, famed for his grand, declamatory style. He portrayed most of Christopher Marlowe's lead characters, including the Scythian shepherd Tamburlaine, who, at the climax of the second part of Marlowe's wildly popular eponymous play written in 1587, curses Muhammad and burns the Qur'an on stage (an act which was notoriously censored when the play was performed at London's Barbican Theatre in 2005 following the London bombings on 7 July of that year). Throughout the 1590s Henslowe's diary contains numerous references to props, apparel and payments received relating to plays that featured and even named 'Mohammed', including an item listed on March 1598 as 'old Mahemetes head'. In 1600 these dramatic fantasies became a reality, as Londoners who had spent more than a decade watching plays filled with raging Turks and duplicitous Moors sporting turbans and brandishing scimitars were now able to see real-life Muslims like al-Annuri moving around London with their entourages, conducting diplomacy and doing business at the highest levels of Elizabethan society. They could even be seen openly practising their religion, with some commentators noting that al-Annuri and his retinue 'turn their faces eastward when they kill any thing; they use beads, and pray to saints'.[21]

Between 1579 and 1624 props and apparel like those bought and sold by Henslowe featured in more than sixty Elizabethan and Jacobean plays with identifiably Islamic characters, themes or settings, many of which mentioned the Qur'an, and some like Marlowe's brought it on stage.[22] Most of these plays have since fallen into obscurity, portraying something that later generations would regard as 'foreign and uninteresting', to use Dr Johnson's phrase. But at least one of those plays has retained an enduring hold on the popular imagination. Some time towards the end of 1601, a few months after al-Annuri's return to Barbary, William Shakespeare began *The Tragedy of Othello, the Moor of Venice*. Produced at the height of his dramatic powers, *Othello* stands alongside Shakespeare's other great tragedies, *Hamlet*, *Macbeth* and *King Lear*, all written during an unprecedented period of intense creativity stretching from 1599 (when he began *Hamlet*) to 1606 (generally agreed to be the year in which *Macbeth* and *King Lear* were written). In contrast to these other plays, with their northern European settings, *Othello* is set in the Mediterranean world and is a largely sympathetic portrayal of the tragic downfall of a soldier from North Africa destroyed by his adopted Christian community. Looking again at al-Annuri's portrait, and retracing his movements across London in 1600–1601, it is possible to discern some of the local raw material on which Shakespeare may have drawn for his portrayal of the 'noble Moor'. Like al-Annuri, Othello is simultaneously admired and feared by his Christian hosts. He is cultivated as a military asset, yet, like al-Annuri, is denigrated as an outsider. These two men, one real, the other fictional, move into a Christian world that first embraces but eventually rejects and expels them. Othello is called 'an extravagant and wheeling stranger | Of here and everywhere',[23] much like al-Annuri. In Shakespeare's play the Moor's obscure origins and paradoxical identity are lost in his contradictory 'traveller's history'.[24] In a striking parallel with al-Annuri, Othello is also described as seeming to move between paganism, Islam and Christianity, of 'being taken by the insolent foe' – presumably the Ottoman Turks – then 'sold to slavery' before his eventual 'redemption' by Christians.[25]

In less than half a century of Elizabeth's rule Protestant England came closer to Islam than at any other time in its history until today. In early 1601, members of the Moroccan and English courts responsible for al-Annuri's embassy aspired to a new chapter in Anglo-Islamic relations. An agreement to bind together Elizabethan England and the Sa'adian dynasty of Morocco seemed a real possibility, with Spain as the common enemy. Antagonism between Christianity and Islam stretched right back beyond the Crusades to the Muslim invasions of Europe in the early eighth century, but the more recent split between Catholics and Protestants at the Reformation had complicated the simple division between the two faiths, allowing an isolated ruler like Elizabeth to ally herself with the infinitely more powerful Muslim courts of Morocco, Persia and the Ottoman Empire. For many English Catholics and Puritans such alliances were an abomination; to a number of statesmen and merchants they represented profit and made military sense. Such ambivalent and contradictory responses to Muslims and the Islamic world provided a rich source of dramatic material to Marlowe, Shakespeare and their contemporaries, who produced drama that no longer traded in simple pieties but instead provoked the audience and challenged their beliefs in creating characters of previously unimaginable emotional complexity and psychological depth.

This book tells the remarkable stories of the Elizabethans who travelled to the Muslim world, what they learned and how it affected life back home. It shows how, for some, there was real enthusiasm for a Protestant–Islamic alliance to oppose the power of Catholic Spain and the papacy, which were in turn determined to wipe out all forms of what they regarded as heresy, be it reformed Christianity or 'Mahometan' Islam. It reveals how far Elizabethan England – just one generation away from the beginning of a decisive shift in its religious values from Catholic to Protestant – regarded Islam, with its refusal to worship icons and its venerating of a holy book, as a faith with which it could do business. It also shows how the fear, or allure, of converting to Islam, which became known at this time as 'turning Turk', was taken seriously by many men and women who had already experienced one shift in state religion and were certainly capable of imagining another. Catholic Europe reacted with horror at the rapprochement between Elizabeth and Islam, and sought to conflate Protestants with Muslims as two sides of the same heretical coin. In an age when the Ottoman Empire was regarded as the world's most powerful and successful military machine, the possibility of an Anglo-Ottoman alliance was viewed with genuine alarm in Spain and Italy as a direct threat to Catholic hegemony in Europe and the Mediterranean.

Historians and literary critics have usually understood the prevailing Christian responses to Islam to be alarm and fear. The Protestant preacher Thomas Becon voiced many people's dread of Turkish Islam when he wrote in 1542, 'consider how grievously and without all mercy the people of Christ in many places be most cruelly invaded, handled, led captive, miserably entreated, imprisoned, slain, murdered, and all their goods spoiled, brent, and taken away of that most spiteful and Nero-like tyrant the great Turk, that mortal enemy of Christ's religion, that destroyer of the Christian faith, that perverter of all good order, that adversary of all godliness and pure innocency'.[26] For many Christians, Islam was the antithesis to Christianity, regardless of their denomination. But others took a very different view. They included the respected and influential French political philosopher Jean Bodin, who praised Islam and the Ottomans in particular as a religiously tolerant and meritocratic society whose success was based on a belief in civic welfare, social justice, military discipline and charity. Writing in 1576, Bodin ridiculed suggestions that the Habsburg Empire could maintain the imperial mantle of ancient Rome, arguing instead that 'if there is anywhere in the world any majesty of empire and of true monarchy, it must radiate from the [Ottoman] sultan. He owns the richest parts of Asia, Africa and Europe, and he rules far and wide over the entire Mediterranean.'[27] Bodin also knew that such power brought with it many examples of Christian states forging alliances with the Ottomans. After the fall of Constantinople in 1453 the Venetians agreed mutually beneficial commercial treaties with Sultan Mehmed II, and in 1536 the French king Francis I agreed a formal Franco-Ottoman alliance with Sultan Süleyman I in opposition to their common enemy, the Habsburg emperor Charles V. Polemics like

Becon's have tended to drown out more considered voices like Bodin's in most histories of Christianity's relations with Islam. One of the purposes of this book is to show how Elizabethan England performed a delicate balancing act between both faiths that was unique in Europe at the time, and a result of the very specific nature of Elizabeth I's religious and diplomatic policy.

Dramatists thrive on paradox and uncertainty, and in the late sixteenth century England's unsettling encounters with the Islamic world provided Shakespeare and his contemporaries with a rich variety of characters, settings and scenarios. Rather than being simply ignorant or hostile to the Muslim world as many critics have previously assumed, these writers responded to Islam in a number of ways: as a theology that might just save England from Catholicism, as a military empire that could overrun all of Christianity, and as an international commercial power capable of enriching those who worked with it. The stories of violent, tyrannical and lustful Ottoman, Moroccan and Persian sultans appalled many diplomats and clerics, but to dramatists they offered fantastic raw material from which to fashion some of the theatre's greatest characters. Playwrights offered yet another perspective on Islam to that of thousands of English merchants, diplomats, sailors, soldiers, preachers, exiles, artisans and servants who spent time in Muslim countries from North Africa to Persia and Mughal India. At a time when Islam inspired fear and awe, as well as admiration and hope, Elizabethan playwrights took such disparate emotions and created a drama that was unique in celebrating its ambivalence towards Islam. Their stories cast new light on Elizabeth's reign, during which virtually every key moment – from her accession and excommunication to her relations with favourites like the earls of Leicester and Essex, Sir Francis Drake's circumnavigation of the globe, her policy towards Spain and the papacy, the defeat of the Armada and her attitude towards Calvinism – was affected by various Anglo-Islamic alliances. It is only by making sense of this history that we can understand why almost every playwright working in London from the 1580s put a Turkish, Persian, Moorish or Saracen character in at least one of their plays.

The book first describes how, in the early decades of Elizabeth's reign, relations with various Muslim lands and rulers took such a decisive shape. The story of Tudor men and women engaging with the Muslim world has never been part of the so-called Elizabethan World Picture, which has always assumed that Shakespeare's England, what he called in *Richard II* 'this sceptred isle',[28] existed in splendid isolation from much of the rest of the world, and encountered Turks, Saracens and Mahometans only at the furthest limits of its literary imagination and on the margins of its world maps. This was far from being the case. The Elizabethans were, rather, peripheral players on the margins of a geopolitical world dominated by the empires of Spain, Persia and the Ottomans, and at various moments they openly acknowledged the superiority of the Muslim powers with which Elizabeth repeatedly put England on friendly terms. This does not mean that England under Elizabeth was part of a halcyon world we have lost in which Christians and Muslims got on famously together; it would be misleading to assert amity between the religions where very little actually existed. There is little doubt that the relationship was based on mutual suspicion, misunderstanding and ambivalence. Its consequences were various and sometimes contradictory, but those involved did not seem to believe they were playing out some profound clash between civilizations. It is a subtle and complicated history that illuminates the Elizabethan period, and also our own.

I

Conquering Tunis

Unseasonably stormy weather greeted England's first Spanish king in waiting as he sailed up the English Channel in June 1554. Under the terms of his imminent marriage to Mary I, Queen of England, the Habsburg prince Philip (the future King of Spain and Portugal and ruler of much of the New World) was about to become King of England and Ireland *jure uxoris* – by right of marriage – in an alliance that would have a lasting effect upon the subsequent history of Tudor England. At the age of six, Mary, the eldest daughter of King Henry VIII by his first wife, the Spanish Catherine of Aragon, had been betrothed to her mother's nephew, the Holy Roman Emperor Charles V, but in a classic example of incestuous dynastic marriage alliances, it was eventually Charles's son that she married. Before Henry VIII's decision to separate the Church of England from the Roman Catholic Church, such alliances between Spain and England would have been regarded as a convenient formality between royal cousins. But the impact of the Reformation precipitated by Martin Luther's Ninety-Five Theses challenging papal authority (1517) and Henry's determination to divorce Catherine, as he did in 1533, had changed everything. By the time Mary's radically Protestant but sickly and childless younger brother, King Edward VI, had died in 1553, England and Spain were on opposite sides of a deep-seated religious divide.

Just five days before the marriage Philip had landed at Southampton in a Spanish flotilla escorted into harbour by a fleet of twenty-eight English vessels. As he stepped on to English soil, the lord steward, Francis Talbot, Earl of Shrewsbury, ceremonially presented the twenty-seven-year-old Spanish prince with the Order of the Garter, the highest chivalric honour an English monarch can bestow. Its ceremonial insignia included a garter strapped to the left calf, and a jewelled brooch of St George, the patron saint of England, slaying a dragon, worn suspended from the collar. Philip's Spanish advisers were on their best behaviour, but they remained suspicious of a country that for five years had broadly embraced John Calvin's reformed religious beliefs as official state policy. The English, as one Spaniard observed privately, were 'a barbarian and highly heretical people' who, he claimed, murdered monks and were contemptuous of God and his saints. Simon Renard, Spain's resident ambassador, expressed the difficulty of selling the marriage of Mary and Philip to a deeply divided country, with many English men and women fearing they were 'going to be enslaved, for the queen is a Spanish woman at heart and thinks nothing of Englishmen, but only of Spaniards and bishops. Her idea, they say, is to have the King crowned by force and deprive the Lady Elizabeth of her right, making the operation of the law subject to her own will.'[1] Philip had been told to avoid alienating his hosts and trod as diplomatically as he was capable of in front of the English. He spent three days in Southampton recovering from his journey, before riding to Winchester with a magnificent retinue of 2,000 English and Spanish nobles on horseback. The lord chancellor and Bishop of Winchester, Stephen Gardiner, met him at Winchester Cathedral with an English audience of no fewer than five other prominent English bishops, who lavished him with 'as much love as one could say'.[2]

That evening Philip met his future wife Mary for the first time. Mary was immediately taken with her young fiancé. He was regarded as a 'well-favoured' youth with 'a broad forehead, and grey eyes, straight-nosed and manly countenance', who had yet to manifest the pronounced and infamous Habsburg nose, prognathous jaw and sullen demeanour so visible in his later portraits.[3] Philip and his entourage were less flattering about Mary. Although she was described rather diplomatically by the Spanish as 'a perfect saint' (and someone 'who dresses badly'), the first meeting with the thirty-eight-year-old queen led one of Philip's advisers to observe drily that she was 'older than we were led to believe'. Others were less diplomatic, finding her 'small, and rather flabby'. But publicly the encounter was reported as a great success, as the two 'pleasantly talked and communed together under the cloth of estate',[4] Philip speaking Spanish, and Mary, who understood her mother's tongue but spoke it poorly, using French.

Whatever the public rhetoric, for Philip this was a marriage not of love but of expediency, undertaken on the orders of Philip's father, Charles V. Ruy Gómez, the prince's adviser and confidant, brusquely explained the reasons. 'The king', he wrote, 'understands that this marriage was effected not for the flesh but for the restoration of this realm and the conservation of those states [in Flanders]':[5] that is, the marriage would bring England back under papal jurisdiction and would give Charles greater leverage over his troublesome dominions in the Low Countries. It would also draw England into an alliance against his imperial rival, Francis I, who as we have seen had already allied himself with the Habsburgs' other great adversary, the Ottoman Empire and its sultan, Süleyman I, known to Christians as 'the Magnificent'.

For Mary, notwithstanding what became an obvious infatuation with Philip, the marriage offered the personal and political stability that had eluded her for most of her life. When she was just seventeen her father had married Anne Boleyn, and had nullified his marriage to her Spanish mother, Catherine of Aragon, pronouncing Mary illegitimate. Having remained devoutly committed to her mother's Catholic faith, Mary was barred from inheriting the crown by her brother, Edward. At his death in 1553, she led a successful rebellion to depose Edward's nominated successor, his first cousin the Protestant Lady Jane Grey. Once crowned queen, Mary faced further opposition, having made clear her intentions to pursue marriage to the Spanish, Catholic Philip. In January 1554 Sir Thomas Wyatt led a rebellion against the proposed alliance with Spain. Although it was quickly suppressed and Wyatt executed, the rebellion captured the mood of a country polarized between those who supported an English Reformation and opposed the Spanish match, and those who remained loyal to papal authority and welcomed the marriage as signalling the end of a twenty-year religious aberration.

Mary and Philip were married by Bishop Gardiner in front of a packed congregation in Winchester Cathedral on Wednesday 25 July, the Feast Day of St James, or Matamoros (the 'Moor-slayer'), the patron saint of Spain. A raised scaffold was erected in the aisle for the procession of the bride and groom, the walls lined with rich tapestries and cloth of gold, and two wooden stages or 'mounts', 'her Majesty standing on the right side of the said mount, and the king on the left side'.[6] Mary and her advisers ensured that it was she, not Philip, who took precedence on the right, the dominant position usually reserved for kings. Philip assumed the supplicant position of a queen, to the left, a decision that was not lost on either Spanish or English observers. Before the service began the Spanish presented Gardiner with a patent designating Philip King of Naples, a title relinquished by Charles V and given to his son, ensuring that Mary was marrying Philip as a king and an equal. The nuptials concluded, heralds pronounced Mary's and Philip's titles in Latin, French and English (though not Spanish). The list reflected the religious and international dimension of the marriage. They were now King and Queen of England, France, Naples, Jerusalem and Ireland, Defenders of the Faith; Princes of Spain and Sicily; Archdukes of Austria; Dukes of Milan, Burgundy and Brabant; Counts of Habsburg, Flanders and Tyrol. To ease any potential qualms about the marriage, the English circulated celebratory verses reminding everyone that Philip was descended from King Edward III, so was, as one writer put it, an '*English* Philip'. They 'tell us that he is English and not Spanish', wrote one of Philip's advisers, while noting with equal satisfaction that Mary was of course Spanish through her maternal line. On 31 July the newlyweds left for London on a tide of public goodwill. Philip stopped at Windsor on 3 August to be installed officially as a Knight of the Garter, and on the 18th they made their triumphant entry into London. The gallows erected to execute supporters of the Wyatt Rebellion were taken down, and replaced with stages hastily erected to display pageants and tableaux celebrating the union of Mary and Philip. Philip admired the elaborate displays created in his honour, boasting that throughout the city he was greeted 'with universal signs of joy and love'.[7]

The procession ended at Whitehall Palace, where the couple entered the privy apartments to find one of the most astonishing of all wedding presents, from Philip's father Charles. Hanging from the walls were twelve vast tapestries, woven from the finest gold, silver and silk thread. Each one was over 16 feet high, ranging in width from 23 to 40 feet, a physically overwhelming presence even in such grand chambers. They were what one onlooker called 'those most beautiful tapestries representing the Tunis expedition', a woven account of Charles V's 'proceedings and victories against the Turks'.[8] Known today as the *Conquest of Tunis* tapestries, the cycle now hangs in the Palacio Real in Madrid. It provided a blow-by-blow account of one of the sixteenth century's greatest clashes between Islam and Christianity: Charles V's military expedition to Tunis in the summer of 1535 to crush the Turkish pasha and grand admiral of the Ottoman fleet, Kheir-ed-Din Barbarossa.

'Barbarossa' means red beard in Italian, though by conflation with 'barbarous' the name was also an acknowledgement of Kheir-ed-Din's fearsome reputation for raiding Christian towns and destroying Christian ships across the Mediterranean. In 1534 Süleyman the Magnificent appointed Kheir-ed-Din head of the Ottoman fleet, encouraging him to plunder the Italian and North African coasts, an assault that culminated in his capture of the strategically important city of Tunis in August. Kheir-ed-Din had deposed the city's king, the tyrannical Mulay Hassan, a vassal of the Habsburg emperor. Worse still for Charles, Barbarossa's campaign was supplied with arms by Francis I as part of a strengthening Franco-Ottoman alliance that threatened Spanish influence in the Mediterranean basin. Charles needed to respond decisively. The prospect of a latterday religious crusade against the infidel in North Africa also appealed to Charles, who saw himself as 'Defender of the Faith', with its echo of the assault on Tunis in 1269 led by the French king Louis IX (and including the future King Edward I of England), whose death from dysentery while unsuccessfully besieging the city had led to his canonization. Charles seems to have had his eye not only on succeeding where Louis had failed, but also on achieving sainthood. In the autumn of 1534 he began assembling a huge armada. The recently discovered wealth of the New World financed the expedition, particularly Incan gold sent back to Spain by conquistadors to be used, as one put it, 'in the holy enterprise of war against the Turk, Luther and other enemies of the faith'.[9]

A combined fleet of over 400 ships carrying 30,000 Spanish, Italian, Portuguese, Flemish and German soldiers set sail on 14 June 1535, reaching Tunis later that month. After a punishing siege and battle on the city's outskirts that left an estimated 30,000 dead, Kheir-ed-Din fled and Tunis fell to Charles's forces on 21 July. Habsburg despatches claimed that around 20,000 Christian slaves were freed, although many more Muslims were slaughtered in the three-day sack and pillage of the city, with a further 10,000 (it is estimated) sold into slavery.[10]

Charles was so confident about the outcome of this raid that he took the Flemish artist Jan Vermeyen with him to record events in meticulous detail. He then commissioned Willem de Pannemaker, Brussels' finest tapestry maker, to weave twelve enormous tapestries of events based on Vermeyen's drawings. The series began with a panoramic map of the Mediterranean theatre of operations, and followed key moments in the campaign, culminating in the final graphic scenes of the fall and sack of Tunis. It took forty-two weavers many years to complete the set, at the enormous cost of 15,000 Flemish pounds. When the tapestries were finally completed in Brussels in the summer of 1554, they were packed up immediately and sent to London, where they were unveiled for the first time, to celebrate the union of Mary and Philip.

In vivid and often shocking detail, each tapestry emphasized the awesome military might and financial power of the Habsburg Empire. For the English and Spanish entourage looking at them in Whitehall that August, the message was obvious: the empire would go to any lengths to protect its religious and imperial interests, including the annihilation of the heresy of Islam in North Africa. For many of the English gazing up at these beautiful but intimidating scenes, the tapestries provided the first eyewitness depictions of Muslims in such realistic detail. For generations of English men and women, Muslims had seemed distant and exotic people, glimpsed on the edges of hazy world maps or in literary romances. Suddenly they were confronted with images of life-size turbaned Turkish and Berber soldiers bearing down on their victims, their women and children shown being slaughtered and sold into slavery. Displaying the Catholic Habsburgs in the act of crushing the 'infidel' in London at the celebrations of an alliance between a Spanish prince and an English queen twenty years after the 'heretical' break from Rome provided a stark warning to English Protestantism that the reformed religion advanced by Mary's brother Edward would not be tolerated now that Philip II was King of England. Either by accident or by design, displaying the tapestries indicated that Islam and Protestantism were both heresies, to be eradicated where possible by political unions like that of Mary and Philip, or if necessary by direct military action like Charles's conquest of Tunis.

For Catholics, such a message seemed a blessed salvation from the seemingly irresistible rise of the twin spectres of Lutheranism and Islam. In direct contrast, to English Protestants such scenes confirmed their worst fears of being enslaved by alien Spanish rulers. As one Protestant commentator observed in July 1555, Mary and Philip's religious advisers were arguing that 'the Turks are one and the same thing as we who embrace the pure doctrine of the Gospel'.[11] Mary had already made the connection between Protestantism and Muslim 'heresy' in North Africa as early as the autumn of 1535, when she took the dramatic step of imploring her cousin Charles V to lead a crusade against her father following his divorce from her mother and the split from Rome. 'In so doing', she wrote to the Emperor, he 'will perform a service most agreeable to Almighty God, nor will he acquire less fame and glory to himself than in the conquest of Tunis or the whole of Africa'.[12]

In the context of Henry's appalling treatment of his elder daughter and her Spanish mother Catherine, Mary's emotional plea was not as shocking as it might first appear. But the comment had a longer history. As it was for so many Christians in the sixteenth century battling with profound changes to their faith, Mary's understanding of Muslim Turks had been shaped by misconceptions of Islam that had endured for centuries, and went right back to its origins in seventh-century Arabia. Following the death of the Prophet Muhammad in Medina in AD 632, Christians provided a variety of inconsistent and contradictory responses to Islam, ranging from indifference and bemusement to horror and disgust. The first problem for many Christians was the rapid success of Islam as a religious and political force in the seventh and eighth centuries. At its height the Umayyad caliphate (AD 661–750) stretched from Pakistan and Afghanistan through Syria, the Arabian peninsula and North Africa all the way to Spain and Portugal, and established one of the world's largest ever theocratic states with Damascus as its capital. In direct contrast to Islam's political strength and theological unity, Christianity had suffered centuries of persecution under a pagan Roman Empire, only to emerge from the fall of Rome divided between the eastern Orthodox Church based in Constantinople and the western Latin Church in Rome.

Islam's early political and military success also came with a theological belief system that claimed to supersede Christianity. Like Judaism and Christianity, Islam traced its origins as a monotheistic faith to at least as far back as Abraham. Noah, Abraham, Moses and Jesus were all regarded as prophets who had imperfectly described the word of God; the Torah, the Psalms and the Gospel were also acknowledged as holy texts prefiguring the ultimate divine revelation provided by the Prophet Muhammad in the recitation of the Qur'an. Christians had claimed that Jesus' message supplanted that of Moses and the Jewish faith: Muslims now claimed that Muhammad's prophecies had succeeded those of Jesus. Their austere simplicity was based on the five pillars of faith: *shahâda*, the recitation of the foundational belief, 'There is no God but God, and Muhammad is his Messenger'; *salât*, daily prayers and ablutions; *zakat*, redistributing wealth by giving alms; *sawm*, fasting through the month of Ramadan; and hajj, the pilgrimage to Mecca.

Unlike Christianity, Islam rejected sacramental rites and holy intercessors. Most significantly, the Qur'an dismissed the Christian belief in the Holy Trinity and Incarnation. Jesus was regarded as a holy prophet, but he had not been crucified, nor was he the Son of God or part of a consubstantial divine body. To worship him as God was, as far as Muslims were concerned, a blasphemous error. As People of the Book, Jews and Christians retained the right to freedom of worship even within the *dâr al-Islam* ('House of Islam'), where they were known as *dhimmi*, or protected minorities.

Most of the theological detail of Islam was lost on early Christian commentators, and for understandable reasons. Access to the culture and language of the Islamic world was difficult: by the mid-sixteenth century the Qur'an had been translated into Latin only three times.[13] Then there was the partiality of early Christian responses to Islam.

Faced with an expanding, seemingly irresistible Muslim empire, some early Christian communities decided to convert, but remained understandably silent about the reasons behind their decision. Those who did not convert had to try to offer a persuasive account of the superiority of Christian providential beliefs, when the political and religious events of the seventh and eighth centuries seemed to suggest that if God supported any religion, it was probably Islam. The result from the eleventh century and onwards was a stream of written apologetics – defences of Christianity – that made little attempt to understand Islam as an independent faith. Instead, they presented it as a scourge sent by a Christian God to test his followers' faith. These writings produced a series of insults, caricatures and myths about Islam that laid the foundations of many of today's stereotypes. Muslims, they claimed, were barbaric, licentious and gluttonous, practising a bellicose, tyrannical and murderous religion. Muhammad was condemned as a lecherous, drunken, epileptic trickster with deviant sexual tastes, and the Qur'an derided as a fraudulent amalgamation of Jewish and Christian beliefs.[14]

The names Christians used to describe Muslims show that religion was only one of many ways to understand this new faith. As the terms 'Islam' and 'Muslim' appeared in English in their theological sense only in the seventeenth century, ethnic terms like 'Moor' and 'Arab' were used instead, though such was the importance of the Ottoman Empire that 'Turk' was commonly applied to Muslims of any and often all ethnic origins. Where religion was mentioned it was in relation to the 'law of Muhammad'. But the faith's rise to prominence had to be explained through the Bible in some way, which gave rise to the medieval use of the nouns 'Saracen', 'Ishmaelite' and 'Hagarene'. This cluster of names came from Abraham's offspring. In the Old Testament, Ishmael was Abraham's son, born illegitimately of his wife Sarah's handmaid, Hagar. Ishmael lived to father twelve princes whom Christian and Jewish writers regarded as founders of the twelve Arab tribes (and which are named in Genesis 25: 12–16). For medieval writers such terms – particularly 'Saracen' – became synonymous first with Arabs, then with Muslims.

By the time of the Crusades (1095–1291), the 'Saracens' were regarded primarily as a military threat to Christianity's dominions, rather than as posing a direct challenge to its religious beliefs. Christian misconceptions of the rival faith hardened into two kinds. The first was that Islam was a pagan religion. Saracens were idolatrous *perfidi* – unfaithful, or treacherous, from where we get 'infidel' – who worshipped a variety of idols, including Apollo and Muhammad. Over time, as Christians began to realize that their adversaries in the Holy Land were monotheists rather than pagans, the idea emerged that Islam was just another heresy of the true faith, a confused amalgamation of Christian and Jewish theology which accepted God but rejected intercession and the Trinity. Muhammad was ridiculed as the ultimate heresiarch, a fraudulent prophet who had tricked his followers with the promise of a debauched paradise using demonic magic and feigned miracles.

It was easier to understand Islam as part of Christianity's more familiar struggles with heretical communities from the second to seventh centuries AD than to provide a comparative explanation of its beliefs. Describing Saracens as heretical enabled the faithful to accept them as part of God's plan, a terrifying but necessary prefiguration of the Book of Revelation's Apocalypse, the Day of Judgement and humanity's redemption. Even the rise of the Ottomans – misunderstood as descendants of the Trojans or Scythians – and their conquest of Constantinople in 1453 were regarded as divine punishment for Christianity's inability to unify its eastern Orthodox and western Latin churches.[15] What Christians saw when they looked at Islam was not a rival religion but a distorted image of themselves, a muddled and fearsome projection of their own hopes and fears glimpsed through a warped glass, very darkly.

These glimpses – often confused, usually contradictory, invariably wilful and rarely attempting an accurate account of Muslim belief – endured for centuries. Medieval England may have seemed a long way from Arabia, from where the Muslim tribes had first emerged in the seventh century, but events involving 'Saracens' had already impressed themselves on the medieval Christian imagination throughout Europe. English scholars were integral to the schools and learning of the Latin West, centred on modern-day France, and many of them were at the heart of debates and reflections on the rise of Islamic culture.[16] The Arabs had only been defeated in the middle of France at

Tours in 732; they had conquered the whole of Spain and by 1187 they had taken Jerusalem. In 1143 the Lincolnshire-born theologian and Arabic scholar Robert of Ketton completed the first ever translation of the Qur'an into Latin while studying Arabic in Spain. As its title suggested, *Lex Mahumet pseudoprophete* ('The Religion of Muhammad the Pseudo-prophet') was designed to show Islam as a Christian heresy – or what Robert calls a 'death-dealing' religion – and convert Muslims to Christianity. Despite drawing on Arabic Qur'anic *tafsīrs* (commentaries), Robert's translation was little more than a loose paraphrase of the original and had little or no success in converting Muslims. It survives in twenty-five medieval copies, and remained the standard version of the text in Europe until the mid-seventeenth century.

In William Langland's poem *Piers Plowman* (c. 1360–87) the Prophet is described as a 'Cristene man', a pseudo-Christian schismatic whose followers can find salvation only if they understand their heretical error in worshipping the 'wrong' Messiah (Muhammad), and convert instead to Christ and 'oure bileue, *Credo in deum patrem*' ('our belief, *I Believe in God the Father*').[17] In contrast to this learned and literary approach to Islam as heretical, more popular English traditions continued to draw on older traditions that regarded Muslims as pagans. The mystery-play cycles performed in York and Chester were full of Greek and Roman emperors, as well as Herod and Pontius Pilate, who were all shown worshipping Muhammad as a pagan idol. Heresy, paganism, conversion and millenarianism had all defined Christian responses to Islam for generations.

The religious controversies between Lutheran reformers and Roman Catholics which followed Luther's demands in Wittenberg in 1517 had many far-reaching effects, but one of their unintended and often overlooked consequences is how Christianity's perception of Islam was affected. In 1518 Luther criticized the sale of indulgences to raise money for a new crusade in the Holy Land by arguing provocatively that 'to make war on the Turks is to rebel against God, who punishes our sins through them'.[18] Like many medieval theologians, Luther saw the 'Turk' as another word for ungodliness, a scourge sent by God to punish a wicked, divided Christianity, part of a mysterious but irresistible divine plan.

In 1542, the Swiss publisher Johann Herbst was thrown in jail in Basel for printing Robert of Ketton's translation of the Qur'an in a revised, updated (though still very sketchy) volume by Theodore Bibliander (a Protestant reformer whose real name was Theodor Buchmann) under the title *Machumetis Saracenorum principis vita ac doctrina omnis* ('Life and Teachings of Muhammad, Prince of the Saracens').[19] Luther intervened, petitioning the Basel authorities to release Herbst and offering to write a preface to the new edition, arguing that it was necessary to understand Islamic theology to refute it. In making this argument in his subsequent preface, entitled 'In Alcoranum Praefatio', Luther described Catholics, Muslim and Jews as all heretical. 'Therefore,' he wrote, 'as I have written against the idols of the Jews and the papists and will continue to do so to the extent that it is granted to me, so also have I begun to refute the pernicious beliefs of Muhammad.' In his typically blunt manner he went on:

> Accordingly I have wanted to get a look at the complete text of the Qur'an. I do not doubt that the more of the pious and learned persons read these writings, the more the errors of the name of Muhammad will be refuted. For just as the folly, or rather the madness, of the Jews is more easily observed once their hidden secrets have been brought to the open, so once the book of Muhammad has been made public and thoroughly examined in all its parts, all pious persons will more easily comprehend the insanity and wiles of the devil and will more easily refute them.[20]

Trying to understand Islamic theology by using a twelfth-century paraphrase of the Qur'an was never going to get Luther very far. Besides, his Catholic opponents had pounced on his apparent unwillingness to support a crusade against the Turks as proof of the Lutheran 'heresy' (Luther had argued that Christianity should fight its own internal demons before turning on the Turks). When Pope Leo X threatened Luther with excommunication in 1520, his position on the Turks was cited as just one of his many 'heretical' teachings. In January 1521 Luther was formally excommunicated in the papal bull *Decet Romanum Pontificem* ('It Pleases the Roman Pontiff') and was himself named as a 'heretic' and 'schismatic'.[21]

Luther later changed his mind about waging war on the Turks,

Caricature of Luther with seven heads, including a turbaned Turk (1529).

arguing that this was the prerogative of rulers, not of clergy. He continued to describe Catholicism, Islam and Judaism as conjoined
enemies of the 'true' Christian faith, reserving his bitterest polemic
for Pope Clement VII and the Ottomans: 'as the pope is Antichrist',
he wrote in 1529, 'so the Turk is the very devil'.[22] Catholics responded
by depicting Luther as a divided monster with seven heads, one sporting a Turkish turban. Francesco Chieregato, one of the pope's advisers
at the Diet of Nuremberg (convened to discuss church reform), wrote
in January 1523 that he was 'occupied with the negotiations for the
general war against the Turk, and for that particular war against that
nefarious Martin Luther, who is a greater evil to Christendom than
the Turk'.[23] When Thomas More, author of *Utopia* and privy counsellor to Henry VIII, was asked to respond to the Lutheran challenge,
his *Dialogue Concerning Heresies* (1528) referred to 'Luther's sect' as
worse than 'all the Turks, all the Saracens, all the heretics'.[24]

More's close friend the great humanist scholar Erasmus of Rotter-
dam tried to find a middle way between Catholic and Protestant
sectarian divisions in his *De bello turcico* ('On the War against the
Turks'). Erasmus' treatise was written in 1530 to coincide with the
Diet of Augsburg, a general assembly called by Charles V to discuss
what he regarded as the two greatest threats facing Christendom:
Lutheranism and Islam. Charles's advisers encouraged him to use the
assembly to pursue the policies adopted by his grandparents Ferdinand II of Aragon and Isabella I of Castile towards Muslims in Spain:
forced conversion or expulsion. 'Luther's diabolical and heretical
opinions', wrote Cardinal Lorenzo Campeggio, 'shall be castigated
and punished according to the rule and practice observed in Spain
with regard to the Moors.'[25] But Luther was only one half of Charles's
problem: the other was the spectacular rise of the Ottoman Empire,
which by 1530 was knocking on the door of Christendom. Having
taken Constantinople in 1453, the Ottomans had conquered Egypt
and Syria, and were challenging the Portuguese in the Indian Ocean.
During the 1520s a series of military campaigns across the Balkans
led to the capture of Belgrade and the invasion of Hungary, creating
an Islamic empire that spanned three continents and ruled an estimated 15 million people. Just months before Erasmus wrote his
treatise, Ottoman imperial expansion into Europe reached its zenith,

with an Ottoman army at the gates of Vienna. Süleyman the Magnificent taunted the besieged Christian forces by parading outside the gates wearing an extravagant, bejewelled helmet made for him by Venetian goldsmiths that consciously emulated the Habsburg and papal imperial crowns.[26] It had proved almost impossible to unite Christendom against the Ottomans: Venice remained on amicable commercial terms with them, while the French pursued repeated diplomatic and military alliances with Süleyman as a bulwark against the Habsburgs. Worse still, there were rumours that Süleyman, having learned of the threat posed by Luther to his great enemy Charles V, was encouraging his imams in the mosques of Constantinople to pray for Lutheran success.[27]

With many of the German states in the grip of Lutheranism on one side and the Ottomans in control of much of eastern Europe on the other, this was a critical moment for Catholicism, and Erasmus knew it. How, he asked, had the Ottomans 'reduced our religion from a broad empire to a narrow strip?' The answer reverted to medieval commonplaces about Islamic paganism and heresy. Referring to what he called 'this race of barbarians, their very origin obscure', Erasmus argued that the Ottoman 'sect' was 'a mixture of Judaism, Christianity, paganism, and the Arian [non-Trinitarian] heresy. They acknowledge Christ – as just one of the prophets.' As was true of his medieval theological predecessors, Erasmus' interest in Islam was secondary to the assumption that it was just a projection of a divided Christianity. 'They rule because God is angered,' Erasmus continued; 'they fight us without God, they have Mahomet as their champion, and we have Christ – and yet it is obvious how far they have spread their tyranny, while we, stripped of so much power, ejected from much of Europe, are in danger of losing everything.'[28]

Erasmus' solution to the Turkish problem, which would have seemed harmless enough in the thirteenth century, took on far greater significance when set against sixteenth-century Christian divisions. 'If we really want to heave the Turks from our neck,' he concluded, 'we must first expel from our hearts a more loathsome race of Turks, avarice, ambition, the craving for power, self-satisfaction, impiety, extravagance, the love of pleasure, deceitfulness, anger, hatred, envy.' Writing as a Catholic, but sounding very much like a Lutheran, Erasmus implored his readers to 'rediscover a truly Christian spirit and then, if required, march against the flesh-and-blood Turk'.[29] Christianity needed reformation, but it also needed unification, otherwise the Turk buried within the heart of all believers, be they Catholic or Lutheran, would triumph. Trying to please both sides of a divided Christendom, Erasmus enabled Catholics to castigate Protestants as akin to Turks (meaning all Muslims) for dividing the faith, while also enabling Protestants to condemn Catholics as the worst representatives of 'Turkish' avarice and impiety.

Those assembled at Augsburg responded as they usually did to humanist advice and ignored Erasmus' treatise, which was, for all its theological eloquence, studiedly vague in its practical application. The Diet did little other than keep the Habsburgs on a collision course with both Luther and the Turk, although the pressure to confront the Ottoman threat enabled Lutheranism to survive and prosper in these crucial early years of its emergence. Throughout the 1540s Charles V fought the dual 'heresy' on two fronts and with mixed success. In 1541 he tried to follow his conquest of Tunis with an attack on Algiers, but the campaign was a complete disaster, with the loss of over 4,000 men. By 1545 he was at war with Lutheran forces in Germany, which this time culminated in victory at the Battle of Mühlberg in 1547.

The arrival of the *Conquest of Tunis* tapestries in London in 1554 not only reminded those who saw them of Charles's earlier victory over Islam, but invited inevitable comparisons also with the defeat of Lutheranism at Mühlberg. Within weeks of seeing the Tunis tapestries, Mary and Philip set about stamping out the Lutheran 'heresy' that had taken hold under Edward VI's reign. Legislation was prepared restoring papal authority in ecclesiastical matters, and in November an act was passed for the 'avoiding of heresies which have of late arisen, grown and much increased within this realm'.[30] By February 1555 the first public burnings began of 'heretical' Lutherans, which would secure the queen's enduring historical notoriety as 'Bloody Mary'.

History is rarely kind to the losers, and Mary is no exception. Her short-lived restoration of Catholicism would forever pale in comparison with her half-sister Elizabeth's forty-five-year Protestant reign which became a touchstone of English national identity. For centuries Mary was condemned as a religious zealot who had pursued a murderous crusade against Protestants, prepared to sacrifice her crown to the Spanish Catholics rather than see the Reformation triumph in England. Much of this reputation was the result of the Protestant theologian John Foxe's *Acts and Monuments* (1563), popularly known as *Foxe's Book of Martyrs*, a polemical account of Catholic persecution of Protestants, particularly under what he called 'the horrible and bloody time of Queen Mary'.[31] More recent evaluations reveal a more complex picture of her reign.[32] Although she passed legislation relinquishing her title as head of the church and giving the pope jurisdiction over English ecclesiastical matters, Mary maintained a clear distinction between her religious and secular power. She quietly retained Henrician statutes defining England as an empire over which she, and not the papacy or Philip, exerted *plenum dominium* (complete ownership), and ensured in all official documentation and on public occasions that she took royal precedence over Philip in their controversial co-monarchy. In a country that remained in most areas predominantly Catholic despite the reformed experiments of Edward VI's reign, Mary's marriage to Philip was welcomed by at least as many as opposed it. Eager to ensure the city's position at the centre of a commercial network that looked to Spain and the Low Countries for much of its export market, London's merchant community were so supportive of the marriage that they designed and paid for the couple's carefully choreographed entry into London in August 1554.[33]

Such elaborate spectacles were also used by the newly married couple in the courtly festivities that took place during their London residence in the winter of 1554–5. On Shrovetide, 26 February 1555, there were pageants involving a score of actors dressed as Turkish magistrates, Turkish archers and Turkish women. Exactly what they performed was not recorded, but they presumably represented vices of some kind, intended as foils to Christian virtues, and reminiscent of the Turks seen in the *Conquest of Tunis* tapestries. The clothing used in these pageants survived and was used throughout the 1560s in performances under Elizabeth I.[34]

Upon her accession Mary moved quickly from symbolic to practical matters. She acted to encourage international trade by stressing a surprising degree of continuity with her father's and half-brother's foreign and commercial policies. Henry VIII's merchants had advised him as early as the 1520s that the dominance over global trade of the Spanish, Portuguese and Ottoman empires gave them little room in which to pursue their own commercial interests. To the west, Spain dominated the newly discovered Americas and exploited their silver and gold. To the south Portugal monopolized Africa and the eastern trade routes, having already objected to English merchants trying to establish trade with Morocco and Guinea. The overland route to Asia lay in the hands of the Ottomans. In 1527 Robert Thorne, an English merchant based in Seville, had written to advise Henry that the only way to outmanoeuvre his imperial rivals and reach the Indonesian archipelago's spice islands was to order his merchants to sail north. By 'sailing northwards and passing the Pole, descending to the Equinoctal line', Thorne explained, 'we shall hit these islands, and it should be a much shorter way, than either the Spanish or the Portuguese have'. He claimed that the northern polar region contained a navigable temperate belt beyond the freezing Norwegian seas that sailors knew already. Also, English merchants could develop an export trade 'profitable to our commodities of cloth', while importing spices.[35]

With the collapse of costly English cloth exports in the early 1550s, the crown and city had to decide 'how this mischief might be remedied'. Although it seems mere folly today, going north to reach the east seemed the most obvious solution to many merchants, who began advocating Thorne's 'new and strange navigation', a route that would become known as the north-west passage.[36] In May 1553 Edward VI's counsellors had concluded an agreement with London's merchants and the explorer Sebastian Cabot, issuing 'ordinances, instructions and advertisements of and for the direction of the intended voyage to Cathay', led by Cabot, the governor of the 'Mystery and Company of the Merchant Adventurers for the Discovery of Regions, Dominions, Islands and Places Unknown'. It was a grand title for an amorphous organization with only a vague idea of where it wanted to go. The ultimate destination was Cathay – an Anglicization of the name given to China by Marco Polo – but its supporters were driven by a broader desire for the 'discovery of regions' and 'places unknown' en route. Even more importantly, the Merchant Adventurers' ordinances represented the first attempt to formalize the terms of an English joint-stock company. As its name suggests, a joint-stock company is an association jointly owned by shareholders in proportion to the amount of money they invest. The capital is then deployed to a common purpose – such as a commercial voyage – with the profits (or losses) split between shareholders. There were medieval examples of guilds coming together across Europe to form joint-stock companies, but never in England. Where the physical distances and financial expenditure involved in trading to places like Cathay were too great for individual merchants, the joint-stock company's collective capital mitigated the risks. It was also a sign of the growing power and unity of London's merchant community that they were able to initiate such a project free of royal influence (though with the crown's tacit assent). A total of 240 subscribers including many merchants and some of Edward's closest political advisers invested £25 each to raise the £6,000 required to outfit Cabot's Cathay voyage. It was a global initiative which could establish Tudor England as a significant player on the sixteenth-century world map.

When the expedition set out on 10 May 1553, led by Sir Hugh Willoughby (rather than the aged Cabot) and his pilot Richard Chancellor, it sailed past Greenwich Palace and fired off a salute to the king within. Many on board knew that Edward was mortally ill, and suspected that, should they manage to negotiate the frozen northern wastes successfully, they would return to find a new monarch on the throne (although who it would be remained a source of anguish for all concerned in England). Striking out for the Norwegian seas, the three ships faced treacherous weather, and Chancellor became separated from Willoughby, who found himself stranded on the Lapland coast. Willoughby was painfully ill equipped for such a climate and with temperatures dropping to minus 30 degrees Fahrenheit he and his crew of seventy froze to death in the winter of 1553/4. Their bodies were recovered the following summer, alongside Willoughby's diary; it ends abruptly, describing search parties sent out to seek help, but which 'returned without finding of people, or any similitude of habitation'.[37] Chancellor was luckier, sailing on to the White Sea on Russia's north-west coast, then continuing to Moscow by sleigh, where he met the Tsar of All the Russias, Ivan IV Vasilyevich, better known as Ivan the Terrible.

Having extracted from Ivan English rights to trade in Russia, Chancellor returned to London in triumph in the summer of 1554, to discover Mary and Philip installed as England's new monarchs. While Chancellor had gone north to Russia, other members of the Merchant Adventurers went south into West Africa, establishing a lucrative trade in gold, pepper, ivory and slaves. Philip had no wish for this enterprise to threaten the Spanish monopoly of the Atlantic slave trade or to antagonize Portuguese control of West African commerce, so he persuaded Mary to support her merchants' pursuit of the northern trade routes instead. On 26 February 1555, the 'Charter of the Merchants of Russia, granted upon the discovery of the said country', was granted 'by King Philip and Queen Mary'. Effectively superseding King Edward's 1553 ordinances, this was the first formal charter for an English joint-stock company, described as 'one body and perpetual fellowship and communality'; it would come to be known simply as the Muscovy Company. Its merchants were given a monopoly on 'sailing northwards, northeastwards, and northwestwards' to 'traffic in and out' of Russia, for the 'increase of the revenues of our crown, and general wealth of this and other of our realms'. The monarchs made some gesture towards requiring the merchants to 'subdue, possess and occupy all manner of cities, towns, isles and mainlands of infidelity', but this was primarily a document of trade and exchange, not of plunder and conquest.[38]

The company's original aspiration had been to reach Cathay and the spice islands by heading northwards, but it settled instead on cultivating Ivan the Terrible's Russia as an intermediate trading partner. In the process, however, another destination emerged. In 1557 Mary and Philip wrote to Ivan confirming their new commercial alliance and requesting safe passage for the Muscovy Company's representatives to the neighbouring imperial power and commercial powerhouse, the Safavid dynasty of Persia.[39] Having begun their reign with the express intention of eradicating the heresy of Protestantism at home, economic and international imperatives pushed

Mary and Philip into pursuing tentative relations with a denomination of that other perceived heresy: Islam.

In August 1555, little more than a year after his wedding, Philip left England for Brussels. His father, weary of the political struggles of nearly four decades of rule, was preparing to abdicate and divide the increasingly unwieldy Habsburg dominions between Philip, as King of Spain and the Netherlands, and his younger brother Ferdinand, who would become Holy Roman Emperor. Philip was pleased to escape his troublesome new kingdom, to which he would never return for any significant period of time, but Mary was bereft. Knowing her husband's fondness for maps, she commissioned the Portuguese mapmaker Diogo Homem to create a lavishly decorated atlas for him as a reminder of their personal and political union. Known simply as the Queen Mary Atlas, its nine richly decorated, hand-drawn maps show the world in Mary and Philip's image. The Habsburg imperial eagle flies over the Americas and northern Europe, French and Portuguese political ambitions are diminished, and the threat of Lutheranism is not even acknowledged. The Mediterranean map shows the region in the aftermath of Charles V's Tunisian and Algerian campaigns against the Ottomans. North Africa, adorned with Islamic banners, is labelled 'Mahometania'; off the coast a Christian galley flying the flag of St John engages a Turkish battleship; and to the north the crescent banner of the Ottoman Empire dominates the Balkans. The inference is that only Mary and Philip's Anglo-Spanish alliance could unify a fractured Christendom and rid it of Muhammad's heresy.

The map of northern Europe on the previous folio tells a somewhat different story. The largest escutcheon over England depicts the entwined heraldic devices of England and Spain, surmounted by an imperial crown in acknowledgement of Mary and Philip's union. But on closer inspection it is clear that the Spanish coat of arms has been scratched out from this escutcheon. Having begun work on the atlas in late 1555, Homem laboured over its exquisite decoration for three years, completing it too late to present to Mary, who died on 17 November 1558 and was succeeded by her half-sister Elizabeth. Philip also never saw the atlas, which was presented instead to the new queen. Elizabeth I was the only person with the authority to scratch out the Spanish escutcheon from a royally commissioned book.[40] Whether or not Elizabeth herself was the originator of this stroke of political iconoclasm, it symbolized a decisive end to the brief Anglo-Spanish union, terminating Habsburg influence and with it hopes of returning England to papal jurisdiction. Mary bequeathed her half-sister a country divided politically and religiously in complex ways. Some of its elite had followed the European theological lead in deciding that Protestantism was a heresy akin to Islam, an amalgamation (as we will see) that would come to dominate political and religious language for the rest of Elizabeth's reign. However, that same elite – albeit for strictly pragmatic reasons and via a circuitous route that embraced Russia – had allowed English merchants to reach out to the Muslim world. Elizabeth would exploit this divided legacy to the full as she tried to survive as a Protestant ruler in a predominantly Catholic Europe.

2

The Sultan, the Tsar and the Shah

Within days of her accession in November 1558, the new queen Elizabeth began plans for her coronation, which took place in Westminster
Abbey on 15 January 1559. Superficially the event bore many similarities to Mary's coronation just five years earlier, but there were
some striking theological differences, as Elizabeth began the delicate
task of steering a course between the Protestant reforms of her
half-brother and the Catholic restitution of her half-sister. Breaking
with tradition, the coronation mass was read in both the traditional
Latin and the English vernacular. Even more controversially, while
conducting the mass, George Carew, dean of the Chapel Royal, stuck
to the Catholic ritual of performing the elevation of the bread and
wine, at which point Elizabeth seems to have followed her reformed
principles by silently refusing communion and withdrawing. It was in
fact a carefully rehearsed scene that tried to appease both sides of
Elizabeth's divided theological inheritance. But, as the reign progressed, the religious and dynastic realignments that took place
across Europe would conspire to prevent Elizabeth's attempt to find a
godly 'middle way' through the period's sectarian conflict.

With his wife Mary dead less than two months, Philip, now entitled
King of Spain and Lord of the Netherlands but ever the political
pragmatist, gallantly proposed to his sister-in-law as a noble but
rather half-hearted 'service to God' to keep England Catholic.[1] He
was also anxious to prevent the pro-French Scottish queen Mary Stuart from claiming the English throne and creating what for the
Habsburgs would have been a disastrous Anglo-French alliance. The
even wilier Elizabeth politely declined her brother-in-law's offer with
the argument that he was, well, her brother-in-law. She wanted to

end Philip's influence over English affairs, but she was also keen to
avoid alienating Spain, which she knew could easily interdict her
merchants' trade with the Low Countries. Just three months later, on
3 March 1559, Philip and the French king Henry II signed the Treaty
of Cateau-Cambrésis, which after decades of conflict united the two
kingdoms in peace and concerted opposition to Protestantism.
Although the treaty also formalized peaceful relations between
France and England, no one was fooled. Elizabeth proceeded to
reform the Book of Common Prayer and reinstate an oath of supremacy, established by her father Henry but repealed under Mary,
acknowledging her as 'Supreme Governor of the Church' in England.
These initiatives only increased her isolation from the rest of Catholic
Europe, which responded by starting to assemble a loose alliance
against her new English brand of Protestantism.

This hostility made it more imperative than ever for the new queen
to circumvent the continental powers by pursuing new markets via
the north-east passage advocated by Edward first and then Mary. But
Elizabeth and the Muscovy Company, her newly inherited joint-stock
company, were faced with a serious shortage of personnel. As we
have seen, Hugh Willoughby had frozen to death in Lapland in early
1554; his lieutenant, Richard Chancellor, had repeated the journey
the following year. He again reached the White Sea, but drowned in
a storm off the Scottish coast on his return voyage in 1556. To make
matters worse Sebastian Cabot, the company's director and guiding
light, had died in 1557. However, there was one man with the experience and credentials to develop the fledgling Elizabethan trade with
the east. Unfortunately, as Elizabeth was being crowned queen in
January 1559, he was on Muscovy Company business nearly
4,000 miles away in Bukhara (in modern-day Uzbekistan), a guest of
the Islamic khanate's Shaybanid ruler, Abdullah Khan II. His name
was Anthony Jenkinson.

Although scarcely remembered today, during his lifetime Jenkinson
was regarded as one of the great pioneers of Elizabethan travel. Born
at Market Harborough in Leicestershire, he trained as a merchant,
and as was common at the time spent his apprenticeship working
with English factors (commercial agents) in the Low Countries and

the Levant, where he specialized in textile fabrics. In 1546 he left England and went to Flanders, Germany, Italy, Portugal and Spain, before travelling across North Africa and the Mediterranean islands and throughout what he called the 'holy land'.[2] By November 1553, aged just twenty-four, Jenkinson reached the Syrian city of Aleppo. Together with its neighbour Damascus, Aleppo was one of the oldest cities in the world. It stood at the western end of the Silk Route and, renowned for its trade in Iranian silk and Indian spices, had drawn merchants from east and west for centuries. The city came under the Ottomans' control following their victory in 1517 over the Mamluks (the ruling Egyptian military caste), and quickly attracted resident communities of Jewish, Armenian and Italian merchants who estab-lished permanent trading posts there. By the time Jenkinson arrived, drawn by the volume and quality of silk passing through the city's fifty-six markets and the colossal central *suq*, it was already displac-ing Damascus as the region's premier trading centre, and was widely regarded as the Islamic world's equivalent to Venice.

But on 4 November a very different visitor came marching into the city. Jenkinson was there as Sultan Süleyman I entered Aleppo at the head of a vast Ottoman army which was embarking on a campaign against the neighbouring Persian Safavid Empire. Jenkinson watched in wonder as one of the sixteenth century's great armies swept past, led by 'the Great Turke himself', Sultan Süleyman, 'with great pomp and magnificence'. Jenkinson's experience as a mercer ensured that his description of the scene reads more like a fashion show than a military campaign. Watching an estimated 88,000 men march past, he noted that the cavalry were 'clothed all in scarlet', the infantry 'all in yellow velvet, with hats of the same, of the Tartary fashion, two foot long, with a great robe of the same colour about their foreheads'. The sultan's elite fighting corps, the Janissaries, were wearing 'silk, and apparelled upon their head with a strange form, called *Cuocul-lucia*'. This was the famed Turkish *bork* hat 'in the manner of a French hood', topped with 'a great bush which wavereth up and down most bravely when he marcheth'. Finally, Süleyman himself appeared, 'mounted upon a goodly white horse, adorned with a cloth of gold, embroidered most richly with the most precious stones'. As it was for many European painters of the time (including Bellini, Dürer, Titian and Veronese) it was the sultan's headgear that fascinated Jenkinson. With a mercer's eye for gauging cloth, he noted that Süleyman wore 'upon his head a goodly white tuck [turban], containing in length by estimation fifteen yards, which was of silk and linen woven together, resembling something of Calicut [Indian] cloth, but is much more fine and rich, and in the top of his crown a little pinnach [plume] of white ostrich feathers'.[3] It was such dazzling displays of power and panache that earned Süleyman the soubriquet 'the Magnificent'.

Jenkinson concluded his awed account by observing that Süleyman's army, 'intending to march into Persia, to give battle to the Great Sophie', Shah Ismail I, would winter in Aleppo. The title 'Sophy' came from the Safavids' founder, Safi ad-din Ardabili, and his self-proclaimed designation *çafī-ud-dīn* or guardian of 'purity of religion'. But it was also combined in the Christian Renaissance imagination with the Greek word 'sophia', wisdom, which led many scholars to regard the Persian rulers mistakenly as venerable magi. Little did Jenkinson know that what he was witnessing was a chapter in a conflict between the Ottoman and Persian empires that would have a profound bearing on subsequent Anglo-Islamic relations. It was a conflict that also bore an uncanny resemblance to the religious Reformation convulsing Christendom, including Jenkinson's England. This was the Ottomans' third military campaign against the Persian Safavids, arising out of the centuries-old enmity between the Sunni (Ottoman) and Shi'a (Persian) branches of Islam, whose origins can be traced right back to the struggle for political control of the *umma*, the Muslim community, after Muhammad's death in 632.

The issue revolved around the title of 'Khalifat Rasul Allah', or 'the successor to the messenger of God' – that is, the caliph. The question that consumed Islam throughout this period was whether the caliph should be appointed by the community or follow Muhammad's direct line of descent. As tensions mounted and factions hardened, the *umma* descended into a period of civil wars, known as *fitna* ('strife'). In 656 'Ali ibn Abi Talib, Muhammad's cousin and husband to his daughter Fatima, claimed the caliphate as his hereditary right, but was immediately challenged by Mu'awiyah, the governor of Damascus and part of the Umayya clan that was not directly related to Muhammad. When 'Ali was assassinated by one of his own hard-line former followers in Kufa, south of Baghdad, in 661, Mu'awiyah became the uncontested caliph, and the first of the Umayyad dynasty based in Damascus, shifting the centre of Muslim imperial power away from the Arabian peninsula for the first time in its short, turbulent history.

The majority of Muslims who accepted Mu'awiyah's leadership became known as Sunnis, taking their name from 'Sunnah' – the traditional teachings of Muhammad. However, a significant minority, the 'Shī'atu 'Ali or 'the party of 'Ali', rejected the elective succession of the subsequent Sunni Umayyad, Abbasid, Mamluk and Ottoman caliphates. Their political objections over the succession gradually hardened into a theological schism dividing them from Sunnis after 'Ali's remaining son, Husayn, had been killed by the Umayyads at the Battle of Karbala in Iraq in 681. To the Shi'a, as these minority believers became known, Husayn was a Christ-like figure who had martyred himself in anticipation of a final, divine revelation that would fulfil the prophecies of Abraham, Muhammad and 'Ali. In contrast to Sunnis, the Shi'a invested absolute authority in a line of imams descended from Muhammad through his daughter Fatima and endowed with divine and infallible knowledge. When 'Ali's line disappeared in the ninth century, the largest branch of Shi'a, known as 'Twelvers', developed a belief that God had hidden the twelfth, 'lost' imam, who would one day reveal himself as the Mahdi ('divine guide') or messiah, and unify Islam in its millenarial triumph over all other religions. Sunni theologians condemned these messianic beliefs in eschatology and revelation as *bid'a*, or 'religious innovation', schismatic and heretical beliefs in salvation. Their condemnations sounded strikingly similar to the language with which sixteenth-century Catholics condemned Protestants.

Having rejected the authority of the caliphate, the Shi'a also regarded with suspicion any form of political governance before the return of the hidden imam. However, the fragmentation of Persia under the Timurid dynasty in the late fifteenth century encouraged the rise of various Shi'ite rulers espousing Sufism (a mystical dimension of Islam), the most militant of whom were the Safavids from Ardabil in north-west Iran. In 1501 their fourteen-year-old spiritual and political leader, Sheikh Ismail Safavi, completed a victorious campaign throughout Azerbaijan and Iran, proclaiming himself the first shah of Iran and founding the Safavid Empire in his newly conquered imperial capital, Tabriz. In a defining moment in Iran's history, Ismail proclaimed Twelver Shi'ism the empire's official religion, and announced himself as the long-lost Mahdi. His followers worshipped him as a god, and he immediately launched a jihad against his neighbouring Sunni rivals, the Ottomans, marching into Anatolia and Syria, conquering Baghdad and destroying Sunni holy sites wherever he found them. Persian chroniclers described how, when Ismail conquered Tabriz, he commanded 'that Abu Bakr, Umar and Usman [Sunni caliphs] should be cursed in the bazaars, on pain of death to him who refused. In those days men knew not . . . of the rules of the twelve Imams [but] . . . day by day the sun of the Shi'a faith rose higher.'[4]

In response the alarmed Ottoman sultan, Selim I, declared war on the Safavids as the biggest political and religious threat to his commercial power and title as 'Protector of the Holy Cities' of Mecca, Medina and Jerusalem. As Islam officially forbade war between Muslims, Selim was required to issue a fatwa against Ismail's Shi'a followers, which condemned them as 'infidels and heretics' and asserted that 'to kill them and to destroy their communities is an implicit and essential obligation for all [Sunni] Muslims'.[5] As news of the Ottoman–Safavid conflict reached Europe's capitals in late 1501, Venice, France, Portugal and even the papacy began corresponding with Shah Ismail in an attempt to build an anti-Ottoman alliance. Venetian merchants in Damascus wrote to the city's senators following Ismail's accession, advising them that it was an 'opportune moment to form an alliance among the Christian princes and Persia to engage in the most holy war to throw the Turk out of Europe'.[6] A mixture of political expediency and a garbled understanding of Shi'a beliefs led others to justify such an alliance by mythologizing Ismail as a warrior saint who led his pious warriors into battle against 'infidel' Sunni Muslims, not unlike crusading Christians. In 1502 the Venetian spy Constantino Laschari returned from an encounter with Ismail and reported to the city's senate that the shah's 'Sophi [Sufi] religion has always fought against the Ottoman royal house because the Ottomans are heretics and usurpers of the territories of many

Muslims'. Turning to the shah himself he concluded, 'Ismail is considered a prophet, rich, just generous, and divinely inspired. He is much beloved of his sect which is a certain religion – Catholic in their way.'[7] Venice saw the advantages of securing its eastern Mediterranean trade against Ottoman aggression by allying with Ismail, and the Portuguese sought his favour in their naval battles with the Ottomans in the Indian Ocean. None of Ismail's Christian suitors was concerned to enquire too deeply into the exact nature of his Shi'a faith; one Venetian thought him 'more Christian than otherwise', an erroneous but expedient assumption: as one historian has argued, 'a political alliance with a Sufi saint was easier to justify than one with a Muslim king'.[8]

When a vastly superior Ottoman army equipped with artillery defeated Ismail at the Battle of Caldiran (in modern-day eastern Turkey) in 1514, the shah's divine invincibility was shattered. With his capital overrun by the Ottomans, Ismail retreated eastwards, taking refuge in hunting and drinking (known in Persian poetry as *bazm u razm*), never to regain sufficient authority to challenge the Ottomans seriously. After his death in 1524 he was succeeded by his son, Shah Tahmasp I, who was faced with a series of attempted Ottoman invasions throughout the 1530s and 1540s. In the late 1550s Tahmasp responded with incursions into eastern Anatolia. Süleyman replied by mobilizing his army in 1558 and marching towards Aleppo. But the sultan was not free from his own domestic problems. In his early sixties, he was beset with illness and domestic squabbles between various wives and eight politically ambitious sons, and was particularly suspicious of his youngest, Prince Mustafa. Just weeks before Jenkinson marvelled at his forces marching into Aleppo, Süleyman camped in Konya, central Anatolia, and called Mustafa into his tent, where his eunuchs strangled him with a bow-string as his father looked on.

There is no evidence to suggest Jenkinson knew much about any of these theological and political dimensions to the Muslim world, which makes it all the more remarkable that within weeks of watching Süleyman entering Aleppo he had not only engineered an audience with the sultan but came away from it with the kind of formal trading privileges usually granted only to heads of state, and signed by

Süleyman himself. Without any diplomatic training or credentials and no history of English relations with the Ottomans, Jenkinson had secured virtually unprecedented rights to 'lade and unlade his merchandise wheresoever it shall seem good unto him' throughout the Ottoman Empire, free from 'any other custom or toll whatsoever'. Even the sultan's long-standing commercial allies France and Venice (one of which probably provided Jenkinson with safe passage into Aleppo) were told not 'to intermeddle or hinder his affairs'.[9] One wonders what Süleyman and his advisers made of this precocious (some might say foolhardy) young Christian mercer from a small, peripheral Christian island standing in front of them, with no diplomatic credentials and unable to speak Turkish, boldly negotiating exceptional commercial access to their vast dominions (presumably speaking in a mixture of Italian and French, the Levant's lingua franca). If the history of Anglo-Ottoman relations begins anywhere, it is with the twenty-four-year-old Jenkinson's extraordinary achievements in Aleppo in the winter of 1553–4.

In the spring of 1554 Süleyman and Jenkinson both left Aleppo. The sultan headed east, marching into Persia, while Jenkinson went west, returning home to London, where the following year the Mercers' Company acknowledged his success in the Levant by making him a full member. Two years later, with Willoughby, Chancellor and Cabot all dead, his commercial and diplomatic experience made him the obvious person to lead the Muscovy Company's next Russian voyage, which was given royal assent by Mary and Philip. Jenkinson, still only twenty-seven but already described by the Muscovy Company directors as 'a man well travelled, whom we mind to use in further travelling',[10] was appointed captain general of a fleet of four ships heading back to Russia via the forbidding White Sea to take advantage of the trading rights granted to Chancellor by Ivan the Terrible. In May 1557 Jenkinson set sail, reaching the White Sea in the relatively clement month of July, before travelling overland to Moscow and the tsar's court, where he arrived in December.

Once again, Jenkinson found himself dealing with a powerful emperor ruling an eastern empire that was in transition; once again, he managed to charm his way into the ruler's affections and extract unprecedented access to him and his kingdoms. On Christmas Day

1557, Jenkinson was given an audience with Ivan. He kissed the emperor's hand, presented letters from Mary and Philip, and sat down for dinner with 'diverse ambassadors and other strangers, as well as Christians and heathens'. Ivan's advisers then told him almost immediately that 'the emperor would give me that I desired': unfettered commercial access to the Caspian Sea and trade with Persia.[11] It was a perfect time for both men to do business. England needed to reach the east by avoiding both the overland routes through mainland Europe and the seaborne routes controlled by Spain and Portugal. Ivan had recently conquered Kazan and Astrakhan, Turkic Muslim khanates that had controlled the regions around the Volga Delta and Caspian Sea. This enabled him to offer European traders unrestricted access to Persia and, by optimistic extension, China, in exchange for closer commercial and military ties. But ongoing hostilities with Poland, Lithuania and Livonia on his western borders made it difficult to establish an overland trade route to the Low Countries' markets. Jenkinson and the English seemed to provide a solution by offering a sea route via the White Sea. Tortuous though it might seem, Jenkinson and Ivan agreed to establish a trading route that involved a 1,700-mile sea voyage from London to the White Sea, followed by a 3,000-mile overland route to Persia.

Sailing to Russia and reaching Moscow was the easy part of Jenkinson's expedition when compared to the daunting Persian journey via the Caspian Sea that now faced him. On St George's Day 1558, he left Moscow (now wearing Russian dress) with just two English companions and a Tatar (Turkic) translator provided by Ivan. He headed south-east to Kazan, where he picked up the Volga River and headed south towards Astrakhan. As he travelled by horse, boat and camel, he was appalled by the devastation, including 'famine and plague', that had been wreaked on the local khanates by Ivan's brutal military campaigns. In July he reached the recently conquered city of Astrakhan, less than 60 miles from the Caspian, but was disappointed to find that 'there is a certain trade of merchandise there used, but as yet so small and beggarly, that it is not worth the making mention'. The following month he became the first Englishman to reach the Caspian Sea, knowing that its southern shores marked the beginning of the Persian Empire.[12] The intrepid Englishman was now beyond

Ivan's jurisdiction, and faced repeated harassment, theft and extortion as he travelled in caravans, leading a train of camels with his meagre merchandise, brokering deals as he went with local Tatar warlords who were at perpetual war with both Russia and Persia. Finally, in late December 1558, just weeks after Mary's death and Queen Elizabeth's accession (both of course unbeknown to him), Jenkinson reached Bukhara and the relative security of its Muslim Shaybanid ruler, Abdullah Khan II.

Jenkinson was now within touching distance of Persia. But as he began to grasp the region's complex political, commercial and religious tensions, it became clear to him that, at least on this occasion, he could go no further. The main impediment to his progress was the sectarian divisions between his Muslim hosts. In describing the history of Bukhara, Jenkinson wrote that it 'was sometimes subject to the Persians, and [its people] do now speak the Persian tongue, but yet it is a kingdom of itself, and hath most cruel wars continually with the said Persians about their religion, although they be all Mahometists'. The Shaybanids were Sunni, while their Persian rivals were Shi'a, a distinction grasped somewhat vaguely by Jenkinson through recourse to pogonology. 'One occasion of their wars', he wrote, is 'that the Persians will not cut the hair of their upper lips, as the Bukharians [Bogharians] and all other Tartars do, which they account a great sin, and call them *caphars* [from the Arabic *kafir*], that is, unbelievers, as they do the Christians'.[13] To a mercer obsessed with sartorial appearance, it was the Sunni injunction to trim the moustache as opposed to the Shi'a practice of letting it grow that commanded Jenkinson's attention, rather than any deeper understanding of their theological difference. Nevertheless, it is the first surviving English eyewitness account of distinctions between the two branches of Islam.

Ultimately Jenkinson was far more concerned by Bukhara's disappointing commercial potential than by the varieties of its faith (and beards). In peace there had been 'great resort of merchants to this city of Boghar [Bukhara], which travel in great caravans from the countries thereabout adjoining, as India, Persia, Balgh, Russia, with diverse others, and in times past from Cathay, when there was passage'. But now in times of 'incessant and continual wars', Jenkinson feared that 'these merchants are so beggarly and poor . . . that there is no hope of any good trade there to be had worth the following'. Even worse, the hot central Asian climate meant its merchants had little interest in the coarse, heavy woollen English cloth offered by Jenkinson. Instead, Indian and Jewish merchants traded in silk and cotton, 'but of kerseys [coarse woollen textile] and other cloth, they make little account', and despite his best efforts, 'they would not barter for such commodity as cloth'.[14]

He considered pushing on to China, but seems to have grasped the unlikelihood of successfully realizing such an arduous and dangerous venture. He noted that the route was treacherous because of the 'great wars that had dured three years before my coming hither' between Tatar and Persian warlords, making it 'impossible for any caravan to pass unspoilt' to China. Besides, he concluded, 'it is nine months' journey'. This was a gross exaggeration, but a sign of just how far away Jenkinson certainly felt he was from the legendary 'Middle Kingdom'. Even his attempt to reach Persia was beset with difficulties. His local sources told him that Abdullah Khan had left Bukhara to defend it from an imminent siege by the Prince of Samarkand; beyond the city 'rovers and thieves' were robbing and murdering merchants en route to Persia; Jenkinson's safe-conduct letters had been confiscated by the Bukharan authorities, and as he had already concluded rather glumly, his heavy English cloth was (once again) 'not vendible in Persia'.[15] Perhaps the Bukharans had had enough of the tenacious Englishman, and wanted to get rid of him; perhaps Jenkinson had little appetite for further danger after nearly two years of constant travel. Whatever the reasons, on 8 March 1559 he left Bukhara and headed for home. When he reached the Caspian he 'set up the red cross of St. George in our flags, for honour of the Christians which I suppose was never seen in the Caspian Sea before'.[16] By September he was in Moscow, where he planned to spend the winter before heading for the White Sea and then on to England.

Upon his arrival in Moscow he wrote to his fellow Muscovy Company agent Henry Lane, who had travelled to Russia on Chancellor's second expedition and was now based in Volgograd in southern Russia. He conceded that 'although our journey hath been so miserable, dangerous and chargeable with losses, charges and expenses', there was still a profitable 'trade of merchandise to be had in such lands'. Jenkinson signed off his letter to Lane, 'giving you most hearty thanks for my wench Aura Soltana'. When the Elizabethan geographer and travel writer Richard Hakluyt published Jenkinson's letter in the second edition of his *Principal Navigations, Voyages, Traffics and Discoveries of the English Nation* (1598/9–1600), he added a marginal note that reads, 'This was a young Tartar girl which he gave the Queen afterward.'[17] In the midst of all the loquacious accounts of heroic derring-do and profit and loss, Jenkinson's casual aside gives a sobering insight into the traffic in men and women as slaves that was also part of his commercial mission and that of most other merchants operating in central Asia at this time. He may have bought the unfortunate 'Aura Soltana' while in Astrakhan in July 1558, where he had noted of the local Muslim Nagayan people that 'I could have bought many goodly Tartar children, if I would have had a thousand, of their own fathers and mothers, to say, a boy or a wench for a loaf of bread worth six pence in England, but we had more need of victuals at that time than of any such merchandise.'[18] Having bought the girl and sent her as 'merchandise' to his friend Lane, he seems to have reclaimed her while in Moscow in preparation for bringing her back with him to England as the first recorded Muslim woman to enter the Tudor kingdom and, if Hakluyt is right, presented as a gift to Queen Elizabeth.

By the late autumn of 1560, Jenkinson was back in London. He had spent two and half years away from home, negotiating with some of central Asia's most powerful rulers, some who were Russian Orthodox, others who were Sunni Muslim and Shi'a. The England he had left behind was a formally Catholic country ruled by Mary and her Spanish consort; what he found on his return was a nascent Protestant nation with a new queen, Elizabeth, trying to impose a new religious settlement on a country still deeply divided along religious lines. Whatever he thought of all this – especially the country's official change of denomination – he kept to himself. He reported back to the Muscovy Company's directors on the possibility of further trade with Persia. If the English could somehow exploit the Sunni and Shi'a conflict in the region and access commercial traffic through the Persian Gulf, it could be of huge financial benefit to the new

Protestant kingdom. Elizabeth came to the throne facing a national debt of nearly £300,000 incurred by her late father's wars with France, poor harvests and a slump in the cloth trade, which prompted creditors to threaten to repossess English assets abroad.[19] Neither the company's directors nor Elizabeth needed much convincing to support an immediate return voyage to Persia via Russia, and by the following spring preparations were advanced for a new expedition by Jenkinson, with the ultimate aim of reaching Persia's ruler, Shah Tahmasp.

The Muscovy Company had extracted royal assent from Mary and Philip for its northern ventures but could not encroach upon Spanish imperial dominions in Africa and the Americas to the south and west. Elizabeth had no such scruples in prescribing who her merchants traded with, be they Russian Orthodox or Muslim. Supported by her counsellors – many of whom had invested heavily in the Muscovy Company, so had an interest in its success – Elizabeth wrote letters to both the 'Emperor of Russia' and the 'Great Sophy of Persia' requesting safe conduct and trading privileges on Jenkinson's behalf.

Both Elizabeth's letters drew on a standard template used in such royal correspondence, praising the recipient and requesting safe passage and commercial preferment for Jenkinson through their realms. But the letter to the Persian emperor, which was the first she wrote to a Muslim ruler, required some significant amendments. The queen and her advisers knew little about the religion, politics or even identity of the Safavid Shi'a ruler, Shah Tahmasp. Whatever Jenkinson had conveyed about Safavid rule was scarcely reflected in Elizabeth's letter. It began: 'Elizabeth, by the grace of God, Queen of England, &c. To the right mighty and right victorious Prince, the great Sophy, Emperor of the Persians, Medes, Parthians, Hyrcanes, Carmanarians, Margians, of the people on this side, and beyond the river of Tigris, and of all men, and nations, between the Caspian sea, and the gulf of Persia, greeting.'[20]

With – unsurprisingly – almost no contemporary understanding of the Safavids and their ruler, Elizabeth's address fell back on classical and biblical assumptions about the region. What she describes is not Shah Tahmasp and his Safavid dominions, but the Achaemenid Empire founded by Cyrus the Great (r. 559–529 BC), who was venerated by Christian theologians for conquering Babylon and freeing the Jews in what was regarded as part of the faith's providential history. Unlike the Ottoman Turks, who seemed to have sprung out of nowhere, the Persians could be put within biblical history, which also enabled Elizabeth to avoid any mention of the fact that she was seeking a commercial alliance with a Muslim empire. Despite 'the huge distance of lands' between the two countries, Elizabeth promised the shah that Jenkinson's 'enterprise is only grounded upon an honest intent to establish trade with your subjects'. Taking care to avoid references to explicitly Christian beliefs, she anticipated that if Jenkinson were granted 'good passports and safe conducts' through Persia, 'the almighty God will bring it to pass, that of these small beginnings, greater moments shall hereafter spring . . . that neither the earth, the seas, nor the heavens, have so much force to separate us, as the godly disposition of natural humanity, and mutual benevolence have to join us together'.[21] Written in Hebrew, Latin and Italian, signed and sealed on 25 April 1561 'in our famous city of London', the letter was presented to Jenkinson as he boarded his ship, the *Swallow*, at Gravesend on 14 May, laden with '80 fardles [parcels] containing 400 kerseys', as he prepared to sail for Russia.

Jenkinson's second voyage out passed without great incident. On this expedition it was politics, not geography, that would present him with his biggest challenge. Upon his arrival in Moscow in August 1561 his attempts to see Ivan were frustrated by an obstructive imperial secretary and the tsar's imminent marriage to Maria Temryukovna, a Circassian princess who was, according to Jenkinson, 'of the Mahometicall law'. Ever resourceful, Jenkinson used his time in the freezing city to sell most of his woollen cloth, waiting until the following April, when he finally obtained an audience with the tsar. A clearly relieved and delighted Jenkinson wrote that Ivan showed him special favour and 'committed matter of importance & charge unto me, to be done when I should arrive in those countries whither I intended to go'.[22] Jenkinson had been appointed the Muscovy Company's factor, Queen Elizabeth's de facto ambassador, and was now tasked with acting as Ivan's representative once he reached Persia. After yet more delay, he finally left Moscow on 27 April and headed for the Volga in the company of a Persian ambassador, with whom he 'had great friendship and conference all the way'.[23]

Over the next few months Jenkinson retraced the route of his first journey, travelling through Astrakhan to the Caspian Sea. As he moved on south-east and passed into Safavid territory, he seemed to travel back in time, describing regions through events and individuals from the classical past. In August 1562 he reached the Caspian town of Derbent at the foot of the Caucasus Mountains. His only point of reference was to identify it as part of the ancient Persian province of Hyrcania, and admire the ancient wall that Muslims and Christians believed Alexander the Great had built to keep out the monstrous races of Gog and Magog. Just weeks later he arrived at Shirvan and met its Shi'a *beglerbeg* (governor), Abdullah-Khan Ustajlu, Shah Tahmasp's cousin and one of his closest advisers, whom Jenkinson called 'Obdolowcan'. Yet again the Englishman appears to have made a good impression on his Muslim host, who provided lavish entertainment, including feasting and hawking. And as usual Jenkinson assiduously itemized every opulent fabric and object he saw, including the golden silken garments 'of that country fashion' which he wore for the rest of his time in Persia. When Abdullah-Khan asked 'whether we of England had friendship with the Turks or not', Jenkinson's response was consummate. 'I answered that we never had friendship with them, and that therefore they would not suffer us to pass through their country into the Sophy his dominions, and that there is a nation named Venetians, not far distant from us, which are in great league with the said Turks.' Those awful Venetians had made a friend of the shah's sworn enemies, the Ottomans, and were responsible for blocking the honest English from reaching their obvious allies, the Safavids. When combined with Jenkinson's charm and plausibility, there was just enough truth in such claims (as the Venetians had a history of allying themselves strategically with the Ottomans, from just after the fall of Constantinople in 1453 to the renewal of trading privileges following the Ottoman conquest of Egypt in 1517). Abdullah-Khan was persuaded that the Englishman was not only to be trusted but could even be an asset to his cousin. When he pressed Jenkinson further, 'touching religion, and also the state of our countries' and 'whether the emperor of Almaine [probably a reference to Philip II] or the great Turk were of most power', Jenkinson nimbly 'answered as I thought most meet', probably evading the (rather tricky) questions and turning discussion towards the prospect of meeting the Sophy 'to entreat friendship and free passage'.[24]

Having secured the governor's 'great favour' and being supplied with letters of safe conduct, camels and horses, Jenkinson went on his way. On 16 October he reached Ardabil, another historically charged place where past and present collided, 'wherein the princes of Persia are commonly buried, and there Alexander the Great did keep his court when he invaded the Persians'. It was here that Jenkinson observed that the 'late prince [Shah] Ismail lieth buried in a fair *Meskit* [mosque] with a sumptuous sepulchre', although he does not say if he managed to enter the mosque and see the shah's tomb.[25] Jenkinson was now at the very centre of the ancient biblical (and Qur'anic) world, the holiest site too of Safavid Shi'a belief. He was also close to his ultimate goal of reaching the shah's court. Finally, on 2 November 1562, he arrived at Shah Tahmasp's imperial capital of Qazvin, 90 miles north-west of modern Tehran.

The shah that Jenkinson was about to meet was very different from his fanatical, charismatic father. Born just six months before Ismail's catastrophic defeat by the Ottomans at the Battle of Chaldiran, Tahmasp grew up in the shadow of a ruler whose followers believed he was the messiah, but who died a broken man when the prince was just ten. During Tahmasp's turbulent minority he faced civil wars among his followers, and constant threats from the Ottomans to the west and the Uzbeks to the east. In the pursuit of more conciliatory and pious foreign and domestic policies he signed the Peace of Amasya with the Ottomans (1555), followed by an Edict of Sincere Repentance (1556) which attempted to formalize Shi'a laws by banning painting, wine and many Sufi rituals that had been central to Safavid belief. In direct contrast to his father's fervent millenarianism, Tahmasp regarded himself as a pious king trying to consolidate his empire's political and religious boundaries, rather than expand them.[26] As Jenkinson arrived in Qazvin the shah had recently completed an ambitious programme of public works designed to transform it from a Sunni city into the centre of Shi'ite political and religious power. Royal baths, cisterns and bazaars were built, as well as an entirely new royal garden complex to the north of the city, known as Sa'ādatābād, with palaces, promenades, canals and parade grounds for practising polo and archery.[27]

When Jenkinson was finally granted an audience with the shah in his new palace on the afternoon of 20 November 1562, he was clearly unimpressed. Gone were his usual observations of sartorial elegance and domestic opulence. Instead he immediately pronounced the Safavid ruler – whom he called 'Shaw Thomas' – as 'nothing valiant', so that 'through his pusillanimity the Turk hath much invaded his countries'. What really fascinated him was the shah's Shi'a religion. 'He professeth a kind of holiness,' he wrote, 'and saith that he is descended of the blood of *Mahomet* and *Murtezallie*', Murtezallie being Muhammad's cousin 'Ali ibn Abi Talib. He went on: 'although these Persians be Mahometans, as the Turks and the Tartars be, yet honour they this false fained *Murtezallie*, saying that he was the chiefest disciple that Mahomet had, cursing and chiding daily three other disciples that Mahomet had called *Omar* ['Umar ibn Al-Khattab], *Usiran* [Uthman ibn Affan] and *Abebecke* [Abu Bakr ibn Qhuhafah]', Jenkinson's rather approximate transliterations of the names of the first three caliphs. While confusing his early Islamic history in claiming that 'these three did slay the said *Murtezallie*,' Jenkinson grasped that it was this struggle between the Shi'a and Sunni branches of Islam, 'and other differences of holy men and laws, [that] they have had and have with the Turks and Tartars mortal wars'. This was apparently as far as Jenkinson could delve into the complex distinctions between Sunni and Shi'a theology, and he concluded that to 'entreat of their religion at large, being more or less Mahomet's law and the Alkoran, I shall not need at present'.[28]

After charming Sultan Süleyman and Tsar Ivan, and spending nearly five years (on and off) in pursuit of the Persian Sophy, Jenkinson's luck with eastern potentates finally ran out. Even his eloquence could not prevent the audience with Shah Tahmasp from turning sour. Upon entering the shah's presence he was given shoes so 'I might not be suffered to tread upon his holy ground – being a Christian, and called amongst them *Gower* [from the Persian *gaur*, or non-Muslims], that is, unbeliever and unclean: esteeming all to be infidels and pagans which do not believe as they do, in their false filthy prophets *Mahomet* and *Murtezallie'*. Jenkinson presented the shah with Elizabeth's letter, and spoke of his hope of 'friendship, and free passage of our merchants and people, to repair and traffic within his dominions, for to bring in our commodities, and to carry away theirs, to the honour of both princes'. The shah was having none of it. He demanded to know why Elizabeth's letter was written in Latin, Hebrew and Italian, when he claimed to 'have none within our realm that understand those tongues'. He also 'demanded of me what country of Franks [Christian Europeans] I was, and what affairs I had there to do'. The interview was going from bad to worse: nobody at the shah's court knew anything about this tiny place called England, its female ruler or its 'famous city' of London. As with Abdullah-Khan, what interested Shah Tahmasp far more than insignificant England was 'the Emperor of Almaine [Germany], King Philip [II], and the great Turk, and which of them was of most power'. Jenkinson judged that this was not the time to criticize the Ottomans, as he had in response to Abdullah-Khan's questions, answering the shah 'to his contentation, not dispraising the great Turk'. But then the shah's interrogation of Jenkinson took a dramatic turn:

> Then he reasoned with me much of religion, demanding whether I were a *Gower*, that is to say, an unbeliever, or a *Muselman*, that is, of Mahomet's law. Unto whom I answered, that I was neither unbeliever nor Mahometan, but a Christian. What is that said he unto the king of Georgia's son [the Muslim convert David XI of Kartli], who being a Christian was fled unto the said Sophie, and he answered that a Christian was he that believeth in *Jesus Christus*, affirming him to be the son of God, and the greatest prophet: doest thou believe so said the Sophie unto me: yea that I do said I: Oh thou unbeliever said he, we have no need to have friendship with the unbelievers, and so willed me to depart. I being glad thereof did reverence and went my way.[29]

Thousands of miles from home, the plucky young mercer from Leicestershire stood his ground in front of two Muslim rulers, one the Shi'a shah Tahmasp, the other the Georgian king David XI, a convert from eastern Orthodox Christianity, and affirmed his belief in Christ as the son of God. It must have been a terrifying moment, and one that Jenkinson surely realized placed him in mortal danger. As he made his exit, he was followed by 'a man with a basanet [basin] of sand, sifting all the way that I had gone within the said palace, even from the said Sophie's sight unto the court gate', in a symbolic erasing of the polluting presence of the unbeliever. Jenkinson must have imagined that his audience with Shah Tahmasp would culminate in a trading alliance between the two countries. Instead he found himself effectively banished from the shah's court, his life possibly in the balance, and the Persian adventure wrecked as a result of insuperable religious differences. But he quickly learned that theology was not the sole cause of his expulsion.

Only four days before Jenkinson reached Qazvin, a Turkish ambassador had arrived 'to conclude a perpetual peace betwixt the same great Turk and the Sophy'. Nine years earlier, in November 1553, Jenkinson had watched as Sultan Süleyman marched into Aleppo en route to Persia just weeks after strangling his son Mustafa. The consequences of that murderous decision would eventually scupper Jenkinson's negotiations with Shah Tahmasp. Mustafa's death left Süleyman's sons Selim and Bayezid to fight over the right to succeed their father. The inevitable factionalism and intrigue culminated in Bayezid rebelling against his brother and father. Having been defeated by them at the Battle of Konya in May 1559, Bayezid fled and sought asylum at Shah Tahmasp's court in Qazvin. The shah was initially delighted to shelter such a prestigious rebel from his great enemy, and used Bayezid as leverage in negotiating a favourable renewal of the peace treaty of Amasya. In return, Süleyman and Selim demanded Bayezid's rendition. Finally, in 1561 Shah Tahmasp agreed, and an Ottoman delegation was sent to Qazvin, where Bayezid and his four sons were handed over and summarily garrotted the moment they left the city in July 1562.[30] An appalled Jenkinson reported that with Bayezid 'being slain according to the Turk's will, the Sophy sent him his head for a present, not a little desired, and acceptable to the unnatural father'. It would be inaccurate to say that the shah had ordered Bayezid's execution, but both he and Süleyman certainly displayed murderous duplicity in sanctioning yet another act of political filicide.

As Jenkinson later discovered, the Ottoman ambassador who was in Qazvin to ratify the revised peace treaty with the shah had consulted resident Turkish merchants, who agreed that Jenkinson was bad for business, because his 'coming thither (naming me by the name of Frank) would in great part destroy their trade'. Sure enough, Jenkinson learned that the shah had been persuaded 'not [to] entertain me well, neither dismiss me with letters or gifts, considering I was a Frank, and of that nation that was enemy to the great Turk his brother'. If the shah persisted in pursuing an alliance with the Englishman and it came 'to the knowledge of the Turk, it should be a means to break their new league and friendship'. He was further dissuaded 'because he had no need, neither that it was requisite for him to have friendship with unbelievers, whose countries lay far from him, and that it was best for him to send me with my letters unto the said great Turk for a present'.[31] Having extracted trading privileges from Süleyman in Aleppo, Jenkinson now faced another possible audience with him, but this time as a gift from a rival Muslim ruler. Worse, it was quite possible that he might arrive in Constantinople dead, like Bayezid, rather than alive.

Fortunately, Jenkinson was saved by the intervention of Abdullah-Khan and his son, Shah Ali Murza, who persuaded the shah that 'if he used me evil, there would few strangers resort into his country', which would adversely affect trade. With the Ottoman delegation gone, Shah Tahmasp agreed, and on 20 March 1563 'he sent me a rich garment of cloth of gold, and so dismissed me without any harm'. Jenkinson immediately headed back to Shirvan and the relative safety of Abdullah-Khan's court. The governor explained that if had it not been for Ali Murza's intervention with the shah on Jenkinson's behalf, he would have 'been utterly cast away and sent to the great Turk'. He also claimed that Shah Tahmasp would have granted him trading concessions 'had not the peace and league fortuned to have been concluded between them and the great Turk'.[32] For once in his short but charmed career, Jenkinson had been the victim of monumentally bad timing.

Extracting trading privileges from the ever hospitable Abdullah-Khan was better than nothing, and in May Jenkinson cut his losses and set off on the long journey back to Moscow. He arrived there in August 1563, presenting Ivan with a cache of silk and jewels, as well as 'the apparel given unto me by the Sophy'. In return he received enhanced trading privileges from the tsar. He wintered in Moscow before heading north to the White Sea, which he reached in July 1564. Embarking for England, Jenkinson faced what he described almost casually as 'great and extreme dangers of loss of ship, goods and life' without further explanation, before finally arriving back in London on 28 September 1564, three and a half years after he had left.[33]

Over ten remarkable years, Jenkinson had travelled further and achieved more than any other Tudor adventurer. He had met three of Asia's most powerful and terrifying rulers, survived to tell the tale, opened up trade with Russia and Persia and gained unprecedented insights into the region's Sunni–Shi'a conflict. Eventually, the commercial alliance he had cultivated with the Ottomans in the early 1550s compromised his attempts to establish trade with Persia a decade later, as he stepped into a world of religious and ethnic complexity which he barely understood, and which nearly cost him his life. He probably owed his survival to Süleyman's and Tahmasp's utter indifference to Elizabethan England. They did not seem to know even where it was, dismissing it (if they ever thought about it at all) as a peripheral presence in a much bigger geopolitical situation.

Over the next two decades, five more expeditions followed Jenkinson's foray into Persia. In the late 1560s his immediate successor, Arthur Edwards, spent far longer at the Safavid court than he had, obtaining the prized trading privileges that had eluded his predecessor. Shares in the company that had originally cost £25 now cost £200, but the trade failed to yield a consistent profit. The journey was too far, the returns too meagre and the local conditions too volatile, with repeated skirmishes between Turks, Persians and Tatars leading to the kidnap, ransom, robbery and even murder of successive unfortunate English merchants working in the region.[34]

Jenkinson returned to Russia twice, in 1566 and for the last time in 1571. On both occasions his tact and skill were required to restore amicable trade agreements with Ivan, who took the opportunity of seeing his old friend again to propose a most unlikely marriage with Queen Elizabeth. The queen's court retained one further tangible legacy of Jenkinson's Persian adventure. Records from 1564 detailing Elizabeth's domestic servants describe 'our dear and well beloved woman Ippolyta the Tartarian', who wore dresses made of Granadan silk and introduced the queen to the fashion of wearing Spanish leather shoes. Ippolyta is presumably 'Aura Soltana', the 'young Tartar girl' presented to Elizabeth by Jenkinson in 1560.[35] In the late 1570s Jenkinson returned to England, never to leave again, content to pursue his interests in commerce and property in Northamptonshire, where he died a very wealthy man in 1610.

Over three extraordinary decades, Anthony Jenkinson had met an Ottoman sultan, been sent out to travel to China, settled for Russia where he befriended a tsar, and ended up at the court of the Shah of Persia. Such was the indirect nature of sixteenth-century travel and discovery. Jenkinson's success justified the connection of Russia with Persia in the minds of London's political and commercial elite, and paved the way for further and even closer alliances between Elizabethans and Muslims over the next four decades. Thanks to Jenkinson, the Islamic world had come just a little closer to England. In 1586 the poet William Warner issued a new edition of his celebrated history *Albion's England*, in which Jenkinson was extolled as one of England's greatest explorers, responsible for transforming the country's place in the world under Elizabeth's rule and within Warner's lifetime:

> But where shall we begin his laudes to tell,
> In Europe, Asia, Affrick? For these all he saw, in all
> Employed for England's common good: nor my rejoicing small,
> That from Elizabeth to reign, and I to live begun,
> Hath happened that commerce and fame he to his natives won.[36]

Such high praise might have endured beyond Warner's and Jenkinson's lifetimes, but even as these verses were being written, England's Persian trade was already a thing of the rapidly receding past, and with it Jenkinson's fame. Elizabeth and her merchants were searching closer to home for profitable alliances beyond Catholic Europe. The moment had come to stop looking north and east and turn their attention southwards. It was time to do business with the Moors from Barbary.

3

The Battle for Barbary

In the second edition of his *Principal Navigations* (1598/9–1600) Richard Hakluyt claimed that England's 'first voyage for traffic into the kingdom of Morocco in Barbary' took place as early as 1551.[1] 'Barbary' entered the English language from the amalgamation of Greek and Latin for 'land of barbarians' and the Arabic word 'Berber', describing the local inhabitants. The Elizabethans' vague geography understood Barbary as either the Moroccan kingdom or more usually the entire North African coast as far south as Guinea. What English merchants based in Spain knew was that shipping merchandise direct by sea down the Atlantic coastline, from one port (like Bristol) to another (usually Agadir) in relatively clement conditions at a distance of around 1,800 miles, was relatively easy. This was also an attractive option to Edward VI's fledgling Protestant state because of Morocco's political independence from Spain and Portugal, as well as from the Ottomans. From the late fifteenth century the Berber Wattasid dynasty ruled most of northern Morocco, but was unable to oppose Portuguese incursions into its coastal regions. In the early sixteenth century a new dynasty emerged to the south. The Sa'adians, of Arab descent, claimed Marrakesh as their capital, defeating the Portuguese at Agadir in 1537 and finally overthrowing the Wattasids in 1554.

In 1551, as Wattasid control began to collapse, a group of English merchants financed Thomas Wyndham to sail to Morocco's southern ports, trading English linen, wool and 'diverse other things well accepted by the Moors' in exchange for almonds, dates and the Moroccan sugar that would play such havoc with Elizabeth's teeth.[2] Most of Wyndham's backers regarded Barbary as a natural extension of their established business in Spain, though many also wanted to explore more distant eastern markets – four supporters of Wyndham's voyage soon became charter members of the Muscovy Company. Not everyone was quite so impressed by England's arrival. 'The Portuguese were much offended with this our new trade into Barbary,' admitted one English trader in 1552. The Portuguese still held Tangier, Mazagan near Casablanca, and El Mina in modern-day Ghana. Their claims to a trading monopoly on the 3,000 miles of coastline in between seemed unrealistic, but this did not stop them protesting at the English encroachment. The Spanish were also alarmed, their diplomats reporting that the first ships were loaded with not just linen and wool but also 'pikes and armour', and that a subsequent expedition was 'laden with all sorts of munitions of war'.[3] The Protestant Edward VI and his regents were predictably uninterested in allaying Portuguese and Spanish anxieties that English weapons were arming their Moroccan adversaries, but with the marriage of Mary and Philip in 1554, the English crown agreed to Portuguese demands for a cessation of trade.

In direct contrast, upon her accession Elizabeth had few such qualms about trading with Morocco, and in 1559 her first parliament drew up a series of economic reforms bracing the country for imminent international isolation by restricting imports, but encouraging overseas exports and a stronger navy based on 'new navigations' into regions including 'those to Guinea, to Barbary, to Muscovy'. Within a decade England was importing 250 tons of Moroccan sugar each year valued at £18,000, with imports overall worth over £28,000, nearly 25 per cent more than the entire revenue for trade with Portugal.[4] In 1562, as Portuguese warships and English merchant fleets began clashing off the African coast, the Portuguese ambassador protested to Elizabeth that her merchants were once again selling arms enabling the Moroccans to wage war on Portugal. Elizabeth replied airily in a memorandum drafted by her secretary of state Sir William Cecil that 'the more Christian people that shall resort to the Gentiles and Saracens, the more shall the faith increase', and that she 'cannot allow that more regard should be had to the enriching of any particular person by monopolies and private navigations than to the public utility of the whole body of Christendom'.[5] It was a wonderfully disingenuous answer, especially as it came precisely at the moment when Moroccan forces were besieging the Portuguese in Mazagan. Apart from Elizabeth's studiedly obtuse comment, the English hardly ever mentioned religion directly when pressed on their commercial incursion into Morocco. It was a sign of the trade's profitability – and Elizabeth's growing confidence in foreign policy – that when pressed by the Portuguese to ban it in 1571, she refused on the grounds that Morocco was not a Portuguese possession, and was therefore free to trade with whomever it wished.

There was good reason for Elizabeth to resist such political pressure. The Moroccan trade was becoming very profitable, and involved over thirty of London's most powerful merchants, some acting alone, others in partnerships. In nearly every case, regardless of the commodities involved, the trade was conducted almost exclusively through Jewish intermediaries upon whom the new Sa'adian dynasty came to rely for everything from ransoming Christian captives to running the country's lucrative sugar farms. One of the most powerful of all the Jewish sugar barons in Morocco was Isaac Cabeça. Isaac and his brother Abraham came from a Sephardic family which had fled forced conversion in Spain for Morocco where they reverted to Judaism and flourished under their Muslim patrons first as translators and interpreters, then as merchants and bankers. By the late 1560s Isaac was selling sugar and buying cloth from a consortium of six English merchants led by Sir William Garrard. Garrard, one of London's most influential cloth merchants, had been trading in Morocco since 1552, as well as supporting slaving voyages to West Africa and Richard Chancellor's ill-fated Russian voyage, which led to his appointment as one of the Muscovy Company's founding consuls.[6]

In 1568 Cabeça was pronounced bankrupt and was imprisoned by Sultan Abdullah al-Ghalib for unpaid rents of 50,000 ounces of silver owed on three royal sugar farms. Garrard's consortium was appalled: Cabeça owed them over £1,000 for cloth bought on credit, a standard practice whereby payment – often with interest – was settled in either bills of exchange or sugar. As he had neither, the English merchants' factors struck a bargain with the insolvent Cabeça that 'if he would promise unto them to discharge the old debt' of £1,000 and supplied the consortium with £16,000 of sugar, they would intercede on his behalf with the sultan.[7] They employed 'a certain Moor being chief there about' called Tangarffe to petition Abdullah al-Ghalib to release Cabeça. But first Tangarffe insisted that the English factors had to 'promise to become bound to him' for whatever costs he incurred in settling Cabeça's debts. Two of the English factors agreed, and Cabeça was released, but in the convoluted chains of fractional debts and credits binding Christians, Jews and Muslims together it became so difficult to establish who owed what that the English merchants began suing each other first in the High Court of Admiralty and then in Chancery in a series of tortuous and inconclusive cases which dragged on throughout the 1570s. It is symptomatic of these exchanges that in the depositions undertaken in his absence Cabeça was only ever referred to as 'a famous and jolly merchant', whose religion was largely irrelevant to the financial machinations that threatened to engulf him.[8]

While English merchants traded with Muslims and Jews in Morocco, events thousands of miles away in London and Rome were about to transform England's position within Europe, and with it the country's relations with the Islamic world. In the early hours of 24 May 1570, John Felton, a well-known Catholic sympathizer living in Bermondsey, just south of the Thames, crossed London Bridge and nailed a printed document to the door of the Bishop of London's palace near St Paul's Cathedral. It was a copy of a papal bull issued in Rome on 25 February by Pope Pius V, entitled *Regnans in Excelsis* ('Reigning on High'), declaring the excommunication of Elizabeth I.[9] The bull (so called after its lead seal, or *bulla*), which was named after its *incipit*, or opening words, and written in the third person, condemned 'Elizabeth, the pretended Queen of England' for 'having seized on the kingdom and monstrously usurped the place of Supreme Head of the Church in all England', reducing 'the said kingdom into a miserable and ruinous condition, which was so lately reclaimed to the Catholic faith' under Mary and Philip. It catalogued a litany of perceived sins, based on Elizabeth's legislation of the late 1550s, including the abolition of 'Catholic rites and ceremonies', the introduction of prayer books 'to be read through the whole realm containing manifest

heresy', and other 'impious rites and institutions, by herself entertained and observed according to the prescript of Calvin'. It concluded:
'We do out of the fullness of our Apostolic power declare the aforesaid Elizabeth as being a heretic and a favourer of heretics, and her
adherents in the matters aforesaid, to have incurred the sentence of
excommunication, and to be cut off from the unity of the Body of
Christ. And moreover We do declare her to be deprived of her pretended title to the kingdom aforesaid.' The bull issued one last
particularly divisive edict: 'We do command and charge all and every
noblemen, subjects, people, and others aforesaid that they presume
not to obey her or her orders, mandates, and laws.'[10]

For England's Catholics, the bull created a terrible dilemma, com-
pelling them to choose between their religion and their country. For
Felton, it proved fatal in the most gruesome manner. Within days of
posting the bull he was arrested and imprisoned in Newgate, where
he declared that Elizabeth 'ought not to be the queen of England'.
Such treasonous statements landed him in the Tower of London,
where he was put on the rack and became the first Englishman to be
tortured by the state for his Catholic beliefs. He was found guilty of
treason and sentenced to be hung, drawn and quartered at the scene
of his crime in St Paul's Churchyard. On 8 August he addressed a hostile crowd and a hangman named Bull (a joke not lost on many
Protestant observers), insisting that he had done nothing wrong other
than promote a solemn papal edict. Refusing the ministrations of
attendant Protestant clergy, Felton was hanged, cut down before losing consciousness, and then disembowelled; as the hangman pulled
out his still beating heart he is said to have cried out 'once or twice,
"Jesus"', before he finally expired.[11]

There were various reasons why it had taken the papacy more than
a decade to excommunicate Elizabeth since her accession, though
very few were directly those of religion. Elizabeth's brother-in-law
and old suitor Philip believed he knew England better than most, and
vetoed repeated attempts at excommunication, anxious to avoid
pushing Elizabeth into the arms of the Calvinists in the Low Countries who were already causing him difficulties. As long as Elizabeth
avoided persecuting English Catholics, Spain was reluctant to intervene. However, especially after the introduction of the Oath of

Supremacy in 1559 that required public officials to swear allegiance to the queen as supreme governor of the Church of England, the country's religious reformers were beginning to formulate a series of political and theological attacks on Catholicism. Defending the oath in 1566, Robert Horne, Bishop of Winchester, wrote that 'the Pope is a more perilous enemy unto Christ, than the Turk: and Popery more idolatrous, than Turkery.'[12] As the religious rhetoric escalated and Europe started to divide itself along sectarian lines, Elizabeth found it increasingly difficult to remain neutral. In 1562 she began providing military support to the French Protestant Huguenots, and, though this venture failed, by 1566 she was also funding Calvinist rebels fighting Spanish rule in the Low Countries. Both policies soon ran into trouble. By the late 1560s the Catholic Guise faction in France appeared to be gaining the upper hand over the Huguenots. The Spanish finally lost patience with English privateers raiding its American fleet and Elizabeth's public support for Dutch Calvinism, and in 1568 they impounded English goods in the economically vital port of Antwerp. That same year, Elizabeth's first cousin Mary Stuart, 'Queen of Scots', fled the civil wars engulfing Scotland and sought refuge in England, where she became the focus of English Catholic hopes as a potential successor to Elizabeth. Within a year she was the catalyst for the Northern Rebellion, an uprising led by the powerful Catholic earls of Westmorland and Northumberland, who vowed to depose Elizabeth and enthrone Mary. Although the uprising was crushed, it finally galvanized Pius V to move against Elizabeth.

The pope's decision backfired almost immediately. He had neglected to consult an infuriated Philip II, the only ruler with sufficient military might to enforce the bull's demand for Elizabeth's deposition. In England, it only divided Catholics while strengthening patriotic support for Elizabeth and pushing her towards more aggressive Protestant policies at home and abroad. English suspicions of an international Catholic conspiracy against Protestantism seemed to be confirmed when the House of Guise carried out the infamous St Bartholomew's Day Massacre on 24 August 1572, when over 3,000 Huguenots were slaughtered on the streets of Paris, and thousands more in the rest of France. The news sent shockwaves through Europe: Elizabeth's court went into mourning, condemning the 'cruel murderers of such innocents'. Rome openly rejoiced, and the usually phlegmatic Philip II announced that the massacre 'was one of the greatest joys of my life'.[13]

Emboldened by such isolation and encouraged by the initial forays of London's merchant community into Russia, Persia and Morocco, Elizabeth and her advisers extended their search for alliances beyond Europe. Ever since the eleventh-century Crusades, unscrupulous Christian merchants had traded with the 'Saracens', leading the Fourth Lateran Council in 1215 to threaten with excommunication 'all those faithless and impious Christians, who against Christ Himself and the Christian people provide the Saracens with weapons, iron and wood'.[14] This prohibition, reinforced in councils over subsequent centuries, was honoured more in the breach than in the observance. The Venetians continued to trade with the Ottomans before and after the fall of Constantinople in 1453, and France had proposed commercial agreements with the Ottomans granting its merchants trading privileges as early as 1535. These were known as the 'Capitulations' (from the Latin for 'chapter' or 'paragraph', to describe an agreement with specified terms; the word developed its modern sense of 'surrender' only in the seventeenth century). They gave the French a significant advantage in the Levantine trade, and also cemented a more formal military and naval alliance with Sultan Süleyman designed to check Habsburg imperial expansion.[15] Traditionally England was too small and too far away to matter very much when it came to such edicts. But now, as a Protestant nation led by an excommunicated sovereign placed beyond papal sanction and with some experience of trade with Morocco, England and its merchants were suddenly freer than any other Christian country to trade with the Islamic world with ecclesiastical impunity.

The dawning realization that England could pursue commercial alliances with Muslim rulers was a purely circumstantial response to excommunication, but it was exacerbated by the wider conflicts defining European politics in the late 1560s. In September 1566, just months after the accession of the ultra-orthodox crusading pope Pius V, Süleyman the Magnificent died, ending a forty-six-year reign of relentless Ottoman territorial expansion. His successor, Selim II, immediately set out to prove himself by abandoning war in Persia to confront Christianity in the Mediterranean. With an aggressive pope in Rome and a bellicose sultan in Constantinople, the naturally cautious Philip II was beset with challenges to his rule. In 1568, already struggling with a Calvinist Dutch revolt, within months he faced yet another challenge, this time from the Morisco community in Granada. The Moriscos, or 'New Christians', were Spanish-born Muslims forced to convert to Christianity since the *reconquista* (reconquest) of Iberia from Islam and the mass expulsions by the Catholic rulers of Castile in 1492. Angry at Philip's increasingly intemperate policy towards them, they offered to acknowledge Ottoman sovereignty if Selim provided them with military aid. An exasperated Philip regarded the Moriscos as akin to a fifth column aiding the expansion of Ottoman imperialism and the Protestant cause in northern Europe.[16] As prayers were offered in Constantinople's mosques supporting the Moriscos, the sultan began despatching soldiers and weapons to Granada.

Like Elizabeth, Selim had designs on the Moroccan sultanate, although his interests were more territorial than commercial. From the time of his accession Selim tried to destabilize the Sa'adian dynasty, which had managed to retain its autonomy by playing the Spanish off against the Ottomans. Selim exploited the divisions between the kingdom's ruler Abdullah al-Ghalib and his younger brothers, Abd al-Malik and Mulay Ahmed al-Mansur, offering al-Malik and al-Mansur refuge in Algeria and Constantinople, where they made preparations to retake Morocco from their elder brother. Selim then turned his attention to Tunis. The city's fall to the Habsburgs in 1535 had always rankled with Selim's father Süleyman, and in late 1569 Ottoman forces took it back from the city's Spanish-backed Hafsid rulers. Selim was now in charge of the North African coast as far as Morocco and was poised to push into southern Spain should the Morisco uprising prove successful.

Having taken control of the south-western side of the Mediterranean, Selim now looked east, planning an invasion of Cyprus, knowing that this would almost certainly result in war with the island's Venetian rulers. Legend has it that the decadent sultan wanted the island for the quality of its wine (a questionable assumption on many levels). Cooler heads among Selim's administration knew that whoever held

Tunis and Cyprus controlled the flow of trade across the Mediterranean basin, the geographical flashpoint for what one historian of the region has called the 'forgotten frontier' between Latin Christian and Turkish Muslim communities in the sixteenth century.[17] In 1569, as Selim made preparations for the Cyprus campaign, he ratified the Franco-Ottoman Capitulations of the 1530s in a deft move aimed at ensuring French neutrality in any conflict that might unite Venice, the Papal States and possibly even Spain against him.

Ottoman designs on Cyprus inevitably led to a declaration of war against Venice, in the summer of 1570, and in July a Turkish army of more than 60,000 invaded the island. Over the next sixteen months a brutal campaign was waged between Cyprus's Venetian defenders and the vastly superior Ottoman forces. In May 1571, as the Turkish army besieged the last stronghold of Famagusta, Pope Pius and the Venetian authorities finally agreed a fragile Holy League that also included Spain, the Knights of Malta (fêted since throwing off the Ottoman siege of their island headquarters in 1565) and most of the Italian city states. The league hastily assembled a Christian fleet of over 200 ships led by Philip II's half-brother Don John of Austria, which set sail for Cyprus in August 1571. It came too late for the defenders of Famagusta, who had surrendered just after the fleet started out. When Don John learned of this he headed for Lepanto near Patras in the Greek Peloponnese, where the Ottoman fleet of 300 ships lay at anchor. On the morning of 7 October 1571 the two sides engaged each other in what would come to be regarded as the greatest naval battle of the century. By 4 p.m. the Ottomans had been outgunned and defeated by the Holy League, losing around 210 of their ships with the deaths of an estimated 15,000 soldiers and sailors.[18] For a brief moment, Christendom forgot its divisions and united in celebration of its first victory in nearly a century over the seemingly invincible Turks. Across Europe the news was greeted with an extraordinary outpouring of delight and relief. Festivities, processions and church masses all celebrated the event as divine intervention just at the moment when Islam seemed poised to overwhelm Christianity. Pamphlets, paintings and poems were published celebrating what the Venetian Pietro Buccio described as a 'marvellous and glorious Christian victory against the infidels'.[19]

When the news reached London it sparked public celebrations there too, despite Elizabeth's recent excommunication. Sermons in St Paul's thanked God for the victory, and the English chronicler Raphael Holinshed wrote that 'there were bonfires made through the city, with banqueting and great rejoicing, as good cause there was, for a victory of so great importance unto the whole state of the Christian commonwealth'. As far as Holinshed was concerned, the Ottomans were 'that common enemy of us all, who regardeth neither Protestant nor Catholic'.[20] Although this showed a limited understanding of Ottoman *realpolitik* – which had a very clear grasp of Protestant and Catholic divisions and how to exploit them – Holinshed's observation caught the popular mood. This was a moment, he intimated, when religious divisions could be set aside to unite Christianity against its biggest foe.

The victory at Lepanto would prove hollow within only a few years; sympathy between England and the rest of Christendom evaporated almost immediately. Philip II and Pius V were now in a league that threatened to rid Europe of its Protestant 'heresy', and both Elizabeth's allies and her adversaries knew it. One of England's spies in the Low Countries responded to the victory at Lepanto by reporting that Spain's 'next enterprise shall be to subdue the English Turks',[21] while another English spy, William Herle, wrote from the Low Countries in June 1573 that Philip II hated the English Protestants 'with an immortal hatred never to be reconciled, esteeming them worse than either Turks, Marranos, Jews, or Infidels, the blasphemers of God's holy name and of his son Jesus Christ'.[22]

Elizabeth turned to her most trusted counsellors – Secretary of State William Cecil, now Lord Burghley, and her ambassador to France and ruthless spymaster, Francis Walsingham – who advised her to consider cultivating alliances at both ends of the Mediterranean with Portugal and the Ottomans. The Portuguese might prove difficult considering the recent rifts over Morocco, but there was at least a diplomatic presence in both countries that might allow some compromise to be reached. The Ottomans were a different case altogether. The 1570s represented the apogee of Ottoman imperial power and territorial reach – though Elizabeth and her counsellors, from their limited perspective in London, could not have known it.

To them the Ottomans seemed to be winning and anyone who was able to take on the papacy and the Spanish was to be welcomed, whatever their religious persuasion. But at such a distance from London and with no resident English ambassador or merchants, any attempt to negotiate with the sultan could prove extremely difficult, even dangerous. So the proposal for an Ottoman initiative was quietly shelved and Burghley opened negotiations with Portugal, agreeing to sacrifice English commercial interests in Guinea to retain a foothold in Morocco. By 1576 an Anglo-Portuguese treaty had resolved most of the outstanding commercial disputes, but it failed even to mention Morocco, leaving the English free by omission to continue trading there with impunity.[23]

Even before the agreement was signed in 1576, English merchants were exploiting instability within the Sa'adian dynasty to pursue increasingly formal arms deals with the crown's tacit support. One of the key figures in the trade was Edmund Hogan, a member of the Mercers' Company from Hackney, who had commercial interests in Germany and Spain and was widely admired as one of 'the wisest and best merchants in London'.[24] In 1572 Hogan had sent his factor John Williams to Morocco to check reports of an abundance of high-quality potassium nitrate, or saltpetre, a key ingredient in making gunpowder, which was extremely scarce in western Europe and was imported at great expense from Persia and India. Attempts by the English to make saltpetre artificially were difficult, messy (it usually involved urine and animal excrement) and low yielding. As a result there was much excitement when Williams returned with Moroccan saltpetre that he told Hogan was 'far better than he could provide in any other place where he had travelled'. The only problem was the new sultan, Abu Abdallah Muhammad II, Al-Mutawakkil, who had succeeded his father Abdullah al-Ghalib in 1574, after a brief power struggle with his uncle, Abd al-Malik, a veteran of Lepanto and a former Spanish prisoner. Faced with al-Malik's continued opposition, Abdallah Muhammad was not interested in trading saltpetre for English cloth: he told Williams that 'if we would take upon us to bring him bullets of iron for his great ordnance, we should have saltpetre'. The sultan's counsellors advised him against the trade, arguing that 'although his law was to the contrary . . . no saltpetre should pass to the Christians, considering the commodity of pellets [iron shot or cannon balls] was as needful for him as saltpetre to the Christians'.[25]

In 1575 Williams returned to England with saltpetre samples and took them to Killingworth Castle to show Burghley and the Earl of Leicester, who was entertaining the queen on one of her royal progresses. Both men were impressed with the quality and approved the export of shot, cannon balls and other munitions. But the order came too late for Abdallah Muhammad. As the arms arrived (and just as Cecil was concluding the Anglo-Portuguese treaty) Abd al-Malik marched into Morocco from Algeria at the head of an Ottoman army, defeating Abdallah Muhammad outside his capital city of Fez in April 1576 and proclaiming himself the fourth Sa'adian sultan of Morocco. Abdallah fled to Ceuta where he sought the somewhat unlikely protection of his great adversary, the young Portuguese king Sebastian I.

Having spent many years at the Ottoman court, al-Malik was more urbane and cosmopolitan than his predecessor, and was eager to re-establish links with the English as a bulwark against the Spanish. Assessing his depleted military supplies, he realized he needed to encourage Hogan's proposals, but although the English merchant found craftsmen initially willing to travel to Morocco to cast weapons, he reported that when they were about to embark from Harwich they took fright 'and suddenly fled away'.[26] Why they refused to leave is unclear, but it suggests that not everyone was as enthusiastic as Hogan and Williams about trading with the infidel.

Despite these problems, the wily Hogan believed a deal was on offer from the new and inexperienced sultan. In a memorandum written to Elizabeth's advisers in March 1577, he claimed that al-Malik was prepared to offer the English an exclusive trade in saltpetre in exchange for weapons. According to Williams's intelligence, al-Malik claimed that, 'being desirous of the honour I hear of your queen of England, and the good liking I have of the English nation', he was prepared to 'enter in league as well as for the quiet traffic of her ships and subjects in to this country of Barbary'. Hogan added one further intriguing observation: al-Malik could provide a global market for English cloth by offering an alternative route into Turkey and the vast eastern markets beyond. He argued that 'all Christian commodities that goeth out of Christendom through Germany and Italy to serve the Turk, shall pass through his [al-Malik's] country to Constantinople, being a nearer passage and less charge than the other way, with good safe conduct and passport'. Hogan had watched the Muscovy Company struggle to sustain its Persian trade via the long and inhospitable north-east passage. He now sensed the opportunity to get at least as far as Turkey by going through Morocco then eastwards across North Africa. By transporting cloth 'into Barbary by sea, which is as near as Spain, we shall cut off all strangers from transportation, and therefore maintain our navy to the enriching of the queen's majesty's subjects'. This, Hogan insisted, 'is a matter of great importance because there shall be saved two thousand miles of carriage, and a good direct passage, with no danger of Portugal and Spain'. He concluded by indirectly contrasting the Atlantic sea route to Morocco with the Muscovy Company's gruelling north-east voyage to the Arctic Circle by noting that 'in our time, since the trade hath been in Barbary, the passage is such by sea as no ship hath miscarried that way'.[27]

Hogan's logistics and geography might have been questionable, but his determination was not. He managed to convince Burghley, Walsingham and Sir Thomas Gresham, the queen's financial adviser and founder of the Royal Exchange (who was always looking for new projects to enlarge Elizabeth's coffers) that he should travel to Morocco and meet the sultan as the queen's formal representative. Quite what he was to discuss has been a matter of intense conjecture. As we have seen, Elizabeth had been provided with outdated information back in 1561 when giving Anthony Jenkinson a somewhat naive letter for Shah Tahmasp. She had no intention of repeating her mistake with another Muslim ruler, and on this occasion she furnished Hogan with a letter of introduction (since lost) and detailed instructions, probably drawn up by Burghley, explaining what he should say upon meeting the Moroccan sultan. Elizabeth ordered Hogan to thank al-Malik for allowing the English to trade in Morocco, but also to ask that he address English commercial grievances sparked by disputes with local Jewish merchants over the settlement of payments in 'the matter of sugars'. Hogan should also avoid any discussion of arms deals. If the sultan raised the issue of 'artillery and munition as he shall from time to time have need of (a matter to which we can neither in honour or conscience yield unto), our pleasure therefore is that you make no mention thereof to him'. If the sultan pressed Hogan about why the English could not supply him with arms, he was to say, 'it is a matter that somewhat concerneth the service of our God', and that any attempt at such a trade would 'draw the hatred of all Christian princes our neighbours upon us' and lead to war.[28]

Armed with his instructions and the dual role of private merchant and Elizabeth's first ambassador to Morocco, Hogan set sail from Portsmouth on 6 May 1577 and fifteen days later landed at Safi, where he was met by a Moroccan delegation and English resident merchants. By the end of the month he had reached the outskirts of Abd al-Malik's royal court in Marrakesh. As he rode into the city 'there met me all the Christians of the Spaniards and Portuguese to receive me, which I know was more by the king's [al-Malik] commandment than of any good wills of themselves'. Hardly stopping even to acknowledge his Christian adversaries, Hogan recounted that they 'hung down their heads like dogs, and especially the Portuguese, and I countenanced them accordingly'. On 1 June Hogan was finally ushered into a meeting with al-Malik, where he read out the queen's letter in Spanish, waiting patiently as it was translated into Arabic. The sultan then responded cordially (via a Spanish interpreter), and 'declared that he, with his country and all things therein, should be at your majesty's commandment'. Over the next month al-Malik and the English merchant turned ambassador developed a brief but intense friendship. They dined together, watched plays, listened to music until midnight, messed about on al-Malik's boat, baited bulls with what Hogan called the sultan's 'English dogs', and even watched what the bemused Englishman described as 'a Morris dance'. In the midst of all the fun, Hogan managed to extract an agreement that 'the Jews there resident' should settle their English debts, and he also obtained '300 quintals [13 tons] gross of saltpetre' – with no mention of any weapons in exchange.

It is hardly surprising that Hogan gave an extremely positive assessment of al-Malik's rule in correspondence with London. 'I find him agreeable to do good to your merchants more than any other nation,' he wrote to Elizabeth, although he acknowledged that the sultan still faced internal challenges from the deposed Abdallah Muhammad. 'He is not yet all in quiet within his country,' as Hogan put it, 'for the black king [Abdallah Muhammad] keepeth in the mountains, being of small force.' But what really caught Hogan's attention was al-Malik's apparent antipathy towards Spain and his support of England. He reported al-Malik as saying, 'I make more account of you coming from the queen of England than of any from Spain,' because, as Hogan observed, Philip II 'cannot govern his own country, but is governed by the Pope and the Inquisition. Which religion [Catholicism] he doth wholly mislike of, finding him to be a very earnest Protestant of good religion and living, and well experimented as well in the Old Testament as New, bearing great affection to God's true religion used in your Highness's realm.'[29] Hogan's obviously partial report read more like Lutheran propaganda than the theological confessions of a Muslim ruler avidly reading the New Testament and embracing the 'true' Protestant faith. Just as the Shi'a Safavids were cast by the Portuguese and Venetians as saintly crusaders akin to early Christian warriors, so Protestant English merchants like Hogan refashioned the Sunni Sa'adian rulers in their own theological image to assuage any qualms they may have felt about doing business with them.

After this apparent revelation of al-Malik's supposedly Protestant beliefs, Hogan went on to describe the Morrocan ruler's account of closer Anglo-Moroccan ties. The sultan was prepared to use his influence among the Ottomans to ensure that 'all English ships that shall pass along his coast of Barbary, and through the straits [of Gibraltar] into the Levant seas' would be granted 'safe conduct that the said ships and merchants with their goods might pass into the Levant seas, and so to the Turk's dominions'. As far as Hogan was concerned, he was now dealing with a quasi-Protestant Moroccan ruler offering him free trade across his kingdom, and unfettered access to Ottoman dominions and markets even further east. It was an assumption that sustained trade for the moment, but one that would not stand up to close scrutiny, nor would survive subsequent cataclysmic events in Morocco.

Hogan concluded the account of his trip by writing that 'touching the private affairs entreated upon betwixt her Majesty and the Emperor [al-Malik], I had letters from him to satisfy her highness'. It is most unlikely that Hogan would have left Morocco with a substantial consignment of saltpetre without exchanging it for the arms that the sultan craved, and whose export Burghley, Walsingham and Gresham had already sanctioned, undoubtedly with royal approval. There is a long, undistinguished history of states, whatever their religious or ideological beliefs, being economical with the truth when it comes to selling arms to apparent adversaries, and the Elizabethans were no different. Formal written instructions are sometimes far from transparent or reliable guides to the truth, and it seems that Elizabeth, fearing that her letter to Hogan might be intercepted by Portuguese or Spanish spies, produced a set of written instructions elaborately condemning arms deals, while privately issuing oral instructions authorizing them.

Such a scenario seems to be confirmed by events after Hogan returned to London in late July 1577. He carried letters for Elizabeth from al-Malik that acceded to all Hogan's demands, and proposed the exchange of ambassadors to formalize their new alliance. The Portuguese ambassador in London, Francisco Giraldi, was outraged, and certainly believed that Hogan had exchanged English munitions for saltpetre during his visit. In a formal complaint delivered to Walsingham on 9 August 1577, he also provided an insight into just how much Londoners knew about the Anglo-Moroccan trade. 'I wish respectfully to inform you', he wrote tartly, 'that this city is full of the reception given by that tyrant the Shereef [al-Malik] to her Majesty's ambassador; how he went to meet him, and honoured him with this name by word of mouth, as has been more fully related to me by a Portuguese who came in the ship which brought the news. Also the thousands of stores and arms which that Ughens [Hogan] has taken in the galleon and in two other smaller vessels, which I am certain was little to the taste of the King, my master.'[30] Elizabeth had to tread carefully, and wrote back to al-Malik in September saying she was happy to receive his ambassador, but pleading for secrecy in the matter. It now seemed that a formal Anglo-Moroccan commercial and military alliance might be only a matter of months away.

*

Hogan's insistence that Morocco could provide access to the Otto-man markets had revived English interest in establishing trade with Constantinople, of which Walsingham had been a long-standing advocate. He appreciated that Christian reports of the Ottomans' demise after their defeat at Lepanto were greatly exaggerated. The Holy League rapidly disintegrated as first Pius died in May 1572 and then Venice, desperate to re-establish commercial relations with the Ottomans, signed a peace treaty in March 1573 acknowledging Selim's sovereignty over Cyprus and even paying him financial trib-ute. The grand vizier (in effect the prime minister), Sokollu Mehmed Pasha, dismissed claims that Ottoman naval supremacy in the region was over. He conducted a massive naval rebuilding programme, boasting that the 'Ottoman state is so powerful, if an order was issued to cast anchors from silver, to make rigging from silk, and to cut the sails from satin, it could be carried out for the entire fleet'.[31] As the Ottomans rebuilt, the Habsburgs seized Tunis in 1573, but a year later a new Turkish fleet, now even larger than before Lepanto, retook the city and restored Ottoman domination of the eastern Mediterranean.

As far as Walsingham could tell, the Ottomans were more powerful than ever and looked as though they would control access to Asia via the Mediterranean for the foreseeable future. Nevertheless, there were uncertainties: Selim had died suddenly in December 1574 (having reportedly fallen in the bath), and was succeeded by his son, Murad III. The new sultan's first and most abidingly infamous act was to have his five younger brothers strangled to prevent challenges to his accession. He became notorious for allowing his *haseki*, or consort, Safiye Sultan, to exercise unprecedented political power from within the protected space of the Topkapi Palace's infamous harem. Safiye, one of Ottoman history's most romantic yet enigmatic figures, was believed to be of Albanian origin and had been presented to Murad as a teenager after being captured by Ottoman forces. Murad also gave his mother Nurbanu Sultan, who was a Venetian noblewoman enslaved within the imperial household, the opportunity to adopt the role of queen mother and dictate rival policies to those of her daughter-in-law, with disastrous consequences.[32]

One such policy that particularly interested Walsingham was the

Ottomans' wooing of Protestants by stressing the commonalities between their faith and that of Islam. In an extraordinary letter written by the Ottoman Chancery in 1574 and addressed to 'the members of the Lutheran sect in Flanders and Spain', the reformers were praised because:

> you, for your part, do not worship idols, you have banished the idols and portraits, and bells from churches, and declared your faith by stating that God Almighty is One and Holy Jesus is His Prophet and Servant, and now, with heart and soul, are seeking and desirous of the true faith; but the faithless one they call Papa [the pope] does not recognise his Creator as One, ascribing divinity to Holy Jesus (upon him be peace!), and worshipping idols and pictures which he has made with his own hands, thus casting doubt upon the Oneness of God and instigating how many servants of God to that path of error.[33]

Rather like Hogan's fantasy of al-Malik being 'nearly' Protestant, in the Ottoman appeal Lutherans become *almost* Muslims, apparently sharing their rejection of intercession and their belief that Jesus was a prophet, though not a divinity, a belief ascribed solely to the 'faithless', misguided Trinitarian Catholic pope. Whether this was a calculated or accidental misunderstanding of Protestant belief in the Ottoman Chancery, its aim was clear: the Turks had a consistent geopolitical strategy to exploit the political divisions between Catholicism and what they referred to as the 'Luterān meẕhebi' ('Lutheran sect'), which was described almost like one of the Ottomans' rival Islamic sects.

In 1577 the Ottomans' attention was drawn away from Catholics and Lutherans and back to one of these rival sects: the troublesome Shi'a dynasty in Persia. Wishing to exploit the internal turmoil following Shah Tahmasp's death the previous year, Murad declared war with the aim of conquering the Caucasus, beginning a long and attritional conflict that would define his reign. At a stroke the Turkish invasion of the Caucasus brought the Muscovy Company's faltering Persian trade in the area to an abrupt halt. As far as Walsingham was concerned, the response required from England's merchants was obvious. The Ottomans were a powerful empire sympathetic to Protestants that needed to arm and clothe its armies: they were obviously crying out for two of England's staple commodities: cloth and guns.

Two of London's biggest commercial companies and their leading merchants had come to the same conclusion about trading with Turkey. In 1575 Edward Osborne and his trading partner Richard Staper, both members of the Clothworkers' Company with extensive business interests in Spain, Portugal, Brazil and the Low Countries, proposed to open up Turkish trade through Poland. According to Hakluyt, 'about the year 1575 the foresaid right worthy merchants at their charges and expenses sent John Wright and Joseph Clements by the way of Poland to Constantinople, where the said Joseph remained 18 months to procure a safe conduct from the *Grand Signor* [the phrase used by the English to describe the Ottoman sultan] for Mr. William Harborne, then factor for Sir Edward Osborne, to have free access into his dominions, and obtained the same'.[34] Hakluyt's praise was understandable, as he was in the pay of Osborne and Staper. They were instrumental in granting him a Clothworkers' scholarship at Oxford, which they continued to fund after he left. This was probably why Hakluyt omitted to mention that the rival Mercers' Company had already financed an earlier Turkish venture, this time by sea.

In June 1577, as Clements was in Constantinople, Thomas Cordell of the Mercers' Company obtained an Ottoman licence (or firman) ensuring safe conduct to trade cloth, tin, lead and steel for a voyage bound for Tripoli, Alexandria and Constantinople. One of the ships that was then prepared for the voyage was the *Pelican*, a 120-ton galleon that did not in the end make it, but was instead renamed the *Golden Hind* and became Sir Francis Drake's flagship when he left Plymouth in November 1577 on the first English circumnavigation of the globe. Cordell had probably obtained the licence from French merchants, trading under the Franco-Ottoman Capitulations that had been ratified in 1569. Under these terms the Ottomans regarded Christian merchants as *harbis*, alien non-Muslims, protected by an *aman*, or temporary licence. They were then tolerated as *musta 'min*, a status similar to that of a *dhimmi*, but were excluded from paying taxes for one year.[35] There are no surviving records showing whether or not Cordell reached Constantinople, or how Clements obtained his precious licence. Whatever the reasons, by spring 1578 the English were ready to do business with the Ottomans. But just after Osborne's factor William Harborne set off for Constantinople in July, news from Morocco sent shockwaves throughout Europe and the Mediterranean.

Ever since al-Malik's accession in 1576, the ousted Abdallah Muhammad had been marooned in exile in Portuguese-occupied Ceuta. During his brief reign Abdallah Muhammad had become notorious for his hostility towards Christians, but now in extremis he made Sebastian a remarkable offer. If the young king invaded Morocco, deposed al-Malik and restored him as ruler, Abdallah Muhammad promised to rule the kingdom as a Portuguese vassal state. Any experienced Christian ruler should have dismissed such a cynical proposal without a second thought. But to the astonishment of his counsellors, the pious, naive Sebastian, desperate for an excuse to prove his mettle by embarking on a glorious crusade, could not resist. One of the sixteenth century's more foolish and misguided monarchs, Sebastian might have been a tragic figure had he not been so pompous and impulsive. His great misfortune was to succeed his grandfather King John III aged just three. Under King John the Portuguese Empire had reached its zenith, monopolizing the far eastern spice trade, colonizing Brazil and reaching China and Japan. But by the 1570s, when Sebastian reached his majority, the empire was already in decline, in direct contrast to the neighbouring Spanish Empire ruled by his cousin Philip II. The young Portuguese king's religious devotion and obsession with leading a crusade to rid Africa of the Moors blinded him to the folly of attacking, with a far smaller force and little backing from the rest of Christendom, a Moroccan army that had the tacit support of the Ottomans. By the spring of 1578 Sebastian began assembling a ragtag army of Portuguese conscripts, Moroccans loyal to Abdallah Muhammad, German Calvinist mercenaries and Castilian adventurers. Their number also included one of England's most notorious renegades, Thomas Stukeley (or Stucley).[36]

'Of this man', wrote Burghley, 'might be written whole volumes.' Even by the swashbuckling standards of Elizabethan England, Stukeley – soldier, spy, pirate, explorer, traitor, informer, conspirator – had had an extravagant career. Rumoured to be the illegitimate son of Henry VIII, by the age of thirty he had already fled England to escape arrest for sedition and fraud. He fought with great bravery and distinction on the continent throughout the 1550s, before returning to England and gaining Elizabeth's favour as a privateer attacking Spanish and French shipping. In 1568 he was arrested on suspicion of treason and collusion with the Catholic Irish rebels. Having denounced Elizabeth, claiming scandalously that he 'set not a fart for her, whore, nor yet for her office',[37] he fled, first to Spain then to Rome, arriving in the wake of the papal bull of excommunication. Loyal Elizabethans were appalled by Stukeley's behaviour. Holinshed castigated him as 'a defamed person almost through all Christendom, and a faithless beast', while the historian William Camden condemned him grandly as 'a ruffian, a riotous spendthrift and a vapourer [boastful bully]'.[38] Preaching open rebellion against Elizabeth, Stukeley encouraged first Philip then Pius to finance his personal invasion of Ireland. In 1571 he captained Spanish galleys at the Battle of Lepanto, and by 1578 he finally obtained Pope Gregory XIII's support, albeit circumspect, for his Irish adventure, receiving just one ship and 600 Italian soldiers.

When Stukeley arrived in Lisbon in May en route to Ireland, Sebastian was still desperately short of soldiers. He implored the Englishman to abandon his Irish adventure and join him on his equally improbable expedition into Africa. The king wrote to Rome with typical sententiousness, explaining that he had bigger plans for Stukeley, and that he 'understood the business better than the pope, or any of us, or anyone else in the world, and in fine it was best not to go [to Ireland] at present'. With characteristic opportunism (and the unattractive alternative of sailing on with a leaky boat and mutinous soldiers) Stukeley agreed, abandoning the papacy and Ireland, which he now claimed would have brought him only 'hunger and lice'. Throughout the summer of 1578 the English renegade watched as Sebastian assembled his fractious army of 16,000 soldiers, which were quickly outnumbered by an extraordinary array of non-combatants, described by one commentator as 'an unsavoury company of baggage' that included bishops, priests and 'an infinite number of drudges, slaves, negroes, mulattoes, horse boys, laundresses, and those sweet wenches that the Frenchmen do merrily call the daughters of delight'.[39] Finally in late June the fleet was ready, but Sebastian was wisely advised that midsummer was no time to lead an army of armour-clad knights into a battle with an experienced standing army in the sweltering Moroccan heat. As ever, the impetuous king refused to listen and on 26 June his armada of hundreds of ships left Lisbon and headed for Africa.

On 12 July the fleet made a chaotic landing at Asilah on Morocco's north-west coast in an unsuccessful attempt to take on water. Rather than re-embarking and sailing down the coast for a few more hours to his chosen landing site of Larache, Sebastian chose a suicidal week-long forced march inland to reach his objective. 'A perilous overland march of some thirty-five miles to reach a point only twenty safe miles away by sea', observes one modern historian, was 'an attraction which the scatter-brained youth could not resist'.[40] On Sunday 3 August the exhausted and demoralized army, debilitated by marching for days on end in full armour in midday temperatures of over 100 degrees Fahrenheit and running low on rations, reached the Mekhazen River on a plain north of the town known locally as El-Ksar el-Kebir (in Portuguese, Alcácer-Quibir). There they met and were quickly encircled by al-Malik's formidable army of at least 60,000 experienced Berbers, Arabs, Turks and Moriscos, four times the size of Sebastian's pitiful force. Even worse, it soon became clear that Sebastian's decision to favour infantry with pikes over cavalry and arquebusiers (soldiers equipped with wheel-lock firearms) had little or no intelligence of al-Malik's 30,000 horse and 3,000 crack Morisco arquebusiers, many of whom were probably armed with English munitions. Facing almost certain annihilation, Sebastian's advisers gathered on the night before the battle in a council of war. The consensus was to avoid disaster and beat a dignified retreat to the coast. With continuing rashness the undaunted Sebastian scorned this advice and ordered an engagement early the next day in the hope of exploiting the element of surprise.

The following day, 'the fourth day of August, which was Monday, in the year of our salutation 1578, the battle was begun between the two kings about twelve of the clocke'. Once again Sebastian managed to disable his army, choosing to fight at the hottest time of the day and riding into the blinding sun. What he did not realize was that his adversary, al-Malik, was mortally ill even before he reached the battlefield. Those close to the ailing Moroccan suspected poisoning by disaffected Turkish supporters, others feared the plague; but, whatever the cause, by the time he addressed his troops that morning he had only hours to live. The Moroccan artillery fired first, briefly halting the advance of Sebastian's infantry. Almost immediately 'the arquebusiers on foot on both sides discharged as thick as hail, with such a horrible, furious, and terrible tempest, that the cracking and roaring of the guns did make the earth so to tremble, as though it would have sunk down to hell'. The fighting quickly descended into hand-to-hand combat: the German and Spanish regiments fought with such ferocity that they broke through the opposition, followed by the Portuguese cavalry. As the Moroccans buckled, al-Malik mounted his horse to rally his troops, but the effort was too much. He collapsed onto his litter and died within the hour. If the news had reached the rest of the battlefield Sebastian might have won a most unlikely victory, but instead 'his death was subtly dissembled' by the Moroccans and their troops rallied.

As the fighting raged on, a second king fell. Abdallah Muhammad had led an unsuccessful cavalry charge and seen the way the battle was going. He tried to escape across the Mekhazen, but was thrown by his horse 'and being unskilful to swim, was drowned and perished'. Stukeley also suffered an ignoble end: having deserted his Italian troops at the Moors' first assault, 'there came a piece of artillery that took off both his legs; and so he ended his days'.[41] He might not have given a fart about Elizabeth, but it may have been one of her cannonballs that killed him. Finally, as the waves of Moorish infantry mowed down the last groups of exhausted soldiers, the third king fell on the battlefield. Sebastian had made every mistake possible in pursuing his dream of a crusade against the infidel, but at the last he proved a courageous, even inspirational warrior, who 'forsaketh not his people: thinking it dishonourable to seek safety by flight, and with those few that followed him, behaved himself valiantly. He slew so many, he sent so many to hell, that many called him the lightning.' He was last seen, even as all was clearly lost, charging once more into the heat of the battle, where he was cut down. He was probably unknown to his killers as the last undisputed king of the Portuguese House of Avis that had ruled the kingdom since 1385.

After six hours of brutal conflict the Battle of El-Ksar el-Kebir – referred to in Europe as the Battle of Alcácer-Quibir or the Battle of the Three Kings, known to the Moors as the Battle of Wad el-Mekhazen and reported in English diplomatic correspondence as the Battle of Alcazar – was over. Sebastian's army of 16,000 had been annihilated. But the horror was not at an end. Reports suggested that anywhere between 3,000 and 12,000 soldiers had been killed, but certainly no more than 200 had managed to escape. The rest, including the thousands of non-combatants, were carried off into captivity: the wealthy ones were ransomed, but the vast majority were sold into slavery. Al-Malik was survived by his brother, Ahmad al-Mansur, who fought in the battle and immediately claimed the throne once victory was assured. He ordered the recovery of the bodies of the three dead claimants to his new crown:

> These dead bodies of three kings being brought into one pavilion, made a horrible spectacle, and wrung tears from the beholders. For what more sorrowful and horrible a sight could there be, than to behold three most mighty kings, that died in one battle, lying together. The army of one of whom was vanquished when he lived, and after he was dead did straight away overcome the army of the other two kings: and whereas all three did aspire to the kingdom of Morocco, none of them held it.[42]

When news of the defeat reached Lisbon the following month, a resident German merchant wrote home describing 'how great were the lamentations, the despair and grief, not only in this city, but in all the land. The men went about as if dazed . . . It is a woeful matter to lose in one day the king, their husbands, their sons, and all the goods and chattels they had with them. But what is even more terrible is that this kingdom must now fall under Spanish rule, which they can brook the least of all.'[43] The humiliation was so profound that many Portuguese historians believe the country never recovered. Although Sebastian's body was eventually repatriated and buried in the church of Santa Maria in Belém, many refused to believe he was dead, claiming he had fled the battle and would one day return to save the country from its seemingly terminal decline. The messianic belief in 'Sebastianism' was even evoked to defend the Brazilian monarchy in the late nineteenth century, and is still part of the modern Portuguese concept of *saudosismo*, a yearning or nostalgia for what was lost, and might yet be.

Across Europe, rulers assessed the significance of the battle. The Ottomans were annoyed at seeing another Muslim ruler (albeit one that paid them obeisance) destroy a Christian army, especially after their own failings at Lepanto, but they reassured themselves that al-Mansur would remain pro-Turkish and cement their dominion in North Africa. Philip II was officially distraught at the news of his cousin's death, though he immediately saw an opportunity to exploit the subsequent power vacuum in Lisbon. Spain's papal nuncio wrote to Rome to blame Sebastian's defeat on Elizabeth's support of al-Malik: 'there is no evil that is not devised by that woman who, it is perfectly plain, succoured Mulocco [al-Malik] with arms and especially artillery', he thundered. Clearly shaken by the loss of their carefully cultivated Muslim ally, the English were dismayed by the prospect of Portugal falling into Philip's hands, as it would give him effective control over the vast wealth of the whole of Iberia, the Low Countries, the New World and the Portuguese possessions in south-east Asia. With no immediate heir, Sebastian was succeeded by his aged great-uncle Cardinal Henry. His succession was contested by Don António, Prior of Crato, grandson of King Manuel I. Don António had fought bravely at Alcácer-Quibir, where he was captured, but had managed to ransom himself. Both England and France backed the Portuguese pretender in a forlorn attempt to stop Philip II, but such foreign support hardly helped his claim, especially when it included English 'heretics' who were blamed for supplying the weapons that had defeated Sebastian. In August 1580 Philip's troops marched into Portugal, defeating Don António's forces at the Battle of Alcántara. Don António fled first to France then to England, in the hope of building political opposition to the Spanish takeover. The following April Philip II of Spain was crowned Philip I, King of Portugal and the Algarve, creating (with the inclusion of Portugal's possessions in the New World) one of the greatest empires the world had ever seen.

In the years leading up to the Battle of Alcácer-Quibir, English merchants had established a precarious understanding with the Sa'adian dynasty, involving questionable religious parallels and the trade of arms for goods, which created the conditions for the first direct alliance between England and a Sunni Muslim kingdom. It was a relationship on which Elizabeth and many of her closest advisers had hoped to build, given the common anti-Spanish feeling of both Protestants and Muslims. Events at Alcácer-Quibir changed everything; the queen's attempts to create an alliance with the Muslim world appeared to be in ruins, and her political isolation more complete than ever. Spain now had the heretic queen in its sights.

4

An Apt Man in Constantinople

As news of the events at Alcácer-Quibir began to reach London in the autumn of 1578, Sir Francis Walsingham assumed that the death of the pro-English al-Malik signalled the end of the fledgling Anglo-Moroccan alliance almost before it had begun. With his usual pragmatism he turned his attention elsewhere – to the Ottomans. By the end of the year, Walsingham had written one of the most important documents in the early history of Anglo-Turkish relations, his 'Memorandum on the Turkey trade', composed for Elizabeth and her counsellors, which would become the blueprint for all subsequent Elizabethan relations with the Ottoman Empire.

With his characteristic attention to detail and unrivalled grasp of *realpolitik*, Walsingham's memo sought to justify the trade as well as to anticipate every eventuality. The English experience in Russia, Persia and more recently Morocco had taught him that it was vital first to establish a trading presence before developing more formal political alliances, so he began by outlining 'the profit that may ensue by trade into the Turk's dominions'. He argued that it would strengthen the navy's role in national defence and international commerce, allow merchants to export English goods direct into Turkish markets rather than through costly middlemen, and enable the importation of duty-free Turkish goods which could then be sold across Europe. However, the obstacles were manifold: he understood that all the great Catholic powers with an interest in Mediterranean trade would attempt to stop the trade, 'by finesse [diplomatic intrigue] and by force'. Walsingham observed drily that Spain, 'being not the best effected towards us', would undoubtedly concoct a strategic diplomatic and naval alliance with the French and Venetians to prevent the English trade. The difficulties would be all the greater once, as Walsingham correctly predicted, Philip 'is possessed of the kingdom of Portugal'.

Walsingham's solution was to 'make choice of some apt man to be sent with her Majesty's letters unto the Turk to procure an ample safe conduct, who is always to remain there at the charge of the merchants'. It was a shrewd proposal. Whoever was chosen would exploit the blurred line between trade and politics, travelling under royal warrant but paid for by London's merchants, giving the queen maximum diplomatic returns on a minimum financial investment. He would remain in Constantinople indefinitely to thwart attempts by resident Venetian, French and Spanish merchants or diplomats to disrupt the English trade. Walsingham stressed that the first visit was 'to be handled with great secrecy' and undertaken overland initially to prevent news of his seaborne departure from London reaching the ears of Constantinople's resident ambassadors. The ambitious long-term plan was for twenty English ships to sail annually through the Mediterranean during the winter months, with sufficient commodities to turn a profit in Turkey. But Walsingham worried: could the English supply enough cloth to load twenty ships? Would such a flotilla flood the Turkish market and cause prices to crash? He also wondered 'whether there shall be that vent of our kerseys during the wars between the said Turk and Sophy as was before the said wars'. Finally he took up Edmund Hogan's plan for connecting the Moroccan trade with Constantinople, believing that it would be vital 'to procure the Turk's letters to the King of Barbary and the rest of the princes of Africa that the ports there may be free for our merchants'.[1] Walsingham was clearly nervous about the Moroccan royal succession following al-Malik's death, and hoped – rather optimistically – that he could use Ottoman leverage to ensure unimpeded English commerce through the region.

The 'apt man' chosen to lead England's hazardous foray into the Turkish trade was William Harborne. Born in Great Yarmouth into a minor gentry family, Harborne began travelling abroad as a factor in 1559, and by the 1570s he was working for Edward Osborne. In 1577, with plans for a Turkish adventure already being mooted, he was named as one of the principal members of the newly formed Spanish Company, alongside Osborne, Staper and Anthony Jenkinson.

Jenkinson's days of travelling to Russia and Persia were over by then, but if he and Harborne met during this period, the older man surely saw a kindred spirit in the younger. They certainly shared many of the attributes required to undertake such gruelling and dangerous long-distance travels into the Islamic world. Both men were charismatic, tenacious and resourceful, both dedicated mercers and both loyal servants of their Protestant queen. Neither was above speaking his mind, even when such frankness threatened their careers and sometimes their lives.

Like many English merchants of his time, Harborne was employed as a government spy before departing for Turkey, which suggests that his selection for the job resulted from the combined effort of Osborne, Staper and Walsingham. Whatever the discussions behind his appointment, in early August 1578, just before the battle at Alcácer-Quibir, Harborne was several weeks into a four-month over-land journey to Constantinople, accompanied by Joseph Clements and just one servant. They travelled through Germany to Poland, where Harborne met his brother-in-law in Lvov (possibly the English factor John Wight), together with an Ottoman dragoman (a diplo-matic translator and envoy) known as Mustafa Beg. In contrast to Jenkinson's bad luck in Persia, it was Harborne's good fortune to arrive just at the moment when an Ottoman diplomatic delegation that included Mustafa renewed a peace treaty between Poland and the new Turkish sultan Murad III. Harborne joined Mustafa's diplo-matic caravan as it headed back to Constantinople, taking a route advocated by Jenkinson back in 1561, through Moldavia, Bulgaria and Romania. He arrived in the Ottoman capital on 28 October 1578.[2]

What Harborne made of his arrival is not recorded, but as a Prot-estant English merchant from Norfolk he must have experienced a combination of exhilaration and trepidation. Constantinople, one of the world's greatest imperial capitals, had changed beyond all recog-nition since it fell to Sultan Mehmed II in 1453, and would subsequently be called Istanbul, from the Greek for 'to the city', although it was also referred to in official Ottoman business for centuries as Kostan-tiniyye, or, as Christians would continue to call it, Constantinople (which is how it is named throughout this book). From a Byzantine city in decline and under siege with a population of just 50,000, the Ottomans had transformed it into the capital of the Islamic world, a vibrant multi-ethnic and multi-denominational city. By the time Harborne arrived it had a population estimated at between 300,000 and 500,000, much larger than London (200,000), Paris (220,000), Naples (280,000) or Venice (160,000). From sheer political and commercial necessity Mehmed had engineered a cosmopolitan capital, repopulating it through the forced resettlement of merchants and craftsmen from various ethnic and religious backgrounds, until it was made up of 58 per cent Muslims, 32 per cent Christians and 10 per cent Jews, which included Greeks, Armenians and various communities deported from the recently conquered Balkans.[3]

To Harborne, the city's skyline must have appeared alien and intimidating. At the command of Mehmed II, the iconic Greek Orthodox cathedral of Hagia Sophia had been transformed into a mosque, and an ambitious programme of public building saw the creation of a new imperial palace, the Topkapi Palace overlooking the Golden Horn, the Fatih Mosque and Külliye (a complex of buildings of characteristic Ottoman architecture) and a commercial district dominated by a *bedestan* (the marketplace today known as the Grand Bazaar) and a series of *khans* (urban caravanserais). On the northern side of the Golden Horn he repopulated Galata – still identified by its imposing Genoese tower – with Jewish and Christian merchants, and this is where Harborne lived during his time in Constantinople. Under Mehmed 190 mosques, 24 madrasas (schools), 32 hammams (bathhouses) and 12 markets were erected, transforming it from a Greek Orthodox city into a Muslim one. Under Sultan Süleyman the urban transformation became even more pronounced, thanks primarily to the extraordinary achievements of the architect Mimar Sinan. During his long career Sinan built some 120 buildings in Constantinople, many of which Harborne would have seen, including the Şehzade Mosque and the monumental Süleymaniye Mosque and Külliye, completed twenty years before the Englishman's arrival.

If the size and splendour of the city dazzled Harborne, his initial encounters with the intensely hierarchical and labyrinthine Ottoman political bureaucracy, of which he had had virtually no experience, must have been completely bewildering. The first problem was one of communication. Harborne corresponded with his Ottoman counterparts in Latin or Italian (in which he appears to have been fluent), which was then translated into Turkish, leaving much room for creative licence and strategic misunderstanding. Then there was the difficulty of gaining appropriate formal access to the Ottoman court. The French had developed the concept of the 'Sublime Porte', the 'High Gate' (in Turkish *Bâbıâli*), through which foreign dignitaries were allowed to enter the Ottoman state buildings in an elaborate and carefully orchestrated procession, where any breach of etiquette could prove disastrous. Once within the imperial complex centred on the Topkapi Palace, visitors were met with a confusing series of layers within the sultan's governance. The Inner Service was dominated by the harem, which was responsible for the sultan's welfare. This included his wives, concubines and slaves, and by the time Harborne arrived it was also, through the power granted to Safiye Sultan, exercising considerable influence over imperial policy. Fiscal and diplomatic responsibilities were delegated to the Outer Service and the so-called Scribal Institution, which was controlled by the grand vizier. The grand vizier was appointed by the sultan with executive powers over an imperial advisory council (the *divan*) composed of viziers and pashas. However, it also had to compete with the demands of various social and economic ministries known as 'institutions'. These included the Religious Institution and the Military Institution, the latter controlling the sultan's feared and often unpredictable fighting corps, the Janissaries. To make matters even more confusing, the Ottoman ruling administration was divided between the Turkish nobility and the *devşirme* class of abducted Christian youths, forcible converts to Islam and by extension loyal to the sultan's administrative or military institutions. Both groups claimed the title 'Osmanli' or 'Ottoman' to signify their membership of the state's ruling class, although in times of conflict each exploited the other's weaknesses for political gain. The sultans had adopted the *devşirme* system as a deliberate method of divide and rule, enabling them to play each group off against the other, but it was a volatile way of doing politics that baffled outsiders.

Harborne's first task was to establish a dialogue with the grand vizier, the seventy-three-year-old Sokollu Mehmed Pasha. Bosnian by birth, the wily Sokollu Mehmed was a product of the *devşirme* system who had risen rapidly through the Ottoman ranks before being appointed grand vizier under Süleyman in 1565. It was testament to his consummate political skill that Sokollu Mehmed had not only survived but prospered in the role for fourteen years and under three different sultans by the time of Harborne's arrival, at which point he was locked in a bitter power struggle with Safiye Sultan.

Harborne was unsurprisingly oblivious to such courtly intrigue, not least because he had a disastrous start to his time in Constantinople. His woes were described in graphic detail in his earliest surviving correspondence, a petition submitted to Sokollu Mehmed, the first ever written to a grand vizier by a foreigner. Harborne wrote the petition in Italian then submitted it via a dragoman to the Ottoman Chancery, where it was translated into Turkish with all the formal conventions (including the plaintiff being presented in the third person) for Sokollu Mehmed's consideration. Harborne complained that within weeks of his safe arrival in Constantinople he had ordered goods and money left in Lvov to be sent to him by one of his servants, only for the servant to be 'assassinated by thieves within one day's journey of this famous city, and they robbed him of his goods and money to the sum of 4,000 ducats [£1,300]'.[4] Considering that an average English ship's cargo was worth around £7,000, this was a substantial loss (the poor servant who lost his life remained anonymous, and was never mentioned again). The goods involved were the ubiquitous kersey cloths, as well as tin and lead, which represented a flagrant violation of the papal ban on such merchandise. Harborne complained that the grand vizier knew the whereabouts of his servant's assassins as well as of his goods, but his *chiauses* (Turkish sergeants) 'have made no effort at all – they did not even wish to go to find the merchandise where the thieves confessed that it was but, rather, wasted their time'. Then, in a remarkable stroke of good luck – at least for Harborne – 'many of the aforesaid thieves have died'.[5] Despite the apparent delicacy of the situation, Harborne managed to end his petition with a request for safe conducts to trade throughout the Ottoman-controlled eastern Mediterranean, and for permission to export lead.

Frustratingly, neither Harborne's subsequent letters nor Ottoman Chancery records reveal if he received compensation for his losses, although he was unlikely to have been able to continue trading without some indemnity. Hakluyt certainly believed that Harborne turned his loss into broader profit, describing the canny Englishman as having 'behaved himself so wisely and discreetly that within a few months after he obtained himself not only the great Turk's large and ample privilege for himself . . . but also procured his honourable and friendly letters unto her Majesty'.[6] This was a very bland account of what really happened. The imperial ambassador to Constantinople, Joachim von Sinzendorf, had been keeping a suspicious eye on Harborne since his arrival. He reported to the Habsburg court in Vienna that 'this so-called merchant Harborne' had 'begun to set this trade going here, with the foreknowledge of the Queen'. Sinzendorf was appalled that, despite having no formal mandate from Elizabeth, Harborne had bribed Sokollu Mehmed 'with a quantity sufficient for three robes of the best English cloth he had' to obtain commercial safe-conduct agreements. Having issued these agreements, Sinzendorf claimed that the grand vizier had asked Harborne's interpreter, Mustafa Beg, 'Does he also want to have a letter from the Sultan to the Queen?', to which a surprised and clearly delighted Harborne is reported to have said: 'Yes, it would be nothing but good.' It seems that the sultan was unaware of the proposed letter to Elizabeth, which was written by Sokollu Mehmed; Harborne had simply struck lucky, having obtained the precious commercial rights as well as the formal letter in return for a relatively cheap bribe. In demanding that the letter be written by the sultan's chancellor, Sokollu Mehmed ignored protocol that insisted the sultan would respond only if a letter was first written to him. It was reported that the grand vizier told the chancellor, 'Of course, write the letter, because they are Lutherans, and good people!'[7] Sinzendorf's report was hardly impartial: he had a vested interest in claiming that Harborne's negotiations with the grand vizier were part of a broader Turco-Protestant conspiracy enabling Murad to establish 'an open, safe port in England, by means of which to set his foot also into the western Empire'.[8] However, he does seem to have understood that Harborne's manoeuvrings had formalized amicable commercial exchanges with the

Ottoman authorities that had put the other European representatives in Constantinople on the defensive.

The letters that followed were the first sustained reciprocal exchange of correspondence between an Ottoman sultan and an English monarch, and would last for another seventeen years. In early March 1579 a letter from the Imperial Chancery was dictated on Sultan Murad's behalf. It was composed in the Diwani script using a particular variant of Ottoman Turkish known as Fasih Türkce ('eloquent Turkish'), the language of poetry and imperial administration. It was written in ink on a large piece of paper, dusted with gold and sealed with an elaborate *tughra* or calligraphic monogram. The letter was a standard Ottoman *hukum*, or command to a subject, addressed as a 'Command to Elzābet, who is the queen of the domain of Anletār'.[9] With Mustafa Beg's assistance Harborne translated the letter into Latin to be read out back in London. It began:

> In greatness and glory most renowned Elizabeth, most sacred queen, and noble prince of the most mighty worshippers of Jesus, most wise governor of the causes and affairs of the people and family of Nazareth, cloud of most pleasant rain, and sweetest fountain of nobleness and virtue, lady and heir of the perpetual happiness and glory of the noble realm of England [Anletār] (whom all sorts seek unto and submit themselves) we wish most prosperous success and happy ends to all your actions, and do offer unto you such pleasures and courtesies as are worthy of our mutual and eternal familiarity: thus ending (as best beseemeth us) our former salutations.[10]

Buried within the letter's honorific rhetoric was some shrewd *realpolitik*. Murad was careful to describe Elizabeth as one of the Christian 'worshippers of Jesus' and part of the 'family of Nazareth', implying the possibility of a Protestant–Islamic alliance based on the mutual acceptance of Jesus as a holy figure. He also ensured that, in praising Elizabeth, she was to understand that he was the active partner doing all the wishing and offering, for which she and her subjects should be grateful. Acknowledging Harborne's arrival 'in the name of your most excellent regal majesty', with 'kindness, courtesy and friendly offices on your part', Murad was prepared to agree that 'our country be always open to such of your subjects, as by way of merchandise shall trade hither: and we will never fail to aid and succour any of them that are or shall be willing to esteem of our friendship, favour and assistance'. Murad assured Elizabeth he had commanded 'all our kings, judges, and travellers by sea' throughout the Ottoman Empire to ensure that 'such aforesaid persons as shall resort thither by sea from the realm of England, either with great or small vessels to trade by way of merchandise, may lawfully come to our imperial dominions, and freely return home again . . . straightly charging that they be suffered to use and trade all kind of merchandise as any other Christians do, without let or disturbance'. In case Elizabeth might feel she was receiving special dispensation, the letter reminded her that 'our familiars and confederates the French, Venetians, Polonians, and the king of Germany, with diverse other our neighbours about us, have liberty to come hither, and to return again into their own countries, in like sort'. The power and magnanimity of the Ottomans was so great they could accommodate anyone, from Catholic merchants and emperors to Protestant English sovereigns. However, in one final caveat which seems to have been added by Harborne (with Mustafa's connivance), the Latin translation reminds Elizabeth that the alliance should be reciprocal, and that 'you likewise bethink yourself of your like benevolence, humanity and friendship towards us, to open the gate thereof unto us . . . and that like liberty may be granted by your highness to our subjects and merchants to come with their merchandise to your dominions'.[11] The original letter contained no such wish, because the Ottomans did not regard the English as a serious political power, an attitude which Harborne tried to mitigate, but which was underscored by the method of delivering its letters to Elizabeth: it was transported in a satin bag tied with a silver capsule – the method used to write to Caucasian princes.[12]

Murad's letter was not the only one that arrived in London from Constantinople in September 1579. Harborne's dragoman, Mustafa Beg, also took the opportunity to break with convention and write an audacious letter to the queen. In it he encouraged Elizabeth to establish 'a league and most holy alliance' between her and Murad, drawing yet again on the potential amity between Muslims and Protestants. 'As I was negotiating in the presence of our Most Mighty Prince [Murad],' writes Mustafa, it occurred to my mind that if by any means I could encourage some kind of understanding and friendship between our Most Mighty Prince and your Sacred Royal Majesty, not only as I know the Sacred Royal Majesty to hold the most Christian faith among all people and that, therefore, Christians throughout the whole world envy the Sacred Royal Majesty and, if they can, try to harm her in every way, but also because I considered it to be beneficial for your Sacred Royal Majesty to be able to establish understanding with so great and so powerful an Emperor [Murad], with whom almost all princes and kings, of their own free will, wish to be closely allied.[13]

Despite its presumptuousness, the letter was taken seriously by Burghley, who filed and annotated it, while Elizabeth regarded it as important enough to write back to Mustafa in October, just weeks after his first letter arrived, imploring him to assist her in obtaining the release of English captives:

> Your letter of March 15 was handed to us by William Harborne, who at the same time recorded your kindness to our subjects. As it has taken the form of promoting the trade of our merchants to the dominions of his Imperial Highness [Sultan Murad] it demands our gratitude and reciprocity of good offices. As by your good means matters are so far advanced that he has begun to incline to Harborne's request on behalf of himself and his partners, and we would not willingly be excluded from the conveniences granted to the subjects of other states, we have written to his Highness to testify our gratitude, and to ask him to allow to all our subjects the same permission that he has granted to a few; promising like liberty to his subjects in our dominions. We beg that you will aid us in obtaining this request. And as we have also dealt with him briefly for the freedom of certain of our subjects who are captive in his galleys we ask you to show your goodwill to us by promoting their cause.[14]

In requesting the captives' release, Elizabeth implicitly recognized Ottoman political legitimacy under international (though unwritten) law.[15] It was unprecedented and highly significant for the future of any Anglo-Ottoman alliance, especially considering how far her excommunication by the papacy had isolated the queen from the rest of Europe.

The resident European merchants and diplomats in Constantinople were horrified by the sudden and apparently inexplicable success of the English interlopers, informed as they were by Mustafa Beg, who seems to have been playing each side off against the other. In September 1579 Bernardino de Mendoza, Philip II's ambassador in London, wrote that Joseph Clements, Harborne's fellow agent, had 'returned recently with a Turk, bringing a letter from his master [Murad] to the Queen, full of endearments, and offering unrestricted commerce in his country to Englishmen if she, on her part, will give the same privileges here to his subjects. I will endeavour to get copies of the letter and their reply to send to Your Majesty.'[16] Mustafa Beg presumably supplied these 'copies', although not all Mendoza's intelligence was as accurate as he might have believed. It seems he had read the Latin translation of Murad's letter, which had been embellished by Harborne and his associates to inflate the significance of the Anglo-Ottoman alliance, and with it hopes of closer trade relations. There is also no record of the arrival in London of the Turkish emissary he mentions.

Nevertheless, the responses of both Sinzendorf and Mendoza reflect the alarm felt by the Habsburgs at the potential political consequences of the rise of English commercial influence in Constantinople. Just two months later, Mendoza reported to Philip II that these fears appeared well founded. 'This queen has received another letter from the Turk by way of France,' he wrote on 28 November. That letter has not survived, but Mendoza claimed that 'in addition to many other offers', Murad 'promises a favourable reception of Englishmen who come to his country, either by land or sea; both on account of his desire for her friendship as for that of the king of France, with whom he requests her to be as friendly as she can. He says that, by reason of his friendship to the king of France, he will be pleased to hear of her marriage with his brother [the Duke of Alençon], from which it may be seen that the French have made it their business to write to him about it.'[17] Elizabeth was indeed embroiled in her famous on–off courtship with Alençon, which if successful threatened the Habsburgs with the prospect of an Anglo-Franco-Ottoman axis capable of dominating Mediterranean naval and commercial movements.

Mendoza went on to explain that 'the Turks are also desirous of friendship with the English on account of the tin which has been sent thither for the last few years, and which is of the greatest value to them, as they cannot cast guns without it, whilst the English make a tremendous profit on the article, by means of which alone they maintain the trade with the Levant'. His intelligence – presumably again gleaned from Mustafa Beg – was that five English ships were already en route to Constantinople, and 'I am told that, in one of them, they are sending nearly twenty thousand crowns' worth of bar tin, without counting what the rest of them take. As this sending tin to the infidel is against the apostolic communion, and your Majesty has ordered that no such voyage shall be allowed to pass the Messina light [a watchtower built by Charles V in 1546 to protect Sicily from Turkish invasion] to the prejudice of God and Christianity, I advise the viceroy of Sicily of the sailing of these ships as I understand they will touch at Palermo, where the tin can be confiscated.'[18] A month later he reported that even more ships were headed to Chios 'carrying bell-metal and tin'.[19] It was a symbolic act of alliance that conflated the iconoclastic faiths of Protestantism and Sunni Islam. With the queen's sanction, Protestant English merchants were removing metal from ecclesiastical buildings – including lead roofing and bell metal – and shipping it to Constantinople to arm Muslims fighting against Catholics.

By now events were moving fast. By late October 1579 Elizabeth had already despatched responses to both Murad's first letter and Mustafa Beg's. The opening of her letter to Murad clearly took the hint about the superficial similarities between Protestantism and Islam:

> Elizabeth by the grace of the most mighty God, the only Creator of heaven and earth, of England, France and Ireland Queen, the most invincible and most mighty defender of the Christian faith against all kind of idolatries, of all that live among the Christians, and falsely profess the name of Christ, unto the most imperial and most invincible prince, Zuldan Murad Chan [Murad III], the most mighty ruler of the kingdom of Turkey, sole and above all, the most sovereign monarch of the East Empire, greeting, and many happy and fortunate years.[20]

Having learned that the Ottomans would give those they labelled 'Lutherans' preferential commercial treatment, Elizabeth and her advisers obviously saw the advantages of presenting her as a religious ruler who rejected both idolatry and those who 'falsely' professed Christ, attributes shared (according to the Catholic powers) by Protestants and Muslims. After establishing her theological credentials, the letter got down to business, asking for trading privileges to be 'enlarged to all our subjects in general', and agreeing that Turks should be allowed 'to come, and go to and from us and our kingdoms'.

The letter concluded with a last request. Murad's 'great affection to us and our nation, doth cause us also to entreat and use mediation on the behalf of certain of our subjects, who are detained as slaves and captives in your galleys', that 'they may be delivered from their bondage, and restored to liberty, for their service towards us, according to their duty: which thing shall yield much more abundant cause to us of commending your clemency, and of beseeching that God (who only is above all things, and all men, and is a most severe revenger of all idolatry, and is jealous of his honour against the false gods of the nations) to adorn your most invincible imperial highness with all the blessings of those gifts, which only and deservedly are accounted most worthy of asking'. Those concerned were probably the crews of the *Peter* and *Swallow*, two English ships captured off Algiers two years earlier. For some the plea brought release and redemption, although it earned for the English a mortal enemy in the shape of the galley slaves' owner, the Turkish admiral Qilich Ali Pasha.

Both sides seemed to be edging towards a closer commercial and political relationship when Harborne was faced with an unexpected crisis. On 12 October 1579, as Sokollu Mehmed Pasha was listening to petitions in the Topkapi's imperial council chamber, a Bosnian dervish suddenly leapt forward and stabbed him to death. Rumours abounded at court that Nurbanu Sultan had ordered the assassination, but whatever the motivation behind his murder Sokollu's death represented a decisive shift in the balance of power within the palace. Over the next two decades the post of grand vizier would be progressively diminished with eleven different incumbents unable to prevent the sultan's harem taking political matters into their own hands. Sokollu's protégés were removed from government, and with them went his more emollient and westward-looking foreign and economic policy.[21]

It is testament to Harborne's determination and resourcefulness that he was undaunted by Sokollu's death and continued his dogged pursuit of an Anglo-Ottoman agreement. His time spent wooing – and probably bribing – subsequent grand viziers to keep hopes of a commercial alliance alive infuriated the other resident European diplomats, including the French ambassador Jacques de Germigny. It was bad enough that Harborne lacked official diplomatic accreditation; even more galling was his skill in playing France off against Spain, while still trading under the cover of the French Capitulations. 'I was informed,' Germigny fumed in a report to Henry III in March 1580, 'that this Englishman had represented to the Grand Vizier the seriousness of the increase of the power of the King of Spain, to the extent that he would take possession of Portugal and the territories dependent on the said kingdom neighbouring to this lord in the Levant.'[22] He also protested that, despite Sokollu's death, Harborne was 'pursuing his negotiation actively in this Porte, and appears to be greatly favoured, as much by reason of the loads of steel, tin, and latten [copper alloys] which he has brought them and promises to bring thereafter'. In June Germigny confessed that it all 'makes me fear that the said Englishman will soon realize his aim' of obtaining full commercial privileges from the sultan. The English advance, together with signs of a growing rapprochement between Murad and Philip II, could leave France dangerously isolated.

It was too late. Murad had already agreed the terms of a peace treaty with Spain, and at the end of May 1580, just days before the despatch of Germigny's letter about Harborne, he also signed a charter of privileges – 'Capitulations' – granting the English full commercial rights in Ottoman dominions. They would prove to be even more important than Walsingham's 'Memorandum' of 1578 and endured for 343 years, until they were dissolved under the terms of the Treaty of Lausanne in 1923, following the collapse of the Ottoman Empire and the birth of the Turkish Republic. The agreement began by praising 'Elizabeth Queen of England, France and Ireland, the most honourable queen of Christendom', to whom Murad agreed to 'give licence to all her people, and merchants, peaceably and safely to come unto our imperial dominions, with all their merchandise and goods without any impeachment, to exercise their traffic, to use their own customs, and to buy and sell according to the fashions of their own country'.[23] It listed in minute detail the privileges granted to the English: their ships were guaranteed security and help in the face of piracy (from Muslims or Christians), shipwreck or even debt; in the event of death goods reverted to the merchant's estate; in case of commercial disputes both sides agreed to abide by the ruling of the local *cadi* (judge) based on sharia law; English merchants were exempt from paying *kharāj* (a local community charge) and were allowed to appoint consuls in Alexandria, Damascus, Tunis, Algiers and Cairo; and if 'any pirates or other free governors of ships trading the sea shall take any Englishman, and shall make sale of him . . . if the party shall be found to be English and shall receive the holy religion [Islam], then let him freely be discharged, but if he will still remain a Christian, let him then be restored to the Englishmen, and the buyers shall demand their money again of them who sold the man'.[24]

For Harborne the Capitulations were the triumphant conclusion to nearly three years of tireless trade, diplomacy and bribery. For the French, they were a calamity. The English agreement was closely modelled on the Franco-Ottoman Capitulations of 1569, which had not been renewed since Murad's accession in 1574. Now the English had trading rights, the Ottomans were in league with the Spanish, and it was the French, preoccupied with their own internal religious strife, who were left politically and commercially isolated. Just weeks after signing the English Capitulations, Murad sent a terse letter to King Henry III, rejecting any suggestion that Ottoman alliances with countries like England violated prior agreements with France, assuring him somewhat disingenuously that 'there is absolutely no refusing or repulsing to the coming and going of anybody', and 'nothing whatsoever to preoccupy you concerning the ancient friendship with you and in the matters of precedence and pre-eminence over the other kings'.[25] As European rulers of various theological persuasions queued up to court Murad, the French risked losing their long-standing influence at the Porte.

As the French floundered, Harborne prospered. From his residence in Galata he exploited the Capitulations to consolidate a thriving commercial network across the Mediterranean. With Osborne's and Staper's financial backing he traded with merchants as far north as

Poland and the Baltic, those from Algiers in the west and Syria to the east, as well as Turks, Egyptians, Greeks and Italians, standing the costs of buying cotton, yarn and carpets from Turkey, flax from Egypt and the Black Sea, wine, oil and currants from Crete and Zante, all the time extending his trade in the ubiquitous English kerseys, lead, tin and copper. He was escorted everywhere by two Janissaries, a sign of the esteem in which the sultan held a man widely recognized as 'the Queen's agent at the court of the great Turk, by whom he is held in the greatest credit'.[26] Harborne even used this 'credit' to visit Ottoman-controlled Jerusalem on a pilgrimage that was probably as good for business as it was for his soul.

Just as it seemed that Harborne had achieved more than anyone in London could have hoped, disaster struck again. In September 1580 the *Bark Roe*, a merchant vessel carrying a cargo of kerseys, tin, brazilwood, madder, lead and broken bell metal from English Catholic churches worth over £1,000, left London for the eastern Mediterranean. The ship's captain was Peter Baker, a servant of Edward de Vere, Earl of Oxford (one of Elizabeth's closest advisers and the man an eccentric minority still believe wrote Shakespeare's plays). Baker was already known in London merchant circles as a 'greedy' and 'evil man' with a reputation for robbing Christians, having seized a ship in the Mediterranean five years earlier laden with salt. He was responsible for a crew of around seventy, including two merchants, and a ship of 160 tons armed with twenty-four cannon. The crew would report much later that Baker had announced they were travelling 'as merchants, though at sea the captain armed himself as a man-of-war', announcing that 'we were sailing for Turkey to act as pirates'. By January 1581, another crew member recalled, they were 'laden with broken bells from England, and when we went to Malta' they made arrangements to sell the metal with its sensitive religious associations to the Maltese Knights of St John. After fifteen days anchored off Malta, Baker 'summoned us on deck. It was bright moonlight; we had not yet unloaded any goods, and he informed us that he wanted to engage in cruising at a venture, plundering the Turks'. The crew was divided, but one member admitted that 'having unloaded the metal of the bells, we had to sail as corsairs'.[27] It was a foolish decision that exposed their inexperience and cupidity – and threatened to wreck the Anglo-Turkish trade just as it began to flourish.

The following month the *Bark Roe* reached the island of Chios, which the Ottomans had taken from the Genoese in 1566. There by pure chance they met Harborne, en route to the Holy Land with a group of French and Flemish merchants. Fresh from his triumph in obtaining the English Capitulations, Harborne was oblivious to Baker's piratical plans. Instead he swaggered around the island, boasting of the terms of the Capitulations, much to the confusion of local Ottoman officials, who assumed that the new agreement ended English merchants' rights to trade under the lapsed French privileges. As the *Bark Roe* prepared to leave in early March 1581, Harborne reported that 'the Jew customer of that port, alleging it unlawful for our nation to use of that [French] country banner and privilege coveted to embargo and detain' Baker's ship until he received clarification from his masters in Constantinople. Harborne hastily produced the new Capitulations, 'not ever before showed', and the Jewish customs official allowed the ship to leave the island free of any charges.[28] Having sold all his cargo, and possibly aggrieved at being detained on Chios, Baker bade farewell to Harborne and set off southwards in pursuit off whatever bounty he could. He chased Turkish and Greek vessels off Rhodes, then sailed westwards across the Aegean, attacking two ships off Methoni in the Peloponnese at the end of March. 'The ships we thought were Turkish,' confessed one crew member, 'but when we captured them we found out they were Greek and that they were carrying a cargo of camlets [woven fabric made of camel or goat hair] and raw silk.'[29] To make matters worse, the cargo was owned by a consortium of Greek and Venetian merchants, and the ships' passengers included Greek Orthodox priests from Patmos, which lay under Ottoman jurisdiction, a jurisdiction that Baker had now violated.

In one foolish act Baker had brought the wrath of the Turkish, Greek and Venetian authorities down upon the English, confirming all their worst suspicions about these gauche interlopers. Seemingly oblivious to the diplomatic crisis he was igniting, Baker quarrelled violently with his crew over the spoils. They insisted that 'he had no authority to take or rob any Christian', and forced him 'to re-enter

Malta to try for justice for fear that piracy would be laid to our charge'.[30] By 22 April the *Bark Roe*, its crew and the two Greek ships were back in Malta, where they were imprisoned in Valetta by Monsignor Federico Cefalotto, the Maltese representative of the Roman Inquisition.

Over the next four months the Maltese authorities began building a case against Baker around claims made by the Greeks (who wanted their cargo back) and the Venetians (who demanded 12,000 ducats to cover their losses). Even worse, the captured Greek priests from Patmos lay within the jurisdiction of the Turkish admiral Qilich Ali Pasha, still smarting from having to surrender English galley slaves to Harborne just two years earlier. The admiral immediately blamed the fiasco on the unsuspecting Englishman, condemning him as a spy and a pirate, and demanding that the sultan imprison and fine him 40,000 ducats and revoke the Capitulations. Horrified, Harborne rushed back to Constantinople to try and clear his name with the Ottoman authorities, from where he also sent a letter to Burghley on 9 June 1581 explaining the situation.

As he wrote, Harborne knew that the future of the Anglo-Ottoman alliance, not to mention his own personal safety, hung in the balance. For the first time in nearly three years, his usually cool and urbane demeanour gave way to fear and self-pity. 'Behold', he wrote to Burghley, 'in what pit of perplexity and snares of unluckiness (almost inevitable) I am entangled through the unchristian and detestable dealings of Peter Baker.' Baker's actions had unleashed 'the slanderous and hellish barking of the maliciously disposed Admiral', who threatened to ruin not only 'our English traffic' in the region, but also Harborne's personal reputation in 'disgorging his long hidden poison against me'. Baker's stupidity had driven Harborne to the brink of despair. 'The intolerable grief of mind which these pirates have caused me, I cannot utter,' he wrote. His greatest fear was how Sultan Murad would respond, and he invited Burghley to reflect on how such accusations would prejudice 'this heathen prince against me, a worm'.[31] Shorn of the usual honorific flourishes and verbose rhetoric that characterized Anglo-Ottoman correspondence, in this moment of extreme peril Harborne's veil slipped, and he was left calling Murad a heathen and seeing himself as little more than a parasite.

Harborne had good reason to panic. Arrested by the Ottoman authorities and subjected to relentless interrogation, he also admitted to Burghley that he had used credit to buy merchandise and send it back to London, but that as a result of Baker's piracy all his assets had been frozen and he had no money to settle his debts. To add to his humiliation he had to beg the French ambassador to act as surety, which Germigny did with grace and, one imagines, some satisfaction, informing Henry III of the remarkable turn of events and noting that Baker's and Harborne's behaviour 'gives a very bad smell to the said English here'.[32] Harborne's pleading with the Ottomans was futile. Murad revoked the English Capitulations and signed new ones with the French. By July 1581 France was once again in control of European trade into Turkey, and Harborne's mission seemed in ruins.

In Malta, things were going from bad to worse for the English. Baker and his crew were put on trial by the Maltese Inquisition. Its usual focus on heresy – an apparently straightforward issue when confronted with English Protestants – and even the settlement of commercial debts was quickly subsumed by darker fears of plots and conspiracies involving those suspected of harbouring reformist religious beliefs. Baker's arrest had coincided with a political crisis on Malta. Cefalotto had been appointed grand inquisitor by Pope Gregory XIII in late 1580 and immediately used his newfound power to accuse those members of the island's Knights of St John who were French of Huguenot sympathies. The crisis was compounded by the decision of a group of Knights in July 1581 to oust their octogenarian grand master Jean de la Cassière, just as Baker was being arraigned. Cefalotto's subsequent report to his superiors in Rome the following spring claimed to have uncovered not just an isolated case of piracy but a vast anti-Catholic conspiracy against the island. 'The plot of the capture of Malta was conceived', he wrote, 'by the English Queen, the Duke of Alençon and the Turks through their intermediary, Peter Baker, who was captain of the English ship *Roe*.' Cefalotto made lurid accusations that French Huguenots and English Protestants were in league with Muslim Turks to destroy what he called 'the Catholic Commonwealth', and that he had uncovered letters proposing an Anglo-Ottoman invasion of Malta that would transform the political balance of power in the Mediterranean. He ordered that

Baker and eight other Englishmen be despatched to Rome where they would stand trial for heresy.[33]

When the news reached London, Burghley advised Elizabeth to sacrifice the renegades such as Baker and apologize to Murad in a bid to salvage something from the imperilled Anglo-Ottoman trade. On 26 June 1581 she despatched a letter to the sultan regretting 'this unfortunate hap'. Scrupulously avoiding specific names or details, she apologized for the 'most injurious and grievous wrong which of late came unto our understanding . . . done unto certain of your subjects by certain of our subjects, as yet not apprehended'. Choosing her words with care, Elizabeth regretted that Baker's actions 'doth infringe the credit of our faith, violate the force of our authority, and impeach the estimation of our word faithfully given unto your imperial dignity'. She implored Murad to 'not withdraw your gracious favour from us . . . to hinder the traffic of our subjects'.[34] Elizabeth must have been furious at having to grovel in this way to Harborne's 'heathen prince' simply because of Baker's witless actions, but unless she did so there seemed little chance of the Anglo-Turkish alliance being renewed.

Even as Elizabeth wrote her letter, Harborne was battling to save his reputation, not to mention his liberty, in Constantinople. He accepted the humiliation of French diplomatic security to help contest the fines levied against him, and used his dragoman, Mustafa, to try to open communications with the current grand vizier, an unimpressed Koca Sinan Pasha. Then Mustafa reported that the Ottomans, perhaps in response to Elizabeth's letter, were prepared to do a deal. They would restore the English privileges on condition that Elizabeth formalized trade and diplomatic relations and appointed an official ambassador to the Porte. Harborne decided to cut his losses and on 17 July 1581 he fled Constantinople. He had spent three arduous and expensive years building up the Anglo-Ottoman alliance from nothing. Now Walsingham's 'apt man' was returning to London with his venture apparently in ruins.

5

Unholy Alliances

By the summer of 1581, events had conspired to frustrate Elizabeth's attempts to establish formal alliances with Muslim rulers in Morocco and Turkey. The death of Abd al-Malik at the Battle of Alcácer-Quibir had robbed the Elizabethan merchants of one of their staunchest allies, and it was unclear if his successor Mulay Ahmed al-Mansur would prove as receptive to English trade. Peter Baker's clumsy piracy seemed to have ended hopes of a commercial alliance with the Ottomans. At their trial before the Roman Inquisition, Baker and his crew were found guilty of heresy, for which most were consigned to the horror of the galleys, although it was reported that Baker had escaped before reaching Rome and was never heard of again, just another renegade who disappeared into the vastness of the Mediterranean. William Harborne meanwhile faced the likelihood, upon his return to London, of public disgrace and humiliation for his handling of the *Bark Roe* incident.

The unregulated trade with Morocco had left the Elizabethan merchants there particularly vulnerable to sudden regime change, and in Constantinople Harborne's lack of diplomatic accreditation had always limited his ability to negotiate with both the Ottomans and the resident Christian emissaries. The Ottomans' demand that Elizabeth appoint an official resident ambassador to the Porte if relations were to continue was the catalyst for a radical change in policy by Elizabeth's advisers and by London's merchants. Walsingham and Burghley had long favoured tacit support for regulated trading companies but without committing the state to full responsibility for their actions, primarily because they lacked the resources. But such a policy wasn't working in Russia, Persia, Morocco or – so it now it seemed – Turkey.

Protests against unregulated commerce had been going on since the late 1560s when the Muscovy Company had asked for a monopoly on trade in the northern region to stop interlopers, asserting that 'this Russian trade will be destroyed as the trade of Barbary is . . . through the greediness of the subjects of this realm carrying thither more of this country's commodities than that country was able to consume, and by that means also causing the Barbary commodities to rise excessively'.[1] In 1601, John Wheeler, the secretary of the Merchant Adventurers' Company, published his *Treatise of Commerce* arguing in favour of joint-stock companies, and claiming that most of London's merchants believed that 'it is most profitable both for the prince and the country to use a governed company, and not to permit a promiscuous, straggling and dispersed trade'.[2] It may have been a partial view that lacked unanimity throughout the city, but it seemed to make sense when trading with particularly remote markets like those in Russia, Persia and the eastern Mediterranean. By the time Wheeler's book came out, London's mercantile community had proposed a series of initiatives to regulate trade in Muslim lands, from the joint-stock model pioneered by the Muscovy Company to regulated companies given exclusive trading rights by government charter in return for a percentage of customs duties on imports.

The shift in government policy precipitated by the *Bark Roe* crisis affected the Turkish trade especially: on 11 September 1581 the crown issued 'The Letters Patents, or Privileges Granted by Her Majesty to Sir Edward Osborne, Master Richard Staper, and certain other Merchants of London for their trade into the dominions of the Great Turk'. Under its terms Osborne was appointed governor of the proposed joint-stock company in recognition both of his 'great adventure and industry' and of the 'great costs and charges' incurred in establishing the Turkish trade. His knowledge of the cloth trade as well as his familiarity with markets as diverse as Brazil, Portugal and the Baltic made him an obvious choice. He would lead a team of merchants including his close associate Staper, Thomas Smith and William Garrett tasked with nominating up to twelve others who were allowed 'during the term of seven years from the date of these patents, freely [to] trade, traffic and use feats [transactions] of merchandise into, and from the dominions of the said Grand Signior'.[3] The company was empowered to create its own internal regulations in return for agreeing to pay £500 of customs duties per annum into the Exchequer. It would call itself the Turkey Company. How its members could inveigle themselves back into the trust of the Ottoman Porte following the *Bark Roe* debacle and Harborne's departure was unclear.

Most of these initiatives took place among the political and commercial elite, but after three decades trading with Muslim powers, Elizabethans living outside such rarefied circles were beginning to express increased interest – and some unease – at what was happening in places like Morocco and Turkey. One outlet for such interests was London's theatre. Since the first commercial playhouses had opened in 1576, the stage had quickly become a touchstone for popular hopes and fears concerning everything from witchcraft and popery to adultery and cross-dressing. Throughout the 1580s and 1590s new theatres were being built across London and, alongside other arenas for public spectacle such as executions, floggings and royal progresses, the Elizabethan public were learning to enjoy their leisure time in the rich and fascinating world of contemporary drama. The various theatre companies running the playhouses boasted some of the country's most powerful aristocrats as their patrons, and their plays were regularly performed at Elizabeth's court. Yet public drama was also regarded with suspicion by London's civic and religious authorities. Preachers condemned theatres as breeding idleness, lust and vanity, and worried that, as institutions driven by profit, and as places where hundreds of people met regularly, they offered a potentially subversive alternative to the church. Writing in 1579, Stephen Gosson, a former playwright and actor and one of the theatre's earliest and sharpest critics, attacked what he saw as its alien and worthless commercial nature, arguing that 'were not we so foolish to taste every drug, and buy every trifle, players would shut in their shops, and carry their trash to some other country'.[4] Gosson, the failed actor, condemned theatre as 'the invention of the devil, the offerings of idolatry, the pomp of worldlings, the blossoms of vanity, the root of apostasy, the food of iniquity, riot and adultery. Detest them.'[5]

In response to such attacks Elizabeth appointed a master of the revels in 1581 to censor any play performed in the city deemed offensive to the church or state. Wary of such opprobrium, the early theatre impresarios built playhouses outside London's ancient Roman walls, in the so-called 'liberties', areas free from the oversight of the city's civic authorities and usually instead under relatively lax royal or aristocratic control. The Rose, the Hope and the Swan were all open-air playhouses erected in the liberties on the south bank of the Thames – or Bankside – an area known for its dangerous and sometimes vicious yet also glamorous atmosphere. People crossed over to the south bank to visit a brothel or a bear pit – or to see a play. In the minds of many Londoners the three activities were interchangeable. When Philip Henslowe first bought the lease of the Rose tavern it was a brothel, whose activities continued to provide a profitable supplement to the theatre that he erected in the building's back yard.[6] He also built the Hope Theatre on the site of a bear garden, where up to a thousand spectators could come and pay a penny to see a play, then return the next day and spend the same amount to watch a bear tied to a stake, whipped and attacked by dogs.[7]

As a result, the theatre inhabited a precarious position in Elizabethan London: it was a vibrant new industry, a contributor to London's financial prosperity, watched by thousands from all walks of life. Yet it was also a theatre of cruelty and danger, subjected to relentless attack from the authorities, situated on the city's periphery, its practitioners living and working in London's poorest areas alongside volatile and marginalized communities of prostitutes, servants, artisans and 'strangers' – people escaping religious persecution and slavery from as far afield as the Low Countries, North Africa, the Ottoman Empire and even the New World. The theatre was drawn to the stories coming back into London from the Islamic world of enslavement, conversion, piracy and heroic adventure experienced and described by aliens and outsiders because they held a mirror up to its own place in society, its own practice and its own people.

In the summer of 1581 a play appeared that dramatized the issues of trade, money, religion and national differences generated by events in and around Turkey in recent years. Its author was Robert Wilson, a talented young actor and playwright attached to a playing company financed by Elizabeth's favourite, Robert Dudley, 1st Earl of Leicester, and it was called *The Three Ladies of London*. In 1583 Wilson would subsequently transfer his allegiance to the Queen Elizabeth's Men and forge a reputation producing plays for Henslowe's Rose Theatre, which opened six years later. But at the beginning of the decade he was still learning his trade with Leicester's Men and writing plays indebted to the medieval morality tradition and classical Roman city comedy whose sobriety might even have satisfied Stephen Gosson.

Wilson's play centres on the struggle between the three ladies of its title, who are personifications of Love, Conscience and Lucre. It begins in London, with Lady Love and Lady Conscience complaining that Lady Lucre and her employees, the vice characters of Dissimulation, Fraud, Simony and Usury, have destroyed the traditional civic virtues and replaced them with the pursuit of money. The problem is identified as foreign goods coming into England purchased with money borrowed at excessive interest rates – a practice condemned as immoral usury. Lady Love complains:

> For Lucre men come from Italy, Barbary, Turkey,
> From Jewry: nay, the pagan himself
> Endangers his body to gape forth her pelf [stolen goods].
> They forsake mother, prince, country, religion, kiff and kin,
> Nay, men care not what they forsake, so Lady Lucre they win.[8]

The overseas trade practised in Muslim kingdoms like Morocco and Turkey by merchants such as Hogan and Harborne is identified as the source of the problem, which is eroding England's time-honoured social relations.

As the play progresses Usury and Simony begin their work on behalf of Lady Lucre. With England's economic problems seen as stemming from imports from the Islamic world, the vices they produce are identified as imported by scheming Italian Catholics infiltrating virtuous Protestant England. Usury explains that he left his birthplace in Venice to come to London because 'England was such a place for Lucre to bide.'[9] Simony admits that his 'birth, nursery and bringing up hath hitherto been in Rome, that ancient religious city' where he had been selling ecclesiastical privileges (including papal indulgences) before English merchants smuggled him into London – where, he tells Lucre, 'I heard in what great estimation you were.'[10] Wilson then introduces

an effete, villainous Italian merchant called Mercadorus with a ludicrous accent. He tells Lady Lucre – addressed as 'Madonna' – 'me do
for love of you tink no pain too mush'.[11] Lucre orders him to 'go
amongst the Moors, Turkes, and pagans' to sell English grain, leather
and beef. In return 'for these good commodities' he must bring back
exotic oriental 'trifles to England' such as amber, jet, coral 'and every
such bauble',[12] expensive objects with little intrinsic value. With comic
relish Mercadorus acknowledges the widespread awareness of – and
concern with – the English trade with Morocco and Turkey:

> Tink ye not dat me have carried over corn, ledar, beef and bacon
>   too all tis while,
> And brought hedar many baubles dese countryman to beguile?
> Yes, shall me tell you Madonna? Me and my countrymans have
>   sent over
> Bell-metal to make ordnance, yea and ordnance itself beside,
> Dat my country and oder countries be so well furnished as dis
>   country, and has never been espied.[13]

The play trades quite literally in the topical unease of laughing at
England's weakness for fripperies in exchange for arming Muslims
with metal taken from churches. The country is seen as sick, venting
its nutritious resources and in return absorbing unhealthy 'baubles',
and even arming its opponents with ordnance.[14] As Mercadorus pur-
sues his villainy, Usury murders the character personifying Hospitality
to ensure that money is spent on 'trifles' rather than the poor, Love is
forced into a marriage with Dissimulation, and Conscience falls into
debt and turns to running a brothel.[15]

Meanwhile, Mercadorus arrives in Turkey, where he is confronted
by Gerontus, described as a 'Jewish usurer in Turkey', who has lent
him money to buy goods in London. Gerontus complains that Mercadorus has broken the terms of his bond. 'You know I lent you two
thousand ducats for three months' space,' he tells Mercadorus, but the
unscrupulous Italian 'fled out of the country'. Gerontus complains
that if Jews behaved like this they would never be trusted, 'But many
of you Christians make no conscience to falsify your faith and
break your day'[16] (that is, a contractually agreed settlement date). He
claims the original capital plus the accrued interest, but Mercadorus

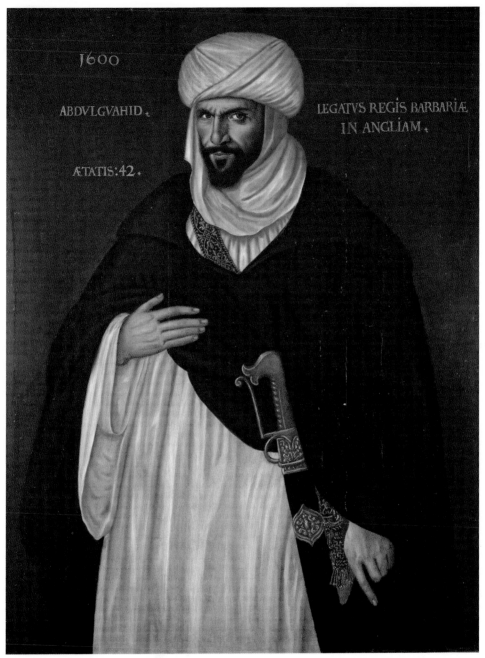

J600

ABDVLGVAHID.

LEGATVS REGIS BARBARIÆ
IN ANGLIAM.

ÆTATIS:42.

1. Muhammad al-Annuri, the Moroccan ambassador and 'Morisco' (Spanish-born Muslim convert) who arrived in London in August 1600 to propose an Anglo-Moroccan alliance. Shakespeare probably started to write *Othello* six months later.

2. Willem de Pannemaker's tapestry showing Catholic Habsburg forces triumphantly sacking Tunis in 1535. These scenes of slaughter and enslavement were first displayed in London following Mary Tudor and Philip of Spain's marriage in 1554.

VICTOREM CAROLVM TER GRATA VOCE SALVTANT.
HASAMVM CAESAR QVAMVIS NIL TALE MERENTEM
OMNIA POLLICITVM CVM RE NEC IVVERIT VLLA.
RESTITVIT MISERVM SOLIOQVE REPONIT AVITO.

3. After his marriage to Queen Mary in 1554, the Catholic Philip of Spain was technically also king of England. This joint portrait was painted in 1558, the year of Mary's death.

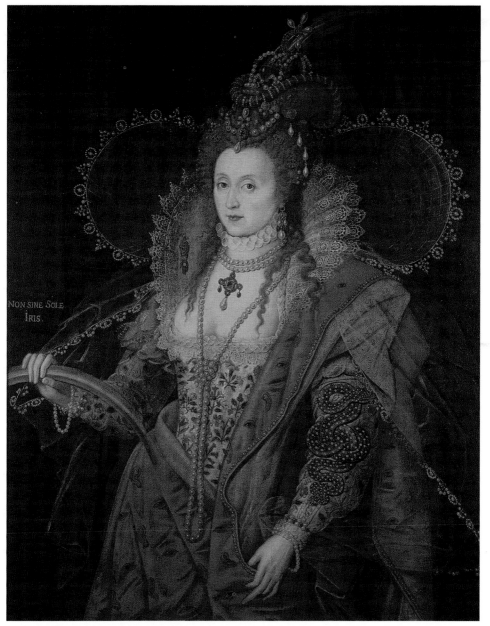

NON SINE SOLE
IRIS.

4. The 'Rainbow Portrait' of Elizabeth I, *c*. 1600. The jewels and fabrics are
all recognizably oriental, a reminder of the extensive Anglo-Islamic trade.

5. Diogo Homem's map of the Mediterranean from the Queen Mary Atlas (1558), showing Ottoman flags flying over North Africa.

6. The idealistic but naive king Sebastian I of Portugal, whose defeat and death (alongside two rival Moroccan rulers) at the battle of Alcácer-Quibir in 1578 sent shockwaves throughout Europe.

7. A view of Marrakesh, the capital city of the Sa'adian dynasty, from a seventeenth-century engraving by the Dutch artist Adriaen Matham.

deceives him, promising to settle in a few more days, while asking Gerontus for 'toys' or 'some fantastic new knack', because 'da gentle-womans in England buy such tings for fantasy'.[17] Seduced, Gerontus offers him perfumes, precious stones and 'many more fit things to suck away money from such green-headed [covetous] wantons',[18] suggesting yet another group to blame for England's consumerism, this time women.

When Mercadorus defaults yet again, Gerontus swears 'by mighty Mahomet' to have him arrested and brings him before a 'Judge of Turkey' to resolve the dispute. The judge is the first Turk recorded on the English stage. Gerontus fears that Mercadorus will appear 'in Turkish weeds to defeat me of my money'[19] by converting to Islam. This is based on a principle pronounced by the Turkish judge who warns Gerontus that 'if any man forsake his faith, king, country and become a Mahomet', then all his 'debts are paid'.[20] Sure enough, Mercadorus enters wearing a turban, announcing repeatedly, 'me will be a Turk',[21] and agrees to swear upon the judge's holy book, possibly the Qur'an. Gerontus is horrified and, fearing that he will be blamed for Mercadorus' apostasy, cancels the debt. A jubilant Mercadorus accepts, but then refuses to 'turn Turk', leaving the judge to offer the following homily before he departs: 'Jews seek to excel in Christianity, and Christians in Jewishness.'[22] Mercadorus exits with his own vicious little moral:

> Me be a Turk? No. It will make my Lady Lucre to smile
> When she knows how me did da scald [scurvy] Jew beguile.[23]

In this convoluted three-way exchange it is the Catholic Mercadorus who is seen as the villain, not the Turk or the Jew, who both try to behave honourably by pursuing the debt in question. Eventually they are all corrupted by money, but this is a Protestant morality play which trades in bad faith: Wilson ends up blaming the Italian Catholic merchant for the play's ills, while exculpating the Muslim and the Jew – both currently in league with Elizabethan England's merchants across the Islamic world.[24] In the final scene a judge named Nemo arraigns Ladies Lucre, Love and Conscience and imprisons them in a forlorn attempt to ensure that 'we be not corrupted with the unsatiate desire of vanishing earthly treasure'.[25] Nemo's name means 'no one' in Latin, which hardly inspires confidence that London's rampant materialism will be curbed.

Wilson's play is a clumsy melodrama, caught between the two-dimensional personifications of medieval morality plays and the more dynamic verisimilitude of later Elizabethan drama, and has not stood the test of time. It is rarely studied and never staged these days, but in late 1581 its topicality was unquestionable. It addressed the hopes and anxieties of a Turkish trade that was enriching England, that aligned it with the Ottomans and their Jewish commercial intermediaries, and that cemented Protestant opposition to Catholicism. But it could come at great cost to the national conscience and its religion. If lucre could corrupt a Catholic into converting to Islam, and enable a Jew to worship Muhammad, then how easily might Protestant Englishmen be seduced into embracing Catholicism, Judaism – or even Islam?

For Wilson, the corrupting influence of international trade in the Ottoman-controlled Mediterranean was symptomatic of the larger problem of usury, which was in turn related to religion. On 19 May 1581 a proclamation had been issued 'Reviving the Statute against Usury' in response to public 'doubts and questions' regarding the Act of Usury passed in 1571, which had fixed the legal limit at which interest could be charged on loans at 10 per cent. The 'doubts' being raised clearly related to moneylenders trying to exceed the set rate, partly in response to the growing volume of overseas trade, including Morocco and Turkey. The statute was therefore not 'against' usury, but simply about redefining its terms. Wilson's play exploited a general confusion about usury. Having been regarded for centuries as an immoral practice condemned by scriptural authority, by the late sixteenth century it was increasingly seen as a necessary evil, mainly due to the expansion of overseas trade. The traditional ways of doing business face to face at market time, with goods bartered or exchanged on the spot for hard currency, were giving way to an international credit network over vast distances and time, where bills of exchange were required to transact goods, and where currency and interest rates dictated profit (or loss).[26] Elizabethan England's economic prosperity depended on usury, but nobody liked to admit it: hiding behind someone else practising it – such as a Catholic, a Jew or even a Muslim – was infinitely preferable.

Protestant merchants like Anthony Jenkinson, Edmund Hogan

and William Harborne had all needed to obtain credit to purchase goods from Muslim merchants, and invariably turned for help to Jewish brokers. Although Christian and Islamic theology officially forbade the practice, the Torah and Talmud tolerated the use of financial loans, so the Englishmen could ask Jewish merchants or moneylenders to lend to them. These religious distinctions over usury lay at the heart of anti-Semitic prejudice in the period. In times of peace and profit, Christian merchants and their Muslim counterparts accepted Jewish merchants and moneylenders as integral to their trade: but when times were bad and losses mounted, the Jews became scapegoats. Wilson's play finds it is easy to blend the usurious and credulous Jew Gerontus with Turkish Muslims, and then encourage his Protestant English audience to laugh at him being duped (or 'cozened') by the Catholic Mercadorus, but over the next decade this portrayal of Jews and international finance on the Elizabethan stage would become darker and more complicated in the hands of Christopher Marlowe and William Shakespeare.

The concerns Wilson's play raised among London's theatre audience about trading with Muslims and Jews struck a chord in the upper echelons of the English church. In September 1582 John Aylmer, Bishop of London, wrote a letter to Thomas Blanke, Lord Mayor of London, complaining about the fate of 'certain miserable captives in Turkey'. Aylmer hoped that these Englishmen could be ransomed with the help of collections held in London's churches, and 'redeemed out of that hellish thraldom where they be, to the great danger of their souls'. Aylmer went on to make the first known attack on the Anglo-Ottoman Capitulations:

> surely in mine opinion it is very strange, and dangerous, that the desire of worldly and transitory things should carry men so far, with such kind of traffic, which neither our ancestors before us knew of, nor can be attempted without selling of souls for purchasing of pelf to the great blemish of our religion and the shame of our country. Wherefore if your Lordship and the rest of your brethren could by your authority stay such intercourse with infidels and save the souls of our people from the Gulf of Mahomet, I think you should do a gracious deed and win an everlasting remembrance.[27]

Complaints like Aylmer's had little discernible impact on the city's merchants or on Elizabeth's advisers, who seemed to have no qualms about entering the 'Gulf of Mahomet'. On the contrary, even as Aylmer was writing, plans were being hatched to expand commerce with Turkey and Morocco by securing commercial monopolies in both regions. When it came to trade, material interests insidiously prevailed over religious ones.

Where the English saw a new commercial opportunity, the Spanish saw a serious threat to their own geopolitical interests. The Spanish ambassador Mendoza had already written a long memorandum to Philip II in 1582 outlining the commercial and geopolitical dangers of England's prosperous alliances with Shi'a and Sunni Muslim kingdoms. 'The English', he wrote, 'settled through the Muscovite with the Tartars on the banks of the Volga to allow the free passage of their merchandise down the river to the Caspian Sea; whilst the Persian, building large ships in Astrakhan, should give them leave to trade and distribute their merchandise, through Media and Persia, in exchange for goods which reach the Persians by the rivers that run from the East Indies to the Caspian Sea. This privilege was granted to the English by the Persian.' He went on to express anxiety about the Anglo-Ottoman trade, reiterating that it was 'extremely profitable' for the English, 'as they take great quantities of tin and lead thither, which the Turk buys of them almost for its weight in gold, the tin being vitally necessary for the casting of guns and the lead for purposes of war. It is of double important to the Turk now, in consequence of the excommunication pronounced *ipso facto* by the Pope upon any person who provides or sells to infidels such materials as these.' Mendoza warned that the English were in discussion with the Ottomans to import merchandise from Persia through Constantinople and overland via Russia, 'without their having to pass, as at present, by Italy'. Mendoza added that with the Ottomans' collusion the English 'might monopolise the drug and spice trades', thus 'weakening the forces of your Majesty, by diverting the English trade from Italy'.[28] In fact the English had nowhere near the resources to achieve such a global monopoly, but Mendoza's letter was a sign of how far their success in the east had rattled the Spanish. As far as Mendoza could discern in the spring of 1582, the scale of their diplomatic achievements in Russia, Persia, Morocco and Turkey suggested that anything was possible.

Nobody was more surprised by Elizabeth's renewed interest in the Ottoman trade than William Harborne. Having arrived back in London as Wilson's play was being performed, the disgraced Englishman must have assumed that his Turkish career was over. He was not mentioned in the articles establishing the Turkey Company that September, but Burghley, Osborne and Staper clearly decided that his experience outweighed his humiliation there and proposed sending him back to Constantinople. A hugely relieved Harborne waited patiently as Osborne and Staper haggled with Burghley over his formal commission as the queen's first ambassador to Turkey. They also wrangled over the financial terms of the Turkey Company's establishment, requesting that the crown settle Harborne's outstanding debts of £600, cover his travel costs and salary for a five-year tenure, and provide an annual budget of £1,000 for buying the sultan lavish 'presents' (thinly veiled bribes). Burghley demurred, knowing that as usual the niggardly Elizabeth wanted all the financial and political benefits of overseas trade without incurring any of its costs.[29] The queen may also have hesitated to take such a momentous step towards formalizing a diplomatic *and* commercial alliance with the Ottomans. Osborne and Staper were interested in trade, not politics, and stood their ground. They reminded Burghley of Elizabeth's promise to Murad 'to send thither her ambassador to gratify his goodwill . . . whose presence is hourly expected'. Any delay risked alienating Murad, who might 'think himself deluded' and refuse to sanction new English Capitulations.[30] Elizabeth would not relent, and the new company's governors were forced to foot Harborne's bills.

The queen seemed pleased to save the cost of paying for Harborne's embassy, and on 20 November 1582 she issued a formal commission to Harborne 'to be her majesty's ambassador or agent in the parts of Turkey'. Praising the 'trustiness, obedience, wisdom and disposition of this our beloved servant William Harborne', the commission ordained him 'our true and undoubted orator, messenger, deputy and agent'. He was also given a letter to present to Murad, reiterating his diplomatic credentials, in the hope that his appointment would cement the 'perfect and inviolable' league between England and

Turkey, and that 'a noble traffic will flourish between these nations'.[31] Within weeks Harborne was aboard the Turkey Company's ship *Susan*, bound for Constantinople. In less than eighteen months he had gone from being a self-confessed 'worm' fearing for his life, to England's first ambassador to the Ottoman Empire and the newly formed Turkey Company's official representative in Constantinople.

As Harborne sailed for Constantinople, London's merchants were also reassessing the attractions of the Moroccan trade in response to the sudden interest of a new and powerful investor: Robert Dudley, Earl of Leicester. The earl was one of Elizabeth's most devoted servants, her greatest favourite, and for many years suitor for her hand in marriage. In 1562 he was appointed to her Privy Council and subsequently made lord steward of the royal household. A keen supporter of the arts and patron of Robert Wilson and his acting company, Leicester was also an enthusiastic advocate of trade and exploration, having invested in the Merchant Adventurers and the Muscovy Company and having acted as the principal promoter for Francis Drake's global circumnavigation in 1578. By 1581, with the Muscovy trade struggling and the Turkey Company about to receive its royal charter, Leicester turned his attentions to Morocco.

The earl had good reason to be interested. Morocco's commercial possibilities were obvious, although still relatively undeveloped in the aftermath of the Battle of Alcácer-Quibir. Equally tantalizing was the possibility of a political and military alliance between Elizabeth and al-Mansur. A year earlier in June 1580 al-Mansur had exchanged letters with Elizabeth (many since lost), in which he flattered her as the greatest adherent of the 'religion of Christ', labelling her 'the majesty in the lands of Christ, the sultana Isabel', and promising a mutually beneficial coalition. 'As you are doing the best to facilitate our affairs', wrote al-Mansur, 'so we will do the same for you here.'[32] If Leicester could broker an Anglo-Moroccan alliance it would fulfil two of his most cherished ambitions: getting closer to Elizabeth and antagonizing the Spanish.

In June 1581 Elizabeth issued a licence to John Symcot, a 'merchant trading into Barbary', allowing him to sell 600 tons of English timber 'and to bring into this our realm so much saltpetre as he shall have in exchange in Barbary for the same wood'.[33] Symcot was Leicester's agent, and it was the earl who had convinced Elizabeth to grant him a lucrative concession that promised to reopen the trade in saltpetre. The commission did not escape the attention of the Spanish ambassador Mendoza, who naturally informed Philip II about Symcot's trade and Leicester's involvement. 'Some Englishmen have arrived in this country,' he informed Philip in October 1581, 'having arranged with the king of Morocco to take him timber from here ready cut to build his galleys. The quantity is so large that, although Leicester is mixed up in the affair for the sake of profit, they have had to send to Holland for some of the wood, as it could not be furnished here.'[34] Unfortunately for Leicester, the whole venture was a disaster from beginning to end. Symcot was already in trouble with the lord mayor and sheriffs of London who arrested him on suspicion of fraud. Leicester was furious and demanded his immediate release, insisting that Symcot was 'bound to her majesty in the sum of two thousand pounds for the bringing over hither certain quantities of saltpetre and other commodities for the maintenance of her majesty's munitions from the country of Barbary'.[35] This was an appeal to the national concern that scarcely concealed the earl's personal interest, but his closeness to the queen meant that it worked. In October 1582 Symcot was released and allowed to sail for Morocco.

The English merchants pursuing respectable if unregulated trade in Morocco were unimpressed by Symcot's arrival. They had quietly sought trade in sugar, cloth and timber with Mulay Ahmed al-Mansur ever since his accession following the Battle of Alcácer-Quibir in 1578. Symcot immediately started to use his royal licence and Leicester's influence as though it were a monopoly, playing on Elizabeth's imprimatur to obtain an agreement from al-Mansur that he should control the trade in iron, lead and tin. He detained certain merchants' cargoes destined for England, and was even accused of opening their letters and sharing them with al-Mansur. An almighty row ensued. A group of English merchants wrote to Walsingham complaining of the 'sinister and undirect dealings of John Symcot and his adherents', to which Symcot responded by protesting against the 'lewd practices and speeches' he claimed were being directed at him, insisting he was only doing the queen's and Leicester's work.[36]

As the dispute escalated throughout the summer, the English merchants wrote again to Walsingham, demanding he redress their grievances. Their position was difficult: as legitimate but unregulated merchants, they were furious with fly-by-night English traders flooding the Moroccan market with goods, driving prices and hence profits down, but they were also opposed to a creeping state monopoly (which is how they viewed Symcot's arrival) that threatened their dissolution. With their future in jeopardy, the merchants justified their complaints by turning to religion. Having shown few qualms hitherto about trading with Muslims, they now told Walsingham that the 'undirect and hard dealing' of unscrupulous English merchants in 'forbidden commodities' into 'the heathen country of Barbary' was causing 'great clamours to be spread in other countries, that out of England there should be suffered to go munitions and other furniture to the aid of the infidels, which causeth our most true and pure religion to be brought into question'. Arming the infidel only strengthened Moroccan pirates and threatened 'captivity to others who profess Christianity, but even also to her majesty's subjects that tradeth [in] Spain'.[37] According to this nervous claim, forbidden Moroccan trade was putting English Protestants in double jeopardy – captivity by armed Muslims and insolvency from antagonized Catholics.

Aside from such fears the complaint painted a halcyon picture of harmonious and profitable Anglo-Moroccan trade 'until the first shippers of unlawful commodities spoiled the same'. This was an illusion, but a powerful one nonetheless: these interlopers were described as inveigling their way into the Moroccan ruler's affections, obtaining from him a 'grant to the Jews, renters of the sugar houses, to give unto them other men's sugars long before paid for, by which hard dealing the Jews bankrupted [them], and thereby her majesty's subjects lost very near £40,000, the circumstances whereof would be tedious to trouble your honour'.[38] A three-way trade between English merchants, Muslim rulers and Jewish intermediaries had been going on in Morocco for decades, with hardly a murmur of religious or sectarian conflict, but once the private trade came under threat, the regulars opposed the monopolists by playing their trump card, theology, disclosing lurid tales of unscrupulous English merchants in league with villainous Muslim kings and greedy Jewish moneylenders. The problem, however, was not really caused by

Muslims or Jews, but by English interlopers like Symcot. He was condemned in the merchants' complaint for trading in 'forbidden commodities, with such others that there doth associate them about some new and secret contract' with al-Mansur, that threatened to end commercial competition and by extension the unregulated trade. The complainants begged Walsingham to write to Symcot as well as to apply pressure on Leicester to stop their high-handed interference. As a close associate of Leicester, Walsingham was unlikely to uphold a protest against the queen's favourite. Besides, he was more interested in the news coming out of Constantinople, where William Harborne had arrived safely on 29 March 1583.

It was a wiser and more circumspect Harborne who returned to Constantinople that spring, where he rented a house he called 'Rapamat' (a corruption of 'Ahmad', from the house's owner, Ahmad Pasha) in the Findikli district along the Bosphorus, a safe distance away from the prying eyes of the other European ambassadors up the hill in Galata. This time he established a formal embassy consisting of his secretary Edward Barton, interpreters, servants, stables and a Janissary guard.[39] He lost no time in paying due obeisance to the grand vizier Kanijeli Siyavuş Pasha and his old adversary Admiral Qilich Ali Pasha. He also visited Hagia Sophia, which he acknowledged respectfully as 'the chief see and church of primacy of this Turk'.[40] On 24 April he was given a formal audience with Murad III at Topkapi Sarayi where he presented an array of gifts, described by the incensed Venetian ambassador as 'a most beautiful watch set with jewels and pearls, ten pairs of shoes, two pretty lap dogs, twelve lengths of royal cloth, two lengths of white linen, and thirteen pieces of silver gilt'.[41] Having this time ensured that he presented the right credentials as ambassador, Harborne was rewarded with the renewal of the Anglo-Ottoman treaty cancelled in 1581. This allowed him to begin appointing consuls across the Ottoman territories to represent English commercial interests. He also boasted of his immediate success in renegotiating the customs duties charged on English goods. 'In my oration to the Grand Signior upon my first arrival for her majesty I obtained of him for the company the release of almost half his custom,' he recalled, reducing the Ottomans' customs duty rate from

5 per cent to 2 per cent, giving the Turkey Company a crucial advantage over its European rivals.[42]

The day after his audience with Murad, Harborne appointed Harvie Millers as 'our consul in Cairo, Alexandria, Egypt and other places adjacent, for the safe protection of body and goods of her majesty's subjects'.[43] Two months later Richard Forster was appointed to Aleppo, Damascus, Amman, Tripoli (in Lebanon) and Jerusalem. Other appointments followed on Chios and Patras, in Algiers and Tunis, creating an impressive network of English residents across the Mediterranean in a vast arc from the Straits of Gibraltar to the Holy Land and into the Ionian Sea. Harborne also reported that Murad had agreed to 'the delivery of captives', English galley slaves, 'freed *gratis* at our request'.[44] Having thought he had seen the back of Harborne, the Venetian *bailo* (ambassador) Gianfrancesco Morosini was infuriated by the Englishman's sudden reappearance. He shared the French ambassador's anger at the 'breach' of their treaty with the sultan, 'which provides that all ships, except those of Venice, must sail under the French flag'. He reported that Harborne 'was escorted by no Christians, only by the Turks', adding rather petulantly that 'even the Turks in contempt call him a Lutheran, and show that they are far from pleased to see him'.[45] However, he confessed that Harborne 'has been well received by his majesty [Murad], who is flattered that such a powerful queen should have sent from four thousand miles away to tell him that she is all for him and desires his friendship. He considers also that she is a very fit instrument to damage the Christians, towards whom in her letters she shows an open ill-will.'[46]

Against all expectations, Harborne had built a network of agents loyal to Walsingham dotted across the Mediterranean, able to facilitate smoother commercial relations (and hopefully avoid incidents like the *Bark Roe* debacle) as well as providing vital military intelligence about Spanish and Ottoman activities. He was also now far more experienced in countering the strategies adopted against him by the resident Catholic ambassadors, including the French and the Venetians, who, he reported, 'have the uttermost opposed themselves against us, but their malice contraried, the Venetian denieth such his proceedings, and dissemblingly pretendeth friendship, having personally visited us', while the French swore 'to renew former amity'.[47]

Staper and Osborne were no doubt relieved to hear of Harborne's success, as they had already funded another team of merchants to head to the Levant, with even greater ambitions to reach Persia, the Mughal court of Jalal-ud-Din Muhammad Akbar, or Akbar the Great, and even China. In February 1583 a group led by Ralph Fitch and John Newberry left London on board the *Tiger*, bound for Syria, with letters from Elizabeth addressed to Akbar, or 'Echebar king of Cambaya', and the 'King of China'. They arrived in Tripoli in April and travelled overland to Aleppo, then on to Basra and Hormuz, where they were arrested by the Portuguese authorities and shipped off to Goa. Having obtained their release thanks to the intercession of local Jesuits, they fled to Agra, where they claimed to have been given the first English audience with Akbar in the late summer of 1585, although what if anything passed between them remains unknown. From here the team split up, and Newberry disappeared. But the intrepid Fitch travelled on, visiting Bengal, Burma and Malacca, before making his return to England in April 1591.[48] The news of Fitch's epic adventures remained in vogue for long enough for Shakespeare to allude to them in *Macbeth* (1606), where one of the witches plots against a sailor's wife, saying, 'Her husband's to Aleppo gone, master o' th' Tiger.'[49] Although the venture failed to yield any concrete commercial breakthrough, it was another sign of the growing confidence of London's mercantile community.

Harborne's good fortune in Constantinople was in stark contrast to the undignified squabbling between the English in Morocco that followed Symcot's arrival. But Harborne's success also diverted the queen's attention from Morocco, and gave Walsingham a space to consider his response to the increasingly intemperate petitions of the regular merchants. Fortunately Symcot died suddenly in the summer of 1583 as he travelled back to England. This took some of the pressure off Walsingham to censure both him and Leicester's aggressive commercial tactics in Morocco, but the larger question of whether to introduce a commercial monopoly remained. With his vast personal wealth and the advantage of Elizabeth's ear, Leicester lobbied ruthlessly for the creation of a regulated company capable of imposing a monopoly on the Moroccan trade – strictly on his terms, of course. In April 1585 Elizabeth wrote to al-Mansur thanking him for the favour shown to Leicester over the Symcot affair, a tacit seal of approval for her favourite's Moroccan policy. It was a pre-emptive decision motivated by knowing that London's merchants were already drafting petitions arguing for and against a monopoly.

On 15 July the petitions were published. Those against a regulated company once more invoked religious differences, arguing that it would be ineffective because the 'King of Barbary and all his subjects are barbarous infidels and without any knowledge of the true God; and his magistrates govern by tyranny; and therefore the danger will be great to execute any ordinance of this corporation within his kingdom, if it shall be understood to him or any of his magistrates'. Their case rested on a question of trust: how could a Christian trust a Muslim, and if the Muslim's ruler refused to abide by the new corporation's terms, how could it work? Finally, they evoked the classic *laissez-faire* economic philosophy: why was regulation needed when there was already a long-standing 'freedom of traffic' in the region where each merchant 'standeth upon his own devise'?[50]

Leicester's pro-regulation merchants adopted a more optimistic common law approach to regulating trade, believing the statutes they proposed would 'keep reasonable men in order and bridle unreasonable men trading into Barbary, by incorporating them'. They pointed to the oversupply of English commodities 'being sold there to much lost advantage', in contrast to the demand for Moroccan goods 'viz. sugar much advanced there', that could be restrained by the creation of a regulated company (an organization with a government charter giving it exclusive rights to trade in a particular region). They also proposed that any English transgressions in Morocco could be 'restrained by order and fear of punishment at home', and that if anyone impeached his countrymen in Morocco 'he must of a Christian become an infidel and abandon his country, which cannot be entered'. Finally, they argued that regulation was a direct response to 'seeing the commodities of that country is in so few men's hands as a few wily heads, with great stocks'.[51] It took an even wilier head, like Leicester's, to argue that a monopoly was required to oppose monopolization.

The result was a foregone conclusion. On the same day, 15 July 1585, the 'letters patent or privileges granted by her majesty to certain noble men and merchants for a trade to Barbary' were proclaimed, providing a charter for the foundation of what would become known as the Barbary Company. Most of them were copied almost verbatim from the privileges granted to the Turkey Company less than four years earlier. But there were two important differences. The first was that the new initiative was not a joint-stock but a regulated company (the former allowed members to trade on their individual capital and at their own risk, whereas the latter formalized and shared collective investments, profits and losses). The second was that Leicester was given unprecedented executive powers so far as a commercial company was concerned. Alongside Leicester and the Earl of Warwick, forty London merchants trading in Morocco were named who, the patent claimed, 'have sustained great and grievous losses'. The way to avoid such losses was to stipulate that 'none others, shall and may, for, and during the space of twelve years, have and enjoy the whole freedom and liberty in the said traffic or trade, unto or from the said country of Barbary', aside from those named. Although there was no official governor, all ordnance was subject to 'the consent of the said earl of Leicester', making the privilege little more than Elizabeth's gift to Leicester and his cronies to run the Moroccan trade as they liked.[52] Leicester could now ship timber and munitions to Morocco with impunity, and in return Elizabeth was guaranteed a resident company agent, at no cost to the crown, capable of pursuing a diplomatic alliance with al-Mansur against the growing threat of Spain.

The wisdom of appointing a resident agent was exhibited by the continued effectiveness of another English agent operating in the Muslim world over 2,000 miles from Morocco, the rejuvenated William Harborne. By January 1583 Harborne had intervened successfully in yet another maritime incident that threatened Anglo-Islamic relations, but this time one committed against the English. In May 1584 the Turkey Company's ship *Jesus* had been seized, its cargo confiscated and its crew imprisoned in Tripoli (Libya). The local authorities believed that a factor had boarded the ship owing a local Turkish merchant 450 crowns, and promptly seized it, hanging its master and one of its crew. The vessel's fate might have remained unknown had it not been for *Jesus'* resourceful boatswain, Thomas Sanders, who managed somehow to smuggle a letter out of captivity in Tripoli to his father in Tavistock in Devon. Sanders provided one of the earliest English accounts of life as a galley slave. He described his 'miserable bondage and slavery' in vivid detail, with lurid stories of how he was sold into the Turkish galleys where 'we were chained three and three to an oar and we rowed naked above the girdle', raiding Greek vessels trading African slaves, and of his compatriots being compelled to 'turn Turk' through graphically described forced circumcision.[53]

When the news reached London, the Turkey Company's directors were outraged by what they saw as a flagrant breach of the resurrected Anglo-Ottoman Capitulations by a Turkish client state. They petitioned Elizabeth successfully to raise the matter with Sultan Murad, who in turn wrote to the Kaid Ramadan Pasha, ruler of Tripoli, demanding that he release the ship, cargo and crew immediately. Emboldened by such royal support from queen and sultan, Harborne himself wrote to Ramadan Pasha in January 1585 demanding immediate restitution. The Englishman condemned his actions as 'contrary to the holy league sworn by both our princes' in the Capitulations, and warned the pasha that unless he redeemed the crew and cargo he would 'answer in another world unto God alone, and in this world unto the Grand Signior, for this heinous crime committed by you against so many poor souls, which by this your cruelty are in part dead, and in part detained by you in most miserable captivity'.[54] Harborne's argument anticipated those calling for a regulated Moroccan trade back in London; here was a Christian demanding that a Muslim abide by the terms of the contractual agreement set out in the Capitulations, regardless of faith or personality. The authoritative tone Harborne adopted towards a Muslim ruler was also in stark contrast to the fretful, self-pitying figure pleading his case during the *Bark Roe* fiasco. It helped that Harborne could use an Ottoman sultan as diplomatic leverage, but there was no doubting that he had finally mastered his brief, and that the English were starting to pull their weight in the Levantine trade. The letter succeeded: the captives were released and mostly melted away into the Mediterranean littoral, never to be heard of again.

Once Harborne had firmly established himself as ambassador with control of a network of English consuls across the Mediterranean, his second period in Constantinople took on a more explicitly political role. He was in regular correspondence with Walsingham, who was briefing him to entice Murad into a desperately needed anti-Spanish alliance. By early 1585 relations with Spain were virtually on a war footing, and England perilously isolated from the rest of Europe. As a consequence Elizabeth had finally agreed with those of her counsellors advising a more aggressive approach towards Spain. Walsingham was foremost among them, and drew up 'A Plot for the Annoying of the King of Spain', which advocated using Drake to launch a preemptive attack on the Spanish fleet. Elizabeth approved, unleashing Drake's squadron of twenty-five ships in a series of assaults on Spanish shipping across the Atlantic and Caribbean. On 10 August 1585 she signed the Treaty of Nonsuch with Dutch Calvinists fighting the Spanish in the Low Countries. Under its terms the queen offered the Dutch £125,000 as well as the support of an expeditionary English army led by Leicester, still preening himself over the successful establishment of the Barbary Company. Philip II interpreted the treaty as a declaration of war against Spain, and in October he informed Pope Sixtus V of his intention to invade England. It was a momentous decision. By December 1585 a plan for a massive armada to sail against the English was being prepared.[55]

Walsingham was keenly aware of the inevitability of a Spanish attack, and had already been corresponding with his agents in the Low Countries as well as with Harborne in Constantinople about the need to create an Anglo-Islamic alliance against the Spanish threat. In December 1585 the spy William Herle wrote to Elizabeth from Antwerp, insisting that the English policy of arming Muslims to fight Catholics was not only expedient but righteous. 'Your majesty in using the King of Fez &c', he wrote, 'doth not arm a barbarian against a Christian, but a barbarian against an heretic [Philip II], the most dangerous that was in any age, the usurper of kingdoms, and the subverter of God's true religion, which you are bound as defendresse of the faith, to defend.'[56] Such arguments added credence to Walsingham's Ottoman policy. Throughout the autumn he encouraged Harborne to agitate for Ottoman military aggression against the Spanish, adding Elizabeth's voice in the matter. 'I did advise you', wrote Walsingham on 8 October:

> of a course to be taken there for procuring the Grand Seigneur, if it were possible, to convert some part of his forces bent, as it should seem by your advertisements, from time to time wholly against the Persians, rather against Spain, thereby to divert the dangerous attempt and designs of the said King from these parts of Christendom. So am I at present, her majesty being, upon the success of the said King of Spain's affairs in the Low Countries, now fully resolved to oppose herself against his proceedings in defence of that distressed nation, whereof it is not otherwise likely but hot wars between him and us, wills me again to require you effectually to use all your endeavour and industry in that behalf.[57]

If Harborne could persuade Murad that it was in his interests for the Ottomans to attack the Catholic Spanish fleet in the Mediterranean, it might hamper Philip's English invasion plans. Ever the realist, Walsingham appreciated that this was very ambitious, and concluded his letter by advising Harborne that 'if you shall see that the sultan cannot be brought altogether to give ear to this advice', then 'procure at least that, by making show of arming to the sea for the King of Spain's dominions, hold the King of Spain in suspense, by means whereof he shall be the less bold to send forth his best forces into these parts'.[58] Like Walsingham, the Venetian *bailo* Morosino understood that a pragmatic approach to religion played its part in all this subterfuge, and he wrote to the Venetian Seignory in 1585 that Murad 'places especially great worth on the friendship of the Queen of England, because he is convinced that, owing to the religious schism, she will never unite against him with other princes in Christendom; she will, on the contrary, always be an excellent instrument for disturbing and thwarting such alliances'.[59] Both Sunni Muslim and Protestant Christian rulers had told each other only half the reasons for their mutual association.

Even as Walsingham was turning a merchant into a spy versed in military matters, Leicester was despatching a soldier to oversee commercial matters in Morocco. Having established the Barbary

Company's privileges on terms of his choosing, it was incumbent upon the earl to appoint England's first official ambassador to Morocco. The man he chose was Henry Roberts, a very different kind of ambassador to William Harborne. Roberts was a client of Leicester's, a soldier with experience of fighting in Ireland and privateering against the Spanish, but little of trade or diplomacy. He would later claim that 'I was forced to take this voyage full sore against my will, for the which cause I was forced to yield up my place where I was settled in Ireland,' and that his relocation cost him £500.[60] Whatever the truth, Roberts's appointment was closely linked to his association with Don António, Prior of Crato, who since losing the Portuguese crown to Philip II in 1580 had used Elizabeth's backing to support his claim to the throne. Elizabeth and Leicester appointed Roberts with a view to establishing not only formal trade relations through the Barbary Company, but also al-Mansur's support for Don António's claim to the Portuguese throne, yet another policy that put both Protestant England and Muslim Morocco on a collision course with Philip II's Spain. Roberts left England with three ships on 14 August 1585 and arrived at Safi on the west coast of Morocco exactly a month later. He was met 'with all humanity and honour' by the local authorities as the first official English ambassador to Morocco. He dined with the resident English, French and Flemish merchants before setting out on the 90-mile journey inland to the Sa'adian capital, the 'Red City' of Marrakesh.[61]

The capital that Roberts encountered in the stifling heat of September 1585 was Morocco's second great city, home to nearly 20,000 people and the gateway to the trans-Saharan caravan trade in salt, ivory, spices, gold and slaves to the south. It had been founded in the eleventh century by the Berber Almoravid dynasty, but had maintained an abiding rivalry with the much older city of Fez, 280 miles to the north, whose madrasas established its fame throughout the Muslim world as one of the great centres of theological and legal scholarship. Until the 1550s Fez remained Morocco's capital city, but with the rise of the Sa'adian dynasty power shifted southwards, and by the time Roberts reached Marrakesh al-Mansur was transforming it into one of Islam's great imperial capitals. In 1578 the Moroccan ruler began work on a palatial complex known as the Dar al-Makhzen, designed to rival the Moorish Alhambra Palace in Granada, and Philip II's El Escorial, then under construction north-west of Madrid. Where Philip's palace was paid for with New World gold and silver, al-Mansur's was built on profits from Moroccan sugar. Carrara marble was imported from Tuscany and 2,000 captives were brought from Fez (including many Portuguese survivors of the Battle of Alcácer-Quibir) to build the palace and new mosques, madrasas, hospitals, factories and even funerary tombs for the ruler's Sa'adian ancestors. António de Saldanha, a Portuguese nobleman captured by the Sa'adians who wrote a chronicle of al-Mansur's reign, claimed that the rebuilding included premises for Christian merchants, and that 'in the streets set aside for their shops, all the goods of France, Italy, England and Spain were sold at lower prices than in the lands where they were produced . . . the town of Marrakesh then attained such greatness as it had never attained before nor ever would again'.[62]

Upon his arrival in Marrakesh Roberts reported that 'I was lodged by the emperor's [al-Mansur's] appointment in a fair house in the Juderia or Jurie, which is the place where the Jews have their abode, and is the fairest place, and quietest lodging in all the city.'[63] Another walled Juderia, more commonly known as the *mellah*, was the first Jewish quarter established in the salt marshes outside Fez in 1438 and took its name from the Arabic *mallah*, or 'salty soil'.[64] Marrakesh's *mellah* had been established in the late 1550s on the same principles as Fez's, but it was very different from the Jewish ghettos created in the Christian cities of Venice (1516) and Rome (1555). In Europe the religious persecution of Jews led to severe restrictions on their rights of employment, property ownership and freedom of movement. Under Muslim rule, Jews (like English Protestants) were granted the status of a protected minority (*dhimmi*) and acknowledged to hold important positions in government and finance, as well as the monopolies over trade in sugar and Christian captives. The vast majority were Sephardic Jews, thousands of whom had started to arrive in Morocco following the expulsions in 1492 of both Muslims and Jews from the Iberian peninsula. Their cosmopolitan experience and ability to broker international political, cultural and commercial deals on behalf of the new Sa'adian dynasty ensured that al-Mansur was assiduous in building a *mellah* in Marrakesh with grand mansions, its own *funduq* (markets) and synagogues, and Christian chapels for other *dhimmi* such as Roberts who found themselves lodged there.

To a soldier like Roberts, used to the monoglot world of England and Ireland and its stark religious divisions between Protestantism and Catholicism, the multi-confessional and polyglot world of Marrakesh must have come as a massive shock. As well as a thriving new capital, it was becoming a multicultural city, containing Berbers, Arabs, Sephardic Jews, Africans, Moriscos and Christians, many of them merchants and diplomats, others slaves and captives hoping to be ransomed, and all of them professing one of a variety of religious persuasions of different hues. Walking through the *mellah* and the city's other quarters Roberts would have heard Arabic, Hebrew, Spanish – the lingua franca of most of the resident Europeans – Portuguese, Italian, French and even German. Marrakesh was also becoming known as a home for a completely new community that was caught between religions: the *renegado*. The Spanish *renegado* (from the Latin *renegare*, 'to deny') meant an apostate, specifically a Christian who had converted to Islam, although it could also refer to Jewish and Muslim apostasy. The word first entered English in the early 1580s, usually with a Spanish inflection – suggesting that it was a phenomenon associated with Spanish Catholicism rather than English Protestantism – just as men like Roberts and Harborne were beginning to experience the full range and complexity of Islam in cities as different as Marrakesh and Constantinople.[65]

Roberts, a Protestant Englishman more used to quashing Catholic insurrection in Ireland than moving in cosmopolitan, multilingual communities, suddenly found himself living in Marrakesh's *mellah* alongside individuals like Estêvão Dias. Born into a Portuguese Jewish family in Tavira around 1545, Dias was a *marrano* or *converso*, a Jew forcibly converted to Christianity. In 1564 he had been denounced as a crypto-Jew by the Lisbon Inquisition, forcing him to emigrate to the Low Countries where he lived as a merchant. He travelled throughout Italy before settling in Marrakesh in 1581. There he reconverted, adopted the name of Rabbi Joseph and began writing an extraordinary defence of his Jewish faith. Known as the 'Marrakesh Dialogues', his apologetic is couched in the form of a dialogue between two Flemish brothers. Both are merchants: one is Catholic, the other, Bernard, converts to Judaism while on business in Morocco and takes the name Obadia Ben Israel, becoming a shopkeeper in Marrakesh's *mellah*. The two brothers debate their respective religions. Obadia criticizes Catholic beliefs ranging from Trinitarianism and idolatry to the recent rise of Lutheranism and Calvinism, which he identifies as a sign of the need for Christianity to embrace Judaism.[66]

Frustratingly, Roberts's own brief account of his time in Marrakesh expressed no interest in describing encounters with individuals like Rabbi Joseph. Instead he limited himself to prosaic details of his domestic arrangements. He occupied a spacious house alongside three resident English factors, Robert Lion, Miles Dickonson and Edmond Mastidge. It included two counting houses, two warehouses and a study, rented for £14 a year. On top of his salary of £100 Roberts could also reclaim from the company various expenses ranging from lodging, food and clothes to furniture, laundry, horses and a Moroccan groom. Lion even claimed the medical costs of treating his 'leg bitten by a dog' (£1 5s 3d). In such a remote and unfamiliar country these expenses were unsurprising, but they would soon begin to diminish the Barbary Company's profits.

Within three days of his arrival Roberts was given an audience with al-Mansur, where he 'delivered my message and her Majesty's letters, and was received with all humanity, and had favourable audience from time to time for three years', discussions which, 'for diverse good and reasonable causes, I forbear here to put down in writing'.[67] Such circumspection was understandable. Roberts spent part of his three years trading munitions on Leicester's behalf (with Elizabeth's tacit support), even though he was officially allowed only to act as the crown's representative overseeing the company's commercial activities. The rest of his time was spent trying to persuade al-Mansur to join an anti-Spanish league in support of Don António's claim to the Portuguese crown.

By now both Leicester and Walsingham were exploiting their alliances in the Islamic world at either end of the Mediterranean in a concerted effort to disrupt Spanish military preparations against England. Just as Roberts in Marrakesh was ordered to press Don António's claims on al-Mansur, in Constantinople Harborne was pursuing a more directly anti-Spanish approach with Murad. By July 1586 Philip had finalized his plans for the invasion of England by a huge Spanish Armada, and the antagonism between the two countries spilled over into Morocco. In October 1586 an English ship called the *Dolphin* arrived in Safi and unloaded its commercial cargo of cloth and metal worth an estimated £5,000. Then, in a piratical act reminiscent of the *Bark Roe* incident, the *Dolphin*'s captain, John Giles, suddenly attacked and captured a Spanish carvel, confiscating all its goods. The Spanish crew escaped and fled to Marrakesh. Fearful of alienating the Spanish, al-Mansur condemned Giles's piracy and threatened to confiscate the *Dophin*'s goods and levy further penalties against the English merchants unless the Spanish carvel and its cargo were released. Roberts despatched two English merchants to Safi to instruct Giles to return the carvel. To the new ambassador's obvious embarrassment Giles refused, claiming that the Spanish ship had been lawfully captured on the high seas. In response al-Mansur immediately arrested all those English merchants with goods on board the *Dolphin*. Roberts again attempted to reach a resolution by asking those involved to stand the cost of the goods on board the Spanish vessel, but as in the case of Isaac Cabeça in 1568, the English merchants began squabbling over their respective contributions.

One of the merchants' servants was 'imprisoned amongst a number of heathens' in 'the infidel's prison' in Taraoudant, 180 miles south of Safi, but managed to write a letter to the Privy Council back in London begging them to intervene in the whole 'unnatural dealing'. The letter was a terrible indictment of Roberts as the crown's agent and of the Barbary Company more generally. Both were condemned as unable to address either the English merchants' factionalism or the complexities of working successfully with al-Mansur. The servant claimed that a 'malicious and envious' faction among the English mercantile community led by William Gore (one of the merchants involved in the Cabeça dispute) were 'affectioned more to the Spaniards' and refused to bear any of the costs involved in settling the dispute, thus 'disobeying the commandments of her majesty's servant', the hapless Roberts. Under duress and facing the prospect of confinement in a Moroccan jail for the foreseeable future unless the Spanish claim was settled, the unfortunate servant launched a bitter attack on everyone from al-Mansur to Leicester's Barbary Company. He began by complaining about 'what small account these heathen people make of us and our English commodities, which proceedeth of the disorderly dealing of the Barbary Company, by overlaying this wicked country of late with abundance of goods'. He then listed the 'great injuries and abuses' that were 'daily offered by the king [al-Mansur] in favour of the Spaniards', which included 'detaining our goods ashore, imprisoning merchants, our masters and mariners of our ships, at the departure of any ship laden by the Spaniards and threatening us that, if their ships miscarry, we shall answer for it, in such cruel manner that no Christian heart would suffer, if we could otherwise remedy it'. He concluded that 'the Barbary Company regardeth little the wrongs and intolerable injuries we abide amongst those cursed people'.[68]

The fate of the poor servant is unknown, but the Spanish carvel's cargo was never returned and the Dolphin's goods were restored (the Barbary Company claimed that this was due to a letter written by the lord high admiral Charles Howard of Effingham to al-Mansur, while Roberts maintained that it was all his own doing – just another example of how far internal relations within the company had deteriorated). Technically it seemed like a victory for the English, but it left the political tensions between England, Morocco and Spain more polarized than ever. The financial balance sheet of Roberts's years in Marrakesh was even less impressive. Leicester had never really tried to make the Barbary Company a going commercial concern: his interests were more political, primarily to monopolize the Moroccan arms trade and by extension persuade al-Mansur into an anti-Spanish alliance. As a result the terms of the company's trade were extremely irregular, in contrast to the Muscovy and Levant companies. By allowing its agents to claim lavish expenses the company immediately compromised its chances of profitability, a problem that was compounded by Leicester's agreement to pay al-Mansur cloth, lead, iron and tin worth £4,000 in the first year's trading to ensure his subsequent monopoly over the import of metals, mainly for munitions. Excluding the £4,000 paid in goods, sales in 1586 amounted to just £2,994, and by shipping more than 2,000 cloths a year the company had saturated the Moroccan market, driving down prices. Worse still, the importation of Moroccan sugar, almonds and gold all registered losses, mainly due to the expense of transportation; hence 7 tons of raw sugar were bought, each at £5 8s, but they cost over £9 to transport back to London, where they also sold at £9, a loss of over £5 a ton.[69] The initial excitement over the importation of saltpetre also evaporated as the costs of refining and transporting it (not to mention the bribes and presents required to sustain the trade) proved prohibitive and led to further heavy losses.

By 1586, despite this financial cost, it seemed that the Barbary and Turkey companies were helping to weaken the threat of anti-English Spanish aggression at both ends of the Mediterranean, even though Philip II had other ideas. Both companies had been established with the dual purpose of trade and politics, to exploit a strategic and potentially profitable commercial alliance between Muslims and Protestants, and to cultivate military alliances in the face of Catholic aggression against a beleaguered Tudor England. But while the political alliances had borne some fruit, the commercial consequences were decidedly mixed. In contrast to the faltering Moroccan trade, the Turkey Company was thriving. The company had put £45,000 into start-up costs, exporting cloth and metal in return for silk, spices, cotton, currants, mohair, carpets, indigo and drugs of various kinds. At the height of Harborne's embassy it was despatching nineteen ships weighing between 100 and 300 tons and crewed by nearly 800 seamen on an average of five voyages a year to trade in ten Ottoman-controlled Mediterranean ports. The profits on some voyages were estimated at over £70,000, producing returns of nearly 300 per cent.[70] Both Murad and Elizabeth were benefiting enormously from the trade, and the strategic anti-Spanish military alliance that came with it. The Spanish were furious with Harborne's success, as were the other Catholic powers, but diplomatically there was little they could do. In 1586 the new French ambassador, Jacques Savary de Lancosme, reiterated his predecessor Germigny's long-standing demands that Murad expel Harborne. The Englishman responded coolly that 'I think he won't be quite strong enough to turn me out.'[71] He was right: in Constantinople at least, the English were there to stay.

6

Sultana Isabel

By the late 1580s hundreds, perhaps thousands, of Elizabethan merchants, diplomats, sailors, artisans and privateers were plying their trade throughout the Islamic world, from Marrakesh and Constantinople to Qazvin in Persia. Slowly the consequences of their adventures began to have a discernible public impact in England, particularly in London. One of the most startling came on 2 October 1586, when the Welsh minister Meredith Hanmer preached a sermon at St Katharine's Church next to the Tower of London, entitled *The Baptizing of a Turke*. This was the first recorded example of a Muslim converting to English Protestantism, which was all the more remarkable given the circumstances. In his sermon Hanmer explained that Chinano (possibly a garbled Anglicization of the Turkish 'Sinan') was a forty-year-old native of 'Nigropontus' on the Greek island of Euboea, which had fallen to the Turks in 1470. 'This Turk', Hanmer claimed, 'was taken captive by the Spanish, where he continued in great misery the space of 25 years, whom the most worthy knight Sir Francis Drake found at Carthaginia.'[1] Drake had set off for the Spanish colonies in the Americas in 1585 with seventeen ships and 2,000 men, pillaging his way across Florida, the Caribbean and the north-west coast of South America. By February 1586 he had reached Cartagena in modern-day Colombia. There he burnt its monasteries, ransomed resident Spaniards and captured local Indian, Moorish and Turkish slaves, including Chinano.[2]

Drake's return to England in July 1586 led the Privy Council to write to the Turkey Company's directors, asking how 'the hundred Turks brought by Sir Francis Drake out of the West Indies (where they served as slaves in the Spanish galleys)' might be 'conveyed home and presented by the ambassador [Harborne] unto the Grand Seigneur, whereby their lordships are persuaded that they may both draw on greater favour and liberties unto them selves than they yet enjoy, and also procure the release of some of the captives of the English nation there'.[3] Both council and company knew that trading repatriated Turkish slaves for English ones in the Ottoman territories made good diplomatic and financial sense. Harborne spent much of his time negotiating the release of English galley slaves throughout the Mediterranean, and later claimed that he had spent £1,203 during his five-year residence in having 'redeemed at Constantinople, Algiers, Tripoli in Barbary and other places fifty four of her subjects [Englishmen] from long miserable captivity'.[4] Over the next few years many of the Turks returned home on Turkey Company ships. But some, like Chinano, clearly stayed in London; and within a matter of weeks Chinano came to Hanmer's attention.

The motivations and sincerity of Chinano's conversion are unclear (not least because he spoke Spanish but no English), although these were of little interest to Hanmer, who seized on the case of what he called 'this silly Turk and poor Saracen' as a way of justifying English Protestantism, refuting Islam and stoking the anti-Catholic and anti-Spanish sentiment that was gripping London. 'I have purposed by God's help, to lay before you', he proclaimed, 'first the original of Mahomet, that false prophet with the nations of Moors, Saracens and Turks; secondly their false doctrine and wicked religion, wherewith they have bewitched infinite souls: with a brief confutation thereof.' What followed was a fairly standard (and very long) denunciation of the Prophet Muhammad and the Islamic faith, riddled with the usual Christian errors, fears, myths, stereotypes and fantasies. According to Hanmer the Prophet was born to a 'heathen' father and an 'Ishmaelite' mother. Ridiculed by Hanmer as a drunken epileptic, Muhammad is described as using magic to 'bewitch the people' and spread 'the law of Mahomet' throughout Arabia, Persia and North Africa. The minister claimed that Muhammad 'patched together his Alcoran of the laws and doctrines of heathens, Indians and Arabians, of superstitious Jews, of Rechabites, of false Christians and heretics', producing a confused theology which denied the Christian Trinity and Jesus as the son of God, but approved of the Gospels. In

Hanmer's mind Muhammad's beliefs betrayed a devilish confederacy with the Jews, who 'continually prick him forward against the Christians'. But the minister reserved his real venom for what he saw as a conflation of Islam and Catholicism. In the 'flocking to tombs and sepulchres, worshipping of dead corpses, bones and relics' and other 'feigned miracles of Romish idolatry', 'we need not say it is popish', railed Hanmer, 'nay, it is Turkish and Mahometicall'. While Elizabeth's merchants and diplomats strategically allied themselves with Muslims in opposition to Catholic power, her preachers took a less flexible position, compounding Islam and Catholicism as two variants of the collective sin of idolatry.

From Hanmer's Protestant perspective, Chinano's conversion was a chink of light in the theological darkness. When questioned on 'what should move him at this present to receive the Christian faith', Hanmer reports that Chinano identified 'his misery and captivity under the Spaniards, his travel hither, and the view of this land, [which] had beaten into him (as he said) the knowledge of the true God. And further he said, that if there were not a God in England, there was none nowhere.' The image of Chinano having knowledge of the 'true' Protestant God 'beaten into him' suggests that his conversion may not have been the joyful and spontaneous decision that Hanmer would have his congregation believe. Warming to his theme of Protestant England's beneficence, Hanmer identified two further reasons for Chinano's conversion: 'before his coming, the virtue, the modesty, the godliness, the good usage and discreet government of the English Christians, and among others (as he chiefly noted) he was most beholden unto the right worshipful knight, Sir Francis Drake, and that worthy captain W[illiam] Hawkins, terming them most worthy Christians'. Drake's and Hawkins's worthy character was in fact rather dubious: Drake was a licensed pirate, a 'corsair', and Hawkins a notorious slave trader, whose recent rampage through the Caribbean had brought death, imprisonment and enslavement to countless Spaniards, Native Americans and *renegados*. Hanmer seemed unconcerned that Chinano's conversion may have been coerced, claiming that upon his arrival in England the Turk 'saw courtesy, gentleness, friendly salutations of the people, succour for him and his countrymen, pity and compassion of the Englishmen, and withal he learned that the poor, the aged, the impotent, the sick and diseased Christians were provided for, whereas in his country and where he had been in captivity, the poor and sick and diseased were scorned, despised, and accounted of as dogs'. When pressed on why he had never converted to Catholicism in twenty-five years of Spanish servitude, he (or more likely Hanmer) gave the reasons every Elizabethan Protestant wanted to hear: the Spaniard's 'cruelty in shedding of blood, and his idolatry in worshipping of images'.

The rest of the sermon descended into a fantastical celebration of Protestantism and a denunciation of Catholicism. Hanmer maintained that Chinano's conversion showed that it was only the political might of Catholic Spain and the papacy that prevented Muslims – who 'know not the purity of religion in the reformed churches' – from converting en masse to Protestantism. 'Let the Church of God be swept then will the heathens, the Jews, the Turks and Saracens the sooner come in,' he declared. Hanmer even used his selective knowledge of the first letters exchanged between Elizabeth and Murad seven years earlier to support his millenarian belief in the mass conversion of Jews and Muslims:

> Mustafa Beg, secretary to the great Turk of Constantinople that now is writing to the Queen of England as appeareth by his letters bearing date the 15 March, and in the year of great Jesu (so he writeth) 1579 sheweth the great affection his master the Turk together with himself beareth to this land and of our religion as it is interpreted he sayeth thus:
>
> 'We know that your sovereign majesty among all the Christians have the most sound religion, and therefore the Christians throughout the world envy your highness.'

This was a clearly misleading interpretation of Mustafa Beg's letter, which had already been amended by Harborne to flatter the queen, but Hanmer had no interest in such subtleties; the political and commercial dimensions of the Anglo-Ottoman rapprochement were of negligible significance when set against what the preacher saw as the Ottoman ruler's obvious acknowledgement of the theological superiority and inevitable triumph of English Protestantism over Catholicism.

The printed version of the sermon ended with a moment of pure

Elizabethan theatre: 'the Turk confessed in the Spanish tongue before the face of the congregation', while from the pulpit Hanmer performed a catechistic dialogue with Chinano, 'propounding the questions and receiving the answers by skilful interpreters'. Chinano 'renounced Mahomet the false prophet of the Moors, Saracens and Turks', embraced the Trinity and 'believeth verily that Jesus Christ was and is the son of God', and finally 'desired he might be received as one of the faithful Christians, and be baptized'. At the conclusion of the service Chinano was led to a table with a basin in the middle of the congregation where he was baptized, having 'desired his name might be William', the Christian name of his liberator, Captain Hawkins.

Throughout Hanmer's oration the voice of Chinano (or William) was mediated by others, and once the sermon was finished he would disappear from the historical record. Like many other sixteenth-century converts and *renegados* his life flickered into public view suddenly for one reason or another, and disappeared again just as quickly. Chinano presented a justification for Hanmer's virulent anti-Catholic position at a moment when a Spanish invasion seemed imminent. The sermon does however reveal that a small but visible group of Chinano's Turkish 'countrymen' were moving around London, and that many Londoners knew about the Anglo-Ottoman alliance and their queen's cordial correspondence with the sultan. While it used Chinano's conversion as a sign of Protestantism's growing ability to redeem its rival religions of the book, it left other concerns about religious conversion unanswered. How genuine was Chinano's baptism, and what could prevent him from reverting? How sincere and enduring was anyone's religion in the face of the sheer variety of forced, strategic or spontaneous conversions taking place between various faiths at this time? This included Protestantism, a theology barely seventy years old, now riven with its own factionalism and fighting for its survival in late sixteenth-century Europe.

Such anxieties were compounded by a growing number of cases in which conversion went the other way, with English Protestants embracing Islam – often coerced, at other times strategic and sometimes possibly even willing converts. Thomas Sanders's sensational account in 1584 of how the *Jesus* and its crew had been imprisoned by the Dey of Tripoli and eventually released thanks to Harborne had also described how English cabin boys 'voluntarily turned Turk'. As Sanders reported, when the dey's son tried to convince two of the *Jesus*' crew to convert to Islam, he turned to one of his father's servants, 'a son of a yeoman of our Queen's guard, whom the king's son had enforced to turn Turk; his name was John Nelson. Him the king caused to be brought to these young men, and then said unto them, "Will you not bear this, your countryman, company, and be Turk as he is?"' Sanders and his crew resisted such demands at their peril: several were forcibly circumcised and dressed 'in the habit of a Turk', while others were thrown into the galleys.[5] But the case of Nelson and the anonymous cabin boys suggests that there were growing numbers of English converts to Islam, some of whom may even have converted willingly, regardless of their Protestant faith.[6]

Reports of even more visible English converts to Islam were also beginning to reach London. In June 1586, just four months before Hanmer baptized Chinano in St Katharine's Church, William Harborne despatched letters from Constantinople addressed to 'Hassan Aga, Eunuch and Treasurer to Hassan Bassa king of Algier'. Hassan Aga was better known to Harborne as Samson Rowlie, his fellow merchant from Great Yarmouth, captured by Turkish pirates off Algiers in the *Swallow* in 1577. Most of the crew had been imprisoned, but Rowlie had been castrated and converted to Islam. Over the next decade he took the name 'Hassan Aga' and rose to become chief eunuch and treasurer of Algiers as well as one of the most trusted advisers to its Ottoman governor, Harborne's old adversary Qilich Ali Pasha ('Hassan Bassa').[7] Like Rowlie, Ali Pasha was himself a Christian convert to Islam. Born a Catholic in Calabria but captured and enslaved in the 1530s by one of Kheir-ed-Din Barbarossa's captains, he converted and became renowned as 'the greatest corsair of them all', and by 1568 had been appointed Ottoman governor of Algiers.[8]

Harborne wrote to Hassan Aga asking him to use his influence to secure the release of the surviving members of the *Swallow*'s crew still imprisoned in Algiers, many of whom had lived and worked with him in his previous life as Samson Rowlie. In direct contrast to Hanmer's account of Chinano's conversion, Harborne acted as though

Hassan Aga's was a calculated act of survival that belied his true and unshakeable Protestant faith. He presumed that Hassan Aga still professed a 'fervent faith' in 'our lord Jesus Christ, by whose only merits and blood-shedding you together with us and other good Christians shall be saved, and also for your faithful obedience like a true subject of Her Majesty, naturally loving your country and your countrymen'. Harborne believed that Hassan Aga's 'true' religion would compel him to intercede with Ali Pasha on behalf of the English captives in 'procuring their redemption', which he assured Hassan Aga would 'manifest to all the world, especially to her majesty and me her ambassador, your true Christian mind and English heart ... that notwithstanding your body be subject to Turkish thraldom, yet your virtuous mind [be] free from those vices'.[9]

A portrait of Hassan Aga that appeared in a traveller's book just two years after Harborne wrote his letter offers little to support the ambassador's conviction that Hassan Aga's conversion was a superficial act driven by self-preservation. Dressed in opulent robes and wearing the white turban of a convert, Hassan Aga reclines on a gilt throne, the picture of a confident, prosperous and successful young Muslim – albeit one who has been castrated and converted from Christianity. Like many other contemporary Christians who, willingly or not, 'turned Turk' in the Mediterranean during this period, Hassan Aga gives the impression that, on balance, a career as a rich and powerful member of the Algerian ruling elite was more appealing than Samson Rowlie's life as a struggling, peripatetic Protestant merchant from Great Yarmouth.

Whether Harborne's petition for the release of the *Swallow*'s crew was successful is unknown, although his failure to mention it in subsequent correspondence suggests that it was not. What happened to Hassan Aga is also unclear, and Harborne's letter is the last we hear of him. Harborne had other matters to attend to, and was unable to act on every single captive, ransom and conversion brought to his attention during his time in Constantinople. One English traveller who did have Harborne to thank for saving him was Edward Webbe. One of the most colourful of all the Elizabethan adventurers in the eastern Mediterranean, Webbe obtained a degree of fame with the publication of his picaresque memoir *The Rare and most wonderfull things which Edward Webbe an Englishman borne, hath seene and passed in his troublesome travailes* (1590). He was born in 1553/4 near the Tower of London, the son of a master gunner, and by 1566 he was in the service of Anthony Jenkinson, spending the next five years travelling throughout Russia. In 1571 he was captured and enslaved by Crimean Tatars. After being ransomed, he returned to England and sailed to Alexandria, where his ship was attacked by Turkish galleys. Following a fierce fight in which most of his crew was killed, Webbe described how he and and ten survivors were 'sent to Constantinople, and committed unto the galleys, where we continued the space of five years'. Somehow Webbe managed to convince his captors of his 'good skills in the gunner's art', and travelled with the Ottoman army to Persia, Damascus, Cairo, Jerusalem, Goa and Ethiopia, and along the Red Sea coast, 'to do the Turk's service in the field'. Returning to Constantinople he organized what he described as 'a cunning piece of firework, framed in form like to the Ark of Noah', for the circumcision ceremony of the sultan's sons. However, as a Christian with no immediate military usefulness, Webbe became once more a 'prisoner in the Turk's dungeons', and was pressed 'to forsake Christ, to deny him, and to believe in their God Mahomet: which, if I would have done, I might have had wonderful preferment of the Turk, and have lived in as great felicity as any lord in the country'. He managed to resist, despite being 'grievously beaten naked' and 'reviled', until 'it pleased God to send thither for the release of me and others, a worthy gentleman of this land, named Master Harborne'. Webbe praised Harborne who 'did behave himself wonderfully wisely, and was a special means for the releasement of me and sundry other English captives'.[10] Unfortunately Webbe's freedom was short-lived: travelling home through Italy he was imprisoned and tortured as a heretic in Rome and Naples before finally returning to England in 1587.[11] He was last heard of in 1592, living in Blackwall, having been made a cannonier for life, presumably living off his pension and his tall traveller's tales.

Despite the success in negotiating the release of captives like Webbe, Harborne's time in Constantinople steadily darkened because of what he rather dramatically called 'the subtle secret devices of my many mighty enemies both Christian and heathen'.[12] His memoirs (written some time after Walsingham's death in April 1590 and never published) conceded that throughout the second half of 1586 he was under intense pressure from London, 'I being certified by the late Right Honourable of worthy memory Mr. Secretary Walsingham, of the said Spaniard his great preparation to invade this realm'. According to Harborne the Spanish were prepared to pay the Venetians 160,000 ducats 'to break off our intercourse and expel us' from Constantinople, as well as encouraging the *bailo* to use his influence over Murad's imperial harem to conclude a non-aggression treaty that would free Philip II to concentrate on attacking England. It was now clear to Harborne that the 'said Spaniards and adherents' jealous suspicion of my proceedings since my second arrival there' went far beyond commercial protectionism, and that he needed to use what influence he had to 'restrain the Venetians from entering the cursed league' with Spain.[13]

Harborne maintained that his strategy drew on his reformed religious beliefs. 'I performed my utmost endeavour', he wrote, 'by setting one enemy of God his church against the other to impair the same.' In a pragmatic echo of Hanmer's denunciation of Catholics and Muslims, the Protestant Harborne claimed to have set Spaniards against Turks to get what Walsingham wanted. His anti-Catholic Protestantism was clearly useful in creating an alliance with the Ottoman court, although privately he was frustrated by the way the sultan and his court teased him about his religious beliefs. 'Everyone, for a joke,' wrote the Venetian *bailo* Morosini, 'calls him Lutheran – even the very Pashas – much to his disgust, as he is a most desperate Calvinist.'[14] Putting aside such annoyances, Harborne's first objective was to build a network of alliances close to Murad. He cultivated his friendship with the sultan's tutor, the great Turkish historian Seadeddin Muhammad Ben Hassan, and made his peace with his old enemy Qilich Ali Pasha, presumably by giving them both substantial 'presents'. This secured their opposition to any plans within the harem for a non-aggression pact with Spain. Harborne's machinations appear to have been at least partially successful as he was able to report that 'the Spaniard dares not withdraw his total forces out of Sicily, Naples and other ports of the Levant Seas', which could then be turned against England. The 'cursed league' was blocked, and

Harborne was triumphant. 'I performed my uttermost endeavour', he boasted, 'not only to break of the same but further to procure the said Turkey navy against him [Philip II], which when (for the streightness [violence] with Persia) I perceived could not be, I yet notwithstanding through God his assistance so prevented his crafty devices in that count, that neither his travel or much exhausted treasure prevailed.'[15] Although he had persuaded Murad to reject an alliance with the Spanish, Harborne believed that any attempt to convince the sultan actually to join with Elizabeth in turning his navy against Philip II was unlikely to succeed, mainly because of the financial and military cost of the Ottomans' campaigns in Persia, which had recently led to the occupation of the former Safavid capital of Tabriz.[16]

On 24 June 1587 Walsingham congratulated Harborne on 'how carefully and discreetly you have proceeded in your negotiations with the sultan and his counsellors'. He also told him that the queen was delighted with his success in preventing the peace treaty, and that:

> her pleasure is that you let the Grand Signor understand that she most thankfully taketh this his stay, by you signified, of renewing the truce desired by the King of Spain which you shall in her name not only persuade him to continue but also show unto him how necessary it is for him to attempt somewhat presently for the impeachment of the said Spaniard's greatness, much more in truth to be doubted than of Persia, against whom his forces seem to be altogether bent, and may be performed by setting such princes as are in Barbary at his devotion upon the King of Spain, furnishing them for the purpose with some number of galleys, which with small cost shall give him great annoyance, whereunto her majesty's hand will not be wanting.[17]

Walsingham then made one final tantalizing offer: 'you may signify unto the Grand Signor that her Majesty hath lying upon the coast of Spain a fleet of very strong, well furnished ships under the conduct of Sir Francis Drake, which the last year spoiled and burned Cartagena and other places in the West Indies, who hath already entered diverse ports of Spain and Portugal'. The implication was clear: England was a naval power to be reckoned with, and if Murad joined forces, they could wipe out Spanish maritime influence in the Mediterranean.

Not that Elizabeth *really* needed Murad's help, as Walsingham was at pains to explain: 'although her Majesty needeth no assistance of other princes yet shall it be a great encouragement and contentation to her Majesty as a more terror to the King of Spain, they having like interest, use like endeavour to abate his power. All which,' concluded Walsingham, 'as well to satisfy and stir up the Grand Signor as also to disgrace your adversaries in that court and country, I leave to your-self to be published, urged and enlarged as you shall see cause.'[18]

Having successfully resurrected his career as ambassador to Con-stantinople and single-handedly wrecked Spain's détente with the Ottomans, Harborne was now faced with the colossal task of engin-eering an Anglo-Ottoman naval attack on Philip II's Mediterranean fleet. He clearly believed that the undertaking was impossible, and inevitably the strain began to tell. In November 1587, when war between England and Spain seemed assured, Harborne wrote an extraordinary letter to Murad, complaining about his reluctance to ratify an Anglo-Ottoman military alliance. It shows how Harborne used religious concordance between Protestants and Muslims to jus-tify a military coalition:

Do not let this moment pass unused, in order that God, who has cre-ated you a valiant man and the most powerful of all worldly princes for the destruction of idol-worshippers may not turn his utmost wrath against you if you disregard his command, which my mistress, only a weak woman, courageously struggles to fulfil. The whole world, with justice, will accuse you of the greatest ingratitude if you desert in her danger your most trusting confederate, who, in the confidence of the friendship and the promises of Your Highness, has placed her life and her kingdom in jeopardy that cannot be greater on this earth. For the Spaniard, since my mistress had declined him peace, is determined to destroy her completely, relying on the maximum assistance of the pope and all idolatrous princes. And when, finally, there will not remain any other obstacle in Christendom, he will direct his invincible military forces toward your destruction and that of your empire and will become the sole ruler of the world. For the pope, whom they con-sider as their God on earth, does not cease to persuade him with his false prophecies that he can and will achieve it. If, however, Your

Highness, wisely and courageously, without delay, will undertake
jointly with my mistress war upon the sea (which the Almighty God,
the pledged faith, the favourable moment, the fame of the glorious
house of Othman, and the salvation of your empire unanimously
advise), then the proud Spaniard and the mendacious pope, with all
their adherents, will not only be cheated of their cherished hope of
victory but will also receive the penalty for their audacity. Since God
protects only his own, he will through us in such wise punish these
idol-worshippers that those of them who might still remain will be
converted by their example to worship the true God in unison with us.
You, however, who are fighting for his true fame, he will grant victory
and shower with other favours.[19]

Harborne's argument is a selective combination of Hanmer's theology and Walsingham's *realpolitik*. Where Hanmer saw Catholicism
and Islam as idolatrous faiths, Harborne's pragmatism proposed an
anti-papal coalition between Protestant and Islamic iconoclasm. The
rest of his arguments are a succinct précis of the brief that Walsingham had urged him to publish and 'enlarge' back in June.

The letter to Murad was an official (if clandestine) statement of
Elizabethan foreign policy designed to flatter and cajole Murad into
action. With the benefit of hindsight, Harborne's memoir of this
fraught period, written towards the end of his life, is altogether more
revealing about his attitude towards the unholy alliance he was
charged with proposing. He grumbled about 'the perverse condition
of those Turkish infidels with whom forcedly so long I was conver-
sant', and admitted that it was 'my continual earnest prayer to God,
which blessed be his holy name he granted, that her Majesty in her
just defence might never need this heathen tyrant his assistance, as
also that during my residence there he might never make him the exe-
cutioner of his fierce wrath and scourge of Christendom for their
sins'.[20] Whatever his public statements, and however timely it may
have been in political and commercial terms, privately Harborne felt
deeply uneasy about trafficking with the 'infidel'.

In early 1588 Harborne began to petition Walsingham and his Turkey Company paymasters for a recall. His five-year embassy was
coming to an end, and his situation was exceptionally stressful, but

his request appears to have been exacerbated by the company's failure to pay him his £200 annual salary regularly. He complained that 'I disbursed there more than I ever charged to account in the advancement of her majesty's service,'[21] and had been paid just £400 over his ten years in Constantinople. The surviving accounts reveal that his expenditure was covered not only by the Turkey Company but also by the sultan himself. Of the £15,341 Harborne spent on wages, household costs, redeeming captives and 'presents' (£1,442), the company covered £13,246, the remaining £2,094 coming out of 'the allowance of the emperor [Murad] in the time of his being in Constantinople'.[22] Such costs were much higher than those incurred by Henry Roberts in Marrakesh, but this reflected the far greater commercial and political investment that Elizabeth's advisers were prepared to make in Constantinople. Although Harborne would claim that such expenditure had contributed towards an alliance between Elizabeth and Murad and the wrecking of another between the sultan and Philip II, it had not produced the firm military axis that Walsingham had hoped for. No Ottoman attack on the Spanish fleet in the Mediterranean was forthcoming, and without it there would be no delay in launching Spain's Armada against England.

In late April 1588, as Harborne was about to be recalled to London by Elizabeth, a Spanish Armada of 130 ships, 8,000 sailors and 18,000 soldiers prepared to sail out of Lisbon bound for the English Channel. It raised its banner in a ceremony reminiscent of that used before the Battle of Lepanto against another of Spain's 'infidel' enemies, the Ottomans. In July 1588, the English fleet led by the lord high admiral Charles Howard, Francis Drake and John Hawkins engaged the Spanish off Plymouth. By the beginning of August, after a series of engagements in different parts of the English Channel, the English were in the ascendant, scattering the Spanish fleet and pursuing it up the eastern coast of England. Much of what remained of the Armada was destroyed in stormy weather on the rocky coasts of Scotland and Ireland. Against all the odds, the Protestant English had prevailed in the face of the overwhelming might of Catholic Spain.

On 1 August 1588, as the remains of the Spanish fleet limped round the Scottish coast in a desperate attempt to reach home, Harborne wrote his final despatch to Walsingham from Constantinople.

Disillusioned and frustrated by the sultan's persistent broken promises of a formal military alliance, Harborne told Walsingham that he
was ready to 'depart presently'. He enclosed his final petition to the
sultan, offering the same accusations and justifications as before. He
believed the Ottomans remained more interested in war with Persia
than with Spain, and offered the forlorn hope that Don António
could lead an anti-Spanish force to recapture the Portuguese throne,
diminishing Spanish power in Iberia, North Africa and beyond.[23] On
13 August, after putting his twenty-five-year-old secretary Edward
Barton in temporary charge of the embassy (partly because he was a
fluent Turkish-speaker), Harborne with his thirty-strong retinue left
the sweltering heat of Constantinople for the last time. When he
reached Hamburg on 19 November he learned of 'her majesty's victory over the Spaniard'.[24] It must have been a bittersweet moment for
the tenacious Englishman. After ten years in Constantinople he had
retrieved a commercial agreement with the Ottomans when all
seemed lost, established England's first official embassy in the Muslim world, founded an extensive network of English factors across
the Mediterranean, and negotiated the release of scores of English
captives from the horrors of galley slavery. Although he had failed to
clinch a deal that would have set Turkish Muslims against Spanish
Catholics, his diplomacy had played its part in unsettling the Spanish
and their preparations for invasion – or so Harborne would insist
upon his return to England. A life of peaceful, obscure retirement in
Norfolk now awaited the former ambassador, who lived for nearly
two more decades before his death in 1617.

In Marrakesh, Henry Roberts had been facing a similar struggle to
convince another reluctant Muslim ruler of the wisdom of backing
Elizabeth in her struggle with Spain. Like Murad, Sultan al-Mansur
seemed unconvinced that the English were worth the risk; they just
did not appear to have the military power and diplomatic status to
match their anti-Spanish rhetoric. Don António was coming to the
same conclusion; in the spring of 1588 he had appealed directly to
al-Mansur for his help in persuading Elizabeth to attack Spain. But
the wily al-Mansur prevaricated, waiting to see what would come of
the Spanish invasion of England. On 12 July 1588 Roberts wrote to

Leicester informing him that 'here came news that the king of Spain's armada is departed for England; the which I well perceive is the case that this king [al-Mansur] doth prolong the times, to know how they speed: for, if the king of Spain should prosper against England, then this king would do nothing; and, if the king of Spain have the over-throw, as by God's help he shall, then will this king perform promises and more'.[25] Don António and Elizabeth were powerless to act in Morocco, or anywhere else for that matter, until the outcome of the Spanish invasion was known.

Across the capitals of Europe and North Africa, statesmen eagerly awaited news of the Spanish Armada. In Marrakesh, the Spanish cir-culated rumours that their fleet had triumphed. But in a letter dated 5 August Elizabeth wrote to al-Mansur informing him of her victory over the Spanish. The letter reached the small community of English merchants in Marrakesh at the beginning of September. The news sparked extraordinary scenes of celebration. They set off fireworks, organized impromptu street banquets and dancing, and led a proces-sion through the city centre. According to eyewitness reports some flew standards showing Elizabeth standing in triumph over a prostrate Philip, while others carried effigies of the Spanish ruler and Pope Six-tus which they set on fire, much to the consternation of the watching Italian and Spanish merchants. The procession then entered the *mel-lah*, where three men challenged them. The first, Diego Marín, was a Spanish diplomat; the other two, the Portuguese nobleman João Gomes da Silva and the Spaniard Juan de Heredia, a survivor of the Battle of Alcácer-Quibir, were living in the city in a state of limbo after having been ransomed. What exactly happened next is disputed, but what is clear is that the three men drew their swords and attacked the English merchants, knocking several from their horses, killing between three and seven of them and wounding many more. The *mellah* descended into chaos, Jews and Muslims watching in horror as Catholics mur-dered Protestants, Europe's Christians replaying their sectarian conflicts on the streets of Marrakesh in faraway North Africa.[26]

Al-Mansur was appalled by such violent scenes which threatened the peace and commercial stability of his capital city, and immedi-ately arrested the assailants. What happened to da Silva and Heredia is unknown, but Marín would spend the next twenty years in prison.

For some of the English merchants, the Armada celebrations had proved fatal, but the Spanish defeat at the hands of the English naval forces had finally convinced al-Mansur of two things: that the mighty Spanish were not as invincible as he believed; and that England and her female ruler could not be dismissed any more as peripheral to the commercial and diplomatic world of North African politics. The Armada's failure prompted Spain's enemies to reassess their diplomacy: suddenly an Anglo-Moroccan alliance seemed like a very real possibility, one which might transform the delicate balance of power in North Africa and Iberia.

The shift in Al-Mansur's approach to relations with England is recorded in the writings of his court scribe and historian, Abd al-Aziz al-Fishtali, who provided the earliest known non-European commentary on the English queen. In his account of events, al-Fishtali pitted Elizabeth, whom he called 'sultana Isabel', against Philip II whom he described as 'the enemy of religion, the infidel (may God increase his sorrow and weaken his hold), the *taghiya* [tyrant] of Qishtala [Castile] who is today against Islam and who is the pillar of polytheism [*shirk*]'. According to al-Fishtali, once the Armada approached the English coast, 'God sent a sharp wind [*reehan sarsaran*] against the fleets of the *taghiya* that broke up their formation and pushed them onto the enemy's lands, bringing down their flags and banners.'[27] Al-Fishtali's use of the phrase 'reehan sarsaran' is particularly telling: it is taken from the Qur'an (4: 16) where it describes the divine winds sent against the polytheistic people of Aad. God punished the Spanish for their sins just as he punished the people of Aad.[28] The Protestant English agreed: the commemorative medal struck to celebrate the English victory bore the inscription *Afflavit Deus et dissipati sunt* ('God blew and they were scattered').[29] Al-Fishtali also interpreted the Armada's defeat as a sign that God was on the side of the Muslims – and the English. And it provided al-Mansur with the opportunity to contemplate a reconquest of Al-Andalus. 'These actions', continued al-Fishtali, 'were, thanks be to God in this dear matter, the harbingers of success and conquest, and a sign for him [al-Mansur] to fulfil his awaited promise, in taking possession, by God's will, of his [Philip's] lands and territories, and in confronting him with the victorious soldiers of God on his own turf.'[30]

Al-Mansur was now convinced of England's military capabilities and signalled his willingness to discuss an alliance that would strike against Spain and instal the Portuguese Don António on the Portuguese throne. Unfortunately, nobody seems to have told Henry Roberts. His patron, the Earl of Leicester, had died suddenly on 4 September after a short illness, just weeks after marshalling the country's defences against the Spanish invasion. His death left Elizabeth utterly distraught, and seems also to have acted as the catalyst for Roberts's decision to leave Morocco after three years. The record of his time there was hardly impressive. As well as failing to conclude a political alliance with al-Mansur, Roberts had overseen only small and irregular profits on exported goods, mainly cloth, but a significant loss on imports, primarily sugar, of £1,689. Neither Leicester nor Roberts had been properly versed or sufficiently interested in business to avoid falling into the traps of selling English cloth too cheaply and buying Moroccan sugar too expensively. Their diplomatic strategy of drawing al-Mansur into an anti-Spanish alliance had failed, and Leicester's death left Roberts more exposed than ever. Having been almost completely ignored by al-Mansur during his time there, he was promptly adopted as a pawn in the canny sultan's change of political direction as soon as news of the Armada's defeat reached him. Roberts was staying outside Marrakesh in one of al-Mansur's garden palaces and presumably oblivious of the attack inflicted on his fellow English merchants in the city's *mellah*. On 14 September he left Morocco 'at the king's charges, with 40 or 50 shot attending upon me for my guard and safety', bound for England.[31]

In the terse account of his embassy, described as being 'written briefly by himself' following his return to London, Roberts recalled that he had left Marrakesh and travelled 150 miles south-west to the port of Agadir. 'In this port', he wrote, 'I stayed forty three days, and at length the second of November I embarked myself and one Marshok Reiz [his real name was Ahmad Bilqasim], a captain and a gentleman, which the emperor [al-Mansur] sent with me upon an ambassage to her majesty.'[32] His own embassy at an end, Roberts was now accompanying Morocco's first ever ambassador to England. What he did not know was that the embassy was just one element in a carefully choreographed exchange of diplomats destined to lead to an Anglo-Portuguese-Moroccan military axis. As Roberts and Bilqasim sailed for England, the Portuguese pretender Don António had agreed to send his brother Don Cristóbal to al-Mansur's court as a hostage to secure his commitment to a proposed military alliance. On 10 November Don Cristóbal left London with four warships and six merchant ships, bound for Morocco. Having passed Roberts and Bilqasim en route, the Portuguese arrived in Marrakesh in January 1589, and immediately petitioned al-Mansur to support Don António in reclaiming his throne. The irony of the situation was not lost on al-Fishtali, who wrote that Don Cristóbal needed 'our swords, made triumphant by God, to regain his lost kingship ... although our imamate swords with their sharp blades had earlier destroyed the edifice of his kingship' at the Battle of Alcácer-Quibir, and 'only with our hands would he recover it'.[33]

Just as Don Cristóbal arrived in Morocco, Roberts and Bilqasim landed in England. As usual, Roberts made a meal of it, complaining that 'after much torment and foul weather at sea, at New Year's Day I came on land at St. Ives in Cornwall'. From there the two men travelled 'by land up towards London, we were met without the city with the chiefest merchants of the Barbary Company, well mounted all on horseback, to the number of 40 or 50 horse, and so the ambassador and myself being both in coach, entered the city by torchlight, on Sunday at night the 12 of January 1589'.[34] The Moroccan ambassador's dramatic arrival in London concluded in a suitably theatrical way a turbulent episode in Elizabethan England's relations with the Islamic world, which had witnessed the success of Harborne's second embassy to Constantinople, the birth of the Barbary Company and the defeat of the Spanish Armada; it also set the stage for another to be played out over the next decade, this time on the stages of London's public theatres.

7

London Turns Turk

In the summer of 1588 London was braced for a Spanish invasion which if successful would lead to the inevitable arrival of a victorious Philip II, returning in public triumph to the city he had ridden through thirty-five years earlier as Mary Tudor's consort. Six months later and with Philip's Armada in ruins, instead of a Catholic conqueror Londoners watched a Muslim ambassador riding in state through the capital. The sight of Ahmad Bilqasim – or Marshok Reiz as his English hosts called him – entering London at the head of an entourage including the Barbary Company's most senior merchants symbolized very publicly an important shift in Elizabethan foreign policy towards the Islamic world. Both the Sa'adian and Ottoman rulers had watched tiny, insignificant England overcome the mighty war machine of the monarch whom al-Fishtali called 'the great tyrant of Castile', and they now regarded Elizabeth with respect as an important political player on the international stage. For their part, Elizabeth and her advisers understood that strategic alliances with both Marrakesh and Constantinople were needed more than ever to combat the inevitable attempt by King Philip to recover from his recent naval humiliation.

Very little documentary evidence remains describing where Ahmad Bilqasim stayed and whom he met during his time in London, but we do have the official diplomatic correspondence describing what both sides hoped to achieve from his mission. A remarkable memorandum written by the ambassador in late January outlined the scale of al-Mansur's projected alliance. It proposed:

> To offer unto your majesty not only to employ in her assistance men, money, victuals and the use of his ports, but also his own person, if

your majesty should be pleased to require it; and to desire, for the better withstanding of the common enemy the King of Spain, there might [be] a sound and perfect league between them.

To let her understand that for the better furtherance of her princely purpose to restore Don António to the kingdom of Portugal, he thought it a good course that the army by sea that she should send with him, should enter into the Straits [of Gibraltar], and there to ship such assistance as he should send; whereby the King of Spain, for the defence of those parts of Spain within the Straits, that coast upon Barbary, should be constrained to withdraw his forces out of Portugal; whereby Don António, finding the country unfurnished of foreign forces, may be better able to recover his country.

Lastly, to offer, when the 100 ships should come upon the coast of Barbary, whereby he might in his own person go into Spain, he would deliver unto her majesty 150,000 ducats.[1]

Al-Mansur was proposing an audacious Anglo-Moroccan military campaign against the Spanish that would put Don António on the Portuguese throne, occupied by Philip of Spain since 1580, and enable him to reconquer the lost Muslim lands of Al-Andalus, in return for which he would pay Elizabeth 150,000 ducats. With his subtle but emotive emphasis on 'recover' and 'restore', al-Mansur suggested a 'perfect league' between the English and the Moroccan rulers that was as much an ideological as a geographical union of the two countries. In the uncertain aftermath of the Spanish Armada's defeat, al-Mansur was proposing an extraordinary unification of Muslims with Christians.

The plan was not solely of al-Mansur's making, but was part of a much larger anti-Spanish axis developed by Elizabeth and her advisers in the immediate aftermath of victory over the Spanish that became known as the Portugal Expedition. In September 1588 plans were being drawn up to launch a bold counter-strike against Spain, with Sir Francis Drake appointed admiral and Sir John Norris as general. Elizabeth approved a military campaign to capture Lisbon, which it was hoped would trigger a popular uprising to put Don António on the throne, then strike at Seville and establish a naval base in the Azores to attack the remnants of the Spanish fleet.

Elizabeth's problem was that she was virtually bankrupt from the cost of defending the realm in the face of invasion. Drake and Norris therefore proposed that the expedition be financed as a joint-stock operation: Elizabeth would contribute £20,000, with £40,000 raised from London merchants who would see a return on their investment in booty, with the Dutch Calvinists asked to provide troops, ships and supplies to the value of £10,000.[2] When she learned that al-Mansur was prepared to pay 150,000 ducats towards the costs – at sixteenth-century exchange rates that was approximately £70,000, or the campaign's entire budget – the possibility of an alliance of Anglicans, Calvinists and Muslims fighting the Spanish must have looked extremely attractive to the impecunious Elizabeth.

With Walsingham ailing and unable to fulfil his role on the Privy Council (he would die in April 1590), it was left to the aged Burghley to lead the negotiations with Bilqasim. Burghley proceeded with his usual caution, worrying about how Elizabeth should advise Don António to respond to al-Mansur's offer, about the exact nature of Moroccan military support and about 'when the money shall be paid'. He also expressed concern at Elizabeth risking her newfound international prestige by throwing in her lot with a Muslim ruler against the Spanish, writing, 'Her majesty is loath to hazard the honour achieved last year.' Eventually Elizabeth agreed to al-Mansur's offer, albeit with some reservations, being 'most ready to requite the same, so far forth as may stand with her honour and conscience'.[3] In January 1589, as Bilqasim settled into his London residence, Drake and Norris were in the Low Countries recruiting Calvinist troops to join their fleet and sail for Lisbon the following month.

Bilqasim was secure enough in his diplomatic role that he also lodged a series of further requests with Elizabeth's advisers. He asked that, should al-Mansur need to defend his realm against other Muslim states while attacking Spain, he be permitted 'to hire for his money certain ships and mariners within this realm', as well as carpenters, shipwrights and 'such provision and commodities' as he required. Bilqasim also requested that Elizabeth 'bestow her reward

A silver 'Geuzen' ('revolt') medal coined during the sixteenth-century Dutch Revolt, with inscriptions 'Rather Turkish than Papist' (*left*) and 'In spite of the Mass' (*right*), dated 1574.

on the poor man of Bristol, who brought him out of Ireland and had his ship cast away in the voyage'. This seems to be a reference to the unfortunate Henry Roberts, until recently England's first ambassador to Morocco, who was now reduced to receiving royal handouts at the intercession of the Sa'adian representative in London. Roberts's fall from grace was all the more humiliating because on his return he spent more than a year embroiled in an undignified and ultimately unsuccessful squabble with the Barbary Company's directors over outstanding pay.[4]

Had the Moroccan ambassador taken time out that winter from his political negotiations, he could have done what so many diplomats have done in London ever since, and gone to the theatre. What he would have seen might have startled him, as the city's commercial playhouses were in the grip of a fascination for staging scenes and characters from Islamic history with which Bilqasim would have been very familiar, even though their version of events would not have been one he recognized.

The most fashionable and popular play the Moroccan ambassador could have seen during his stay was *Tamburlaine*, a play in two parts, the first performed at London's open-air playhouse the Rose in late 1587 by the Admiral's Men (named after their patron, the lord high admiral Charles Howard of Effingham). The play's full title was *Tamburlaine the Great, who, from a Scythian shepherd, by his rare and wonderful conquests, became a most puissant and mighty monarch, and (for his tyranny and terror in war) was termed the scourge of God*. It had been written earlier in 1587 by a precocious young playwright barely out of his Cambridge studies, Christopher Marlowe.

Variously accused in his short yet brilliant life (1564–93) of being a spy, atheist, sodomite and (worst of all) addicted to tobacco, Marlowe quickly saw the limitations of plays like Robert Wilson's *Three Ladies of London*, with their heavy-handed morality and personified characters who bore little relation to the dynamic and exciting world that the mercurial Marlowe saw around him. His response, in both its subject matter and its language, would change the entire direction of Elizabethan drama. Marlowe's inspired choice for his hero was Timur, the Turkic-Mongol Muslim warlord and founder of the Timurid dynasty. In just over thirty years Timur led a series of spectacularly successful and brutal campaigns, laying waste to central Asia, conquering Persia, invading Russia and capturing the Delhi sultanate. In 1402 he marched into Syria, defeating the Egyptian Mamluks and taking Aleppo and Damascus before overcoming and capturing the Ottoman sultan Bayezid I at the Battle of Ankara in 1402. Timur's imperial aspirations were ended only by a fever that killed him in February 1405 as he marched on Ming China.

Timur provided Marlowe with a suitably exotic, violent yet seductive hero, marching across a vast global panorama of the post-classical world in which rival Tatar, Persian, Turkish and Christian empires contended for global sovereignty. In Marlowe's hands much of

Tamburlaine's life is fictional (including his name, which Marlowe adopted from the Latin sources he had read, unaware that 'Tamburlaine' was originally a contemptuous nickname referring to the warlord's lameness from a youthful injury, a disability he lacks in Marlowe's play). He is transformed into a lowly Scythian shepherd, a brilliant orator and charismatic overreacher who delights in humbling the mighty, whatever their beliefs, and whose ceaseless and apparently amoral appetite for conquest simultaneously appalled and enthralled the Elizabethan audience.

Marlowe's play dramatizes the extraordinary ambition and will to power of its eponymous hero. The play begins with Tamburlaine under threat from the Persian emperor, Mycetes, but he is shown quickly seducing, fighting, commanding and conquering his way to lead one of the most powerful empires in history. Most of all, Marlowe wanted to create a heroic character in which his audience could believe. Despite the challenge of staging the vast geographical range of the play (from Persepolis through Africa to Damascus), Marlowe's hero is convincing because of the unprecedented force and power of his language. He is an utterly captivating orator who can perform terrible acts of cruelty and violence while simultaneously persuading the audience of his love for his wife and his absolute commitment to imperial success. In Part Two of the play, Tamburlaine's brutality reaches further extremes. Finally conquering Babylon, and hanging its governor from the city walls, Tamburlaine performs his most audacious and controversial act by burning the Qur'an. Claiming to be greater than any god, he falls ill and commands his sons to conquer what is left of the world before he dies.

Marlowe could create such relentless and riveting drama because of his innovative combination of language and action. Before him, most English poets and dramatists wrote verse that followed a prescribed rhyme and a rhythmic structure dictated by the number of syllables in each line. Marlowe's great innovation was to transform one such rhythmic technique, iambic pentameter, which had been used by earlier dramatists in rhyming couplets to create a stiff and repetitive style that allowed little opportunity for character development or rapid dramatic action. Others like Wilson in *The Three Ladies of London* had used what is known as 'Poulter's measure', rhyming couplets alternating twelve and fourteen syllables. The resulting lines in Wilson's 'Prologue' sound flat and trite:

> To sit on honour's seat, it is a lofty reach,
> To seek for praise by making brags, oft times doth get a breach.[5]

In direct contrast, Marlowe chose to use unrhymed iambic pentameter, what we now call blank verse. From the very first lines of *Tamburlaine*, the difference was audible, and electrifying:

> From jigging veins of rhyming mother-wits,
> And such conceits as clownage keeps in pay,
> We'll lead you to the stately tent of War,
> Where you shall hear the Scythian Tamburlaine
> Threat'ning the world with high astounding terms
> And scourging kingdoms with his conquering sword.
> View but his picture in this tragic glass
> And then applaud his fortunes as you please.[6]

It sounds like a manifesto, which is what Marlowe intended. He tells the audience audaciously to forget the artificial 'jigging' rhymes and clowning of plays like Wilson's, leading them instead halfway across the world into the heart of battle, where the hypnotic beat of the blank verse allows them to 'hear' Tamburlaine declaiming – using transitive verbs and blank verse – in 'astounding terms' how he will match his words with deeds by conquering the world.

Many of Marlowe's contemporaries were either dazzled by or envious of his ability to modulate rhythm by varying the iambic beat and using hyperbolic, polysyllabic language that could shift seamlessly from violence to tenderness in a single line. Ben Jonson captured the power and originality of Marlowe's verse when he wrote of 'Marlowe's mighty line', but he also mocked Tamburlaine's 'scenicall strutting and furious vociferation, to warrant them to the ignorant gapers', vulgar entertainment that did no more than pander to the playhouse's poorly educated audience.[7] Other writers of the period, including Thomas Nashe, ridiculed Marlowe's innovations as 'the swelling

bombast of a bragging blank verse', dismissing them as 'the spacious
volubility of a drumming decasillabon [line with ten syllables]'.[8]
Marlowe's great rival Robert Greene went even further, complaining
that Marlowe's innovations were putting him out of business, 'for
that I could not make my verses jet upon the stage in tragical buskins
[boots often worn by actors], every word filling the mouth like the
faburden [monotonous musical refrain] of Bow-Bell, daring God out
of heaven with that atheist Tamburlaine'.[9] Greene and all Marlowe's
critics reveal that, whether they liked it or not, he had changed the
landscape of drama completely.

According to Greene, Tamburlaine's grand, declamatory style was
notorious for its theatrical impact, and the provocative views it conveyed. Perhaps it could even allow Marlowe to question some of his
audience's most cherished beliefs – including their religion. As the
classical writers of ancient Greece and Rome had shown, the ability
to persuade was one of the most highly regarded talents of public
figures. Marlowe's orator was as skilful as Cicero but as dangerous as
Satan, who had shown in the Book of Genesis that artful and persuasive language had the ability to change the future of mankind. From
this perspective, Tamburlaine becomes even more ambiguous. Is he
the brave hero who conquers the Turkish, Persian and Egyptian
enemies of Christianity in Part One, or the monstrous, tyrannical
atheist who will even march against heaven in Part Two? In Part One,
as Tamburlaine prepares to go into battle with the Ottoman sultan
Bajazeth (Bayezid I), he congratulates his lieutenant Theridamas for
his rousing anti-Turkish rhetoric:

> Well said, Theridamas! Speak in that mood,
> For 'will' and 'shall' best fitteth Tamburlaine,
> Whose smiling stars give him assurèd hope
> Of martial triumph ere he meet his foes.
> I that am term'd the scourge and wrath of God,
> The only fear and terror of the world,
> Will first subdue the Turk, and then enlarge
> Those Christian captives which you keep as slaves.[10]

Tamburlaine sounds and acts like a Christian agent sent to vanquish
the Ottoman Turks, ridding the world of their Islamic faith and

promising to release the captives enslaved in Turkish galleys. Just as Marlowe was writing, William Harborne was struggling to free Christian galley slaves too, albeit using more peaceable methods. Within two scenes Tamburlaine defeats Bajazeth and imprisons him in a cage, adding to his humiliation by using him as a footstool to step on to his throne. Bajazeth asks in vain that the 'holy priests of heavenly Mahomet'[11] poison Tamburlaine, who responds by declaring, 'let the majesty of heaven behold | Their scourge and terror tread

Henry VIII using Pope Clement as a footstool in John Foxe's *Acts and Monuments* (1583).

on emperors'.[12] The moral ambiguity of Tamburlaine made him a captivating hero: simultaneously tormentor and saviour, Marlowe created something more than a type – he made a character.

Trampling an enemy underfoot held powerful and immediate religious associations for Marlowe's audience who would have heard in Marlowe's lines the verse from the Psalms, where God says, 'Sit thou at my right hand, until I make thine enemies thy footstool' (Psalms 110: 1, King James Version). The 1583 edition of Foxe's hugely popular *Acts and Monuments* gave a particularly English twist to the idea through a woodcut showing Henry VIII in the guise of Solomon, using Pope Clement as a footstool. Henry's reforming ministers and clergy surround him (including Cromwell and Cranmer), while the pope's supporters look on in despair as Clement loses his mitre and crown. Marlowe knew that many Protestant theologians – including Foxe – conflated the pope with the Turk as two versions of the same Antichrist, but Tamburlaine was no reformed Christian. At every turn Marlowe confounds his audience's expectations about where their sympathies lie by creating a hero who is simultaneously Muslim and antagonistic towards Christianity, and a conqueror of the Turks who liberates Christians.

Perhaps Greene was right that both Tamburlaine and his creator were atheists. In Part Two Tamburlaine spends much of his time taunting any deities he can, including the Prophet Muhammad. Despite this mockery, Marlowe shows extensive knowledge of both medieval assumptions and more recent reports about Islamic theology. Indeed his mention of the 'Zoacum' tree in Act II scene 3 suggests that he may even have read the Qur'an, where the tree is mentioned in surah 37.[13] In the opening scenes to Part Two, Tamburlaine's lieutenant Orcanes signs a peace treaty with Sigismund, King of Hungary, promising:

> By sacred Mahomet, the friend of God,
> Whose holy Alcoran remains with us,
> Whose glorious body, when he left the world,
> Clos'd in a coffin mounted up the air,
> And hung on stately Mecca's temple roof,
> I swear to keep this truce inviolable.[14]

Tamburlaine himself proves less respectful. Much later in the play, after he captures Babylon and orders the slaughter of its inhabitants, he asks Usumcasane, King of Morocco:

> where's the Turkish Alcoran,
> And all the heaps of superstitious books
> Found in the temples of that Mahomet
> Whom I have thought a god? They shall be burnt.[15]

Boasting that 'I live untouch'd by Mahomet,' Tamburlaine then taunts the Prophet, calling out as he watches the Qur'an burn:

> Now, Mahomet, if thou have any power,
> Come down thyself and work a miracle.
> Thou art not worthy to be worshippèd
> That suffers flames of fire to burn the writ
> Wherein the sum of thy religion rests.[16]

Continuing his diatribe he asks:

> Why send'st thou not a furious whirlwind down
> To blow thy Alcoran up to thy throne
> Where men report thou sitt'st by God himself,
> Or vengeance on the head of Tamburlaine,
> That shakes his sword against thy majesty
> And spurns the abstracts of thy foolish laws?[17]

He tells his soldiers that 'Mahomet remains in hell,' unable to respond to such mockery, and that they should 'Seek out another godhead to adore'.[18] However, within twenty lines he feels 'distemper'd suddenly', and two scenes later he is dead. Is it just coincidence or is Marlowe finally bringing down the wrath of God upon his anti-hero – and if so, which one, Christian or Muslim? As he enters the play's final scene Tamburlaine addresses his general Techelles and his other close advisers and rails against all religions, monotheistic or polytheistic:

> What daring God torments my body thus
> And seeks to conquer mighty Tamburlaine?
> Shall sickness prove me now to be a man,
> That have been termed the terror of the world?

Techelles and the rest, come, take your swords,
And threaten him whose hand afflicts my soul.
Come, let us march against the powers of heaven
And set black streamers in the firmament
To signify the slaughter of the gods.
Ah, friends, what shall I do? I cannot stand.
Come, carry me to war against the gods,
That thus envy the health of Tamburlaine.[19]

According to Robert Greene this and the burning of the Qur'an show Tamburlaine 'daring God out of heaven'. But Marlowe makes it quite clear here that Tamburlaine is the scourge of *any* divinity, not just the God of Islam or Christianity. He cannot be reduced to the status of atheist, Muslim anti-hero or even Christian hero; in the audience's imagination he seems to embrace all of these beliefs at different moments in the play. Here, finally and majestically, the body of the man and the mind of a god collide: the 'terror of the world' has a soul but he will die in 'war against the gods'. Only they, Marlowe suggests, can defeat such a man.

None of Marlowe's provocations would have been possible without the invention of the lowly 'Scythian shepherd' from central Asia. Marlowe was fully aware of Elizabethan England's close relations with the rulers of Persia, Morocco and the Ottoman Empire that people his play. While he was still studying at Cambridge and writing *Tamburlaine* he was already associating with the intelligence networks run by Cecil and Walsingham, and might well have been privy to aspects of the ambiguous and conflicted policy of Elizabeth's advisers towards the Islamic world that had existed over the previous two decades.[20] Marlowe's play had little interest in either celebrating or condemning Elizabeth's strategic alliances with the Islamic world. It explored the contradictory and ambivalent emotions inspired by creating associations with a traditional enemy that could be – and had been – quickly transformed into an ally, and possibly even a saviour. The result was a new kind of drama that embraced duality and encouraged the audience to revel in both the horror and the delight of identifying with a charismatic oriental character like Tamburlaine. The play created a shiver of pleasure rather than a sombre moral lesson; it asked the audience to make up their own minds about its eastern hero and 'applaud his fortunes as you please'. Judging by the 'sundrie times' the play was 'showed upon stages in the city of London', they could not get enough of it.[21]

Almost immediately *Tamburlaine*'s success spawned a new generation of playwrights, eager to exploit not just Marlowe's style but also his exotic settings. One of the first was Thomas Kyd. Kyd's life was nearly as mysterious as Marlowe's: they were close friends and former roommates who soon became embroiled in the murky world of Elizabethan espionage. Kyd would subsequently be arrested, tortured and imprisoned on charges of blasphemy arising out of documents that he said in fact belonged to Marlowe. They died within little more than a year of each other, Marlowe in May 1593, Kyd in August 1594. Kyd probably wrote his celebrated revenge play *The Spanish Tragedy* within months of *Tamburlaine*. The backdrop for Kyd's violent and bloody drama was the political struggle between Spain and Portugal, a prescient issue in the late 1580s considering Elizabeth's support for Don António. It also featured a play-within-the-play dramatizing the Ottoman sultan Süleyman the Magnificent's fictional pursuit of the Greek beauty Perseda. Kyd's play set a new benchmark for revenge tragedy and was so successful that in 1592 he rushed out a follow-up, *Soliman and Perseda*, that focused exclusively on the Ottoman sultan's invasion of Rhodes, his capture of Perseda and his eventual downfall.

Another of Marlowe's contemporaries, George Peele, took a different approach to the dramatic fashion being established by Marlowe. Instead of staging a play in the Ottoman Empire, he chose places and events closer to home. Either just before or just after the Armada's defeat, Peele returned to an earlier moment of conflict involving Iberia, writing *The Battle of Alcazar* and recounting the events that had taken place at Alcácer-Quibir ten years earlier. If the Moroccan ambassador had seen this play on one of the many occasions it was performed by Lord Strange's Men at the Rose Theatre on Bankside, he would have been perplexed to see his sovereign Mulay Ahmed al-Mansur being played by an English actor and renamed 'Muly Mahamet Seth'. Eschewing the liberties taken by Marlowe and Kyd

in describing distant Ottoman history, Peele took the innovative decision to dramatize a relatively recent historical event like Alcácer-Quibir
by drawing on publications that described the battle. The result
looked and sounded more like war reportage than epic drama, a play
indebted to Marlowe's style but strikingly different in its setting and
subject matter. It was the first play in English theatrical history to use
a Presenter to introduce each act, and the first set exclusively in
Morocco to put a Moor on the English stage. What Peele did with his
'Moorish' characters would have a profound effect on all subsequent
Elizabethan drama.

Peele named the ruling sultan Abd al-Malik I 'Abdelmelec, also
known as Muly Molocco, rightful King of Morocco', in contrast to
his scheming nephew, the exiled Abu Abdallah, whom Peele called
'Muly Mahamet, the Moor' (not to be confused with Muly Mahamet
Seth). This opposition is made all the more explicit in that, while
Abdelmelec is regarded as the legitimate 'brave, Barbarian lord Muly
Molocco', Abu Abdallah is characterized as 'the barbarous Moor, |
The negro Muly Mahamet', a 'tyrant', 'Black in his look and bloody
in his deeds'.[22] The term 'Moor' was derived from dual meanings of
the Greek root Μαῦρος, the first describing an inhabitant of Mauretania, the second an adjective meaning 'dark' or 'dim'. During the
Middle Ages the Latin derivation 'Maurus' took on a more ethno-
graphic sense of blackness, which following the Islamic conquest of
North Africa also become a synonym for 'Mahomet's sect' (Muslims).[23] The word was thus an explosive mix of religion and ethnicity
that Peele exploited to the full as he contrasted the two contenders for
the Moroccan throne. But he went further than other dramatists,
drawing on contemporary sources which argued that Moors 'are of
two kinds, namely white or tawny Moors, and Negroes or black
Moors'.[24] With his face made up with burnt cork and oil and wearing
black gloves, the actor playing Muly Mahamet was easily transformed into the devilish, scheming 'blackamoor', while Abdelmelec
was his complete antithesis, a virtuous 'tawny Moor', possibly even
swathed in white robes, a suitable figure for English merchants to do
business with.

Peele showed Abdelmelec as a noble, tawny Moor distanced from
associations of blackness and Islam because eventually it would be

his son, Ahmed al-Mansur (renamed by Peele as 'Muly Mahamet Seth') who would inherit the kingdom and establish an alliance with Elizabeth. But this is where the play began to run into problems. Despite their apparent differences, both men are acknowledged as Muslims and 'descended from the line | Of Mahomet'.[25] Although Abdelmelec is seen as the legitimate ruler, he also announces that 'I do adore | The sacred name of Amurath the Great,'[26] the Ottoman sultan Murad III, with whom he is in league. In a further striking difference, Muly Mahamet is shown allying himself with the Christian king, Sebastian I. From this point in the play onwards, Peele has to work hard to portray Sebastian as a courageous but tragic figure, flawed by his Catholicism and therefore easily manipulated by the scheming Muly Mahamet.

The play's anti-Catholic bias intensifies with the introduction of Peele's dramatization of Thomas Stukeley, surrounded by Irish clergy and Italian soldiers, heading for Ireland and hoping to 'restore it to the Roman faith'.[27] Sebastian persuades Stukeley to join his Moroccan crusade, but the bombastic Englishman's thundering, sub-Marlovian speeches reveal him to be a pale, opportunistic version of Tamburlaine:

> There shall be no action pass my hand or my sword
> That cannot make a step to gain a crown,
> No word shall pass the office of my tongue
> That sounds not of affection to a crown,
> No thought have being in my lordly breast
> That works not every way to win a crown.
> Deeds, words and thoughts shall all be as a king's,
> My chiefest company shall be with kings,
> And my deserts shall counterpoise a king's.
> Why should not I then look to be a king?
> I am the Marquess now of Ireland made
> And will be shortly King of Ireland.
> King of a mole-hill had I rather be
> Than the richest subject of a monarchy.[28]

The vain and conceited Stukeley lacks the ambition and linguistic prowess of Tamburlaine. Instead he is fixated on the pursuit of a king's crown, preferring to be king of an Irish 'mole-hill' rather than anyone's subject.

At the end of Peele's play, his historical sources dictated that everyone dies, though not before Muly Mahamet demands 'A horse, a horse, villain, a horse' in the climactic battle scene, prefiguring the demise of another tragic villain, Shakespeare's *Richard III*, four years later. The only man left standing is Muly Mahamet Seth, Elizabeth's future ally, but even he does little more than order the mutilation of Muly Mahamet's body followed by a Christian burial for Sebastian (which not did happen historically). Like Marlowe's *Tamburlaine*, there is no obvious lesson from Peele's play as it ends with no Chorus to provide a simple moral, and no character with which the audience can identify. Instead they are offered a choice between the pompous Abdelmelec, the pious Sebastian, the scheming Muly Mahamet and the mercenary Stukeley.[29]

This lack of simple identifications in Peele's play came about in part through the contradictory nature of Elizabeth's relations with Iberia and Morocco in the late 1580s. These contradictions provided an alternative to the prescriptive history of classical Rome and Greece, and allowed Elizabethan dramatists to develop their own idiom, enabling them to address contemporary English hopes and fears by staging them in a faraway land where the horrors of warfare, murder, atheism and tyranny could be explored in relative safety, free from the suspicious eyes of Elizabeth's censors. We might think the play more conventionally recommends the avoidance of Catholic–Muslim conflicts, and advises Elizabeth against pursuing an alliance with al-Mansur (Peele's Muly Mahamet Seth). But Tudor dramatists were obviously not foreign policy advisers. First and foremost they wanted to exploit the contradictory associations, ambivalent emotions and theological conflicts created by English experiences in Morocco and beyond as spectacular, exciting, captivating drama, regardless of morality or ideology.

The Battle of Alcazar was not, however, Peele's only foray into contemporary events in Iberia and North Africa. At the same time he also produced a poem entitled 'A Farewell to Sir John Norris and Sir Francis Drake', written in anticipation of the departure of Norris and Drake's Portuguese Expedition in spring 1589. Where *The Battle of*

Alcazar had shown Catholic Portugal destroyed by its ill-fated Moroccan adventure, Peele's poem imagined an English Protestant crusade taking on the might of Spanish Catholicism. He describes the fleet leaving behind 'England's shore and Albion's chalky cliffs' as they head for 'the spacious bay of Portugal' and the 'golden Tagus'. Bidding farewell to all they hold dear, Peele even glances backwards at his own recent play alongside those of Marlowe and Greene:

> Bid theatres and proud tragedians,
> Bid Mahomet's poo [poll, or head], and mighty Tamburlaine,
> King Charlemagne, Tom Stukeley, and the rest,
> Adieu. To arms, to arms, to glorious arms!
> With noble Norris, and victorious Drake,
> Under the sanguine cross, brave England's badge,
> To propagate religious piety.

Peele used the evocative image of the 'sanguine' red cross, the traditional symbol of Christian militancy since the time of the Crusades, in anticipation of an English victory as part of a wider religious crusade which will 'propagate religious piety'. Clearly, the hope was that Drake and Norris's heroic exploits would eclipse those of characters seen in London's theatres such as Marlowe's Tamburlaine and even Peele's own version of 'Tom Stukeley'. Drake and Norris's mission 'to deface the pride of Antichrist | And pull his paper walls and popery down' in the name of 'Christ, and England's peerless Queen', was one which, if successful, Peele seemed ready to stage himself.[30]

Disappointingly for Peele, however, by January 1589 preparations for the Portuguese Expedition were beginning to show signs of strain. In the Low Countries the Dutch and English commanders quarrelled over how many troops could be spared. The final number of 1,800 minus cavalry was half Norris's original request, as was the eventual supply of arms and munitions. Popular enthusiasm for the venture throughout the south-east of England swelled the army's numbers to nearly 20,000, but many of these were inexperienced adventurers who all needed feeding, adding to Drake and Norris's financial headaches. Running out of money but determined to continue, the two men issued the order for their fleet of 180 vessels to leave Plymouth on 18 April 1589, with provisions to last them less than a month.[31] On board were Don António and the returning Moroccan ambassador Bilqasim, disguised as a Portuguese nobleman. It was yet another awkward alliance of Portuguese Catholics and Moroccan Muslims, with echoes of what had happened at Alcácer-Quibir, but this time with the intention of overthrowing a kingdom in Lisbon rather than in Marrakesh.

Almost immediately things went wrong. Despite Elizabeth's orders to attack the Spanish fleet at Santander, Drake and Norris first plundered La Coruña on the north-western Spanish coast instead, wasting valuable time and manpower and alerting the Spanish. The queen was furious, complaining bitterly that 'they went to places more for profit than for service', but she was powerless to change their course.[32] By the time the fleet reached Lisbon in May the city was heavily defended, and the promised revolt in support of Don António never materialized. The siege turned into a fiasco, as the English forces dwindled to just 6,000 in the face of sickness and desertion. In late June the English withdrew and made their way home, having failed to achieve any of their objectives, and in the process losing a huge number of men (an estimated 11,000 died) and a great deal of money, much of it Elizabeth's. Drake and Norris were in deep disgrace, Don António returned to England yet again, his last opportunity to regain the Portuguese throne apparently gone, while Bilqasim exploited the chaos to discard his Portuguese outfit and slipped away to Marrakesh.

Elizabeth's best chance of ending the Spanish military threat for a generation had been missed, lost in the face of mismanagement, greed and mutual recriminations. The queen blamed everyone for the expedition's ignominious end, including al-Mansur who was accused of duplicity in failing to support the fleet during the critical attack on Lisbon. In August al-Mansur wrote to Drake and Norris, protesting weakly that he had not been informed of the fleet's departure from England, and so was unable to help them. The truth was that al-Mansur's support could not have saved the disastrous campaign and that his sudden withdrawal was not duplicitous but pragmatic, as it transpired that the Moroccan was not the only ruler holding hostages. After the Battle of Alcácer-Quibir, Philip II had taken charge of two Moroccan princes who had fled the fighting: Muley al-Shaykh, the son of Abu Abdallah Muhammad, and al-Mansur's nephew, Muley al-Nasr. As news of the Anglo-Moroccan alliance reached Philip, he moved the princes to Seville, a veiled threat to send them back to Morocco, where they would undoubtedly have unleashed a civil war. In the face of such an imminent challenge to his rule, al-Mansur's dream of jihad and *reconquista* dissolved almost immediately. To reward him, Philip agreed to return the strategically important towns of Asilah and Larache on the Moroccan coast.[33] By the autumn of 1589, Catholic Spain, Protestant England and Muslim Morocco were locked in a three-way power struggle, each side playing off the others in a complex dance of politics, religion, money and military one-upmanship, with the first round going to the wily Philip.

Still, the English refused to give up on a Moroccan alliance. Faced with the collapse of the Portugal Expedition, Don António had sent an envoy to Marrakesh called John de Cardenas (alias 'Ciprian') to plead with al-Mansur to give him money to support his claim to the Portuguese throne. Cardenas, however, was a double agent who was also working for Walsingham, and in October 1589 he wrote a long letter to his English paymaster providing a remarkably frank assessment of the political situation and of al-Mansur's intentions. Cardenas appears to have been made of far sterner stuff than predecessors like Hogan and Roberts. As a spy rather than a merchant or a soldier he clearly had greater experience of the slipperiness of rulers like al-Mansur, although he was not without his own braggadocio. He reported to London that he had been kept waiting nearly a month before meeting al-Mansur, and Cardenas complained that when he finally entered his presence he was 'twice or thrice interrupted in the midst of my tale; which had been clean cut off, if I had not resolutely insisted to be suffered to say what I had to say. I delivered my message to the Moor, urging him, by all the reasons I could, to the performance of his promise' to assist Don António and Elizabeth in their anti-Spanish league. Al-Mansur responded by offering what Cardenas dismissed crisply as 'his pretended forward disposition to assist the king of Portugal'. As far as Cardenas was concerned, al-Mansur had failed 'to perform what he had promised' and 'went about to fill my ears with wind only'. He claimed rather grandly to have issued the Moroccan ruler with an ultimatum: unless he committed to financing another military strike against Portugal by the winter, 'I would take his delay thereon for a plain refusal.' Boasting that he had 'driven him to the wall', Cardenas extracted al-Mansur's agreement 'to take a final resolution in the matter', but events suggest that Cardenas's bluster had absolutely no effect on al-Mansur. Just days later the frustrated spy reported that the Moroccan's 'former promise made to me was performed only by sending his Jew without unto us', an unnamed official offering yet more vague assurances of political support.[34]

A clearly frustrated Cardenas then turned on al-Mansur for the way he conducted business. 'The Moor', he protested, 'doth rob the Jews' by demanding that they run the sugar mills for hardly any profit, leading them to default on their contracts with English merchants. But the English were not exempt from criticism either. In a withering attack on the policies of the likes of Henry Roberts, Cardenas attacked the English merchants for having 'been the causes of their own harm and spoiling of the trade', because they had 'bred a glut of and discredit of their commodities, and partly also by outbidding one another in the price of Barbary commodities through the envy and malice that reigneth among them'. He then raised the unspoken issue of religious difference, taking a swipe at Protestant Elizabethan foreign policy by reflecting that it was 'to be lamented that Christians should furnish the sworn enemies of Christ with iron, with brimstone, handguns, with firelocks, with swordblades, and such like'.[35]

Although Cardenas had been sent to Marrakesh to resurrect the faltering Anglo-Moroccan alliance, he offered further cynical opinions on al-Mansur and his attitude towards Elizabeth, concentrating again on religion. As far as he was concerned, 'the Moor doth not purpose the performance of his promise, I judge by his ill usage of me . . . whereunto I may add the natural hatred he beareth to Christians, and his cowardly and extreme covetous disposition'. He denounced al-Mansur for trying to draw Elizabeth into a war in which he never had any intention of participating: 'the proof hereof appeareth both by the untruth of some of his promises, which his country cannot perform, and by the consideration of his own estate and disposition: for how can it agree with reason that the cowardliest man in the world, another Sardanapalus in life, a man generally hated of his subjects, should hazard himself and his fortune at home to undertake a needless and endless war abroad?'[36] For Cardenas, the best way of explaining al-Mansur's actions to Walsingham was to compare him to a semi-fictional Assyrian ruler renowned for his licentious and indolent behaviour who became a byword for oriental despotism. Such an exotic, polysyllabic character could have stepped right out of a scene from Marlowe's *Tamburlaine*. Cardenas's insistence on calling al-Mansur 'the Moor', and his repeated references to the Sa'adian ruler's ability to 'perform' his 'role',[37] also evoked the Moorish characters in Peele's *Battle of Alcazar*. Perhaps Cardenas had been watching Scythians, Turks and Moors on London's stages before he left for Marrakesh. What is certain is that by the beginning of the 1590s the concept of 'the Moor' was part of the common language of not just the Elizabethan theatre but diplomacy too.

When Cardenas's report reached London, Elizabeth reacted with a fury born of political impotence. In August 1590 she wrote to al-Mansur complaining about what she regarded as his bogus friendship. Not only had he failed to support the English during the disastrous attack on Lisbon, but his promises of money and the return of English captives had failed to materialize. In an uncharacteristic fit of pique, Elizabeth then threatened to go over his head to the Ottoman sultan Murad. 'If you would not grant us what we so reasonably ask from you, we will have to pay less attention to your friendship,' she wrote in exasperation. 'We know for sure also that the Great Turk, who treats our subjects with great favour and humanity, will not appreciate your maltreatment of them in order to please the Spaniards.'[38] Sounding more like a childish taunt than a diplomatic manoeuvre, it was nevertheless a revealing comment: a Protestant English monarch trying to play one Muslim kingdom off against another, assuming that al-Mansur dreaded the Ottomans far more than he feared Spain and England. Elizabeth had in fact already written to Murad about al-Mansur. But the wily Moroccan ruler brushed off the threat of Ottoman intervention, writing back a delightfully patronizing letter, mollifying the queen and assuring her of his love and friendship. By January 1591 even Murad was becoming annoyed by al-Mansur's behaviour, writing to Elizabeth about his irritation with the 'faithless prince of Fez'.[39]

Al-Mansur seemed indifferent to such threats. He was preoccupied with fulfilling a messianic project that had exercised him since his accession: extending his empire into the Muslim kingdom of Songhai in modern-day Niger. When Elizabeth's letters reached him in the autumn of 1590, his army of 5,000 soldiers including Moriscos, *renegados* and European mercenaries had already set off to cross 2,000 miles of Saharan desert to march on the Songhai capital, Gao, on the Niger River. On 13 March 1591 the Moroccan troops equipped with muskets massacred 80,000 Songhai warriors armed with only lances and javelins. As the Songhai soldiers fell they are reported to have shouted, to no avail, 'We are Muslims, we are your brothers in religion.'[40] The Moroccan victory brought al-Mansur vast wealth from controlling a key stretch of the trans-Saharan trade route, generating an annual tribute from the Songhai of 1,000 slaves and 100,000 gold pieces.[41] European merchants flocked to Marrakesh in their droves as gold poured into the imperial capital. Politically and financially al-Mansur seemed more secure than ever. He even wrote to Elizabeth apologizing casually for not having done so earlier, excusing himself because of the small matter of the invasion of Niger, but promising her that the money rolling into his imperial coffers would help their joint effort to defeat the Spanish. His victory was also chronicled by his court historians in terms that illuminated his rivalry with the Ottomans: al-Mansur was now regarded as the Mahdi, the legitimate heir of the caliphate descended from the Prophet Muhammad (unlike the Ottoman sultans), who would unify Islam and lead a holy war against Christianity. If New World gold and silver had enabled Spanish Catholic imperial interests to fight Protestants and Muslims throughout Europe and the Mediterranean, gold from Central Africa would be used to confer imperial and religious legitimacy on al-Mansur. The English were of course oblivious to these quasi-spiritual claims, but Elizabeth appreciated that al-Mansur's success in Niger, in contrast to her own military failure, meant she needed his support more than ever, whatever she thought of his real motivations.

*

The political histories, diplomatic reports, travellers' tales and sermons being published in London describing epic military victories and heroic defeats, gold plundered from fabled African empires, captive princes, ransomed slaves, political skulduggery and apocalyptic claims of universal empires across the Mediterranean and Asia were the raw material that quickly became a recipe for theatrical success in London's commercial playhouses. The fascination with the mixture of faith, ambition and ethnicity in the early plays of Marlowe, Kyd and Peele developed into staple theatrical fodder throughout the 1590s, as almost every Elizabethan dramatist attached to an acting company began to include despotic sultans, deceitful Moors, renegade Christians, murderous Jews and vulnerable princesses in their plays. An endless variety of recusants, pagans, converts, apostates and atheists parading the political and personal power of their beliefs (or lack of them) became central to the commercial success of Elizabethan theatre.

Of more than sixty plays featuring Turks, Moors and Persians performed in London's public theatres between 1576 and 1603, at least forty were staged between 1588 and 1599. Of the thirty-eight extant plays performed between 1587 and 1593, at least ten acknowledge explicit debts to Marlowe's *Tamburlaine*.[42] But the line between simply imitating Marlowe and exploiting Elizabethan fascination with the Islamic world became increasingly blurred as playwrights drew on a growing body of humanist, diplomatic, commercial and religious writings describing Muslim kingdoms from Morocco to Persia. Robert Greene, who had implied that Marlowe was an atheist, responded almost immediately to *Tamburlaine*'s popularity with plays for the Queen's Men that took the Ottomans as their main interest. *The First Part of the Tragicall Reign of Selimus, Sometime Emperor of the Turkes, and Grandfather to Him that now Reigneth* (c. 1588–90) was an explicit attempt to imitate *Tamburlaine* by envisaging a two-part play chronicling the life and reign of the Ottoman sultan Selim I (r. 1512–20).[43] In Greene's hands Selim became the first Ottoman sultan to get his own play on the English stage, and it was the first one set exclusively in the Ottoman Empire. Selim is shown poisoning his father Bayezid II and murdering his brothers in the pursuit of absolute power. He is a combination of Tamburlaine (who is mentioned on three separate occasions) and Machiavelli's prince, with little interest in what he calls 'the holy Prophet Mahomet', the 'sacred Alcoran' or 'gods, religion, heaven and hell', which he dismisses as 'mere fictions' and 'bugbears to keep the world in fear'.[44] In keeping with medieval Christian stereotypes, Greene portrays Islam as irreligious in its affinity to paganism and its love of idolatry. Selim buries his father at the 'Temple of Mahomet' and tries every theatrical trick known to Greene to compete with *Tamburlaine*'s success, from exotic settings and epic battles to deathbed conversions, poisoning, strangling, the severing of one character's hands and even a graphic eye-plucking scene that anticipates a similar moment in *King Lear* (1606). The play ends much like the first part of *Tamburlaine*, with 'victorious Selim' preparing to march against the Egyptian sultan, and Greene's Chorus angling for a recommission:

> If this first part, gentles, do like you well,
> The second part shall greater murthers tell.[45]

Unfortunately, it seems the audience did not like it well at all. Greene lacked Marlowe's rhetorical flair and ability to manipulate the audience's emotions: instead he had put a murderous and unsympathetic Turk in Tamburlaine's clothing, with none of the Scythian shepherd's epic allure. No second part was forthcoming.

Greene tried again with *Alphonsus King of Aragon*, which went further back in time to the fifteenth century and the life of the Spanish Alfonso V, King of Aragon and Naples, and his defeat of a fictional Ottoman sultan, the bombastic Amurack. The depiction of Islam in Greene's play was even more outlandish, with a theatrical device that went beyond Tamburlaine's burning of the Qur'an. The 'God Mahomet' is brought on stage as a brass idol, 'a brazen head set in the middle of the place behind the stage, out of the which cast flames of fire, drums rumble within'.[46] Mahomet's false prophecy leads to Amurack's defeat at the hands of Alphonsus. The sultan offers his daughter Iphigina to the Spanish king, promising in a bizarre fantasy of Christians triumphing over the Ottomans that for her dowry he 'shall possess the Turkish empery'.[47]

Like other playwrights of the early 1590s, Greene continued to exploit the fascination for all things coming out of Islamic lands.

Many attempted to outdo Marlowe, but most of them failed not because their audience's appetite for such plays was diminishing, but because their plays were unable to build character and action beyond types or images. Writers like Thomas Dekker, Fulke Greville, John Day and William Haughton all tried, each one producing ever more overblown plays set throughout Africa and Asia, all featuring violent, despotic characters, strutting, stamping, ranting and bellowing their way across the stage as they simultaneously conquered and murdered. They wore turbans or 'Turkish caps', flowing robes, ostentatious scimitars and 'moustachios'. The result was an outlandish style of histrionic orientalism, whose affected, stagey performance by melo-dramatic actors has become an enduring characteristic of the English theatrical tradition. It is a convention that first developed out of a combination of Marlowe's 'mighty line' and the contemporary reports reaching London from Elizabethans living and working throughout Africa, the Mediterranean, the Ottoman Empire, Russia, Persia and even India.[48]

But as Marlowe's followers churned out ever more lurid imitations of *Tamburlaine*, the mercurial young playwright followed that work's success with a complete change of direction: in 1589–90 he wrote *The Jew of Malta*. While *Tamburlaine* was a recognizable figure from world history, this new play was an explosive and unpreced-ented leap of the imagination. There are no direct (or at least obvious) sources for the play, but the name for its central and wholly unscru-pulous character was taken from the Bible, which relates the story of Barabbas, a violent mobster who is released from prison by Pilate instead of Jesus (Matthew 27: 16–27). In Marlowe's hands, Barabas (spelled differently from the biblical original) becomes one of the most outrageously immoral characters in Elizabethan drama: a wealthy Jewish merchant who relishes the riches of trade and the murder of those who threaten it. Out went the epic, restless geo-graphical sweep of *Tamburlaine* and in came the insular setting of Malta, a Mediterranean island so apparently insignificant that Tam-burlaine never even mentioned it in his thundering speeches of imperial conquest. Gone too was Tamburlaine's mighty rhetoric and military ambition, replaced by a middle-aged Jew who first appears on stage counting his 'infinite riches' and confessing that his people 'come not to be kings'.[49] However, within two scenes the island's Christian authorities confiscate Barabas's wealth to settle the annual tribute demanded by the Ottomans of Malta. His response is to embark on a gleeful rampage of deception and murder to recover his wealth. He buys a Turkish slave called Ithamore and forms a murderous alliance with him based on their shared religious identities. Barabas tells Ithamore, 'Both circumcised, we hate Christians both.'[50] He proceeds to poison his own daughter Abigail (as well as a convent of nuns) when she converts to Christianity. He then plays off the Maltese Christians and the invading Ottoman army against each other to ensure his own survival, before they both realize what he is up to and turn on him, boiling him alive in a cauldron as he rails against them:

> had I but escap'd this stratagem
> I would have brought confusion on you all,
> Damn'd Christians, dogs, and Turkish infidels![51]

Marlowe's play partly drew on Malta's importance in recent geopolitical events, from the unsuccessful Ottoman siege of the island in 1565 to the *Bark Roe* incident of 1581 and the wider role of Jewish merchants acting as commercial intermediaries between Christian and Islamic interests. Although these events and individuals provided Marlowe with some of his raw material, what really interested him as a dramatist was not the mechanics of trade and the price of commodities, but the issues that such activities generated: trust and betrayal, faith and apostasy, conversion and exchange. These were problems that English merchants like Hogan, Harborne and Roberts had been struggling with in North Africa and the Ottoman territories for decades, but it took Marlowe's genius to give them full voice in *The Jew of Malta*. Here was a play that put the three religions of the Book on stage, each found to be more rapacious, duplicitous and hypocritical than the other. In a wonderful declaration of villainy, Marlowe sets Barabas up to revel in the prejudices of an Elizabethan audience:

> As for myself, I walk abroad a-nights
> And kill sick people groaning under walls;
> Sometimes I go about and poison wells;

And now and then, to cherish Christian thieves,
I am content to lose some of my crowns,
That I may, walking in my gallery,
See 'em go pinioned along by my door . . .
And with extorting, cozening, forfeiting,
And tricks belonging unto brokery,
I filled the gaols with bankrupts in a year,
And with young orphans planted hospitals,
And every moon made some or other mad,
And now and then one hang himself for grief,
Pinning upon his breast a long great scroll
How I with interest tormented him.[52]

Here is the self-confessed villain playing to the playhouse's ground-lings, as this most notorious of Jews declares himself to be quite as terrible as Christian lore believed. Marlowe evokes every myth asso-ciated with anti-Semitism, but most particularly apostasy, murder and money. The pun on 'interest' would not have been lost on its audience: simultaneously meaning advantage, profit and fascination, Jewish 'interest' was never far from the public imagination. Although Jews had been officially expelled from England in 1290, a small but significant community still lived in London.[53] From the outset of the play, Marlowe translates the geographic scope of Tamburlaine into the symbolic weight of wealth. As he picks over his riches, Barabas declares:

Give me the merchants of the Indian mines,
That trade in metal of the purest mould;
The wealthy Moor, that in the eastern rocks
Without control can pick his riches up,
And in his house heap pearl like pebble-stones,
Receive them free, and sell them by the weight.[54]

The rich and exotic world of imperial conquest comes to rest 'as infinite riches in a little room'.[55] In this play more than any other, Marlowe demonstrated how charismatic characters like Barabas could transcend established boundaries of morality, religion and eth-nicity. Marlowe had little interest in the specific nature of Barabas's

Jewish faith, or Ithamore's Islamic beliefs; instead he wanted to show that their behaviour was just as rapacious and unprincipled as that of many of those in the London audience.

The Jew of Malta was another great success for Marlowe, but his dominance of London's stage was to prove tragically short-lived. On 30 May 1593 he was stabbed to death in a house in Deptford, ostensibly over a dispute concerning the settlement of a bill. The exact circumstances of and reasons for his murder have remained shrouded in mystery ever since, but what cannot be doubted is that his death brought to an end the career of one of Elizabethan theatre's most promising talents.[56] Marlowe's genius was to take the fear, hypocrisy and greed surrounding Elizabethan England's relations with the Islamic world and transmute it into electrifying theatre that generated conflict, doubt and anxiety, which always make for better drama than moral absolutism. It all happened in little more than five extraordinarily creative years that altered the course of the English theatre. It was difficult to imagine that any of his imitators would ever manage to surpass his brilliance, and certainly not before the decade was over. But one man, born like Marlowe in 1564, had been quietly learning his stagecraft by observing his fellow playwright, absorbing his style and working out how he might take Elizabethan theatre in a new direction. His name was William Shakespeare.

8

Mahomet's Dove

In his diary entries for the Rose Theatre's spring season of 1592, Philip Henslowe noted that Marlowe's *Jew of Malta* was a popular hit performed on at least ten occasions, but its success was soon eclipsed by a new play called *Henry VI*. Henslowe recorded that the play's first performance took place on 3 March 1592, and that during the rest of the season it was performed on fifteen occasions, often on alternate days with *The Jew of Malta*.[1] Today few people read Shakespeare's earliest forays into English history, but during the first half of his career the three parts of *Henry VI*, written in rapid succession in the early 1590s, were enormously popular with audiences, offering a distinctive new style that challenged Marlowe's theatrical supremacy.

Shakespeare did not try to compete with Marlowe by imitating his 'high astounding terms' and exotic settings. Instead he looked closer to home, to the Plantagenets, the flawed and often tragic line of medieval English kings. London's commercial theatre had never thought of itself as grand and secure enough to put recent English history on stage, let alone humanize it by transforming the vulnerabilities and frailties of inadequate kings like Henry VI and Richard II into tragic figures. Marlowe had emphasized his male characters' relentless will to power, but they were not heroes. Shakespeare, on the other hand, succeeded in making historic failures into figures of empathy, insight and deep pathos. As if to acknowledge this shift, he began the first part of *Henry VI, Part 1* with an event similar to the one with which *Tamburlaine* ends, the death of a fabled warrior – in Shakespeare's play 'the King of Kings'[2] Henry V – with no obvious successor strong enough to fulfil his legacy.[3] What follows is a catalogue of English woe, as the young Henry VI proves powerless to prevent English civil strife and the loss of French territories conquered by his father. Central to the play are its portrayal of the French mystic and warrior Jeanne La Pucelle, known in Britain as Joan of Arc, and the death of the famous English warrior John Talbot, Earl of Shrewsbury, said to have caused the shedding of 'the tears of ten thousand spectators' when Lord Strange's Men performed the play in spring 1592.[4] Many of the audience would have known this story well and have anticipated a certain version of English chronicle history, in which the alleged visionary Joan claims she can defend France.

In Act I scene 2, the French dauphin Charles tries to raise the siege of Orleans but is beaten back by the 'famished English', complaining that 'rather with their teeth | The walls they'll tear down than forsake the siege'.[5] He is then introduced to Joan, who, 'by a vision sent to her from heaven, | Ordained is to raise this tedious siege | And drive the English forth the bounds of France'.[6] Marlowe's ghost was never far from Shakespeare's early plays, and here, in an obvious parallel with Tamburlaine, Joan describes herself as 'by birth a shepherd's daughter', who is 'black and swart'.[7] Challenged to single combat with the dauphin to prove her worth, she wins and he makes her leader of the French army. Looking on this self-confessed swarthy visionary, Charles exclaims:

> Was Mahomet inspirèd with a dove?
> Thou with an eagle art inspirèd then.
> Helen, the mother of great Constantine,
> Nor yet Saint Philip's daughter's, were like thee.
> Bright star of Venus, fall'n down on the earth,
> How may I reverently worship thee enough?[8]

The dauphin struggles to understand Joan's strength and capabilities before he alights on an analogy that expresses her singular power: if Mahomet had a mystical dove, then she must have an eagle. Both the eagle and the dove have obvious symbolic resonance in a play about war: peace has no place in the dauphin's ideology and Joan, famed for her prowess on the battlefield, is associated with a spectacular bird of prey. But, more significantly, the allusion to Islam puts France within a context of holy war. Joan is recruited because she demonstrates divine powers comparable to those of Emperor Constantine's visionary mother, and St Philip's prophetic daughters, and it is this divinity that establishes her role in French history as a crusader. For Shakespeare, however, such divinity extends beyond Christianity and into an irresistible synthesis of mysticism and power.

This is Shakespeare's only explicit reference to the Prophet Muhammad and the Islamic faith and refers to the apocryphal Christian belief, widely held since medieval times, that Muhammad was a fraudulent apostate mimicking divine intercession. In Meredith Hanmer's recent sermon *The Baptizing of a Turke* (1586) (see chapter 6), Hanmer described how Muhammad 'taught a dove to feed at his ear, wherein he was wont to put grains of corn [and] persuaded his wife and others that he was a prophet, that the spirit of God fell upon him and that the Angel Gabriel, in the form of a dove, came to his ear and revealed him secrets'.[9] Sir Walter Raleigh also reproduced the myth in his voluminous *History of the World* (1603–16), where he described it as 'Mahomet persuading the rude and simple Arabians, that it was the Holy Ghost that gave him advice', attacking it as a fraudulent mimicry of the apparition of the Holy Spirit as a dove at Jesus's baptism.[10] Thomas Nashe, widely regarded as one of Shakespeare's collaborators on *Henry VI*, also wrote about Muhammad's dove in *The Terrors of the Night* (1593), where he refers to 'the dove wherewith the Turks hold Mahomet their prophet to be inspired',[11] and he may have had a hand in drafting this particular exchange.

It is a joke at France's expense, but for it to work Charles must believe in his reference to Mahomet's dove. In the English chronicles Joan is an impostor, but in French history she is a saint. The references to mystical ornithology make the French look deluded and sharpen Shakespeare's representations of national difference. From the perspective of a Protestant English audience watching the play in 1592, it made sense to compare the Catholic French with the Prophet Muhammad, based on the misapprehension that Muslims worshipped false idols: after all, that is what Robert Greene and most of his contemporaries had assumed when staging plays like *Alphonsus King of Aragon*, with its brass head of 'Mahomet'. The 'false' prophecy of Muhammad is then emphasized further by Charles's description of more obvious Catholic prophets – John the Apostle's eagle, St Helen and the True Cross, and Philip the Apostle's vatic daughters. The fusion of these Islamic and Catholic associations damns the French Charles and Joan in the Protestant English audience's eyes; it goes even further when Charles promises Joan a grander urn than the 'rich jewell'd coffer' given to Darius, a reference to Darius III, last ruler of the Achaemenid Empire of Persia. Darius was of course not a Muslim, but to the Elizabethan audience he conjured up the oriental grandeur and despotism associated with Persia and the Ottomans. Marlowe had exploited Islamic characters and settings to create a suitably epic and histrionic drama; Shakespeare's use of them now highlighted the religious and sectarian differences confronting the Elizabethans in the early 1590s.

The anxious and seditious atmosphere of *Henry VI* captured the mood of a nation whose optimism since victory over the Spanish Armada in 1588 had evaporated. The failure of Drake and Norris's Portuguese Expedition in the summer of 1589 was the first of several foreign policy setbacks which suggested that, now in her mid-fifties and having ruled for over three decades, Elizabeth's political powers might be on the wane. Walsingham was in the last months of his life, and Leicester was dead, as were many of her other most trusted advisers. Only Burghley remained, but he was in his seventies. The news from France, so central at a different period to Shakespeare's play, was also bad. King Henry III's attempt to mediate between the Catholics and Huguenots led to his murder in August 1589 and to the contested succession of the Huguenot Henry of Navarre as King Henry IV. Henry IV's elevation split France, and the outraged French Catholic League rose up against him as he marched on Paris. The possibility of the French capital falling into Protestant hands after the defeat of the Armada was too much for Philip of Spain, who ordered Spanish forces to invade France through the Low Countries. Elizabeth could not countenance the possibility of a Spanish-controlled northern France being used as a launchpad from which to try and invade England again, so she despatched an English army of 3,600 men to support Henry's campaign in Normandy. In May 1591, just as Shakespeare was probably working on *Henry VI*, she sent another 4,000 soldiers under the command of the rehabilitated veteran Sir John Norris. Once again Norris was compromised by the vagueness of his orders. At the whim of Henry's command he spent the next twelve months in pointless sieges and skirmishes, his force dwindling by the spring of 1592 to just 600 sick and hungry men. As Shakespeare's *Henry VI* described in graphic detail the political mis-management of an English campaign in France in the 1420s, his audience was painfully aware of the disastrous campaigns of the last three years, which had left thousands of English soldiers dead or returning home as invalids, with nothing to show for their support of the French Protestant cause.[12]

The turmoil in France was even felt in Constantinople, where Har-borne's successor Edward Barton was assiduously exploiting divisions within the French diplomatic community. Since his appointment the industrious if somewhat intemperate Barton had proved remarkably successful, having cultivated a close personal relationship with Murad's powerful *haseki*, Safiye Sultan. In a letter written to Burgh-ley in July 1591 Barton had boasted, 'such an eyesore I am to the Christians here resident and so well esteemed by the Turks', that it was assumed Murad was preparing a new Turkish fleet to sail against the Spanish in league with Elizabeth.[13] The resident French ambas-sador was Jacques Savary de Lancosme, a firm supporter of the Catholic League, who now found himself compromised by the acces-sion of the Huguenot Henry IV. Barton accused Lancosme of working for Philip II against Ottoman, French and English interests, and had him arrested by the Ottoman authorities. When Lancosme was released into Barton's charge in 1592 the triumphant Englishman sent him as a prisoner to Henry IV.[14]

Just as Barton believed he had cemented a three-way alliance between France, England and the Ottomans, Henry IV was making plans to break the religious stalemate in France by converting to Catholicism. Throughout the spring of 1593 the king was locked in discussions with theologians about how to present his conversion to both sides of the religious divide. His Catholic advisers finally agreed solemnly that 'His Majesty was not a Turk . . . that he should be led gently from error to truth.'[15] An oath abjuring his Huguenot faith and embracing Catholicism was agreed, and on 25 July 1593 before enter-ing the capital Henry celebrated high mass in the Abbey of St-Denis just outside Paris. Elizabeth had feared that Henry would try to cement his political position by choosing what one of her counsellors called his religious 'metamorphosis', and responded to the news of his conversion by refusing him any further military support.[16] As far as the French Catholics were concerned, Henry's transformation might have saved him from turning into a Turk, but to the Protestant English this was what his conversion amounted to.

Shakespeare's warning of the supposed French admiration for 'Mahomet's dove' must have seemed prescient as the first instalment of *Henry VI* and its subsequent parts were performed throughout the 1590s. But the phrase also had a more uncomfortable resonance for the English. In March 1592, just as *Henry VI* was first being performed, the English Catholic propagandist and exile Richard Verstegen circulated a pamphlet entitled *A Declaration of the True Causes of the Great Troubles, Presupposed to be Intended against the Realm of England*, in which he attacked Elizabeth's privy counsellors, Burghley in particular, for what he saw as England's political difficulties. He criticized the counsellors for 'the assisting of the Huguenots of Navarre', which was just one aspect of England's 'general discord with all the Catholic Christians of the world'. He continued:

> Thus the realm of England, being brought into breach of amity, not only with the Church of God, but with all their old allies and friends, if we now consider with whom they are joined in true friendship, we shall find them to be so few as none at all, since they have neither spared, to offend friend nor foe. But if we look what new confederates they have chosen, instead of the old, we shall see them to be the great Turk, the kings of Fez, Morocco, and Algiers, or other Mahometains and Moors of Barbary, all professed enemies to Christ.[17]

Having condemned Elizabeth's alliance with the Turkish and Moroccan 'Mahometains', Verstegen then mocked English support for a variety of Protestant groups across northern Europe. 'They are also in league with a few beer-brewers and basket-makers of Holland and Zealand,' he wrote scornfully, as well as 'a company of apostates and Huguenots of France'. Verstegen revealed that he was fully aware of Walsingham's and Harborne's attempts to draw the Ottomans into a closer military alliance during the previous decade, warning his readers, 'the great Turk and his consorts, may be by the English excited to invade some parts of Christendom, near unto them adjoining (as already upon such persuasion they have attempted) but good unto England they can do none albeit the English would exchange their Geneva Bible for the Turkish Alcoran, because their situations are so far distant'. The attack on England's Protestantism was clear enough: 'the English thus leagued with infidels, heretics and rebels' would only make them increasingly isolated within Christendom.[18] The conciliatory language of religious accommodation that characterized the Anglo-Ottoman Capitulations had come back to haunt Walsingham and its English adherents.

Elizabeth's counsellors were so concerned about the possible damage of Verstegen's pamphlet both at home and abroad that they commissioned Burghley's nephew, the future lord chancellor Francis Bacon, to write a refutation entitled 'Certain Observations made upon a Libel Published this Present Year, 1592'. Towards the end of his lengthy response Bacon directly addressed Verstegen's claim that 'England is confederate with the great Turk.' Firstly, he asked rhetorically:

> if he mean it because the merchants have an agent in Constantinople, how will he answer for all the kings of France since Francis I which are good Catholics; for the Emperor; for the King of Spain himself; for the Senate of Venice; and other states, that have long time ambassadors liegers [residents] in that court? If he mean it because the Turk hath done some special honour to our ambassador (if he be so to be termed) we are beholding to the king of Spain for that; for that the honour we have won upon him by opposition hath given us reputation through the world.

This was a standard justification based on commercial exigency that had been used ever since William Harborne's arrival in Constantinople: every Christian ruler had ambassadors and merchants in the city, and Harborne's opposition to Spanish aggression in the region had also won rather than lost friends. Bacon's next claim was more theologically ambiguous: 'If he mean it because the Turk seemeth to affect us for the abolishing of images, let him consider then what a scandal

the matter of images hath been in the church, as having been one of
the principal branches whereby Mahumetanism entered.'[19] As far as
Bacon was concerned, Islamic aniconism was not responsible for Protestant iconoclasm; instead the flagrant idolatry of Catholicism had
enabled heresies like Islam to thrive. His argument went right back to
Erasmus' claim in his essay 'On the War against the Turks' (1530)
that Islam had flourished because of Catholic disunity, and was a
scourge sent by a Christian God to punish the church's sins. But it
was hardly a convincing justification of the deeply entrenched historical alliances that Elizabeth had cultivated with the Islamic world
over the previous three decades. Then, as now, ideological differences
could always be put to one side in the pursuit and justification of
trade.

Bacon had good reason to be reticent because, even as he wrote,
Elizabeth's relations with 'the great Turk' were taking on a new
dimension. Rumours were circulating through Europe's royal courts
that Elizabeth was providing financial and military support 'to help
the Great Turk to invade Christendom', partly inspired by the success
of Barton's embassy.[20] Barton was also petitioning Burghley to send
Murad gifts from the queen to endorse his appointment. In September 1593 Burghley relented, and the *Ascension* of London docked in
Constantinople laden with offerings for the sultan. As well as presenting gifts of gold plate, cloth and satin to Murad and his entourage,
Barton also conferred gifts upon Safiye Sultan, described by him as
'the Sultana or empress who (by reason that she is mother to him
which was heir to the crown imperial) is had in far greater reverence
than any of his other queens or concubines'. One of Barton's retinue
described the gifts 'sent in her majesty's name' as:

> a jewel of her majesty's picture, set with some rubies and diamonds,
> three great pieces of gilt plate, ten garments of cloth and gold, a very
> fine case of glass bottles silver and gilt, with two pieces of fine Hol-
> land, which so gratefully she accepted, as that she sent to know of the
> ambassador what present he thought she might return that would
> most delight her majesty: who sent word that a suit of princely attire
> being after the Turkish fashion would for the rareness thereof be
> acceptable in England. Whereupon she sent an upper gown of cloth of

gold very rich, an under gown of cloth of silver, and a girdle of Turkey work, rich and fair, with a letter of gratification.[21]

The transaction was conducted by the two royal women's intermediaries: Barton represented Elizabeth while Safiye delegated everything to her *kira* (a Jewish agent or intermediary), the Spanish-born Esperanza Malchi, whose power in the imperial harem was second only to her own. A delighted Barton valued the sultana's gifts at £120 before sending them on to England.[22] No record of Elizabeth's present of her bejewelled portrait remains, but other surviving examples provide some clue to the kind of object she sent. They include Nicholas Hilliard's magnificent golden locket of the queen encrusted with diamonds and rubies, which showed her as 'Defender of the Faith', a title she had used repeatedly in her correspondence with Murad.

The presentation of these luxury items was a carefully rehearsed diplomatic act designed to celebrate the Anglo-Ottoman alliance, a point underlined by a translation of Safiye's 'letter of gratification', which reached Greenwich Palace with her presents in August 1594. The letter provided an unequivocal statement of Ottoman political supremacy. It began by praising God and 'the pure soul of Lord Muhammad' before listing Murad's numerous titles as 'emperor of the seven climates and of the four parts of the world', then reminding the queen that the correspondence was initiated 'on the part of the mother of Sultan Murad Khan's son', Safiye, the sultan's consort and mother of his presumptive heir. The letter then managed to praise Elizabeth while also stressing her subservience to Murad:

> Sultan son of Sultan from all the sons of Adam to this time, the shadow of God, the protector of faith and state, Khan Murad, the support of Christian womanhood ... who follow the Messiah, bearer of the marks of pomp and majesty, trailing the skirts of glory and power, she who is obeyed of the princes, cradle of chastity and continence, ruler of the realm of England, crowned lady and woman of Mary's way – may her last moments be concluded with good and may she obtain that which she desires![23]

As far as Safiye was concerned, regardless of the presents exchanged between them, Elizabeth came under Murad's imperial and theological protection. Her letter unwittingly confirmed the accusations levelled against Elizabeth and her Protestant counsellors by Verstegen and the exiled English Catholic diaspora: England was being treated as a vassal state of the Islamic Ottoman Empire, prepared to trade anything from cloth and pictures to its faith.

Just as this exchange of gifts and letters began in late 1593, London learned of the outbreak of war between the Ottomans and the Habsburgs following the sultan's invasion of Hungary in July. The conflict would drag on for another thirteen years with no decisive outcome, and news of its campaigns would dominate English publications for the rest of Elizabeth's reign. Reports of the conflict also coincided with London's playhouses reopening after a year of closures prompted by a particularly severe outbreak of plague. On 24 January 1594 Henslowe had a resounding commercial success with another new play by Shakespeare performed at the Rose Theatre by the Earl of Sussex's Men: *The Most Lamentable Roman Tragedy of Titus Andronicus*. Having found early success in 1592 staging the prehistory to the triumph of the Tudors, now Shakespeare cast his creative net further back to the decline of the Roman Empire and the brutal, bloody tragedy of a fictional general.

The play shows Titus returning to Rome in triumph after a ten-year campaign against the Germanic Goths, in which twenty-one of his sons have died. As tradition demands, he attempts to appease the gods by sacrificing the son of the imprisoned Tamora, Queen of the Goths. The new Roman emperor Saturninus makes Tamora his empress, and she vows revenge on Titus for her son's death. Tamora's sons rape and mutilate Titus' daughter Lavinia, leading to a grisly and unrelentingly violent cycle of atrocities that culminates in Titus feeding Tamora her dead sons in a pie before killing her, his own daughter and himself. The play ends having shown or described fourteen killings (ranging from ritual murder to infanticide and suicide), six severed body parts (including heads, hands and tongues), a rape, one live burial, one bout of madness and one case of cannibalism. Shakespeare adapts Lavinia's rape and Tamora's enforced cannibalism from the story of Tereus and Philomel in book six of Ovid's Latin poem the *Metamorphoses*. The sixteenth-century translation of Ovid used by Shakespeare begins with the line 'Of shapes transformed to bodies strange I purpose to entreat.'[24] For Shakespeare, Ovid's stories of transformation and mutability were an endless source of inspiration for his own drama, with its ability miraculously to transform the stage and its humble actors into myriad protean characters, places and situations. But as in his relations with all his classical sources, Shakespeare's emulation of Ovid also involved surpassing him. In *Titus Andronicus*, instead of one rapist there are two, where Ovid has one murdered child Shakespeare has five, two children are eaten rather than one, and Lavinia has not just her tongue severed but also her hands.

In imitating the classics, Shakespeare also borrowed from his contemporaries. Robert Greene's *Selimus* gave him the idea for the sickening scene where Titus is tricked into cutting off his hand to ensure the release of his sons, unaware that Saturninus and Tamora have already beheaded them. It leads to one of the grisliest stage directions in all of Shakespeare: 'Enter a messenger with two heads and a hand'.[25] Marlowe's *Tamburlaine* influenced the creation of Titus as an aged and tragic version of the Scythian shepherd, a histrionic anti-hero railing about his military valour and honour, yet blind to the consequences for him and his family. But if the play began mimicking Tamburlaine's humourless swagger, its spectacular violence also borrowed the black humour Shakespeare saw Marlowe inject into *The Jew of Malta* with the murderous exploits of Barabas. When Titus' brother Marcus discovers the raped and mutilated Lavinia, he asks her, 'Cousin, a word,'[26] before realizing she has no tongue. Marcus also squabbles with his brother over which of them should sacrifice his hand to save the sons, while Titus asks the messenger, 'Lend me thy hand, and I will give thee mine.'[27] At the play's climax Titus appears dressed as a cook about to feed Tamora her sons in a pie, which audiences often see as a gruesome joke about getting your 'just desserts'.

Shakespeare's bloodiest and most violent play, *Titus Andronicus* has had a mixed critical history. Despite its initial success it fell out of favour in the later seventeenth century, and from the eighteenth its extreme violence led many critics to dismiss what they regarded as its 'bad taste'. They included T. S. Eliot, who in 1927 called it 'one of the stupidest and most uninspired plays ever written, a play in which it is incredible that Shakespeare had any hand at all',[28] although his pun was probably unintentional. Later twentieth-century responses to the play witnessed a slow rehabilitation as the atrocities of the Second World War left many directors and critics agreeing with Harold Hobson that 'there is absolutely nothing in the bleeding barbarity of *Titus Andronicus* which would have astonished anyone at Buchenwald'.[29] Since the 1980s it has experienced an extraordinary theatrical and critical revival. Today it is as popular as when it was first performed in 1594, and in 2014 the English press reported with some relish that a new Globe Theatre production had seen five members of its audience faint.[30]

In a play where violence seems to be the rule rather than the exception, the distinction between civilization and barbarism becomes increasingly tenuous. Initially Rome represents everything that is civilized, but once it allows the outsiders and barbarians like the Goths inside its gates, it too can turn on itself and, as Titus says, become 'a wilderness of tigers'. Distinguishing between civilization and barbarism was a problem that had preoccupied Elizabethan Protestants in their relations with Catholic Europe and the Islamic world for decades. To Elizabeth and her advisers, it was difficult to see who was more barbaric: idolatrous Catholics trying to eradicate heretical Protestantism, or Muslim infidels offering military and religious salvation.

Into this situation Shakespeare introduced one of the most striking characters in the play: the central villain, Aaron the Moor. Aaron is the ultimate outsider, an amoral and unrepentant villain who unlike the Goths refuses to be assimilated into Rome or any other society. He first appears as part of the triumphal procession of Goth prisoners that Titus leads into Rome, though why a North African Moor should be in league with Germanic Goths is never explained. Aaron is Tamora's lover, a relationship that continues after her marriage to Saturninus, and which leads to the birth of a 'blackamoor' child, described as 'a joyless, dismal, black and sorrowful issue'.[31] Once Tamora is established as Roman empress, Aaron is allowed to go on a spree of 'murders, rapes and massacres | Acts of black night, abominable deeds',[32] encouraging Tamora's sons to rape Lavinia, framing Titus' sons for murder, and tricking Titus into cutting off his own hand. Aaron's only loyalty is to his 'first-born son and heir'.[33] At the end of the play the surviving Romans deem death too good for him: he is buried 'breast-deep in earth'[34] and left to die.

Classical texts by writers such as Seneca and Ovid often included the intrusion into the civilized city state of a destructive barbaric outsider who causes chaos, but Shakespeare invigorated and developed this tradition by drawing on Elizabeth's fraught relations with North Africa's Moors. Recent stylometric analysis of *Titus Andronicus* also suggests that, as with *Henry VI*, he was not alone in writing it, and that several key scenes including many featuring Aaron were written by George Peele.[35] To what extent Peele was involved may never be known, but Aaron was clearly modelled on his evil, duplicitous blackamoor Muly Mahamet in *The Battle of Alcazar*. Like Peele's character, Aaron is a 'blackamoor' and an 'irreligious Moor'[36] who conflates his own skin colour and evil with villainous relish. As he plots Lavinia's rape he compares himself to a snake, his 'fleece of woolly hair that now uncurls' like 'an adder when she doth unroll | To do some fatal execution'.[37] In helping Titus to chop off his hand he laughs:

> Let fools do good, and fair men call for grace
> Aaron will have his soul black like his face.[38]

Aaron becomes one of the earliest Elizabethan stereotypes to represent black men as duplicitous, lustful and evil. But in naming him Aaron, Shakespeare also associates his character with more immediate Elizabethan anxieties about Muslims and Jews. Aaron, the Old Testament prophet and elder brother of Moses, is common to all three Abrahamic religions. The Qur'an venerates him as related to the Virgin Mary, while Judaism celebrates his Levite descendants as upholders of Jewish ritual law. Many in Shakespeare's audience would know that the biblical Aaron's youngest son was called Ithamar, an obvious allusion to the villainous Turk Ithamore in Marlowe's *Jew of Malta*.

But where Aaron's name and ethnicity recall Marlowe's Turk/Moor, his speech and actions imitate Barabas. Towards the end of the play when he is confronted with his crimes and asked if he is 'not sorry for these heinous deeds', Aaron responds:

Ay, that I had not done a thousand more.
Even now I curse the day – and yet I think
Few come within the compass of my curse –
Wherein I did not some notorious ill,
As kill a man, or else devise his death,
Ravish a maid, or plot the way to do it,
Accuse some innocent and forswear myself,
Set deadly enmity between two friends,
Make poor men's cattle break their necks,
Set fire on barns and haystacks in the night,
And bid the owners quench them with their tears.
Oft have I digg'd up dead men from their graves,
And set them upright at their dear friends' doors,
Even when their sorrows almost were forgot;
And on their skins, as on the bark of trees,
Have with my knife carved in Roman letters,
'Let not your sorrow die, though I am dead.'
Tut, I have done a thousand dreadful things
As willingly as one would kill a fly,
And nothing grieves me heartily indeed
But that I cannot do ten thousand more.[39]

The relish with which Aaron recounts his random brutality is reminiscent of Barabas's attitude to his own villainy. Even when he is buried in the ground, Aaron mocks those who would turn to conscience or prayer:

I am no baby, I, that with base prayers
I should repent the evils I have done.
Ten thousand worse than ever yet I did
Would I perform, if I might have my will.
If one good deed in all my life I did
I do repent it from my very soul.[40]

This is the expected end of a villain whose barbarism is so profound he is buried before and not after his death. Aaron encapsulates all the fears associated with his non-Christian character. He is black, a Moor, but also 'irreligious'; however, by associating him with Barabas and

Ithamore, Shakespeare also conflates him with Turks and Jews as well as Moors and atheists. He is everything the audience should despise; and yet they are also drawn irresistibly to him. Then as now, we watch and listen to Aaron – often as he speaks directly to us in soliloquy or asides – but, by the very nature of being an audience, we are powerless to intervene even if we wanted to, becoming appropriately 'mute' accomplices, colluding in his outrageous villainy.

In creating such a formidable character, Shakespeare exploited every available stereotype he knew; but in the process he also asks his audience to see the Moor as a creation of the failings of the apparently 'civilized' Roman world. By incorporating Tamora and by extension Aaron into the body politic, the Romans invite their own destruction. As much as the Elizabethans aspired to emulate the Roman Empire, they also regarded it as the citadel of Catholicism which since the Reformation had represented the barbaric idolatry of the papacy. Such a double perspective emerges towards the end of the play when Roman soldiers capture Aaron while he is hiding with his newborn son in 'a ruinous monastery'.[41] When he is presented to Titus' sole surviving son Lucius, Aaron promises to confess everything if the Roman will 'swear to me my child shall live'. Lucius refuses, saying, 'Who should I swear by? Thou believest no god.'[42] Aaron responds:

> What if I do not? – as indeed, I do not –
> Yet for I know thou art religious
> And hast a thing within thee called conscience,
> With twenty popish tricks and ceremonies
> Which I have seen thee careful to observe,
> Therefore I urge thy oath; for that I know
> An idiot holds his bauble for a god,
> And keeps the oath which by that god he swears,
> To that I'll urge him: therefore thou shalt vow
> By that same god, what god soe'er it be
> That thou adorest and hast in reverence.[43]

In a sudden moment of metamorphosis, the audience is transported from imperial Rome to post-Reformation England, in a scene from Henry VIII's dissolution of the monasteries, with a Moor captured by 'popish' Roman Catholic soldiers and condemning their idolatrous 'tricks and ceremonies'. The audience is put in an invidious position, agreeing with Aaron's dismissal of Catholicism, only to realize that they are identifying with an 'irreligious Moor' who regards faith as nothing more than a 'bauble'.

Titus Andronicus is not a play designed to elicit sympathy for Aaron the Moor. His villainy remains indebted to an older tradition of medieval morality plays, but Shakespeare adds a new dimension by making him ethnically different, funny and, crucially, unrepentant. The play manipulates a profound ambivalence about the role of such 'barbarians' in a confused post-Reformation world of shifting political and theological alliances. Shakespeare combined classical fears about such outsiders with Elizabethan England's even more ambiguous relations with Moors and Turks to create gripping drama filled with conflicts and contradictions. As in Henry VI, he offered a new kind of drama different from Marlowe's. Nobody really cares about Barabas, as he kills his own children and gleefully attacks any religious belief, but Aaron is a sadistic, murderous atheist who nevertheless cares for his child and attacks Catholicism, leaving the audience then as now confused about whether to admire or revile him.

Even as Titus Andronicus played to large crowds throughout the 1594 season, negotiations between Elizabeth and al-Mansur were under way for a second Moorish delegation to visit England. In May 1595 Edward Holmden, master of the Grocers' Company and a prominent merchant in the Venice and Turkey companies, wrote to the Privy Council from Morocco. He reported that it 'is still given out that the king's ambassador shall go for England, being a man of account, and two alcaids [military governors or chiefs] with him, and carrieth a retinue of twenty-five or thirty persons . . . he will be here before Michaelmas [29 September]. The cause is not known.'[44] Although Holmden claimed that the embassy's 'causes' were unknown to him, its leader, Ahmad bin Adel, was clearly on his way to England to propose further Anglo-Moroccan military operations against the Spanish.

Perennial diplomatic tensions between England and Spain were once more leading both sides towards open conflict. Tit-for-tat naval raids throughout 1595 led Philip II to sanction yet another invasion of England, which this time involved landing a Spanish army in Catholic Ireland ahead of a full-scale military assault on the English mainland. When news reached London, Elizabeth's Privy Council authorized a pre-emptive strike at Cadiz, Spain's main Atlantic seaport and home to the Indies fleet. The Moroccan delegation was designed to negotiate logistical support for Elizabeth's naval operations, including Moroccan ships and soldiers, and the creation of a fort at Agadir from which the English could attack the Spanish gold fleet en route to and from the Americas. No records survive of the delegation reaching London that autumn, but although al-Mansur eventually refused English access to Agadir, he sent several galleys and supplies to support the English attack on Cadiz.

Having coordinated an unlikely alliance involving Muslim Moroccans and Dutch Calvinists, Elizabeth's fleet of 150 ships and 6,000 soldiers left Plymouth in June 1596 under the joint command of the loyal veteran Charles Howard, now lord lieutenant general of England, and the queen's new favourite, the dashing thirty-year-old Robert Devereux, Earl of Essex. Others involved included Sir Walter Raleigh on one of his last great naval campaigns, and seeking political rehabilitation after returning empty-handed from a long and dangerous voyage to Guyana. There were younger men too, in search of booty and adventure, including the royal physician Roger Marbeck, and the twenty-four-year-old poet John Donne. In late June the fleet reached Cadiz and attacked it immediately, first by sea then by land.[45] In the short but fierce naval exchange that followed, the English destroyed several Spanish galleons including the *St Philip*, which Roger Marbeck watched being blown up by a 'Moorish slave' who set fire to the ship's gunpowder store before seeking refuge alongside thirty-eight other Moroccans among the English forces. Marbeck wrote that Howard and Essex agreed 'to furnish them with money and all other necessaries, and to bestow on them a bark and pilot, and so to have them freely conveyed into Barbary, willing them to let the country to understand what was done and what they had seen. Whereby I doubt not but, as her majesty is a most admirable prince already over all Europe and all Africa, Asia and Christendom, so the whole world hereafter shall have just such cause to admire her infinite princely virtues.'[46] The English also captured two Spanish galleons, the *St Matthew* and the *St Andrew*, both of which had run aground, although the Indies fleet laden with a cargo worth an estimated 12 million ducats' worth of bullion was destroyed before the English could reach it. They then sacked the city, ransomed hostages and sailed away on 4 July, leaving Cadiz on fire and a large part of Philip's Indies fleet at the bottom of its harbour.

News of the English victory spread quickly across Europe and North Africa. Although the expedition had failed to capture the vast wealth of the Indies fleet, its commanders celebrated it as a great triumph. William Monson, one of the English naval commanders, proclaimed, 'Spain never received so great an overthrow, so great a spoil, so great an indignity at our hands as in that journey to Cadiz.'[47] But the English did not have a monopoly in claiming victory. When the survivors freed by the English reported back to Marrakesh, al-Mansur was quick to insist on his part. In characteristically astounding terms his court historian al-Fishtali described how 'the sky darkened with dissension against the tyrant of Qishtala [Philip II], and the kings of the nations of the Christians attacked him like wild dogs. The most ferocious against him, and the one most daring in attacking his kingdoms and tightening the noose around him, was Isabella the sultana of the kingdoms of the lands of England.' Al-Fishtali claimed that the Cadiz victory was thanks to al-Mansur's diplomatic and logistical support. It was al-Mansur who 'had lured her with his support and sharpened her will against him [Philip II]; he showed her his willingness to confront him [Philip II] by supplying her with copper to use in cannons, and saltpetre for ammunition which he permitted her to buy from his noble kingdom . . . With God helping him, he pitted her against the enemy of religion.'[48] It is unclear just what the Moroccan galleys had achieved during the battle, but according to al-Fishtali's account, England and Morocco were now joined in a holy war against Catholic Spain.[49]

Philip II responded by preparing yet another armada, this time one that would land first in Ireland and exploit the Catholic rebellion there before invading England. A fleet of more than sixty ships carrying over 10,000 soldiers left Lisbon for Ireland on 25 October 1596, but off the north-west Spanish coast it ran into a terrible storm, losing half its ships and thousands of lives. Defeated at home and overstretched abroad, Philip II was forced to declare his kingdom bankrupt just weeks later. He would try to raise another armada the following year, but the weather wrecked his plans once more.[50] Even some of Philip's Spanish advisers felt that, when it came to invading England, Divine Providence had deserted them. It seemed that on this matter God was indeed on the side of the English Protestants.

Although the Moroccan delegation led by Ahmad bin Adel never materialized, another Moor did appear in London – not at London's royal court, but on its stage. In late 1596 Shakespeare wrote *The Merchant of Venice*, or to give it its full title when it was first published in 1600, *The Most Excellent History of the Merchant of Venice with the Extreme Cruelty of Shylock the Jew*. Shakespeare's portrayal of Shylock, the Jewish moneylender who demands a pound of flesh from the Venetian merchant of the play's title, Antonio, in settlement of a bad debt, has divided audiences for generations. Antonio borrows the money to help his feckless friend Bassanio pursue the wealthy heiress Portia, who is in turn being wooed by a series of suitors, including the Prince of Morocco. The play reaches its climax with the famous courtroom scene where Shylock prepares to cut out a pound of Antonio's flesh, only to be prevented by Portia, disguised as a lawyer, who argues that 'if thou dost shed | One drop of Christian blood, thy lands and goods'[51] will be confiscated by the Venetian state. Unable to act, Shylock is then condemned as an 'alien' who has sought the life of a Venetian. He is stripped of his wealth and required to 'presently become a Christian',[52] leaving the stage a broken man and agreeing to all the Christians' terms.

Shakespeare had several inspirations for writing his play. The Cadiz expedition was clearly on his mind because scholars base their dating of the play on an explicit reference to the captured Spanish galleon *St Andrew* in the play's opening lines. The Venetian merchant Salerio talks about 'my wealthy Andrew dock'd in sand' – the ship had run aground when it was captured in Cadiz, and nearly did so again when it was taken back to England in the summer of 1596. In terms of dramatic precedents Shakespeare was responding to Marlowe's *Jew of Malta* and Wilson's *Three Ladies of London* with their contrasting depictions of Jewish merchants – as well as Muslims. There was also one other recent event that may have inspired Shylock's creation. In January 1594 Elizabeth's personal physician, Dr Roderigo Lopez, a Portuguese-born Jewish convert to Protestantism, was arrested on charges of treason and conspiring with the Spanish to poison the queen. Although Lopez had indeed been paid to spy for the Spanish, the charges of attempted murder were completely fabricated by the Earl of Essex, who was eager to prove his loyalty to the queen and gain an advantage over his great rival Burghley. Lopez was a pawn caught up in Essex's and Burghley's machinations, and he never stood a chance. At his trial he was accused of accepting 50,000 crowns from Philip II to poison Elizabeth. One of his prosecutors, Sir Francis Bacon, captured the suspicion that Lopez's conversion had generated by describing him as 'of nation a Portuguese, and suspected to be in sect secretly a Jew (though here he conformed himself to the rites of Christian religion)'. Sentenced to death, Lopez was executed in June 1594. According to the historian William Camden he protested from the scaffold 'that he loved the Queen as well as he loved Jesus Christ; which coming from a man of the Jewish profession moved no small laughter in the standers-by'.[53] For those who watched Lopez being hanged, drawn and quartered, his profession of innocence was seen as a comically equivocal admission of guilt, the duplicity of a convert who spoke of love when he meant hate.

The cruel but uneasy laughter that accompanied Lopez's violent demise also permeates Shakespeare's play. It seems that Shakespeare even intended it to be a comedy (which is how it was listed when published in the Folio of 1623) and at various times over the past 400 years audiences have felt able, or perhaps been incited, to laugh at Shylock's downfall and the anti-Semitic abuse from Portia and Antonio that comes with it. But the laughter is not of the quality associated with Aaron's or Shylock's direct predecessor, Marlowe's Barabas. Like Barabas, Shylock watches his daughter Jessica being converted to Christianity, but despite his murderous designs on Antonio, he never engages in the wicked depravity of Marlowe's character. Shakespeare provides Shylock with a depth of humanity not out of some secret liberal desire to express toleration towards the Jewish faith, but to sharpen the dramatic ambiguity and the power of his character.

Shylock appears in only five of the play's scenes, but in one of the most significant he utters the lines that suggest Shakespeare's plea for a common humanity. 'I am a Jew,' he tells Solanio and Salerio. 'Hath not a Jew eyes? Hath not a Jew hands, organs, dimensions, senses, affections, passions; fed with the same food, hurt with the same weapons, subject to the same diseases, healed by the same means, warmed and cooled by the same winter and summer, as a Christian is? If you prick us, do we not bleed?'[54] But the speech's conclusion also reminds the audience that Shylock is a creation of Venice's society and its Christians, and he is no better or worse than them: 'if you wrong us, shall we not revenge? If we are like you in the rest, we will resemble you in that. If a Jew wrong a Christian, what is his humility? Revenge. If a Christian wrong a Jew, what should his sufferance be by Christian example? Why, revenge. The villainy you teach me, I will execute, and it shall go hard but I will better the instruction.'[55] Shylock is just as vicious and acquisitive as Antonio, a point made inadvertently by Portia when she enters the courtroom dressed as a lawyer and, unable to distinguish between them, asks, 'Which is the merchant here, and which the Jew?'[56]

Portia refers to Shylock contemptuously as 'Jew' on no fewer than ten occasions during the courtroom scene. But he is not the only alien that feels her wrath. Under the terms of her father's will, she can only marry the man who identifies which of three caskets of gold, silver and lead contains Portia's portrait. The play's second scene opens with her recalling those suitors who have already failed, including an arrogant Italian, a drunk German, a capering Frenchman, a quarrelsome Scot and a badly dressed Englishman. It is then announced that a new suitor is about to try his luck: the Prince of Morocco. Upon hearing this Portia immediately recoils at his skin colour, joking, 'If he have the condition of a saint and the complexion of a devil, I had rather he should shrive me [hear confession] than wive me.'[57] But when Morocco enters he is not what the audience might expect. He is a tawny Moor dressed in white, who sounds more like Tamburlaine than Aaron. In a speech that anticipates Shylock's plea for humanity he implores Portia:

> Mislike me not for my complexion,
> The shadowed livery of the burnished sun,
> To whom I am a neighbour and near bred.
> Bring me the fairest creature northward born,
> Where Phoebus' fire scarce thaws the icicles,
> And let us make incision for your love
> To prove whose blood is reddest, his or mine.[58]

Having created an evil blackamoor in the shape of Aaron, Shakespeare now produced his opposite, a virtuous, heroic, tawny Moor, one that has no apparent qualms about marrying into the Christian world of Portia's fictional Belmont. His religion is never mentioned, but he retains an element of sexual frisson sometimes associated with Moors, boasting to Portia:

> I tell thee, lady, this aspect of mine
> Hath fear'd the valiant; by my love I swear
> The best-regarded virgins of our clime
> Have loved it too: I would not change this hue,
> Except to steal your thoughts, my gentle queen.[59]

His virile boastfulness turns into fantasy when he swears to win Portia:

> By this scimitar
> That slew the Sophy and a Persian prince
> That won three fields of Sultan Solyman.[60]

The audience knew that nobody even from the Islamic world had been able to slay a Persian ruler and prince, as well as defeat the Ottoman sultan Süleyman the Magnificent. Nevertheless, here was a Moroccan warrior arriving in a Christian country claiming to have defeated Ottoman and Persian forces, bearing a striking resemblance to al-Mansur's diplomatic and military overtures to Queen Elizabeth. Officially these proposals were known only to Elizabeth's innermost circle, but one wonders how far awareness of the Anglo-Moroccan rapprochement had spread into the public domain.

However, Morocco's suit fails, he chooses the wrong casket and Portia ushers him hastily off the stage and out of the play with the devastating couplet:

A gentle riddance. Draw the curtains, go.
Let all of his complexion choose me so.[61]

There is no real reason why a Prince of Morocco should be in a supposed romantic comedy about Venetian merchants and Jewish moneylenders. But Shakespeare had at least two precedents for putting Muslims into plays about conflicts between Jews and Christians. In Wilson's *Three Ladies of London* the honourable Jewish moneylender Gerontus complains to a Turkish judge about the hypocrisy of the villainous Christian merchant Mercadorus, while in Marlowe's *Jew of Malta* Barabas forms a murderous alliance with the Turkish Ithamore. As usual Shakespeare took the middle way between the two, putting a Jew and a Moor on stage who are not saints, but are expelled ruthlessly by the Christian world as soon as they threaten to challenge the status quo.

At a theological level Christendom had always conflated Muslims and Jews as apostates who denied Christ as the Son of God, heretics representing two sides of the same religious error. At a commercial level they were intimately related, Jews as we have seen acting as the mediators in most Elizabethan mercantile transactions with the Muslim courts in Morocco, Turkey and Persia. In fact the English had much greater experience of Jewish merchants, moneylenders and political intermediaries in Morocco in the 1590s than of those in Venice at the same time. Examples like the highly publicized case of the Moroccan Jewish sugar baron Isaac Cabeça's insolvency in 1568 and the subsequent trials in the High Court of Admiralty and Chancery would have been far more familiar to Londoners watching Shakespeare's play than any Jewish Venetian merchant's activities. Perhaps through the guise of the Prince of Morocco the play casts a topical eye on the burgeoning Anglo-Moroccan alliance. But it is also likely that Shakespeare was moving away from the purely villainous Jews and Muslims of Marlowe's plays to allow the more ambiguous Shylock and Prince of Morocco to question the precarious version of multiculturalism in sixteenth-century Venice and London. Both were places where the exigencies of politics and trade required alliances with Jews, Turks or Moors. While everyone profited, everything was fine, but when trouble arrived, the laughter stopped and the villainy one side taught was executed upon the others. By the end of Shakespeare's play, the audience is placed in the uncomfortable position of being as repelled by its self-righteous Christians as it is by its haughty Moroccan and vindictive Jew. Within just over two years of Marlowe's death, Shakespeare had modulated his 'high astounding terms' and violent, murderous eastern characters to produce a far more subtle but equally devastating theatre of complicity, where Moors, Jews and Christians and even the audience are all equally culpable for perpetuating a cycle of greed, victimization and vengeance. This, as we shall see, Shakespeare would go on to exploit in some of his greatest later plays.

As *The Merchant of Venice*'s Prince of Morocco left the stage, so did the Barbary Company. In July 1597, just a year after Shakespeare wrote *The Merchant of Venice*, with its charter expired and private trade promising to offer better returns, the company was quietly dissolved.[62] It was now every man for himself in Morocco. With the plans for a formal alliance stalled and the crown's interest in the trade at an end, Elizabeth and her advisers had already turned their attention back eastwards, towards the Ottoman Porte in Constantinople.

9

Escape from the Seraglio

On 15 January 1595 Sultan Murad III died in the Topkapi Palace in Constantinople. In keeping with Ottoman tradition, his death was kept secret until his heir, the crown prince Mehmed, could reach Constantinople and ensure a smooth transition of power. Four weeks later the English ambassador Edward Barton forwarded a letter to Lord Burghley from a man whom he called a 'curious Jew' describing 'what here hath lately passed', the 'death of the late Sultan Murad III and success to this empire of Sultan Mehmed III'.[1] The letter was written by a Portuguese Jew called Alvaro Mendès, better known to the Ottoman court as Salomon Aben Yaèx, an associate of Barton's with privileged access to the imperial *divan*. Mendès reported that on 27 January Mehmed had arrived from Manisa near the Aegean coast to claim the throne and bury his father in Hagia Sophia. What followed next has became one of the most terrible and reviled acts in Ottoman imperial history:

> That night his nineteen new brothers were conducted to the king Sultan Mehmed, they were the male children then living of his father, by several wives; they were brought to kiss his hand, so that he should see them alive; the eldest of them was eleven. Their king brother told them not to fear, as he did not wish to do them any harm; but only to have them circumcised, according to custom. And this was a thing that none of his ancestors had ever done, and directly they had kissed his hand they were circumcised, taken aside and dexterously strangled with handkerchiefs.[2]

The Venetian ambassador added to the horror with a story of even greater pathos. 'They say', he wrote, 'that the eldest, a most beautiful lad and of excellent parts, beloved by all, when he kissed the sultan's hand exclaimed, "My lord and brother, now to me as my father, let not my days be ended thus in this my tender age." The sultan tore his beard with every sign of grief, but answered never a word. They were all strangled.' Salomon acknowledged that such a brutal act of political succession 'certainly seems a terrible and cruel thing, but it is the custom'; he also conceded that the sight of all nineteen coffins – some no bigger than a doll's – when placed next to their father's, brought forth 'the tears of all the people'.[3]

Barton had taken great pains to obtain Salomon's report for Burghley because the sultan's death was a critical moment in Anglo-Ottoman relations. Most of Elizabeth's diplomatic and commercial relations with the Ottomans were based on a cordial personal correspondence with Murad that stretched back over seventeen years, and more recently with his *haseki*, Safiye Sultan, who with his death was now elevated to the role of Valide Sultan (Queen Mother). It was unclear if Mehmed would be as sympathetic towards the English as his father had been, but the signs were not promising. Mehmed vowed to pursue the flagging Ottoman military campaigns in Hungary, but he hardly seemed like a warrior. One English merchant described him as 'a prince by nature of wit and courage: but by accident, dull, timorous, and very effeminate'.[4] Barton needed to act quickly if he was to retain Ottoman favour, and his hope was that by sending Salomon's letter to London Burghley would see the wisdom of despatching a suitable gift to the new sultan to cement his diplomatic position. Unfortunately for Barton, the Privy Council was somewhat dilatory in its response. With no present forthcoming, Barton was obliged to show his support for the new sultan by accompanying him on a military campaign the following year against Archduke Maximilian's Catholic armies in Hungary. Barton set out for Hungary with Mehmed's army in June 1596 accompanied by a large retinue paid for by the sultan, observing the Ottoman campaign and even sending Burghley a detailed account of the dramatic Ottoman victory over the Austrian-Hungarian Habsburg forces at Keresztes in northern Hungary in October 1596.[5] When news of Barton's presence spread throughout Europe and even Russia, Elizabeth was forced to go on a diplomatic charm offensive, sending embassies as far as Prague and

Moscow to deny that she had 'incited the most loathsome enemy of the Christian name to wage war on Christian princes'.[6]

Nevertheless, the Elizabethan alliance with the Ottoman Porte endured because of its importance. Qualms about the relationship ranged from religious differences and fears about Ottoman imperial ambitions to their fratricidal approach to political succession, but it was a partnership that had far-reaching consequences for diplomatic and economic policy. While the sultans acted as a powerful if capricious military bulwark against Spain, at home the trade established by William Harborne and others from the late 1570s had a marked impact on the domestic economy. In contrast to the uneven profitability of the Barbary Company, the success of the Turkey Company led it to merge with the Venice Company in 1592, creating the Levant Company, which by the end of the decade had twenty ships exporting cloth worth £150,000 annually to the Mediterranean.[7]

The impact of all this trade could be seen at various levels of Elizabethan life. In terms of English printed books alone, there was a notable surge of interest in the Muslim world towards the end of the sixteenth century. The registers of the Company of Stationers of London reveal that an estimated sixty books were published in Elizabeth's reign on subjects relating to the Ottomans, and of these half were published in the 1590s. Considering that the registers record only 60 per cent of all books printed in the period, and do not include religious polemics and diplomatic correspondence, the true figures are likely to be much higher.[8]

As well as reading about and watching Turks, Elizabethans could also scrutinize their rulers up close. Portraits of the Ottoman sultans, such as Hans Eworth's painting of Süleyman the Magnificent on horseback (1549), could be found in many of England's great houses.[9] The inventories of the art collections of London's lord mayor Sir Ralph Warren, the Virginia Colony's governor John West and the Oxford scholar Thomas Key all listed pictures of the 'Great Turk'.[10] In 1575 the poet, courtier and soldier Sir Philip Sidney was delighted to receive a 'portrait of Murad the new Emperor of the Turks' from one of his correspondents in Strasbourg.[11] Painted in Venice, this portrait, alongside Sidney's assiduous compilation of intelligence on

Ottoman matters throughout the 1570s, had a significant influence on his poetry and prose. In the opening lines of sonnet 30 of his love sonnet sequence *Astrophil and Stella* (written in the early 1580s) he asks:

> Whether the Turkish new-moone minded be
> To fill his hornes this yeare on Christian coast.[12]

The reference to the Islamic crescent moon is a topical allusion to rumours (which proved unfounded) circulating between March and June 1582 that the Ottomans were about to strike against Spain following Philip II's annexation of Portugal the previous year. Sidney was even able to joke about the Turkish occupation of Greece:

> Love, borne in Greece, of late fled from his native place,
> Forc'd by a tedious proofe, that Turkish hardned heart
> Is no fit marke to pierce with his fine pointed dart:
> And pleasd with our soft peace, staid here his flying race.[13]

Love, finding the Turks too hardened to its advances, flees Greece – or more specifically Cyprus, the home of Cupid's mother Venus, which fell to the Turks in 1573 – in favour of England, only to recoil at the cold weather later in the poem. As well as such references to the Turks in his love poetry, Sidney also used his knowledge of the Ottomans in his earlier *Defence of Poesy* (1579), in which he argues that in contrast to England, 'even Turks and Tartars are delighted with poets'.[14]

As well as depicting figures from the Muslim world, Elizabethan portraiture revelled in reproducing the growing volume of oriental imports flowing into London. These included opulent and expensive Islamic fabrics, rugs, carpets, embroideries and even Iznik pottery made in Bursa in Turkey. The pearls, diamonds, sapphires, silks, brocades and damasks that feature in so many Elizabethan paintings – including those of the queen herself – were self-conscious displays of the Anglo-Islamic trade's success. Ownership of 'Turkey carpets', quilts and Anatolian rugs containing Kufic (Arabic) script were also self-conscious statements of personal wealth and connections to the Islamic world. As well as his investments in the Moroccan trade, the Earl of Leicester's various household accounts show that at the time of his death in 1588 he had amassed a collection of over eighty carpets described as either Turkish or Persian, worth hundreds of pounds (one alone was valued at £5).[15] The similar inventory of another Elizabethan nobleman, John, Lord Lumley, and his household goods in Nonsuch Palace and Lumley Castle list over a hundred 'Turkey carpets of silk'. Like many other contemporary noblemen, Lumley also owned depictions of the Ottoman capital Constantinople.[16]

This luxuriousness was not confined to queens and noblemen. The importation of cotton wool from Turkish merchants stimulated a burgeoning textile industry in Lancashire, and by the end of Elizabeth's reign the manufacture of raw silk from Iran provided employment for hundreds of workers who produced clothes 'in the Turkish manner' and household furnishings for middle-class consumption.[17] The resulting objects were such a common feature in wealthy Elizabethan homes and domestic life that Shakespeare felt confident enough to make casual references in his comedies written in the 1590s to 'Turkey cushions bossed with pearl' in *The Taming of the Shrew*[18] and to 'Turkish tapestry' in *The Comedy of Errors*.[19] The English even began to imitate imported textiles: in 1579 Richard Hakluyt had sent the dyer Morgan Hubblethorne to Persia to find 'carpets of coarse thrummed [twisted] wool, the best of the world', asking him to return with 'the art of Turkish carpet making'. It is unclear if Hubblethorne came back with what Hakluyt wanted, but by the 1590s English craftsmen (and women) were copying Persian and Turkish carpets with cheaper and simpler 'Turkey work', which involved tying woollen knots on to linen or hemp.[20]

The Muscovy, Turkey and Barbary imports enabled Elizabethans to wear silk and cotton in new designs, drink sweet wines and incorporate myriad condiments into their diet, including aniseed, nutmeg, mace, turmeric and pistachios. The demand for currants alone from Ottoman-controlled Greek islands was so great that at the height of Elizabeth's reign 2,300 tons were being imported annually.[21] The activities of John Sanderson, a Levant Company merchant working in the Ottoman territories from 1585, also show how far oriental goods percolated through Elizabethan society. Sanderson gave his sister Grace a wedding present of 'a Turkey carpet, more worth than £1.10.0', and his clergyman brother received 'Six Turkey painted books' (probably a reference to Ottoman costume books), worth £3, and 'Four Turkey carpets' worth over £5.[22]

Nor was the display and consumption of objects and artefacts from Muslim lands limited to London. By 1601 Elizabeth Talbot, Countess of Shrewsbury, better known as Bess of Hardwick, had amassed a collection of oriental embroidery, tapestry and needlework of a quality and size to rival those of Leicester and Lumley, which she displayed in her two great Derbyshire homes, Chatsworth House and Hardwick Hall. It included forty-six 'Turkey carpets', as well as a remarkable set of three large embroidered wall hangings depicting personifications of the cardinal virtues and their opposites, dating from the 1580s.[23] The first showed Hope triumphing over Judas, the second Temperance prevailing over Sardanapalus (to whom Cardenas compared al-Mansur), while the final hanging shows Faith subduing her contrary, the unfaithful 'Mahomet'. All three were based on a series of Dutch engravings of traditional Christian 'Virtues and Vices' dated 1576 that were adapted by the embroiderers to suit the prevailing theology of the day and, more practically, to fit the best bedchamber in Hardwick Hall, where they can still be seen on public display.

The hanging of Faith and Mahomet shows Faith modelled closely on Queen Elizabeth. She stands in front of a backdrop of ecclesiastical architecture, next to a large crucifix, holding a Bible in her right hand with the word 'Faith' picked out on its spine in gold twist, a communion chalice in her left hand, and 'Fides' embroidered on her arm. She towers over Muhammad, a turbaned, moustachioed figure crouching down as if in subjection at her feet, resting his face on his hand in a melancholy pose of apparent despair at his faithlessness, with a copy of the Qur'an ('Acoran') on the floor in front of him. Above him are what appear to be scenes from the life of Muhammad. In the foreground two groups of turbaned Turks with scimitars are shown in deep discussion, while in the background Muhammad appears again in what seems to be a sixteenth-century English idea of a mosque. He stands holding a book (presumably the Qur'an) in a canopied arch resembling a Gothic church. Angels float above pulling back the curtains in a moment of religious revelation – surprising for a scene involving the Prophet Muhammad, as such iconography was usually reserved for Catholic images of Christ or the Virgin and Child. Perhaps the embroidery was meant to suggest the idolatry that many Protestants believed united the papacy and the Prophet Muhammad.[24]

The Hardwick embroideries capture Protestant English ambivalence towards Islam, and the Ottomans in particular, as the sixteenth century drew to a close. Bess of Hardwick wanted to display her wealth by acquiring expensive and elaborately crafted Turkish rugs and carpets, but she also wanted to show off her Christian piety, reproducing a standard image of biblical faith over that of the Muslim Qur'an, and offering the faithless Muhammad in the foreground the possibility of salvation through the cross and communion. As with so much of Elizabethan visual art, the embroidery was a carefully crafted delusion; Protestants across North Africa and the Mediterranean like Samson Rowlie were more likely to bow down before the Qur'an and convert to Islam than Muslims such as Chinano were to embrace Christianity. Like many other Elizabethan misrepresentations of Islam, the Hardwick embroidery was a wishful fantasy. Its depiction of Muhammad, the Qur'an, mosques and even Muslim dress were all based on second-hand sources, and it is unlikely that either Bess or her anonymous embroiderers knew how far their sovereign was advanced in forging an alliance with the Muslim rulers of Morocco and Turkey.

For an elite member of the Elizabethan establishment like Bess of Hardwick, the allure and horror of Islam could be resolved only by faith, ultimately the dream of converting heathen Muslims to the true faith of Protestantism. Such contradictory emotions were also proving an irresistible source of raw material for Elizabethan London's dramatists. Unlike many of his contemporaries, Shakespeare never put a Turkish character in any of his plays (with one peculiar exception which we shall discuss later). But throughout the mid-1590s, just a few years after Bess of Hardwick's embroideries were completed, he wrote a series of plays mainly about English history that are haunted by the spectre of the Turk. He refers to Turks in thirteen plays written in this decade, more than a third of these references appearing in his history plays. Having established his reputation with a first tetralogy about the reigns of Henry VI and Richard III in the early 1590s, in the latter half of the decade he began a second tetralogy, four plays dramatizing the lives of Richard II, Henry IV (in two parts) and Henry V. He wrote about this turbulent period of English political history, characterized by conflicts over royal succession, deposition, rebellion and civil war against the backdrop of a new genre of English 'war books' describing conflicts between Christians and Muslims in central Europe, and in particular the Ottoman incursions into Hungary. Inevitably the spectre that came to Shakespeare's mind time and again was the tyrannical, fratricidal, faithless yet inscrutable Turk.[25]

The second tetralogy begins with *King Richard II*, probably written in 1595. The play culminates in the climactic moment of King Richard's deposition by the Plantagenet Henry of Bolingbroke, the future King Henry IV. In the play's fourth act, as Bolingbroke prepares to accept the crown after forcing Richard to stand down, the Bishop of Carlisle warns his followers of the dire consequences of dethroning a legitimate king. He utters a prophecy that reverberates through the rest of the tetralogy:

> My Lord of Hereford [Bolingbroke] here, whom you call king,
> Is a foul traitor to proud Hereford's king;
> And, if you crown him, let me prophesy
> The blood of English shall manure the ground,
> And future ages groan for this foul act.
> Peace shall go sleep with Turks and infidels,
> And in this seat of peace tumultuous wars
> Shall kin with kin and kind with kind confound.[26]

Carlisle condemns Bolingbroke's attempt to seize the crown as religious and political apostasy, the kind of murderous and illegitimate behaviour that was all too familiar to Elizabethan theatregoers who had watched various 'Turkish' sultans strutting, murdering and conquering their way across London's stages throughout the early 1590s. If Bolingbroke deposes an anointed king, he will lead the country into a perpetual war that will 'kin with kin and kind with kind confound'. Carlisle's point is that deposing a king breaks the bonds and laws of nature, defined and decreed by God. Identifying 'Turks and infidels' as similarly unnatural, the bishop predicts chaos and disaster through the language of religious difference. The Turk is political shorthand for a breakdown in the natural order of things.

Carlisle's prophecy is ignored. Bolingbroke is crowned and Richard II murdered. Over the next two parts of *Henry IV* Carlisle's prediction is fulfilled as the country descends into a series of civil wars. *Henry IV, Part 1* (1596) begins with Bolingbroke as the new king bemoaning the way his kingdom is being torn apart by 'the intestine shock | And furious close of civil butchery'.[27] To atone for his sins in deposing Richard, Henry promises to launch a crusade:

> As far as to the sepulchre of Christ –
> Whose soldier now, under whose blessed cross
> We are impressed and engaged to fight –
> Forthwith a power of English shall we levy,
> Whose arms were moulded in their mother's womb
> To chase these pagans in those holy fields
> Over whose acres walked those blessed feet
> Which fourteen hundred years ago were nailed,
> For our advantage, on the bitter cross.[28]

Henry announces himself to be a crusader using the language of Christian righteousness, prepared to fight a holy war in the name of Jesus. He is not the least bit convincing, but he conveys Shakespeare's vision of national identity shaped by faith and belonging. It does not matter that Jesus never actually walked on the 'holy fields' through which Henry's army will chase their enemies: what is important is that the king develops national unity through a shared faith, and a common enemy. Having overthrown Richard and pitched England into a Turkish hell, the new king seems to be acting like a pious Christian prince, trying to exorcise his sins by recovering the Holy Land from what Carlisle had earlier called 'black pagans, Turks, and Saracens'. The ending of *Richard II* had associated him with murderous, usurping Turkish sultans; at the opening of this, the first play of his reign, Henry looks like either the penitent Christian ruler or the scheming, Machiavellian prince, tainted with Turkish tyranny.

As in his earlier histories and comedies, Shakespeare was becoming increasingly adroit at manipulating these contradictory analogies

to exploit the audience's allegiances. In the second tetralogy this enabled him to create a more ambiguous and multifaceted king whose
power is tenuous and exercised strategically. He was also becoming
sufficiently confident to begin exorcising the ghost of Marlowe. In
Part 1 the leader of the rebellion against Henry IV is Henry Percy
(nicknamed 'Hotspur'), the Earl of Northumberland's son. As his
nickname suggests, Hotspur is an impetuous warrior who uses the
hyperbolic language of Tamburlaine, declaiming before one battle
that 'we live to tread on kings',[29] an explicit reference to Tamburlaine's treatment of Sultan Bajazeth. But speaking in a tavern in
London's Eastcheap, Hal (Henry IV's heir apparent) mocks Hotspur's bombastic Marlovian pretensions, observing drily, 'I am not
yet of Percy's mind, the Hotspur of the north; he that kills me some
six or seven dozen of Scots at a breakfast, washes his hands, and says
to his wife "Fie upon this quiet life! I want work." '[30] Viewed from
London's taverns and brothels, the heirs of Marlowe's 'mighty line'
like Hotspur start to look like a throwback to an older, semi-mythical
world of pagan heroes and heroic conquests that has been supplanted
by the new world of opportunistic rhetoric and cunning represented
by Henry IV and his even more inscrutable son.

In both parts of *Henry IV* Shakespeare moves between the elite
courts of Henry and the rebels to London's murky underworld, the
taverns and fleshpots of Eastcheap, where Prince Hal consorts with
Sir John Falstaff, Mistress Quickly and their confederates. In *Henry
IV, Part 2* (1597–8) Shakespeare goes out of his way to parody the
dramatic vogue for exotic stories and characters. In Act 2 scene 4, the
cowardly soldier Pistol mangles a series of mock-heroic references to
Peele's *Battle of Alcazar*, to the same writer's lost play *The Turkish
Mahamet and Hiren the Fair Greek* and to Marlowe's *Tamburlaine*.
'Have we not Hiren here?' he asks of Doll, then mimics Marlowe's
'hollow pampered jades of Asia', before telling Mistress Quickly to
'feed and be fat, my Calipolis', a direct quotation from *The Battle of
Alcazar*.[31] Shakespeare was wittily showing Marlowe and Peele the
exit, in the process building on their portrayal of Moors and Turks to
create his own kind of central dramatic character: charismatic but
withdrawn, ironic yet violent, a leader who remains unfathomable,
perhaps even to himself.

Towards the end of *Henry IV, Part 2*, with his father dead and himself about to succeed to the throne, Hal suddenly makes a striking negative comparison to an Ottoman sultan that has puzzled critics for decades. As Hal enters Westminster Palace dressed as the new king, he turns to his three brothers and tells them:

> This new and gorgeous garment, majesty,
> Sits not so easy on me as you think.
> Brothers, you mix your sadness with some fear.
> This is the English, not the Turkish court;
> Not Amurath an Amurath succeeds,
> But Harry Harry.[32]

Initially Hal's first pronouncement as king seems straightforward enough. He assures his brothers that his accession is as strange to him as it is for them and that they have nothing to fear. Hal promises his younger brothers that they will not be murdered like Murad III's five younger brothers in 1574 or – in a striking echo of Edward Barton's report – Murad's nineteen sons, strangled just a couple of years earlier on the orders of Mehmed III. But perhaps the prince doth protest too much. The speech's awkwardness betrays the problem. Hal uses the rhetorical technique known as *germinatio*, where 'Harry' and 'Amurath' are repeated in the same sentence. Hal claims he will imitate his father, not Murad. But the audience have already experienced one version of Henry IV as the calculating pretender whose political usurpation triggers civil war. If young Harry is just the same as old Harry, then perhaps he will reproduce the same sectarian divisions. By trying to erase associations between his family and despotic Turks, Hal succeeds only in reminding us of the comparison. Everyone watching hopes the reformed son will metamorphose into the perfect Christian prince; the fear remains that he might still turn Turk.

The anxiety recurs throughout the tetralogy's final play, *Henry V*, written in the summer of 1599. For generations of English-speaking readers the play has represented England's greatest warrior king, a patriotic celebration of Henry's plucky English 'band of brothers' triumphing over the French at Agincourt in the face of impossible odds. But perceptive critics have identified a more ambivalent side to Henry. The great essayist William Hazlitt saw in Hal 'a very amiable monster, a very splendid pageant',[33] who preferred brute force over right or wrong. More recently the American critic Norman Rabkin discerned in the young king an embodiment of the duck/rabbit gestalt illusion, where the viewer can see a duck or a rabbit, though not both at the same time. Rabkin believed that the play similarly points in two different directions: Henry can be seen as the militant Christian warrior, or as the scheming Machiavellian prince.[34] Today, in an age when the idea of a crusade is less persuasive than ever before, audiences are similarly attuned to Henry's unsympathetic slipperiness.

This ambivalence was built into Henry's character from the moment Shakespeare first conceived him. As he leads the English into a morally questionable war with the French, the young English king begins to reveal a latent 'Turkish' side to his character. In the scene where his forces are besieging Harfleur, Henry warns the town's inhabitants that failure to surrender will lead him to unleash rape and murder:

> Your naked infants spitted upon pikes,
> Whiles the mad mothers with their howls confused
> Do break the clouds, as did the wives of Jewry
> At Herod's bloody-hunting slaughtermen.[35]

The threat is reminiscent of Tamburlaine's massacre of the virgins of Damascus, and the image of infants spitted on pikes was associated persistently with Turkish atrocities in central Europe in pamphlets published across the continent at this time. But it also draws on a much older theatrical traditional: the fourteenth-century mystery play, Coventry's fourteenth-century mystery play *The Pageant of the Shearmen and Taylors*, in which the Slaughter of the Innocents was depicted. The play shows Herod, King of Judaea, slaughtering Bethlehem's newborn infants to prevent a future King of the Jews threatening his position. By associating Henry with Herod, Shakespeare presents him as a raging, pagan tyrant. But the Coventry *Pageant*, which Shakespeare may well have watched as a child, also showed Herod embracing idolatry, or '*maumetrie*' – worshipping and swearing by Muhammad ('Mahound') – while dressed in 'Saracen' clothing.[36] Through these associations Henry is given many faces, simultaneously the heroic English king defeating the French, the pagan Herod menacing the Jews, and the idolatrous Muslim 'Mahound', threatening to slaughter the innocent Christians 'spitted upon pikes', and perhaps prompting the rapt audience to reconsider his denial of any association with the murderous sultan Murad upon his accession in *Henry IV, Part 2*.

Of course unlike Tamburlaine, Herod or Murad, Henry does not slaughter the innocents of Harfleur. Any qualms we have about him are soon alleviated by his adoption of what became that most quintessential of English icons, St George, the national patron saint. Before Harfleur, after exhorting his soldiers to adopt the ruthless 'action of the tiger', he combines patriotism with religion in his famous rallying call, 'Cry God for Harry, England and St George!'[37] His transformation from the dissolute Prince Hal seems complete. But even his adoption of George's militant purity would not have convinced everyone.

St George is a particularly significant example of how far Christian and Islamic traditions were entangled in the late sixteenth century. The saint had little place in the reformed beliefs of influential theologians, not least those of John Calvin and John Foxe, both of whom attacked the veneration of saints as another example of popish 'idolatry'. In his *Institutes* (1536) Calvin condemned those who regarded God's 'intercession as unavailing without the assistance of George and . . . other such phantasms'.[38] Foxe was similarly dismissive. In his chapter on the 'History of the Turks' published in the 1570 edition of the *Acts and Monuments*, he argued that 'if God have determined his own Son only to stand alone, let not us presume to admix with his majesty any of our trumpery. He that bringeth St. George or St. Denis, as patrons, to the field, to fight against the Turk, leaveth Christ, no doubt, at home.'[39] If London's mainly Protestant audience watched Henry deny the association with 'Amurath' and the temptation to turn Turk, perhaps they also saw in his assumption of the role of St George that he could have fallen into another trap, this time of Catholic idolatry.

To make matters even more complicated, St George is not an exclusively Christian saint: he is also a key figure in the Islamic faith. In Christian iconography St George is shown as a resurrected martyr who appears from the Crusades onwards slaying the heretical 'dragon' of Islamic militarism.[40] But in Islam he is associated with Al Khidr, identified in the Qur'an as a servant of God who meets Moses, and an associate of Elijah in subsequent Hadith literature. In Sufism he is known as 'the Verdant One', a mystical warrior whom some sources claim to have been an officer in the army of Alexander the Great. Some versions of his life declare that, like St George, Al Khidr was resurrected after his death at the hands of a pagan king. In the 1550s the Habsburg diplomat Ogier Ghiselin de Busbecq travelled through the Ottoman Empire, recounting stories of a similar figure revered by Turkish dervish communities in central Anatolia, 'a hero called Chederle, a man of great physical and mortal courage, whom they declare to be identical with our St. George and to whom they ascribe the same achievements as we ascribe to our saint, namely, that he rescued a maiden by the slaughter of a huge and terrible dragon'.[41] Busbecq observed that 'the Turks are much amused at the pictures of St. George, whom they declare was their own Chederle, in the Greek churches', and that when they saw such pictures 'they prostrate themselves in adoration and imprint kisses all over it, not omitting even the horse's hoofs. St. George, they declare, was a man of might, a famous warrior, who often in single combat fought with the Evil Spirit on equal terms and was victorious.'[42]

Although he went under various names, St George was shared widely between various Christian and Muslim communities, but it was only around the time that Shakespeare wrote *Henry V* that he began to have a more recognizably English domain. The likelihood is that Shakespeare had no idea of the Islamic version of St George, but many of his contemporaries placed the saint in a nebulous Muslim context even as they tried to reclaim him for a more parochial version of English Protestantism. The most famous example of St George moving between east and west can be found in the poetry of Edmund Spenser and especially in his vast unfinished epic, *The Faerie Queene*, one of the longest in the English language, the first half of which was published in 1590, the second in 1596. Today *The Faerie Queene* is rarely read, but with the publication in 1590 of its first three books it soon became one of the most influential poems in English. Written in archaic, medieval language, it is a difficult, complicated, largely plotless and seemingly interminable allegory variously interpreted as being about Elizabeth, England and Protestantism. It is set in what Spenser called a 'Faerye land', a mythical landscape inspired by Arthurian legend and Italian Renaissance epic poems including Ariosto's *Orlando Furioso* (1516) and Tasso's *La Gerusalemme liberate*, or *Jerusalem Delivered* (1581), both of which describe the clash between Christians and Muslims since the time of the Crusades. Like so many other English writers of his generation, Spenser used Muslim characters, identified through various old-fashioned terms as 'Saracens' and 'Paynims', as foils for dramatizing the clash between Protestantism and Catholicism.

In trying to create an English version of the European epic, Spenser imagined several knights who embark on a series of adventures during which they are tested by a seemingly endless procession of monsters, giants, magicians, pagans and temptresses in their pursuit of six key Protestant virtues: holiness, temperance, chastity, friendship, justice and courtesy. *The Faerie Queene*'s first book is entitled 'The Legend of the Knight of the Red Crosse, or of Holiness'. Its opening lines seem to identify the knight unambiguously because:

> on his brest a bloudie Crosse he bore,
> The deare remembrance of his dying Lord,
> For whose sweete sake that glorious badge he wore.[43]

The 'Gentle Knight' wears the red cross on a white background associated with Christian crusaders, the Knights Templar and of course St George. He travels alongside Una (or 'One'), who is as 'pure an innocent' as her 'milke white lambe', the first of several personifications of Elizabeth in Spenser's poem. Redcrosse's stated task is to 'prove his puissance in battell braue' in protecting Una's holy purity from evil. Spenser was reluctant initially to identify Redcrosse explicitly with St George because his sympathy with Protesant reformers like Calvin and Foxe meant he rejected the veneration of saints. Instead, using his convoluted allegorical method, he spends the rest of the first book refashioning George as a Protestant English Everyman, a knight of the realm more than a Catholic saint.

The result is a series of contorted descriptions of Redcrosse as he embarks on adventures to defend Una. He is drawn eastwards into a world identified as the Holy Land, where the villainous sorcerer Archimago – a Catholic idolator, or 'arch-imagemaker' – disguises himself as the saint. This is the first explicit mention of St George, and Spenser describes Archimago's imitation as so convincing that 'Saint George himself ye would haue deemed him to be' – suggesting the 'false', Catholic idolatry involved in one version of St George. Meanwhile, Redcrosse, 'the true *Saint George*', is described as having 'wandred far away'. His travels finally lead him to confront a series of Muslim warriors (with whom he is often mistaken), beginning with the 'Saracen' Sansfoy (Faithlessness):

> At last him chaunst to meete upon the way
> A faithlesse Sarazin all arm'd to point,
> In whose great shield was writ with letters gay
> Sans foy.[44]

Sansfoy travels with a scarlet woman named Duessa who wears a 'Persian mitre on her head' that evokes a string of associations with the Whore of Babylon, Catholic episcopacy, the Assyrian queen Semiramis and even the red turban of the militant Shi'a Muslim group the Qizilbash. Redcrosse vanquishes both, and then goes off in search of further spiritual enlightenment. He defeats another Muslim warrior named Sansjoy (Joylessness) who is described as a 'Paynim', before he enters the house of 'Holinesse', an allegorical hospice in which seven holy attendants dispense various forms of Protestant charity. It is here that Spenser makes his most explicit topical reference to Anglo-Islamic relations – the ransoming of English captives by the Ottomans:

> The fourth appointed by his office was,
> Poore prisoners to relieue with gratious ayd,
> And captiues to redeeme with price of bras,
> From Turkes and Sarazins, which them had stayd.[45]

This was the kind of 'charity' – paying for the release of English captives with money ('bras') – that John Aylmer, Bishop of London, had called for in 1582, and which had consumed so much of William Harborne's time in Constantinople throughout the 1580s. Spenser uses it here as part of Redcrosse's spiritual education, which prepares him for the revelation of his destiny towards the end of Book 1, when another allegorical figure named Contemplation suddenly describes

Redcrosse as 'thou faire ymp, sprong out from English race', and tells him to travel to the Holy Land:

> Then seeke this path, that I to thee presage,
> Which after all to heauen shall thee send;
> Then peaceably thy painefull pilgrimage
> To yonder same *Hierusalem* do bend,
> Where is for thee ordaind a blessed end:
> For thou emongst those Saints, whom thou doest see,
> Shalt be a Saint, and thine owne nations frend
> And Patrone: thou Saint *George* shalt called bee,
> Saint *George* of mery England, the signe of victoree.[46]

By this point Redcrosse is deemed to have purged himself of the sins of pride and idolatry that Protestants like Spenser associated with Catholic accounts of St George, and is ready to face martyrdom and return as the defender of the (Protestant) faith of 'mery England'. It was hardly a ringing endorsement; Redcrosse disappears from the rest of the poem, to be replaced in the next two books by the more convincingly English figure of King Arthur who continues the battle against various 'Saracens'.[47]

While Spenser wrestled with the problem of transforming St George from a Catholic icon into an English hero, he also found other ways of conflating what he regarded as Catholic duplicity and political tyranny with that of Islam. In Book 5 of *The Faerie Queene* Arthur comes to the aid of a female ruler called Mercilla – another surrogate for Queen Elizabeth – who is menaced by a 'Souldan' (sultan) of 'lawlesse powre and tortious wrong'[48] modelled on Philip II and his plans for the Armada of 1588. The Souldan is depicted as 'Swearing, and banning most blasphemously' – a reference to Philip II's and Pius V's collusion in excommunicating Elizabeth in 1570 – and his iron chariot with its 'hookes arm'd dreadfully'[49] evokes the armed galleons of the Spanish fleet. Arthur, who initially confronts the Souldan by impersonating 'a Pagan knight', is able to defeat his adversary only when he reveals his 'sunlike shield'. The Souldan's chariot collapses and 'tost the Paynim'[50] to his destruction in an elaborate echo of the fate of the Spanish fleet off Calais.[51]

Spenser was not alone in acknowledging England's and St George's complicated relations with Islam. Others included Richard Johnson, a popular writer of prose romance now largely forgotten. In his *Famous History of the Seven Champions of Christendom* (1596) – a source for *Henry V* – Johnson transferred St George's origins from Cappadocia in Turkey to, perhaps surprisingly, Coventry. In Johnson's book St George is somewhat clumsily turned into an 'English Champion' and Protestant iconoclast, even though his enemies remain polytheistic Persian Muslims. Like Spenser's version of the saint, Johnson's St George travels east in search of adventure and is offered the hand of Sabra, daughter of the Egyptian king, but he insists, 'I am a Christian, thou a Pagan: I honour God in heaven, thou earthly shadowes below: therefore if thou wilt obtaine my love and liking, thou must forsake thy Mahomet and be christened in our Christian faith.' Sabra agrees, but they are betrayed by the jealous 'Almidor the blacke knight of Moroco'.[52] George is sent to Persia for execution, where Johnson depicts him as a militant Protestant iconoclast: 'Upon the day (Saint George entred the sultan's court) when the Persians solemnly sacrificed to their Gods Mahomet, Apollo, Termigaunt, the unchristian procession so moved the impatience of the English champion, that he took the ensigns and streamers whereon the Persian gods were pictured, and trampled them under his feet.'[53] As a consequence George is condemned by a 'Soldan' who swears by 'Mahomet' and hands him over to his 'Janissaries' to be executed. As he is martyred, George vows:

> Let tyrants think if ever I obtain,
> What now is lost by treason's cursed guile:
> False Egypt's scourge I surely will remain,
> And turn to streaming blood Moroco's smile.
> The damned dog of Barbarie shall rue,
> The baleful stratagems that will ensue.
> The Persian towers shall smoke with fire,
> And lofty Babylon be tumbled down:
> The Cross of Christendom shall then aspire,
> To wear the proud Egyptian triple crowne,
> Jerusalem and Juda shall behold,
> The fall of Kings by Christian Champions bold.[54]

Like Spenser's Redcrosse knight, Johnson's St George has to go through a series of encounters with Muslims in the Holy Land before he can be martyred and finally adopted as England's patron saint.

Much of what Spenser and Johnson wrote about St George's complex heritage in the 1590s finds its way into Shakespeare's *Henry V*, culminating at the end of the play in one final striking identification between Henry and St George. After his victory at Agincourt, Henry makes peace with the French by marrying their princess, Katherine. His rather awkward wooing concludes with his proposal: 'Shall not thou and I, between Saint Denis and Saint George, compound a boy, half-French half-English, that shall go to Constantinople and take the Turk by the beard?'[55] Henry offers to combine the blood of the English and French patron saints to 'compound' a crossbred crusader who can fulfil a version of his father's original desire to reclaim Jerusalem (although in this case it is to conquer Constantinople and its Turkish rulers). It is hardly a romantic proposal, but rather one of militant Christian expansion, where the compound French and English heir can establish his power at the heart of Islam. As Henry augments his power through a dynastic marriage with the French princess he reveals himself as a strategic polyglot: it is hoped that the eagerly anticipated boy will seize the imaginary Turk and fulfil the Christian dream of the reconquest of holy places from Jerusalem to Constantinople. However, the audience knows there will be no crusade because, as the bathetic Epilogue points out:

> Henry the Sixth, in infant bands crowned king
> Of France and England, did this king succeed,
> Whose state so many had the managing
> That they lost France and made his England bleed.
> Which oft our stage hath shown.[56]

In this moment of self-promotion Shakespeare reminds the audience that eight years earlier they have seen his version of what happens to Henry VI. Henry's great victories were all for nothing. The compounded boy would not conquer Constantinople – if anything, quite the contrary, he would lose France and England would sink into yet another civil war. The dynastic cycle of conflict will begin all over again, and the spectre of Carlisle's prophecy of internecine strife where 'Peace shall go sleep with Turks and infidels' will return like a ghost that cannot be exorcised. Shakespeare intimates that even at the core of England's greatest ruler there is a little touch of Turkish tyranny. Perhaps, he suggests, the Christian is not so very different from the Turk after all.

By 1600, the ghost of Marlowe was gone from Shakespeare's work, consigned to the occasional comical parody of bombastic and largely ineffectual characters. But the process of exorcism had given Shakespeare a fascinating new compound figure, the Moor–Turk, elements of which he could use to add depth and complexity to creations like Henry V. Shakespeare had no interest in making moral judgements about such characters: Islam was apparently of little interest to him as a theology, but the characters that emerged from Christianity's myths and misunderstanding about it were. Gradually he transformed the stereotype of the Moor–Turk as a murderous villain that he inherited from Marlowe and Peele into something subtler, yet also tragic and conflicted. In keeping with the exchange of goods and people between England and Morocco, Shakespeare's Moors were exotic yet unsettling. Standing on the threshold of Rome and Belmont, they threatened to invade their domestic economies, polluting their women and bloodlines. For an Elizabethan audience with some awareness of Moors, such face-to-face encounters were a distinct possibility. In contrast, Shakespeare's Turks were more spectral figures, metaphors more than roles, rarely seen on England's shores, representative of an overwhelming political power, military might and religious difference that was still closely related to the Elizabethan body politic. They would soon coalesce to help create one of his most enduring tragic heroes.

Even as Shakespeare finished *Henry V* with its unlikely proposal of a crusade against the Turks, a group of Englishmen were involved in a far less heroic but no less extraordinary adventure in Constantinople that would put Elizabeth's relationship with the Ottomans back at the top of the international political agenda. In January 1598 Edward Barton had died of dysentery aged just thirty-five, ending abruptly his short but colourful tenure as English ambassador to the Porte. He was buried with little fanfare in a Christian cemetery on the island of Heybeli Ada, a short boat ride away from Constantinople. The sultan had never officially ratified Barton's position because his controversial Hungarian adventure had further delayed the despatch of royal presents from London that Mehmed had been asking for since his accession. It was left to Barton's successor, Henry Lello, to request gifts and letters patent from London, as well as to renegotiate England's commercial Capitulations in the face of renewed French opposition. Unfortunately Lello possessed neither the tact nor the dynamism of his predecessors; his colleagues nicknamed him 'Fog' and could hardly restrain their glee in reporting his shortcomings. During one of his earliest audiences with the sultan he stood 'like a modest midwife, and began a trembling speech in English . . . sounding like the squeaking of a goose divided into semiquavers'.[57] Although he struggled to adapt to his position in Constantinople, he managed to convince London that if reasonable Anglo-Ottoman relations were to continue, gifts and letters patent confirming his position must be sent immediately.

As Elizabeth's advisers debated how to satisfy Lello's and Mehmed's demands, Richard Hakluyt was in the final stages of preparing the publication of the second edition of his *Principal Navigations*. Hakluyt had dedicated the first edition to his patron Walsingham, and would soon dedicate the second to Burghley's son Robert Cecil, who became Elizabeth's leading minister following his father's death. Cecil probably asked Hakluyt to use the opportunity to try to forestall criticism of England's Turkish alliance. Hakluyt wrote a dedicatory epistle to Cecil, drawing on Bacon's earlier defence. It turned first to ancient history, arguing, 'if any man shall take exception against this our new trade with Turks and misbelievers, he shall show himself a man of small experience in old and new histories, or wilfully lead with partiality, or some worse humour. For who knoweth not, that king Solomon of old, entered into league upon necessity with Hiram the king of Tyrus, a gentile?' It was a carefully chosen Old Testament analogy. Just as King Hiram of Tyre had provided Solomon with the timber needed to build the Holy Temple of Jerusalem, so Elizabeth would do business with whoever enabled her to erect the Protestant Temple of God in England. Turning to the hypocrisy of England's Catholic opponents, each of them with merchants based in Constantinople, Hakluyt went on, 'who is ignorant that the French, the Genoese, Florentines, Ragusans, Venetians, and Polonians are at this day in league with the Grand Signior, and have been these many years, and have used trade and traffic in his dominions?' He concluded by taking a global perspective to ask:

> who doth not acknowledge, that either hath travelled the remote parts of the world, or read the histories of this later age, that the Spaniards and Portugales in Barbary, in the Indies, and elsewhere, have ordinary confederacy and traffic with the Moors, and many kinds of Gentiles and Pagans, and that which is more, do pay them pensions, and use them in their service and wars? Why then should that be blamed on us, which is usual and common to the most part of other Christian nations?[58]

In other words, nobody could blame the English for working with the Turks or the Moors because everyone was at it.

Nevertheless, as news began to circulate in January 1599 that a ship carrying a consignment of gifts was ready to leave London for Constantinople, many onlookers expressed their anxiety. The inveterate gossip and diarist John Chamberlain wrote that a 'great and curious present is going to the Grand Turk, which will scandalize other nations, especially the Germans'.[59] Elizabeth chose the gifts personally and they were indeed 'curious'. One was a coach worth £600 intended for Safiye Sultan, a shrewd decision that not only continued their reciprocal exchange of gifts but also enabled Elizabeth to cultivate the woman who it was believed had wielded ultimate power at the Turkish court since her son's accession. The other gift was even more elaborate – a clockwork musical organ, built and already played before the queen (much to her satisfaction) by a musician and blacksmith from Warrington in Lancashire called Thomas Dallam. Edward Barton had written to Elizabeth back in 1595 suggesting she send Mehmed a 'clock in the form of a cock'. Elizabeth clearly felt that a clockwork organ was better than a cock (perhaps it sounded better), and the following month, along with the coach, a consignment of cloth and a team of artisans including Dallam himself, the organ was packed up and put on board the *Hector*, a 300-ton Levant Company ship bound for Constantinople.

On 28 August 1599 the *Hector* reached its destination. The Venetian *bailo* Girolamo Capello's report on its arrival was mixed. He noted that the ship's cargo 'consists of an organ very cunningly designed, which serves as a clock and can play several airs by itself, of a carriage and fittings for the sultana, of some silver vases and many suits of cloth which they say are mouldy and ruined'.[60] The reality was even worse. Lello was horrified to discover that Dallam's organ had been damaged on the long sea journey, alongside the consignment of ruined cloth, and with it possibly his hopes of receiving Mehmed's formal blessing as ambassador. Dallam saw that the 'gluing work was clean decayed on the organ' and 'his metal pipes were bruised and broken', blaming 'the working of the sea and the hotness of the country'. Lello's French and Venetian counterparts turned up to laugh at the pile of broken pipes. Aside from the fuss over presents, the Venetian *bailo* remained concerned about Lello's longer-term ambitions to establish Protestantism in the shadows of the Ottoman capital's minarets. Several weeks after Dallam's arrival Capello wrote to his superiors:

> The English Ambassador will kiss hands tomorrow morning. He goes working away at various chimerical schemes, principally the idea of asking the Grand Signor to give him one of the churches in Galata for the use of a preaching minister whom he has brought with him. Both the French Ambassador and myself considered this design of his to be obviously important in its effect on the honour of the Holy Church, and we accordingly approached the poor Mufti on the matter. He promised us every support; but now we have had recourse to the Chief Eunuch; nor shall we fail to make every effort in order to thwart this excessive and arrogant pretension of the English, who would endeavour to sow even here the perversity and impiety of Calvin.[61]

While the French and Venetians worried about Lello's religious ambitions, the querulous Englishman was more concerned about Dallam. It must have been with mixed feelings that he watched the industrious Lancastrian quickly overcome the initial setback with his organ, spending the next month repairing then reassembling it in front of a curious and increasingly expectant Turkish audience at the Topkapi Palace. At least the coach had arrived unscathed and proved to be a success, as Lello later described the somewhat incongruous sight of the sultan and his mother riding around the city in it. When the organ's repairs were complete, Dallam was called to perform before an audience with the sultan. On 25 September he and his organ were ushered into the inner sanctum of the Topkapi. As the sultan entered he demanded silence, and the twenty-four-year-old blacksmith from Lancashire began to play the organ in front of the most powerful ruler in the world. Dallam recounted what happened next:

> All being quiet, and no noise at all, the present began to salute the Grand Signor [Mehmed]; for when I left it I did allow a quarter of an hour for his coming thither. First the clock struck 22; then the chime of 16 bells went off, and played a song of 4 parts. That being done, two personages which stood upon two corners of the second storey, holding two silver trumpets in their hands, did lift them to their heads, and sounded a tantara. Then the music went off, and the organ played a song of 5 parts twice over. In the top of the organ, being 16 foot high, did stand a holly bush full of black birds and thrushes, which at the end of the music did singe and shake their wings. Diverse other motions there was which the Grand Signor wondered at.[62]

Mehmed was so enchanted that he demanded Dallam play for over two hours, while the humiliated Lello was left outside, fuming as he waited in vain to kiss the sultan's hand.

The recital was a triumph for Dallam. He was given gold worth £20 by Mehmed, and was implored by the sultan's advisers 'to stay with them always, and I should not want anything, but have all the content that I could desire'. He was taken into Mehmed's 'privy chambers' where he was allowed to draw his sword in imitation of the sultan, and was offered the pick of the sultan's harem, 'either two of his concubines or else two virgins of the best I could choose my self'. To whet his appetite he was even allowed to see the harem women by spying on them through 'a grate in a wall', where he saw 'thirty of the Grand Signor's concubines', and 'very pretty ones indeed'. Young Dallam was clearly delighted to report that the concubines wore 'fine cloth made of cotton wool, as white as snow and fine as lane [muslin]; for I could discern the skin of their thighs through it'. It all proved too much for his furtive guide, who 'stamped with his foot to make me give over looking; the which I was very loath to do, for that sight did please me wondrous well'.[63] Dallam was the first recorded Englishmen ever to see the sultan's harem. It must have all seemed a long way from Warrington.

Somewhat surprisingly, none of these enticements persuaded Dallam to stay, and he made plans to leave. Both Mehmed and Lello were determined to keep him, and removed him from the *Hector* as it was about to sail for England in December 1599 with Safiye's gifts and diplomatic correspondence for Elizabeth. The furious organist eventually persuaded the dithering ambassador to let him slip away under pretence of illness and travel to Zante where he could rejoin the *Hector*. As he left Constantinople never to return, Dallam had one final poignant encounter. To guide him through Ottoman territory he was assigned a dragoman, whom he described as 'an Englishman, borne in Chorley in Lancashire; his name Finch. He was also in religion a perfect Turk, but he was our trusty friend.'[64] As he reached the Greek coast, Dallam took his leave of Finch: two men from Lancashire, briefly united as friends, standing together on the Greek coast, one, a Christian, headed west, the other, a Muslim convert who had 'turned Turk', headed back east. Dallam had spent nearly a year travelling more than 3,500 miles from London to Constantinople and through Greece to meet a man born in Chorley, not much more than 20 miles away from his home near Warrington. We will probably never know what they discussed on their ten-day trek, or whether they spoke of their lives, their beliefs and the choices they had made that separated them. But whatever passed between them, it seemed that they were not so very different, whatever their putative religion.

In May 1600 the *Hector* docked in England, with Safiye's gifts and letters to Elizabeth. At first, all seemed well. Safiye's translated letter acknowledged that 'you sent us a coach; it has arrived and has been delivered. It had our gracious acceptance.' It also itemized the gifts sent in response: 'a robe, a sash, two gold-embroidered bath towels, three handkerchiefs, and a ruby and pearl tiara'. Even more importantly, the elaborate gift exchange seemed to have had its desired diplomatic effect of persuading Mehmed to ratify the Anglo-Ottoman Capitulations. Safiye assured Elizabeth that 'I will take action in accordance with what you have written. Be of good heart in this respect. I constantly admonish my son, the Padishah [Mehmed], to act according to the treaty. I do not neglect to speak to him in this manner. God willing, may you not suffer grief in this respect.'[65] Unfortunately, on closer inspection it transpired that the original letter had been so hastily written in Constantinople that it was addressed to 'the king of England, may his last moments be concluded with good'.[66] And undeniably, Safiye's gifts paled in comparison with the lavish coach and organ sent to Constantinople. Safiye's *kira*, Esperanza Malchi, who it transpired had already been accused of withholding some of the gifts despatched to Elizabeth six years earlier, also had the temerity to address a letter directly to the queen, asking if she could send Safiye 'rare distilled waters of every kind for the face and odiferous oils for the hands' and offering her services, despite being 'a Jewess by faith and of a different nation from your Majesty'.[67] Perhaps unsurprisingly, no record survives of any response from Elizabeth to this request for perfume and hand lotion.

The exchange would prove to be the zenith of Anglo-Ottoman relations under Elizabeth. Although the Capitulations were agreed and Lello's embassy ratified, the querulous Englishman failed to reproduce the kind of friendship the increasingly pro-Venetian Safiye Sultan had enjoyed with Barton. He was also persistently outwitted by his French opposite number. He struggled on until 1607 when he was recalled to England and replaced by the more capable Thomas Glover, who was promptly accused by his vindictive predecessor of bigamy, adultery, sodomy, domestic violence and – worst of all – wearing too many jewels and feathers in the sultan's presence.[68]

In Constantinople, Esperanza Malchi's luck ran out even before the *Hector* reached London. Fed up with what they regarded as the political control and financial corruption exercised by the harem, the Turkish imperial cavalry rose up against the Safiye Sultan, venting their fury on Esperanza. A Levant Company official called Humphrey Conisby described what happened to her. The cavalry 'drew the *kira* out of her house (this was a Jew woman most dear to the Sultana, who by such grace, with her accomplices, governed in effect, the whole empire; and was worth at her death millions). Her they hauled through the streets, forth at Adrianople Gate, and there killing her (after she had offered more for her life than their pay came to) they cut her into small pieces, every one, that could get, carrying back through the streets to their houses a piece of her flesh upon his knife's point.'[69] Safiye had sacrificed Esperanza to the mob to ensure she clung to power, although the incident severely diminished her influence. She lived for another five years, during which she conspired with Mehmed to have his son Mahmud strangled when the youngster began to question his grandmother's continued influence over his indolent father.

Nothing quite so dramatic awaited Thomas Dallam. Having returned home he got married, had six children and spent the next thirty years building some of the period's finest organs for King's College Chapel in Cambridge, St John's College in Oxford, Eton College, the Scottish Chapel Royal and the cathedrals in Norwich, Worcester and Bristol. According to his entry in the *Oxford Dictionary of National Biography*, Dallam's greatest achievement was 'the consolidation of the two-manual "double organ" with twelve to fourteen flue stops (without reeds, mixtures, or pedals) as the norm for English cathedrals and for larger collegiate churches during the pre-civil war period'.[70] Perhaps. But he probably never forgot his grand performance in front of the sultan, nor his glimpse of the harem and escape from the seraglio.

10

Sherley Fever

By the end of the sixteenth century, many Londoners had heard stories of English merchants, diplomats and artisans like Edmund Hogan, William Harborne and Thomas Dallam and their travels and adventures throughout the Muslim world. But their accounts were often circulated in random and unreliable ways, by gossip and word of mouth, in private diplomatic correspondence or in handwritten manuscripts passed from hand to hand. Few of these men had sufficient social standing or financial resources to publish printed books about their travels. Dallam may not have forgotten his time in Constantinople, but there is no evidence that Shakespeare ever met this modest Lancastrian artisan, or read about his organ. There was, however, one Englishman living in Islamic lands at the turn of the century who had sufficient stature to broadcast news of his exploits so widely that he could be casually mentioned in a Shakespearean comedy and everyone knew who he was. His name was Sir Anthony Sherley, an English knight whose notoriety epitomized the desire and peril associated with English relations with the Islamic world in the final years of Elizabeth's reign.

Sherley's name appears on the London stage on the first of several occasions in Shakespeare's *Twelfth Night*, early in 1601. *Twelfth Night* is one of Shakespeare's most accomplished comedies and a world away from the crusading rhetoric of *Henry V*. The play is set in Illyria on the Dalmatian coast (stretching from modern-day Croatia down to Albania). It seems to be a never-never land where near-identical twins Sebastian and Viola are shipwrecked and spend their time trying to find each other in a comical reworking of Shakespeare's earlier *Comedy of Errors* (which was set in Ephesus, a town in modern-day Turkey and an Ottoman possession since the early fif-teenth century). Viola cross-dresses as 'an eunuch',[1] a young male page named Cesario, to secure a position of service at the court of Countess Olivia, who employs her as go-between with Orsino, Duke of Illyria. Olivia falls in love with Viola, who in return falls for Orsino. In the chaos of mistaken identity that ensues, the delusion of Olivia's pompous steward Malvolio that he could marry his mistress is comically yet brutally exposed by her roguish kinsman Sir Toby Belch and his friends. The play ends with betrothals and reconcili-ation, though not for the humiliated Malvolio, who exits comparing himself to a bear baited by dogs, warning 'I'll be revenged on the whole pack of you.'[2]

For all its wit and humour, *Twelfth Night* is characterized by moments of unrequited love, loss, mourning, melancholia and tra-gedy. Some critics have explained its darker side by noting that it was written at the same time as *Hamlet*. But it also contains a surprising number of references to the 'Orient' and Islamic worlds that had pre-occupied Shakespeare and his contemporaries throughout the 1590s. At the time he wrote the play Illyria was no fantasy but a region under the control of the Ottoman Empire, which by this time con-trolled most of Hungary, the Balkans, Mesopotamia (modern-day Syria, Iraq and Kuwait), Egypt, Palestine, western Arabia, much of the Caucasus and western Iran. Its tributary states and semi-autonomous principalities included Transylvania, Moldavia, the Crimea, Tripoli, Tunis and Algiers. The extent of the empire was clearly in Shake-speare's mind as he wrote *Twelfth Night*, a play replete with references to Egyptian thieves, 'the gates of Tartar', 'notable' pirates, a 'renegado', heathens and even a 'new map with the augmentation of the Indies'.[3] This was the Cambridge mathematician Edward Wright's world map made to illustrate the second edition of Richard Hakluyt's *Principal Navigations* (1598/9–1600). Wright's map was widely celebrated as the most up to date of its time, incorporating the latest Spanish, Portuguese and Dutch discoveries in the East and West 'Indies'.[4] Shakespeare also alluded to the Ottomans in the loaded reference to Viola early in the play as 'an eunuch', a phrase which the audience associated with the emasculation and submission which took place throughout the Ottoman Empire and which as we have seen had been a feature of Elizabethan travellers' tales and plays for over a generation.

Twelfth Night also included two highly topical allusions to the Persian 'Sophy'. Halfway through the play Sir Toby and his cowardly friend Sir Andrew Aguecheek deceive Malvolio with a fake letter from Olivia proclaiming her love for him. Sir Andrew is so pleased with the trick that he says, 'I will not give my part of this sport for a pension of thousands to be paid from the Sophy.'[5] Later in the play when Sir Toby goads Sir Andrew into a duel with the cross-dressed Viola, he teases him with dire threats about his adversary:

> Why, man, he's a very devil, I have not seen such a virago. I had a pass with him, rapier, scabbard and all, and he gives me the stuck in with such a mortal motion, that it is inevitable, and on the answer, he pays you as surely as your feet hit the ground they step on. They say he has been fencer to the Sophy.[6]

The terrified Sir Andrew is tricked into believing he is about to face a deadly warrior renowned for teaching swordsmanship to the fearsome Persian emperor, rather than the equally petrified Viola dressed as Cesario, who the audience know is of course a young female servant, hardly capable of holding a rapier.

Sir Toby Belch was alluding to two real aristocratic rogues, Sir Anthony Sherley and his brother Robert. The audience would have heard immediately that he was punning on their name – 'surely' – and evoking their adventures in Persia. By early 1601, thanks to at least a dozen books and pamphlets printed with the tacit support of the vain and ambitious Sir Anthony prior to his death in the 1630s, the Sherleys' adventures were the subject of gossip throughout London. Sir Anthony had left England in the summer of 1598 bound for Italy, but within months he appeared with his brother Robert at the court of Shah Abbas I, the fifth Safavid ruler and grandson of Anthony Jenkinson's old adversary, Shah Tahmasp. The Sherleys' extraordinary enterprise was described in several travel books published just before Shakespeare wrote *Twelfth Night*, claiming among many other things that their mission was so successful that Robert was appointed the shah's fencing master and Sir Anthony given a substantial pension of 30,000 crowns a year to train the shah's army.[7]

The brothers were part of a family already famed for their escapades and misdemeanours. Their father, Sir Thomas Sherley, was a notorious courtier and treasurer-at-war who embezzled hundreds of thousands of pounds from Elizabeth's military campaigns in the Low Countries, for which he was declared bankrupt and imprisoned in the Fleet debtors' prison, his estate of Wiston in Sussex sequestered by Elizabeth. His eldest son, Thomas, was an almost comically incompetent soldier and terrible pirate also imprisoned for various misdemeanours in London and Constantinople who tried (but failed) to poison himself before being elected a member of Parliament later in life. The youngest brother, Robert, was held hostage in Persia for a decade thanks to his abandonment by the middle brother Anthony. Despite such travails Robert managed to change his religion, marry a princess, return to Europe, work for the papacy and have his portrait painted by Van Dyck wearing full Persian dress before he died in Qazvin and was buried in Rome.

Between them, over five decades, the brothers visited the Low Countries, Ireland, Scandinavia, Italy, Spain, Turkey, Africa, Persia, India, Greece, Russia, Newfoundland, the Caribbean, Mexico, the Azores and the Cape Verde Islands. At various times they worked for English queens and earls, French kings, Persian shahs, Russian tsars, Ottoman sultans, Habsburg emperors (one Spanish, the other Austrian), Moroccan kings and the Venetian state. All three were knighted outside England in dubious circumstances: Thomas in Ireland, Anthony in France and Robert in Prague. Each one was associated with recusancy and embraced Catholicism at some point in their lives. From their earliest mention in *Twelfth Night*, the brothers' exploits were celebrated throughout their lifetimes and beyond in a vast number of plays, pamphlets, magazines and books. In 1625, Samuel Purchas, Richard Hakluyt's successor as the great chronicler of England's voyages and discoveries, wrote, 'Amongst our English travellers, I know not whether any have merited more respect than the honourable, I had almost said heroic gentlemen, Sir Anthony & Sir Robert Sherley.' For Purchas, their adventures exceeded those of classical myth, because 'if the Argonauts of old, and Graecian worthies, were worthily reputed heroical for European exploits in Asia, what may we think of the Sherley brethren, which not from the nearer Greek shores but from beyond the European world, *Et penitus toto divisus Orbe Britannia* ["even to Britannia, that land completely separated from the world"], have not coasted a little way (as did those), but pierced the very bowels of the Asian seas and lands, unto the Persian centre'.[8]

By using a Latin quotation from Virgil's epic poem the *Aeneid*, Purchas hoped to wrap the Sherleys in the mantle of heroic empire-builders, spreading the word of English decency and common sense across the globe. He also saw their support of Persian military expansion as ridding the world of the troublesome Turks: 'the mighty Ottoman, terror of the Christian world, quaketh of a Sherley fever, and gives hopes of approaching fates. The prevailing Persian hath learned Sherleian Arts of War, and he which before knew not the use of ordnance hath now 500 pieces of brass and 60,000 musketeers.'[9] It was an early example of the belief that superior Christians brought technology to the backward orientals. Unsurprisingly, the Victorians embellished Purchas's sentiments with romantic gusto. The *Gentleman's Magazine* of 1844 lauded 'Those three brave Sherleys! Each separate history a romance! How proud must the old knight their father have been, living at Wiston with his noble sons! What heart-breaking partings; what sorrowful misgivings as son after son left the paternal home to seek honour and renown in distant lands!'[10]

Such praise was generated by the Sherleys' genius for self-promotion in their memoirs and correspondence and in their patronage of various printed publications extolling their adventures. Not everyone was impressed by the brothers' heroic ambitions. Accusations of the family's flagrant personal aggrandizement and corruption began to circulate as early as the 1580s, and more sober recent biographical studies have uncovered a dizzying trail of betrayal, debt, embezzlement, dishonesty, espionage, conversion, heresy, privateering, incarceration, treason, drunkenness, elopement and murder wherever the brothers went.[11] Of all the attacks levelled at the Sherleys, none were more consistent and vituperative than those directed at Sir Anthony. Even his biographers find it hard to admire him. One of the earliest, the renowned orientalist scholar and linguist Sir Edward Denison Ross, conceded that Sherley possessed great courage and charisma, and 'rare insight into the Oriental mind', but concluded that he was 'an inveterate and unscrupulous intriguer, being incapable of single-minded devotion to any person or cause. He had all the natural instincts of a buccaneer, and his cupidity was only equalled by his extravagance.' He 'passed without compunction or regret from one employment to another and surely it is seldom that one man has served so many monarchs', at least seven according to Ross's calculations: three Protestants, two Catholic, one Sunni and one Shi'a Muslim. Not only was Sir Anthony 'quick-tempered and quarrelsome'; worse, he gave 'no evidence of possessing a sense of humour'.[12] A subsequent biographer managed to go even further, condemning Sherley as 'a born intriguer, a complete opportunist, a man whose word could never be relied on and whose personal dishonesty leaves us gasping'. At best, 'he was a completely sinister person, to be avoided by all who valued their reputations or their fortunes'.[13]

The garrulous Sherley was himself partly responsible for these damning assessments. Unlike so many anonymous travellers to the Muslim world, he left behind a mountain of correspondence, pamphlets and even a rambling vainglorious memoir, entitled *Sir Anthony Sherley: His Relation of his Travels into Persia* (1613). Although it is often difficult to extract the facts from Sherley's fanciful self-fashioning, supporting evidence reveals his egotistical opportunism from an early age. Like most young aristocratic Elizabethan men, Sherley went to fight the Spanish in the Low Countries, along with his father and elder brother Thomas. By 1586 they were all serving there under the Earl of Leicester, but his father began embezzling money from the war effort, and the Spanish slaughtered his brother's company one night after the foolish Thomas had spent all day drinking with them. With his father and brother in disgrace, Anthony went on to distinguish himself in battle – bravery was one virtue he did not lack – and after Leicester's death attached himself to Elizabeth's new favourite, the equally intemperate Earl of Essex. In 1591 he was part of Norris's expeditionary force to France, where the French king Henry IV awarded him a knighthood of the Order of St Michel. Sherley was delighted, but when Elizabeth heard he had accepted a foreign honour without her permission she threw him in jail. Sherley refused to relinquish the title with what would become his characteristic verbosity, insisting that 'this matter concerned his reputation, more dear to him than his life, and that his life and all that he had was at Her Majesty's commandment, and that he had rather lose his life than lose his reputation, desiring rather to die than live with disgrace, which he accounted the yielding up of this would bring him'.[14] He was marched straight back to jail. A compromise was reached and he was released, but from then on he would only ever answer to the title of Sir Anthony.

A spell in prison seems to have done nothing to temper Sherley's ambitions. Almost immediately he incurred the queen's wrath again by secretly marrying Essex's cousin in 1594, and was exiled from court. He turned to privateering and in 1596 he persuaded his father to channel an exorbitant amount from the war effort in the Low Countries to outfit a fleet of ships to attack the Portuguese island of São Tomé in the Gulf of Guinea. It was an ill-fated expedition from the outset. Bad weather and illness forced Sherley to abandon his initial plans and launch a feeble attack on the Cape Verde Islands. Fearing a Portuguese counterattack Sherley took the ludicrous decision to cross the Atlantic and head for the Caribbean. In early 1597 the fleet tried unsuccessfully to plunder Dominica and Jamaica, but was beset by mutinies and limped home empty-handed via Newfoundland. By June Sherley was back in England, poorer than when he had left and overshadowed by Essex's success in Cadiz. In an attempt to recoup some money and escape from his estranged wife, he joined Essex and Raleigh's unsuccessful summer expedition against the Spanish-held Azores, alongside the young poet John Donne. He returned in October 1597, impatient for his next escapade.

As one adventure ended, another opened up. In late 1597 Essex sent Sherley to Ferrara in a misguided scheme to help Don Cesare d'Este, the last surviving member of the city's ruling d'Este dynasty, hold on to the duchy in the face of Pope Clement VIII's claims. Essex hoped to tie up Spanish and papal forces in the crisis that would otherwise be turned against England. Sherley was the obvious choice to bribe, flatter and generally cause chaos, and in early 1598 he slipped out of London without the queen's permission, leading a party of twenty-five volunteers. He would never set foot in England again. Not satisfied with a substantial budget of £8,000 from Essex, before he left Sherley duped his father out of jewels worth over £500. Sir Thomas, having only just been released from debtors' prison, wrote to Burghley on 30 December, declaring that 'against my will I am driven to complain of the cruel dealing of Anthony Sherley towards me' and protesting about the theft of the jewels. 'When my man called then, Anthony had gone out of town, we hear, with purpose to go beyond the seas, but whether with the Queen's licence, or not, I do not know. After wounding my estate by his voyage [for São Tomé] he has now the more undone me in my present desperate state by thus cozening me of the money which I am in no way able to repay . . . For this indeed is wickedness to add to the affliction of his poor aged parents.'[15] So much for the proud old knight and his noble sons.

In January 1598 Sherley crossed the Channel and travelled with his party on to Germany, where he learned that Don Cesare had fled Ferrara, which was now under papal control, apparently bringing his mission to an end before it had begun. Seemingly unconcerned, Sherley made instead for Venice in search of even greater opportunities. The city's network of spies and informants was abuzz with the arrival of the pompous Englishman and his intentions. In March 1598 one wrote:

> Here, one finds a gentleman named Sherley . . . He passed through Holland while on his way here, and he was (or so he says) well-regarded and received there. Nevertheless, he hardly speaks better of the Estates [the Dutch Calvinists], and, on the contrary, he unceasingly extols the greatness of Spain, and even more that of the Pope, and says that he has received great offers from the one and the other . . . If he were wise and of good counsel, he would talk less and would be more feared . . . he is a spendthrift who has spent all his means, and those of his father who he has ruined, and he lives here on what he has borrowed.[16]

These comments distilled the characteristics that Sir Anthony displayed throughout his life: the profligacy, boastful claims, suspect religious and political allegiances, empty threats and unscrupulous opportunism.

It did not take long for Sherley to spot an opportunity. Venetian overland trade with south-east Asia had been hit hard by the

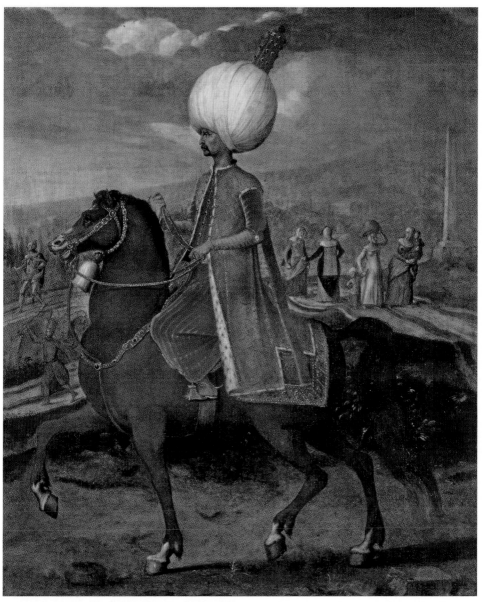

8. Hans Eworth's portrait of sultan Süleyman the Magnificent on horseback (1549), one of many pictures of Islamic rulers owned by the Elizabethan elite.

9. Sultan Selim II, surrounded by his army, receiving homages after the death of his father sultan Süleyman in 1566.

10. Samson Rowlie, a Norfolk merchant captured by the Turks in 1577. As the Latin inscription states, he was castrated, converted to Islam, renamed Hassan Aga and became Chief Eunuch and Treasurer of Algiers.

11. Needlework hanging showing a personification of Faith – looking remarkably like Queen Elizabeth – and Muhammad, commissioned by Elizabeth Talbot, Countess of Shrewsbury at the height of the Anglo-Ottoman accord.

12. A portrait of Sultan Murad III from an Ottoman album of 1588–9. Murad and Queen Elizabeth corresponded about politics and commerce for over two decades.

13. Copy of a letter from Sultan Murad III to Queen Elizabeth dated 20 June 1590 in praise of the queen, with the Ottoman calligraphic *tughra* at the top.

14. Nicholas Hilliard's Heneage Jewel, *c.* 1595, made of gold, diamonds, crystal and rubies. Elizabeth sent jeweled portraits like this to the Ottoman court in the 1590s.

15 & 16. Sir Anthony Sherley and his rival ambassador the Persian cavalryman Husain Ali Beg Bayat, engraved by Aegidius Sadeler during their joint embassy to Emperor Rudolph II in Prague in 1600 to propose a Euro-Persian alliance. The two men quarreled violently before Ali Beg finally abandoned Sir Anthony and returned to Persia.

17 & 18. Sir Robert Sherley and his wife Teresa painted in opulent oriental style by Sir Anthony Van Dyck during Sherley's embassy to Rome in 1622. Teresa was the daughter of a Circassian chieftain baptised into the Catholic faith.

19. The Persian shah, Abbas I, the Safavid ruler of Iran, from a seventeenth-century Mughal painting. Falconry was one of his passions, shared by his friend Sir Anthony Sherley.

20. Constantinople, the Ottoman capital, in the early seventeenth century. The skyline is dominated by minarets, characteristic of the Ottoman architecture that redefined the Byzantine city after it fell to Mehmed I in 1453.

21. The Somerset House Conference (1604), which brought about reconciliation ...n and marked the end of Elizabethan engagement with Islam. The ...elegates are on the right, the Spanish and Flemish on the left; on the ...ween them is an Ottoman rug.

Portuguese discovery of a sea route to the same markets following Vasco da Gama's voyage to India in 1497–9. Since Portugal's annexation by Spain in 1580, Philip II's empire had monopolized the seaborne eastern trade. Its Portuguese fortress at Hormuz on the Persian Gulf controlled maritime traffic in and out of the Gulf and much of the Red Sea, which was ruining Venice. However, in 1597 news reached London and Venice that a Dutch fleet had broken the monopoly by sailing to Java via the Cape and returning to Holland with a consignment of spices and pepper. Essex, always keen to develop an international strategy that would expand his political influence and challenge Spain, began to explore the feasibility of an Anglo-Dutch maritime alliance that could establish seaborne and overland relations with Persia and break the Iberian stranglehold over the region. The result was an Anglo-Dutch-Persian coalition capable of challenging the dominance of not only the Spanish and Portuguese but also the Ottomans.[17] In this, Essex was at odds with Elizabeth's pro-Turkish policy, but his more militant advisers were pushing the earl to challenge what they regarded as the queen's and his adversary Burghley's more emollient foreign policy. The Essex faction's increasingly bellicose strategy would, as we will see, culminate in one of the most serious crises faced in the course of Elizabeth's reign; but it also found itself in unlikely alliances with Catholic sympathizers like the Sherley family, unhappy with Elizabeth's Anglo-Ottoman friendship. It was this unlikely association that gave the restless Sir Anthony his next glorious opportunity: in the late spring of 1598 he would strike out for Isfahan and befriend the Shah of Persia.

It is unclear who first suggested the venture. In his *Relation* Sherley naturally claimed that it was his idea, sanctioned by Essex, who, he wrote, 'proposed unto me (after a small relation, which I made unto him from Venice) the voyage of Persia'. He described the decision in his characteristically prolix and neologistic style as 'a profitable experience of my seeing those countries, limiting upon the king of Spain's uniall [united] parts, and answering to her majesty's merchants' trade in Turkey and Muscovy; and besides, being not unlikely but some parts might have been found fit for the Indian navigation, then principiated [initiated] in Holland, and muttered of in England'. He could not resist adding that he was plotting 'some more private designs, which my fortune, being of the condition, which my persecutions have brought it unto, counselleth me not to speak of'. Other evidence suggests that the wily Venetians had planted the seed of a Persian adventure in Sherley's overactive imagination. Using the hyperbolic terms Sherley loved, the Venetian statesman Giacomo Foscarini encouraged him to go because it would be 'beneficial to all Christendom and in particular to Venice, which by the traffic overland from thence was mightily enriched before the Portugals were lord of those parts'. It was undoubtedly no accident that Sherley was subsequently introduced to a Persian merchant who told him about 'the royalty of the Sophy, his king, which pleased Sir Anthony very well'. He also met 'a great traveller, newly come to Venice from the Sophy's court, whose name was Angelo [Corrai], born in Turkey, but a good Christian, who had travelled sixteen years, and did speak twenty-four kind of languages'. Corrai also appealed to Sherley's vanity, telling him 'of the worthiness of the King of Persia, that he was a gallant soldier, very bountiful and liberal to strangers, and what entertainment he had at his court; assuring Anthony that, if he would go thither, it would be greatly for his advancement'.[18]

Sherley needed little further encouragement, and in May 1598 left Venice for Persia. His small entourage included Angelo Corrai as guide and interpreter, the Frenchman Abel Pinçon (a spy working for Burghley), several English gentlemen including George Mainwaring, William Parry (both of whom survived to write about their adventures) and his brother Sir Robert. Their elder brother Sir Thomas was unavailable, having extracted money from his long-suffering father and Burghley to fund a privateering adventure that was to prove disastrous. Even before he left Falmouth one of Sir Thomas's six ships sprang a leak, another was damaged and several of its crew killed by a botched cannon salute. A mutiny in which 400 sailors absconded forced him to sell four ships and sail with just two. If his departure was a farce, the outcome was an embarrassment. He tried to attack the south-west coast of Spain, but anchored too far offshore and the landing party got stuck on a sandbar at the entrance to the bay. He finally abandoned the whole humiliating affair and returned home to the scorn of the diarist John Chamberlain, who sneered that Sherley's only achievement was 'two or three peasants to ransom, of whom when he saw he could raise nothing [for them] he would not bring them away for shame'.[19]

A talent for logistics clearly did not run in the family. As Sir Anthony departed Venice for Persia he left behind him the inevitable debts, and he also failed to obtain sufficient provisions (although the two may have been related). Within weeks of his voyage to Zante he ran out of food, begging provisions from the Italian passengers, although it was a group of Persians who came to his rescue and shared their food. The enraged brothers took their revenge on one unfortunate Italian, accusing him of slandering the queen. Sir Anthony ordered him to be beaten brutally, and when the captain intervened, Sir Robert attacked him. It was symptomatic of their behaviour all the way to Persia. Arriving in Zante Sir Anthony wrote to 'Foggy' Sir Henry Lello in Constantinople, insisting that he was heading for the Red Sea on the queen's official business while posing as an English merchant. He demanded that the hapless ambassador send him passports and money to enable him to travel unmolested through Ottoman territory.

Over the next six months Sherley lied, bullied and borrowed his way across Ottoman territory, travelling through Crete, Tripoli and Aleppo, where he obtained more money from the English consul. News of his behaviour was already reaching London, where in December 1598 John Chamberlain noted, 'Sir Anthony Sherley has wrung £400 from our merchants at Constantinople, and has scraped together £500 more at Aleppo, with which he has charged Lord Essex by his bills, and is gone away to seek his fortune.'[20] But as old Levant hands like Harborne knew, Sherley's route was a dangerous one, and his retinue faced repeated harassment from the Turks they met along the way. While in Aleppo, George Mainwaring recounted that 'to my hard fortune, I met with a Turk, a gallant man he seemed to be by his habit, and saluting me in this manner: took me fast by one of the ears with his hand, and so did lead me up and down the streets'. As onlookers watched, laughed and threw stones at Mainwaring, the Turk 'gave me such a blow with a staff, that did strike me to the ground'. Once Mainwaring had returned to the safety of the English consul's house bloody and beaten, the resident Janissary sought out the Turk, and 'ran fiercely at him, and threw him on his back, giving him twenty blows on his legs and his feet, so that he was not able to go or stand'. According to Mainwaring such attacks and their violent retribution, symptomatic of the enduringly fragile nature of English relations with the Turks, occurred 'diverse times'.[21]

On 2 September 1598 Sherley's retinue left Aleppo and travelled east through Raqqa and Fallujah before reaching Ottoman-controlled Baghdad at the end of the month. News of his unofficial Persian embassy quickly spread, and English merchants refused to honour his debts unless assured that Elizabeth or Essex had sanctioned his trip. Even worse, Baghdad's suspicious Turkish governor impounded Sherley's goods, and in November the Englishman and his party fled after a tip-off from a sympathetic Florentine merchant that they were about to be arrested on orders from Constantinople. They were pursued by a party of Ottoman Janissaries whom they shook off as they travelled towards Persian territory with a group of Shi'a pilgrims returning from Mecca. As they went, George Mainwaring reported, they 'saw many ruinated places which Tamberlane had conquered, as we were told both by the Jews and the Turks, for his name is had in memory among them to this day'.[22] They had a run-in with some Turks before reaching Babylon, where William Parry assessed its tower, which he called 'Nebuchadnezzar's Tower', as 'about the height of St. Paul's'. When they finally crossed into Persian dominions Parry 'thought we had been imparadised, finding our entertainment to be so good and the manner of the people to be so kind and courteous, far differing from the Turks'.[23] Finally, on 1 December 1598, the group reached the Safavid Persian city of Qazvin.

Sherley could not have timed his arrival better. Thirty-six years earlier, when Anthony Jenkinson had been the first Englishman to enter the city, Shah Tahmasp had just agreed a peace treaty with the Ottomans (as we saw in chapter 2) and had no interest in alliances with Christians; Jenkinson was promptly expelled. Sherley arrived just as Shah Tahmasp's great-grandson, Shah Abbas I, had ended years of internecine conflict by defeating the Safavids' sworn enemies the Uzbeks and was now ready to confront the Ottomans once more. Abbas had overseen a remarkable transformation of the Safavid Empire since his accession in 1588, aged just seventeen, as the fifth

shah. Because of Ottoman expansion in the west and Uzbek depreda-
tions in the north-east, he had inherited a kingdom riven with
factional rivalries and reduced drastically in size and stature since the
glory days of its founder Shah Ismail. A pragmatic and ruthless
leader, Abbas understood that, if he was to survive and the Safavid
kingdom to prosper, he must somehow end division, reorganize the
army and recover lost territory. He immediately made a strategic
peace treaty with the Ottomans, quashed internal dissent and created
a new standing army including musketeers and an artillery corps. He
also took the bold decision to move his imperial capital from Qazvin
to the more central Isfahan. The city underwent a period of enormous urban renewal: Abbas supervised the building of one of Islam's
greatest capitals at a time when other cities like Marrakesh were also
being redesigned on a grand scale. Isfahan's transformation included
new palaces, mosques, bazaars, madrasas, baths, forts, gardens
and public avenues which saw it celebrated in the proverb *Esfahān
nesf-e jahān ast* ('Isfahan is half the world' – the other half being
paradise).[24]

In the spring of 1598, as work began on his new capital, Abbas
made his move against the Uzbeks. He marched out of Isfahan in
April, and on 9 August 1598 his army of 10,000 soldiers defeated the
Uzbeks at the Battle of Rabat-i-Pariyan, seizing Herat, Nishapur and
Meshed. As he returned to Isfahan at the head of a triumphal procession, he heard of Sherley's arrival. Abbas ordered a steward called
Marjan Beg to present Sherley with twenty gold pounds to sustain
him until he was called for. Mainwaring observed with relief that
Sherley's typically contemptuous response delighted rather than
alienated the steward: 'Sir Anthony, according to his princely mind,
turning the money over with his foot, returned this answer: "Know
this, brave Persian, I come not a-begging to thy king, but hearing of
his great fame and worthiness thought I could not spend my time better than come to see him, and kiss his hand, with the adventure of my
body to second him in his princely wars." '[25]

Sherley's rhetoric of fame, adventure and contempt for wealth
seems to have complemented perfectly the ethos of the Persian court,
as Mainwaring claims that Marjan Beg was suitably impressed,
responding, 'Pardon me, brave stranger, for now I see thou art a

prince thyself, for so it seemeth by thy princely answer.' Sherley demurred, but was clearly delighted. He was finally being given the regal treatment he felt he deserved. Equally thrilling, it was also time to dress up. His party was 'furnished with apparel and horses' and prepared for a meeting with the shah.[26]

At the very end of December 1598 Sherley's party was summoned to a royal audience 4 miles outside Qazvin. The Sherley brothers were attired in lavish Persian outfits, 'Sir Anthony himself in rich cloth of gold, his gown and his undercoat, his sword hanging in a rich scarf to the worth of a thousand crowns, being set with pearls and diamonds, and on his head a turban according, to the worth of two thousand dollars, his boots embroidered with pearl and rubies'.[27] As they approached, Abel Pinçon was given a sickening insight into the shah's ruthlessness. Shah Abbas was making a 'triumphal entry' into Qazvin, in which 'he caused to be carried on the end of strong and heavy spears twenty thousand heads of Tartars whom he had defeated in Uzbek'. Mainwaring estimated that it was only 1,200, but whatever the number it was 'a hideous spectacle' designed to impress Qazvin's inhabitants, but which also unsurprisingly intimidated the newly arrived Christians.[28]

At this point, Shah Abbas appeared. Pinçon described him as 'about thirty years of age, small in stature but handsome and well proportioned, his beard and hair is black ... he has a strong and active mind and an extremely agile body, the result of training'.[29] Mainwaring claimed that 'at our first encounter of the king, Sir Anthony and his brother did alight off their horses, and came to kiss the king's foot; for it is the fashion of the country ... after that was performed the king did look upon them both very stately, and afterward did look upon us all, giving never a word unto Sir Anthony'.[30] Sir Anthony glossed over such servility, recalling he 'kissed his stirrup; my speech was short unto him, the time being fit for no other'. Instead he was keen to stress that Abbas told him that the Englishman 'had done him infinite honour, to make such a journey for his sake'.[31] Other sources say he delivered a more fulsome and obsequious oration to Abbas, which sounds more in keeping with his characteristic verbosity. 'I am a soldier whose profession is clean contrary to words, which shall sooner fail me,' he is reported to have begun. He then offered to act as 'a subject for your majesty's most excellent virtues, if my devotion and observances were not sealed with my blood, the which I do humbly and freely offer at your majesty's feet, to be shed and spent, at the least sign and token of your majesty's pleasure'.[32] Again, accounts differ as to Abbas's response, but as they were all from Sherley's party they were unanimous that it was positive. Mainwaring claimed that the shah embraced and kissed the brothers, 'and taking Sir Anthony by the hand, swearing a great oath that he should be his sworn brother, and so he did call him always'.[33] Parry even claimed that Sherley immediately 'possessed the king with such a burning desire to invade the Turk's dominions' that he threatened to launch a campaign there and then.[34]

Whatever the truth of these accounts, the English were certainly welcomed royally. They received sumptuous entertainment, spending over two months feasting, drinking and hunting with the shah's court. Gifts of horses, camels, mules, weapons and jewels were exchanged, and, if the reports are to be believed, Sir Anthony and Shah Abbas became virtually inseparable 'in sporting and banqueting', walking arm in arm through the city's streets. The Englishman was even made a *mirza* (prince), a title originally reserved for princes and Muslims. It was hardly surprising that in return Sir Anthony extolled Abbas's virtues, describing him as 'excellently well shaped, of a most well proportioned stature, strong and active . . . his mind infinitely royal, wise, valiant, liberal, temperate, merciful, and an exceeding lover of justice'. He even praised the Persian ruler's approach to political succession: in contrast to the Ottomans, rather than strangling his siblings upon his accession, the magnanimous Abbas only blinded them.[35]

It is difficult to assess the genuineness of the two men's friendship. There are no known records from the Persian archives to tell us what Shah Abbas thought of Sir Anthony, while the Englishman's memoir and the reports of his supporters are either too vague or deeply biased. Nevertheless, though doubtless exaggerated, subsequent events suggest that Sherley's and Abbas's closeness went beyond that of any other Elizabethan Englishman and Muslim ruler. Certainly men like Jenkinson, Hogan and Harborne had never managed such a personal rapport with a Persian, Ottoman or Moroccan ruler. But they had been lowly merchants pursuing ignoble commercial agendas. Sherley would have recoiled in horror at such a comparison: even his diplomatic brief was unofficial, and possibly not even sanctioned by Essex. Instead he revelled in proclaiming his martial, aristocratic status. The relationship between him and Abbas was closer in spirit to that of the Portuguese king Sebastian and the English renegade Sir Thomas Stukeley. But Sherley and Stukeley regarded themselves primarily as warriors with little time for unseemly discussions of money or commerce.

Religion was a far more complex matter. Sherley's party certainly progressed beyond Anthony Jenkinson's grasp of the distinction between the Shi'a and Sunni versions of Islam, concentrating on the contrast between Safavid and Ottoman beliefs. William Parry understood that the Safavid faith was 'as the Turk's, but somewhat different in religion. As the Persian prayeth only to Mahomet and Mortus Ally ['Ali ibn Abi Talib], the Turk to those two and to three other that were Mahomet's servants. Against which three the Persian still inveighs.'[36] Parry also learned that 'Their conceit of Christ is that he was a very great prophet and a most holy and religious man, but in no way comparable to Mahomet: for Mahomet (say they) was that final prophet by whom all things were and are to be perfected and consummated.' Parry did not condemn this belief, he only observed, 'They further say that because God never had wife, therefore Christ cannot possibly be his son.'[37] Pinçon assumed that because his Christian readers were sufficiently familiar with the schism between Sunni and Shi'a it was 'unnecessary to treat of the hatred and discord which exist between them [the Persians] and the Turks over the explanation of the Alcoran and over the precedence and dignity of their false prophets', only saying that 'the Persians hold the Turks in great abomination'. He also made a token gesture to reclaim Abbas for Christianity, acknowledging that he was a 'Mahometan' but that 'round his neck he always wears a cross, in token of the reverence and honour which he bears towards Jesus Christ'. Pinçon's attempted assimilation only went so far: just a few paragraphs earlier he had succumbed to more familiar stereotypes, damning Abbas as a tyrant who tormented his subjects, 'behaving towards them inhumanely and cruelly, cutting off their heads for the slightest offence, having them stoned, quartered, flayed alive and given alive to the dogs, or to the forty Anthropophagi [a mythical race of cannibals] and man-eaters that he always has by him'.[38]

Sir Anthony of course had his own view on Abbas's religion. He had already found the shah's 'government differing so much from that which we call barbarousness' that he compared it flatteringly to Plato's *Republic*.[39] After many weeks in his company, conversing in a mix of Latin, Persian (Farsi), Italian and possibly even Spanish, he reflected on Abbas's theological beliefs, which he saw as positively Machiavellian:

> For the king knowing how potent a uniter of men's minds the self-same religion is for the tranquility of an estate: and the like disuniter several religions are for the disturbance of the peace of an estate, he is exceeding curious and vigilant to suppress through all his dominions, that religion of Mahomet which followeth the interpretation of Ussen [Uthman] and Omar [Umar], and to make his people cleave to that of Aly: not (as I judge) through any conscience, which carrieth him more to the one than the other; but first to extirpate intrinsic factions, then to secure himself the more firmly against the Turks.[40]

It made sense for Sherley to conclude that the shah's Shi'a beliefs were as politically strategic as his suppression of the Sunni followers of Uthman and Umar, but it also revealed more about Sherley's religious predisposition than about that of Abbas.

After Sherley's party had spent nearly three months spent revelling in Qazvin, the shah invited them to accompany him to his new royal capital of Isfahan. When they arrived, Sir Anthony began the delicate task of finding a way to broach the subject of his political mission. For once in his life, he seems to have grasped the sensitivity of a Christian proposing an alliance with a Persian shah 'to move him to war in so fit a time against the Turk', and prevaricated while Abbas showed him the splendour of his new city. Finally, 'taking the opportunity of the king's being alone with me and my brother in a garden' and using increasingly cryptic and periphrastic language, Sherley raised what he called 'the enterprise'. He argued that 'the extreme tyranny of the Turk' continued to threaten the Persians, and that if Abbas wanted 'the recovery of that which was by force and violence usurped from his state', there was a solution: 'if it pleased him to to invite the princes Christian to his amity', Abbas could forge a Shi'a–Christian alliance that would defeat the Ottomans and give the shah control over central Asia.[41]

Once the shah's advisers heard of Sherley's proposals, they were furious, and a protracted debate ensued. Many warned Abbas that 'these Christians . . . were sent to disquiet your majesty's tranquility of your state'. He should not jeopardize a hard-fought peace with the Turks nor intimate any military weakness by having to 'beg an amity of the Christian princes'. Besides, despite Abbas's recent victory over the Uzbeks, his army was still not strong enough to face the mightier Ottomans. Others were more supportive of Sherley's proposals. One counsellor pointed out that 'this Christian hath brought with him a founder of artillery: let him be useful to your majesty,' although there are no records of such an expert in Sherley's team, and it sounds like another of the Englishman's tall tales of what he was able to deliver. As weeks went by without agreement, talk about Sherley's proposals 'did aggravate both the grief of my mind, and unquiet of my body', and he took to his bed.[42] As he did so, a Turkish ambassador arrived in Isfahan, warning Abbas to respect their truce, and demanding that he cede territory to Mehmed III and acknowledge his servility by sending one of his sons as a hostage to Constantinople. It seemed that like Anthony Jenkinson, Sir Anthony might be unceremoniously ejected from Persia in the face of the Ottomans' overwhelming political and military superiority.

At this point Abbas paid Sherley an unexpected visit on his sickbed. If Sherley is to be believed, an extraordinary conversation ensued. The shah began by saying 'he had no great inclination' to demean himself by allying with a divided group of Christian powers, 'God having given him so ample, so rich and so warlike a dominion' as Persia. Sherley responded by arguing that Abbas would have to confront the Turks sooner rather than later, as their political demands and military campaigns against Persia 'were likely rather to increase than diminish'. He conceded that the Christians were divided, but contended that many, including the Spanish and the papacy, were already fighting the Ottomans, and would 'embrace the amity, honour the name of your majesty, and unite themselves in any terms of princely alliance'. He also suggested that the shah could strike at Ottoman hegemony in another way: 'in giving liberty of Christian religion, so much abhorred of their part, and security of trade, goods and person to Christians', Abbas would circumvent Constantinople's control over commercial and pilgrimage routes in the region, and would allow him access to European 'founders of ordnance, makers of all sorts of arms, and munitions'.[43]

Sherley's proposals were optimistic to say the least, but, remarkably, Abbas responded to them. He agreed 'to write to as many of the Christian princes as are greatest amongst them' to 'apply themselves to our purpose' and allow 'their merchants to repair to our dominions'. Abbas made it clear that it was Sherley's responsibility to implement the initiative. 'And because you have been the mover and persuader of this business, you also shall be the actor of it, assuring myself that my honour cannot be more securely reposed in any man's hands, than your own.' Sherley was ecstatic: he now claimed the right to represent the shah's interests in Europe and to act like a Persian *mirza* with the authority to mingle with kings and emperors. Having left England in 1598 in the service of the Protestant Earl of Essex, intent on disrupting Spanish and papal policy in Italy, Sherley was now proposing to broker a grand anti-Ottoman alliance between Persia and Europe's Catholic rulers. Considering that official Elizabethan policy remained broadly pro-Ottoman, this was an extraordinary turn of events. As Sherley took on the mantle of the shah's ambassador to Europe, he must have known he was turning his back on any possible rehabilitation with the queen or her counsellors. Perhaps he believed he could single-handedly change the queen's foreign policy. Perhaps his arrogance and hubris meant he no longer cared.

As before, it is difficult to assess the veracity of Sherley's claims with little or no evidence from the Persian side. The shah may have already decided to despatch an embassy to Europe to antagonize the Ottomans following the Turkish ambassador's provocative demands. Mainwaring recalled that Abbas immediately 'sent away the Turk's ambassador . . . commanding him to tell his master the Turk [Mehmed III] that he would never rest until he were in the field with him'.[44] Whatever actually passed between Sir Anthony and the shah at the

Englishman's bedside, in April 1599 Abbas began a lavish round of feasting in preparation for the departure of Sherley's embassy. The shah prepared formal 'Letters of Credence from the Great Sophy to the Christian Princes', stating that Sherley had come 'of his own free will, out of Europe, into these parts', and that 'when this gentleman comes unto your Christian princes, you shall credit him in whatsoever you demand or he shall say, as mine own person'. Sherley was also given commercial privileges by Abbas 'For all Christians to Trade and Traffic into Persia'. These stated that Persia was 'open to all Christian people and to their religion', and included a 'patent for all Christian merchants, to repair and traffic in and through our dominions, without disturbances or molestations'.[45] These were remarkable concessions that, if set beside Elizabeth's alliances with the Ottoman and Sa'adian rulers, gave England unprecedented commercial and diplomatic relations with the Islamic world stretching over 4,300 miles from Marrakesh via Constantinople to Isfahan.

Sherley, now drunk on his own grandeur, began planning his embassy. He agreed blithely with Abbas that his brother Sir Robert should stay behind in Persia, ostensibly to aid the shah in his military preparations, but obviously as a hostage to ensure that Sir Anthony would return. Perhaps as further insurance Abbas also appointed a member of his trusted tribal cavalry called Husain Ali Beg Bayat to join the embassy as an ambassador with Sherley, alongside four Persian secretaries, including Ali Beg's nephew Uruch Beg. The most surprising member of the party was a Portuguese Augustinian friar named Nicolò de Mello who had arrived in Isfahan claiming to be not only the Spanish procurator to the Indies (an agent responsible for liaising between the Curia in Rome and its missionaries in the Indies), but the long-lost brother of the dead Portuguese king Sebastian I. De Mello intrigued Sherley, who introduced him to the shah, but the friar promptly denounced the Englishman and his mission. Moving quickly to defuse the situation and 'stop this priest's mouth', Sherley explained to him that he 'was sorry that he had not understood my purpose which was the general service of all Christendom, and that he might make himself great, by bearing a part in such a holy service'.[46] While acknowledging that it was a risky plan to travel with a hostile Augustinian friar as well as a Persian cavalry officer, Sherley invited de Mello to join his party.

By May 1599, after spending five months in Persia, Sherley and his embassy were ready to leave. It was an ill-assorted crew of at least twenty-four, excluding servants, boasting two ambassadors (Sherley and Ali Beg), Augustinian and Franciscan friars, a retinue of Persians and the long-suffering Mainwaring, Parry and Pinçon, along with thirty-two crates of gifts for the Christian princes. Their political mission made returning via Ottoman territory impossible, so with Abbas eager to foster closer commercial relations with the new Russian tsar Boris Godunov the embassy headed north towards the Caspian, and from there up the Volga towards Moscow. Divested of his semi-regal status at the Persian court, Sir Anthony started behaving badly almost immediately, although on this occasion it seemed with some justification. Almost as soon as they departed Parry learned that de Mello had 'confessed he was but an ordinary Augustine friar, and in a gamesome vein he further confessed how he would bring men's wives, after he had shriven them, to his bent', and he liked nothing more than to be 'with a whore at night'. When the Franciscans revealed further details of de Mello's duplicity Sherley kept him under armed guard for the rest of the journey. However, the Englishman was also already quarrelling violently with Ali Beg Bayat and the Persians over various unspecified 'misdemeanours'. When they reached the Caspian Sea bad weather threatened to capsize the entire bad-tempered mission. As the storm hit, 'One heard a dreadful medley of voices and prayers,' recalled Pinçon. 'We of the [Protestant] religion prayed in one way; there were some Portuguese monks who threw figures of the *Agnus Dei* [Lamb of God] into the sea to appease it, and muttered certain words, repeating "Virgin Mary", "St. John" and the *In Manus* [Evening Prayer]. The Mahommedans invoked "Ali, Ali Mahomet," but instead of all these I feared that the Devil would come to carry this rabble to Hell.'[47] They survived to reach Moscow in November 1599, but the mood in the party remained tense.

If the plan was to incorporate the new tsar as the first member of Abbas's and Sherley's grand Euro-Persian alliance, it was a miserable failure. Godunov, a shrewd and capable politician, had succeeded to the tsardom following his extinction of the Rurik dynasty, and was suspicious of any diplomatic initiatives that might threaten his questionable accession to power. Upon his arrival Sherley was promptly arrested for ten days by a 'crew of aqua-vitae-bellied fellows, clad in coats of cloth of gold'. When he and Ali Beg Bayat were granted an audience with Tsar Boris, an ambiguity relating to the ambassadors' status arose, causing the first of many diplomatic incidents. By appointing two ambassadors neither with precedence over the other, Abbas had invited obvious confusion, which resurfaced when the tsar requested to see the Persians before Sherley, who 'utterly refused to go in that order . . . especially he being a Christian and they pagans'.[48] Sherley's notorious sensitivity in matters of etiquette and protocol alienated him from both the tsar and the Persian ambassador; Godunov 'vexed and molested' him, while Ali Beg goaded de Mello into accusing Sherley of being a lowborn spy, with no interest in furthering anyone's interests other than his own. Boris's officials seized Abbas's letters of introduction, and their studied vagueness seemed to confirm the Russians' suspicions; once again Sherley was placed under arrest.

Not for the first time, the Englishman's reckless and intemperate behaviour managed to save him. When summoned by Boris to answer de Mello's charges, 'and being by that graceless and ungrateful friar further provoked, he, not able, though instantly he should have died for it, to suppress his heat, gave the fat friar such a sound box on the face, his double cause of choler redoubling his might, desire of revenge withal augmenting the same, that down falls the friar, as if he had been struck down with a thunderbolt'.[49] Remarkably, instead of arresting him for such violent behaviour the Russians were impressed by Sherley's 'courage and high resolution', and promptly dropped the charges against him. In response he mentioned that de Mello had been secretly celebrating the Roman Catholic mass during his stay in Moscow. Catholicism was detested and outlawed by the Russian Orthodox tsar, who immediately banished de Mello to the Solovetsky Monastery on the White Sea (which in the 1920s became one of the earliest labour camps in the infamous Soviet Gulag).

His honour partly restored, Sherley wintered in Moscow and prepared to leave in the spring of 1600. With any pretence of involving

Tsar Boris in a Persian alliance now gone, he wrote to his supporters back in London, justifying his actions and positioning himself for a return to England. In February he wrote to the counsellor of his patron the Earl of Essex, Anthony Bacon, elder brother of the Queen's counsellor Francis. In his letter Sherley boasted of his achievements in Persia. 'I have opened the Indies for our merchants,' he fantasized, with the result that 'they shall have more power than the Portuguese, through Persia they may bring as secure as between London and St. Albans'. Spinning ever more fanciful and grandiose schemes, Sherley professed to be in correspondence with 'the King of Tabur [Lahore]', the 'mightiest king of the Indies', the Mughal emperor Akbar the Great. Sherley claimed Akbar 'hath desired of me some man which knows the wars to discipline his men', and that he was ready to send a Captain Thomas Powell, at that time in Persia with his brother Robert, to assist Akbar in attacking the Portuguese. Sherley's extravagant plans did not end there. He had an even crazier scheme to conquer the Indies that involved the illegitimate children of the unfortunate Portuguese pretender Don António (who had died in poverty in Paris in 1595). He suggested that 'if any of Don António's sons will come into his [Akbar's] country he shall be assisted with money and men, for the recovering of the rest of the Indies'. Unsurprisingly, Bacon did not rise to this lurid fantasy of an alliance between Portuguese renegades and Mughal Indians dislodging the Habsburg-controlled Portuguese in the Indian Ocean. In any case, he had much more pressing matters to deal with back in London. His master Essex's disastrous campaign in Ireland the previous year had left him in deep disgrace with Elizabeth and under house arrest in London. As Sherley spun ever more improbable webs of grand political strategy, one of the few men capable of ensuring his honourable return to England was losing the capacity to do so.

In June 1600 Sherley's party abandoned Moscow and retraced Anthony Jenkinson's steps towards Arkhangelsk on the White Sea. There Sir Anthony wrote to Essex, clearly having been informed of the earl's arrest and political isolation, telling him, 'I am plunged in grief to hear of your Lordship's misfortunes, but my devotion to you is as great as ever.'[50] This did not prevent him from meeting Muscovy Company merchants and writing to Essex's rival Robert Cecil, who had replaced his father as secretary of state in 1596, much to the dismay of the Essex faction. Sherley knew he was in disgrace for leaving England without royal permission and, even worse, brokering a Persian alliance that now threatened to upset Elizabeth's cordial relations with the Ottomans (the queen was currently preoccupied with the elaborate exchange of gifts with Safiye Sultan). With his habitually florid but unintentionally comical style he tried to be contrite: 'Yet do I upon the knees of my heart acknowledge the greatness of my fault in departing from her majesty without the blessedness of her gracious favour.' But then he bragged, 'I have laid open the treasures of other countries for her subjects,' adding that 'I have only used the favour and love of the king of Persia for her glory.' He also apologized for further delaying his return home. 'Neither is it my will', he maintained unconvincingly, 'that I am first gone to the Emperor of Germany,' the Habsburg Holy Roman Emperor Rudolf II. Still, he could not resist offering the queen a little advice, pointing out that Tsar Boris had a daughter and if Elizabeth could find a suitable 'gentleman of spirit whom she will vouchsafe to call cousin' then an Anglo-Russian marriage would be 'to the infinite benefit of her merchants'.[51]

Cecil was unimpressed. He wrote to Ambassador Henry Lello in Constantinople, another victim of Sherley's duplicity, complaining of Sir Anthony's arrogance in having 'taken upon him to be an ambassador to the princes of Europe, to unite themselves in a league with the Persian, for which purpose he came through Muscovy'. Cecil reported that the queen's fury over Sherley's reckless scheme had been intensified because he had 'the audacity to write to the queen for leave to come to her . . . Hereupon her majesty increased her former displeasure towards him . . . as by no means she will suffer him to come into the kingdom.'[52] The way home was now closed. Perhaps Sherley knew, because his behaviour became even more impulsive and erratic. As the embassy prepared to leave Arkhangelsk, the Persians accused him of stealing the shah's thirty-four cases of presents for the Christian princes and selling them off through the local Muscovy Company agents. Sherley denied this, claiming that he had opened the cases and found that the gifts were an embarrassment, and worth only a fraction of their estimated value of 400,000 crowns.

Rather than risk humiliation by presenting them to Europe's rulers, Sherley had quietly sent them back to Persia. Whatever happened they were never seen again, and the imputation that Sherley had profited from them blighted the rest of the embassy.

In late June the embassy sailed out of Arkhangelsk, travelling first to Stade then to Emden on the German coast, where they arrived on 30 August 1600. Over the next three months they travelled in state through Germany, being entertained by delighted and astonished princes as they moved southwards towards Rudolf's court in Prague. They arrived there without much incident on 11 October, and at Rudolf's expense settled into a luxurious lifestyle, Sherley quickly racking up his usual mountain of debt, as well as having his portrait engraved alongside Ali Beg's by the court artist Aegidius Sadeler. The Venetian ambassador Piero Duodo reported that 'what the mission of this Embassy may be we do not know yet', but he believed that 'it is a matter of moment and that there is question of a written treaty. There are other and wilder rumours, that the Persian will become a Christian.'[53] Within weeks the two ambassadors had been granted an audience with the curious emperor Rudolf. Duodo was watching events with a keen interest and on 8 November reported to the Seignory: 'Yesterday the ambassadors from the King of Persia had an audience. The Englishman spoke in Spanish, and the substance of that king's offer to his imperial majesty [Rudolf] was that he would arm against the Turk, and would also make the Arabs and the Georgians take the field with him.'[54] The Venetian noted with satisfaction that the Spanish ambassador was appalled by the proposed alliance, which also threatened Spain's interests by proposing to divert the spice trade overland through Russia and into the Low Countries.

Rudolf was clearly impressed by Sherley and Ali Beg, because he issued a formal response to their orations almost immediately, announcing that it was 'right pleasing' to receive them, and that he would propose an alliance 'with other Christian Princes against the Turk', whom he had 'been struggling against without intermission'. He pointed out that he had 'already attempted to form a league with other Sovereigns. He will do his best to secure such a league; and meantime he promises that he will continue the war with all his might, and will omit nothing which may be needed to break the power of the Turk. He will summon a Diet of the Empire, will raise funds, and will urge all Christian nations to join him; he will send embassies, and will endeavour to prohibit the commerce of Christians with Turks.' If the Persians 'should do much the same on his side with the Georgians and Muscovites', they could anticipate an irresistible military alliance and 'the following spring should see a joint attack'.[55]

Rudolf's bellicose rhetoric was in fact not much more than a minor variation on ineffectual Christian calls for crusade stretching back hundreds of years. The proposals began to unravel almost immediately. Rudolf's advisers suggested that Sherley and Ali Beg report back to the shah, to whom the emperor would send his own messengers with a formal offer of a military and political alliance. Their refusal aroused suspicions: did this vain and profligate Englishman have the authority to propose a pan-European alliance with Persia when everyone knew that Elizabeth was in league with the Turks? Even if it were politically feasible, the Venetian diplomat Duodo noted that the coordination of a perpetual war against the Ottomans was logistically impossible. During the winter of 1600–1601 the astute Venetian was busy discovering Sherley's plans, writing triumphantly to the doge, 'I suspected some secret negotiation, and my suspicions were just.' He provided a devastating assessment of Sherley's threadbare scheme and increasingly straitened circumstances. 'His object is to divert the India trade altogether from Egypt, and send it through Muscovy. Grand schemes, impossible to accomplish. I have seen his credentials; they do not give him the title of ambassador, which the Persian who is with him has. He has spent much and made presents. Although living at his majesty's charges, he has contracted 46,000 thalers of debt; and his creditors are after him.'[56]

It was time for Sherley to move on once more, and in February 1601 he left Prague and his debts behind and headed for Italy. He went with Rudolf's blessing and over 2,000 of his florins. With the proposals for an alliance quietly dropped, it must have felt more like a pay-off, the relieved Rudolf happy to see the back of the troublesome Englishman and his sullen Persians. Slowly but surely, doors started shutting on Sherley. He planned to travel to Venice, but when he sent emissaries ahead to announce his imminent arrival, they returned with news that a Turkish delegation had arrived there, and considering Sherley's anti-Ottoman credentials it would be 'inconvenient' for him to enter the city. They headed instead for Rome via Florence, where a Medici representative gave a damning assessment: 'this Englishman does not appear bodily hale and sound to me. I know nothing about his soul. His face does not strike my fancy. I feel that if we were to go to an inn together for dinner, I would end up with the bill.'[57]

Events seemed to be taking their toll on Sherley, who spent the whole journey to Rome still fighting with Ali Beg over their formal titles and the lost presents. 'They arrived in such a state of hostility over precedence', remarked the Spanish ambassador in early April 1601, 'that they came to blows' and had to be separated.[58] Oblivious to their behaviour, Pope Clement VIII received them with great public fanfare. Like Rudolf II he hoped – somewhat optimistically – that the Persians offered a chance to challenge the Ottomans' military supremacy. The French cardinal Arnaud d'Ossat was not so sure; he reported that 'the Pope has given them lodging in the Borgo, near St. Peter's', over which they fought for the best apartment, and that no audience had been arranged because 'each claims the right to precede his companion'. Sherley claimed priority as a Christian, but Ali Beg accused him of lacking formal diplomatic credentials and reiterated the charge of stealing presents that the Persian might have presented to Pope Clement. Having fought on their arrival they even returned to their lodgings and 'fell on each other on the staircase'. It was another farcical scene, but also tragic for a proud and haughty man like Sherley when a statesman like d'Ossat began to regard him as absurd and his mission as faintly comical. 'Perhaps someone may be found', wrote d'Ossat drily, 'who shall tell them that since they, being but two and sent by the same prince on the same mission, cannot agree between themselves, they will find it difficult to bring about a union of so many Christian princes and others in order to ruin the Empire of the Turk.'[59]

It seemed nothing could be done to resolve their difficulties, until finally a compromise was reached, with both men being named 'orators' and given separate audiences with the pope. On 25 April Sherley went first, sitting cross-legged in the Persian fashion before Clement, assuring him that 'God had so touched the heart of his master [Shah Abbas] that he and all his kingdom might be converted.' The pope's obvious delight at this news evaporated at the following day's audience when Ali Beg accused Sherley of all kinds of 'fraud and craft', from embracing Islam to stealing the pope's gifts. The diplomatic consensus was that Clement took the Persian's side 'because he has always spoken consistently. The Englishman is doubtless a liar and unreliable though a great talker and well informed.'[60]

It was at this time that news from London reached Rome about Sherley's patron the Earl of Essex. On Sunday 8 February 1601 (continuing from the events described at the beginning of the Introduction) the disaffected Essex had left his house on the Strand and marched into the City with 300 armed supporters. But Londoners had refused to support him, and by Sunday evening he was under arrest for treason. On 25 February he was beheaded at the Tower of London.[61] The devastated Sherley had lost his patron, and began to cast around for another. In April the Spanish ambassador wrote to King Philip III (who had succeeded his father in 1598), about Sherley's situation. 'The Englishman was very much bound to the Count of Essex,' he declared, 'and since the latter's imprisonment and death, he is completely without hope of ever again being admitted to the presence of the queen ... [as a result] he is determined to serve your majesty if your majesty should so desire.' However, d'Ossat also told the French court that Sherley had visited him and 'wished to be my servant', offering his services to Henry IV. The wily cardinal advised caution, revealing that the Spanish 'have exploited and interrogated' Sherley already, 'and have made him fine offers in order to win him over to their side, as much by reason of their ancient designs against England as for these affairs of Persia and the Turk. And it may be that he, being far from his own country and in need of money, will accept a post from the Spaniards, who pay more willingly for wrong-doing than for any other thing.'[62]

Another event seems to have propelled Sherley into the arms of the Spanish. On 30 April the Jesuit Robert Parsons, Rector of the English College in Rome, wrote a letter to a fellow Jesuit in England that made extraordinary claims about Sherley. In it Parsons insisted that Sir Anthony 'denieth himself to have been a Protestant ever since his first being at Venice [in 1598] for that there he was reconciled [to Catholicism] . . . And since his being at Prague, and here also, he hath used to frequent confession every seven or eight days.' Parsons also reported that over Easter Sherley had dined at the English College where he discussed the 'likelihood of casting religion [missionary work] in Persia'. Parsons added that Sherley 'hath no great minds to return any more into England as well for that the Earl of Essex and most of his special friends are gone', and that 'the queen resteth £22,000 in his debt'.[63] Honesty and modesty had never been Sherley's strongest qualities, but even by his standards these revelations of conversion and treachery were shocking. He never confessed to the exact time, place and genuineness of his apostasy; maybe it was genuine, but it smacks equally of desperation. Perhaps it was another example of his claim while in Persia that religion was a pragmatic 'uniter of men's minds', a Machiavellian 'toy'. Perhaps he was now lost in such a tangled web of deceit that he could no longer tell the difference between belief and disbelief. Perhaps he no longer cared.

On 10 May 1601 Pope Clement officially dismissed the ambassadors, giving them both a thousands crowns to try to get rid of them as quickly as possible. Their destination was ostensibly Spain, to deliver the shah's letters to King Philip III, but to all intents and purposes the embassy was over, destroyed by factionalism, rivalries and apostasy. The Persian cook, barber and under-secretary all converted to Catholicism and vowed to stay in Rome, while the mortified Ali Beg left immediately for Spain. En route another three members of his surviving retinue converted, including his nephew Uruch Beg, who was baptized Don Juan, settled in Spain and wrote a colourful memoir of his escapades. For some reason Sherley did not travel with them but stayed in Rome. At this stage his activities become more opaque than ever. He wrote offering his services to the Stuart king James VI of Scotland, perhaps aware that James was the most likely candidate to succeed the aged Elizabeth. James appears to have been taken in by Sherley, and would prove to be a remarkably forgiving ally over subsequent years. Sherley wrote darkly that he was about to leave Rome 'and am gone in that sort that, except the Pope himself, no man knoweth whither'. The intimation was clear: despite the dismissal of his embassy, his conversion had led him to offer to spy for

Clement. Whether he had actually made such an offer, and whether, if he had made it, it had been accepted, is unknown. By the end of May 1601 Sherley had claimed at one point or another to be working for England, Scotland, Spain, France, Persia and the pope, representing Muslim, Protestant and Catholic interests. The only significant power missing was the Ottomans, but his path to them was closed (even if he had wanted to take it) because a servant had stolen his Persian letters and sent them to Constantinople.

By the time he left Rome Sherley was a renegade, working (perhaps) for everyone but wanted by nobody. The Persian embassy was over and he needed a new patron and new adventures. His only option was to head for Venice, where he arrived in the late summer of 1601. He had gone there three years earlier as a Protestant Englishman proposing to break the Spanish control over the Persian trade. Now he was working for at least two Catholic powers and was notorious for trying to build a Euro-Persian alliance against the Ottomans. The Venetians were attempting to negotiate yet another entente with Sultan Mehmed III, so they treated Sherley's appearance with the utmost suspicion, as did everyone else. Sherley arrived claiming to represent the Scottish king James's interests as well as those of the Spanish (and probably the papacy), which earned him the attentions of two of Cecil's agents who followed his every move. As usual, trouble soon found him. A bullet was fired into his house, he dabbled in alchemy and there were the inevitable accusations of plots, thefts and debts. In June 1602 one of Cecil's spies wrote with wry scepticism that Sherley 'hath been lately assaulted in this city, or at least maketh it to be given out so, and that one of his company was sorely hurt; himself happily escaping the blow, was borne over a bridge into the water'. Sherley's household muttered darkly that the culprit was probably a Jew in the pay of the Turks, although one of Cecil's spies reported that it was more likely a creditor seeking settlement of a wine bill. Dozens of merchants cheated by Sherley over the years must have wished they had pushed him off the bridge; the only surprise is that it took so long for someone to do so.

By the spring of 1603 Sherley's behaviour was becoming ever more capricious; he proposed increasingly fantastical schemes to the Spanish, demanded he be allowed back to England, and even ingratiated himself with a newly arrived Persian merchant. It was all too much for the Venetians, who arrested and imprisoned him in March 1603. His situation was made all the more precarious when news of his feckless elder brother Sir Thomas reached Venice that spring. In February, after attacking Venetian shipping in the Cyclades Islands, Thomas had been captured by the Ottomans and was now languishing in prison in Constantinople. With Sir Robert still a hostage in Persia, the three brothers were now all being held in captivity, by three different foreign powers. Sir Thomas's privateering was seen as yet another example of the Sherleys' anti-Venetian activities, and can have done his brother Anthony little favour.

Just when all seemed lost, news arrived from England that at least in the short term offered Sherley salvation. In March 1603, Queen Elizabeth died at Richmond Palace. While most of England lamented, Sherley must have celebrated, as the queen's death brought one of his greatest supporters to the English throne, King James VI of Scotland. James, never renowned as a shrewd judge of character, had been flattered by Sherley's prolix correspondence and in May wrote to the Venetian authorities insisting that Sir Anthony 'is not the bad subject he is represented to be'. He asked the Venetians to hand over one brother and intercede with the Ottomans on the behalf of the other.[64] It took another two years to secure Sir Thomas's release, but by June 1603 Sir Anthony was free again. James seems to have realized his mistake almost immediately because by February 1604 he issued a licence permitting Sherley 'to remain beyond the seas some longer time, and recommended to the princes [and] strangers by whom he may pass'.[65] It gave Sherley some formal status as an Englishman abroad, but it was hardly a ringing endorsement, and talk of a return to England was quietly dropped. Sherley reverted to his old ways almost immediately, passing intelligence about Turkish troop movements to Rudolf II in Prague, promising 'I work still for your majesty and am ready for any sacrifice for your cause.'[66] On 1 December the Venetian authorities voted unanimously to banish him from the city for ever. He was given four days to leave on pain of death. Nothing he or James could say would change their minds, and within days Sherley left Venice for the last time.

With King James's accession and Sherley's final exile from Venice, his Persian embassy was well and truly over. James had no interest in pursuing alliances with either Persians or Ottomans; his primary aim was peace with Spain, which left Sherley with little diplomatic leverage (not that his increasingly erratic behaviour left him much of that anyway). But this was not the end of his picaresque story. He returned to Prague from where he went to Morocco in 1605 to propose a Moorish campaign against the Turks in Algiers, but predictably it came to nothing. By 1606 he was working for the Spanish court in Madrid, persuading a gullible Philip III to fund a privateering fleet, with disastrous results. In 1607 the Sherley brothers' stories became so famous that a group of journeymen playwrights wrote a play about their exploits entitled *The Travailes of the Three English Brothers*, although it came nowhere near capturing the sheer strangeness of their adventures. By this time, Shah Abbas had understandably grown so frustrated by the lack of news from Sir Anthony that in 1608 he despatched Sir Robert on a similar mission. Sir Robert had not been idle in his brother's absence, converting to Catholicism and marrying the daughter of a Circassian chieftain, the nineteen-year-old Sampsonia, baptized by Carmelites as Teresa. He travelled across Europe, was made a count by the pope and then travelled to Madrid, where in April 1611 he was finally reunited with his brother Anthony after twelve years. The elder brother's immediate response to their reunion was to denounce Robert as an English spy to the Spanish authorities. The youngest had finally eclipsed the elders: Sir Robert went on to serve King James and his son King Charles I until his death in 1628. Sir Thomas was released from prison and returned to England, depressed and destitute, dying on the Isle of Wight in 1633.

Sir Anthony remained in Spain, an increasingly marginal and pathetic figure, living off a meagre Spanish pension. He remained full of impossible dreams of power and influence, yet was racked with debt, with 'scarce money to buy him bread' and living 'in a *bodegon*, which is little worse than an English ale house'. Somehow he persuaded Robert to take his account of the Persian embassy back to London and publish it as his *Relation* in 1613, but nobody paid much attention. In the 1620s he wrote two similarly sententious treatises addressed to the new king Philip IV's ministers, proposing ever more deluded plans for his and Spain's greater glory. The final damning picture of

Sherley was given by Francis Cottington, England's ambassador to Spain, who wrote, 'the poor man comes sometimes to my house, and is as full of vanity as ever he was, making himself believe that he shall one day be a great prince, when for the present he wants shoes to wear'.[67] His fall from grace was so profound that he died in Spain in complete obscurity at an unknown date in the 1630s.

During the final years of Elizabeth's reign, nobody was better known for his oriental adventures than Sir Anthony Sherley. His exploits were so outlandish that Shakespeare had no need to write a play about them: the passing reference in *Twelfth Night* was all that his audience needed to imagine a bombastic, swaggering, slightly ridiculous nobleman. His was the tragicomic story of a man entangled in a dangerous and unforgiving world who aspired to the international grandeur of advising sultans, shahs and emperors, but who ended life in exile and obloquy without enough money to buy bread or clothes. Ultimately Sherley resembled not the comical, aristocratic rogue Sir Toby Belch but the tragic Malvolio: an avid social climber, humiliated in his schemes of preferment, raging against his enemies, the Persian, Turkish, Russian, even English dogs who conspired against him, still planning to be avenged on the whole pack of them. A recusant Catholic who ended up allying himself with Shi'a Muslims in opposition to a Protestant–Sunni alliance between Elizabethan England and the Ottoman sultans, Sherley exemplified just how complex these relationships had become at the close of Elizabeth's reign. But such relationships were also fraught with danger and disenchantment. Like so many Elizabethans before him, he had gone eastwards in the hope of riches and preferment at the hands of various Muslim rulers, but ended up disillusioned and displaced, a stranger in a strange land, with little sense any more of where home was.

Others built rather more on the connection between Sherley and Shakespeare, though less plausibly. In 1888 the Reverend Scott Surtees of Dinsdale-on-Tees joined in the fashionable debates over the authorship of Shakespeare's plays with the publication of a short pamphlet entitled *William Shakespeare, of Stratford-on-Avon, His Epitaph Unearthed, and the Author of the Plays run to Ground.* Instead of endorsing more obvious candidates like Sir Francis Bacon or the Earl of Oxford, Surtees was drawn to a more cosmopolitan individual, someone with naval and battlefield experience, a background in law, trade, diplomacy and 'the habits and the ways, the customs, dresses, manners, laws of almost every known nation', including Aleppo, Algiers, Bermuda, Cyprus, Greece, India, Mauretania, Mexico, Persia, Rome, Russia, Tunis, Venice, Verona and Vienna, and someone obsessed with naming his characters 'Antonio'. So, Surtees asked triumphantly, 'What is Antonio everywhere but Anthony "writ new"?' As far as Surtees was concerned, the answer to the authorship controversy was obvious: 'Anthony Sherley and no other was he who wrote these plays.'[68]

11

More than a Moor

In June 1599, just weeks after Sir Anthony Sherley had left Isfahan for Moscow, the English merchant and spy Jasper Thomson wrote a letter from Marrakesh to his relative Richard Thomson in London. Jasper's letter described a recent meeting with al-Mansur's principal secretary, al-Caid Azouz, at which Thomson recounted that Azouz had discovered that 'I had been employed some years in Turkey and that, in this last journey into Hungary which the Grand Signor [Mehmed III] made in person, I was present'. Al-Mansur ordered Azouz to spend 'the whole night' questioning Thomson 'upon the many particularities concerning the Grand Signor and his proceedings (for I see nothing is more pleasing to the king than to hear that the Turks' affairs succeeded not well)'. As Thomson related news of recent Austrian victories over the Turks in Hungary, Azouz turned the conversation to England's relations with the Ottomans. He 'was desirous to know what reason or wherefore the queen had required aid of the Turk against the Spaniard'. Thomson protested rather weakly that 'never any such thing was demanded', but after 'much talk' about Elizabeth's policy towards Spain and the Ottomans, as well as about the size of her army in France, Azouz asked the Englishman:

> Whether I thought the queen would be content to make such another army to land in some port in Spain with twenty thousand footmen, and with vessels to transport twenty thousand horses and men from Barbary, and so to join together in conquest of the country; whereof, said he, there is no doubt but it may be performed, if her majesty and his king should join together in the action.[1]

He wanted to know if Thomson had 'friends that could procure by word of mouth to move the queen therein'. The Englishman responded with understandable caution; the Thomson clan were servants of Sir Robert Cecil's and always on the lookout for intelligence they could relay to their London paymaster. Nevertheless, Jasper could not afford to be presumptuous about Azouz's approach. He told the Moroccan that he was unaware of the queen's latest policy towards Spain, especially in the wake of Philip II's recent death in September 1598, but he advised him that, if al-Mansur was serious, 'it were good he sent an ambassador to her majesty, about the negotiation of whom I was assured he should have a princely answer'. He concluded his letter with news of the return of al-Mansur's military commander responsible for the conquest of Songhai back in 1591. 'He brought with him thirty camels laden with tyber, which is unrefined gold,' he wrote, estimating the gold's value at over £600,000, equivalent to Elizabeth's entire annual revenue, and twice the national debt. He also noted the arrival of a 'great store of pepper, unicorns' horns and a certain kind of wood for dyers . . . all which he presented unto the king, with fifty horse, and great quantity of eunuchs, dwarfs and women and men slaves, besides fifteen virgins, the king's daughters of Gago [Songhai], which he sendeth to be the king's concubines. You must note all these be of the coal black hair, for that country yieldeth no other.'[2] Like many of his contemporaries working in the Muslim world, Thomson had no difficulty switching between cool *realpolitik* and lurid exoticism.

Judging by the flurry of correspondence between the English and Moroccan rulers over the next few months, Azouz's proposal was clearly taken seriously in London. In March 1600 Elizabeth wrote to request the release of nine Dutch captives held by the Moroccans; by June al-Mansur told her he was sending a diplomatic embassy disguised as a trade delegation travelling to Aleppo, taking a (somewhat unlikely) route via London. It would be led by Abd al-Wahid bin Masoud bin Muhammad al-Annuri, al-Mansur's adviser. Al-Annuri was given powers to discuss a proposed Anglo-Moroccan attack on Spain 'verbally and in secret'.[3] Nevertheless, news of the plan began to leak out, and speculation soon mounted among the English merchants in Marrakesh. One of them, John Waring, wrote to Cecil about the imminent departure of al-Annuri's embassy, along with the 'nine Dutchmen taken long since captives by the barbarians and became slaves to Mully Hamett, King of Barbary'. He observed that 'it is thought most meet that the said captives do accompany the Moors, until they come one with the other unto her majesty or your honour's presence, to acknowledge her majesty's great bounty and liberality'.[4] The real motives behind the embassy could be hidden under the pretence of trade and the routine repatriation of Christian captives, which also made Elizabeth look good in the eyes of the Dutch Calvinists.

A few weeks later Jasper Thomson's cousin George sent Cecil an even more detailed report of what to expect from al-Annuri and his entourage. Although he confessed that their mission was 'so secret that none knoweth the ground of their going', his personal contacts with most of the Moroccans meant he could provide his master with a fulsome report concerning the whole crew. It included two prominent merchants, 'Side al-Hage Messa [Hajj Musa]', who lost the opportunity to lead the delegation after accusations that he had withheld precious stones from al-Mansur, and 'Al-Hage Bahanet', who were both delegated to represent the embassy's commercial interests. The fourth was a friend of Thomson's called 'Side Abdala Dodar [Abdullah Dudar], an Andalusian [Morisco] who goeth for trudgman or interpreter, who telleth me he will speak Italian to her majesty; but I take it he will use the Spanish tongue, being his natural language'. Thomson also provided a detailed description of al-Annuri. He was 'a natural Moor born, but of the race of Fessians, which the natural Moor holdeth baseness', because Fez was incorporated into the Sa'adian dynasty only in 1548. Thomson warned Cecil that, although al-Annuri possessed a 'sharpness of wit and gift of pen', he was a proud and boastful man, with a 'baseness of mind' that lacked 'gentility'. This condemnation should be treated with some caution. Thomson also told Cecil that al-Annuri 'much relieth on [John] Waring's friends and no doubt but the merchants which trade to this place will be liberal unto him'.[5] As he wrote, three of Jasper's cousins, the brothers George, Richard and Arnold, were embroiled in one of those interminable legal disputes with Waring over goods and money which became so intractable that Elizabeth wrote to al-Mansur asking him to intervene.[6] Whether he did so or not is unclear, but the dispute suggests that if Thomson thought al-Annuri should be treated with suspicion, then so should he be.

Following the arrival of the Moroccan mission in London in August 1600, al-Annuri had two audiences with Elizabeth, the first at Nonsuch and the second at Oatlands, both described in detail at the beginning of this book. The second meeting ended with a proposal for an Anglo-Moroccan military alliance that would involve a joint attack on Spain and its possessions in the Americas and the Far East. Having listened to al-Annuri's proposal at Oatlands, Elizabeth and her advisers demurred over the proposed alliance, probably unconvinced by the likelihood of defeating the Spanish in their homeland and abroad, and countered with their own offer. They seem to have believed that al-Annuri was a Morisco who had 'reverted' to Islam. That he sat for his portrait around this time in contradiction of orthodox Islamic aniconism (when al-Mansur never showed his face and spoke from behind a veil) certainly suggests that the ambassador possessed some Spanish heritage, notwithstanding Thomson's assertion that he was from Fez (which itself questioned his status as a 'true' or faithful supporter of the Sa'adian dynasty). Cecil also knew that al-Mansur regarded the allegiance of the Moriscos with deep suspicion, even though they hated the Spanish as much as the Moors did. Based on this assumption, Elizabeth's advisers offered al-Annuri the opportunity to join the English forces in their more realistic ongoing campaign against Spain, which was being primarily waged at sea rather than on land. It was effectively an attempt to 'turn' al-Annuri into a double agent.[7]

Perhaps they had misjudged his origins or his loyalty, or both, but it seems the ambassador refused to betray al-Mansur. However, at least one of his party, the translator Abdullah Dudar, was unquestionably a Morisco (or 'Andalusian') whose native tongue was Spanish, and it appears that he and Hajj Musa led some kind of revolt against al-Annuri, possibly because they were interested in accepting the English offer. On 15 October the indefatigable diarist John Chamberlain observed, 'the Barbarians take their leave some time this week to go homeward; for our merchants nor mariners will not carry them into Turkey, because they think it a matter odious and scandalous to the world to be too friendly or familiar with infidels.' However, exhibiting the contradictory approach of so many Englishmen towards the Moors, Chamberlain continued, 'but yet it is no small honour to us that nations so far remote, and every way different, should meet here to admire the glory and magnificence of our Queen of Sheba'.[8] The Old Testament story of the oriental Queen of Sheba visiting Solomon is inverted by Chamberlain, who sees Elizabeth as an aged latterday Sheba, awaiting visitations from the other side of the world. Six days later Chamberlain noted, 'the Barbarians were yesterday at court to take their leave and will be gone shortly; but the eldest of them [Hajj Musa], which was a kind of priest or prophet, hath taken his leave of the world and is gone to prophesy *apud inferos* [in the grave] and to seek out Mahound their mediator.'[9] Chamberlain's rather poor joke was followed by subsequent reports making much darker accusations. Stow wrote: 'they poisoned their interpreter being born in Granada, because he commended the estate and bounty of England. The like violence was thought to be done unto their reverend aged pilgrim [Hajj Musa], lest he should manifest England's honour to their disgrace. It was generally judged, by their demeanours, that they were rather espials than honourable ambassadors, for they omitted nothing that might damnify the English merchants.'[10]

Had al-Annuri murdered two rebellious members of his party on the Strand then ordered a hasty departure? Or were the rumours of murder and insurrection among elements of the Moroccan delegation malicious slanders resulting from disagreements between various commercial and political factions? As speculation grew, the Privy Council was debating action against English merchants artificially inflating the price of Barbary sugar, and petitioning the Levant Company to cover the costs of transporting the Moroccan delegation to Aleppo. Elizabeth responded to al-Annuri's initial overtures for a full-scale military alliance by writing a studiedly non-committal letter to al-Mansur, saying nothing about its detail, only thanking him for his 'many effusive expressions of true kindness', and hoping that 'these letters of ours will communicate our deepest gratitude'. She reminded al-Mansur, 'We have always been keenly aware of the great esteem in which Your Majesty holds our longstanding correspondence over many years regarding trade and agreements between our subjects,' but then she raised the issue of 'some considerable monies owed to several of our subjects, who, along with their merchants, have been treated most harshly' in Morocco. She also invoked the release of the Dutch merchants, pointing out that it emphasized 'our undertaking to safeguard the wellbeing of those who, like ourselves, recognize the name of Jesus the Redeemer and Saviour of all men'. This was hardly an attempt to encourage the proposed Anglo-Moroccan alliance against Spain. She went on to hint at the conflicts raised by the embassy both among its members and within the wider London community. 'We have', she wrote, 'taken Your Majesty's request for ships to convey your ambassadors to Aleppo into great consideration and we are loath to refuse this or any other greater courtesy.' However, she admitted, 'we have been informed and advised that such an operation would entail many inconveniences and difficulties both to our ships and to the ambassadors themselves, out of respect to very many great concerns. We have therefore been so bold as to inform your ambassadors of these circumstances and ensure them that Your Majesty will not find any fault with them for having followed our wishes and instructions.'[11] What she did not wish to reveal was that the disgruntled merchants of the Levant Company had refused to pay for al-Annuri's onward journey to Aleppo. Nevertheless, regardless of what was happening behind closed doors on the Strand, the Moroccans seemed to be heading home.

However, a month later on 17 November 1600, al-Annuri and his remaining entourage were still in London, publicly celebrating another remarkable act of political staying power, the forty-second year of Elizabeth's reign commemorated by the Accession Day festivities held in Whitehall. At some point around this time al-Annuri must have sat for his portrait. Perhaps this event and the delay in the embassy's departure were not unconnected. The portrait appears to be designed to mark a specific diplomatic event, with its date of '1600', al-Annuri's Anglicized name and his age ('42') inscribed on the left, and his title ('Legate of the King of Barbary to England') on the right. The picture was clearly tied to Elizabeth's Accession Day triumphs in some way, as it was surely no coincidence that al-Annuri's age, marked so prominently on the painting, was the same as the length of Elizabeth's reign. The portrait could have been painted in response to Elizabeth's and Cecil's attempts to commemorate some aspect of al-Annuri's visit, anticipating an Anglo-Morisco alliance (even though some knew that support for it was waning) or a compromise anti-Spanish union with al-Mansur that stopped short of full-scale invasion. Elizabeth would not countenance an alliance with the Barbary kingdom, but she would consider doing what her sailors did best, which was raiding the Spanish fleet in the Caribbean, if al-Mansur would keep his promise to cover the costs.

Agreeing to such a plan was evidently beyond al-Annuri's authority, and by January 1601 negotiations seemed to have stalled, just as public hostility towards the Moroccans grew more pronounced. One of Cecil's spies, Philip Honeyman, provided one possible explanation when he claimed that al-Annuri's mission was 'to learn here how merchandise went, and what gain we made of their sugars, that he might raise the prices accordingly. The merchants took little pleasure in his being here.'[12] The English antiquarian John Stow offered yet another perspective:

> Notwithstanding all this kindness shown them together with their diet and all other provisions for six months space wholly at the queen's charges, yet such was their inveterate hate unto our Christian religion and estate as they could not endure to give any manner of alms, charity or relief, either in money or broken meat, unto any English poor, but reserved their fragments and sold the same unto such poor as would give most for them. They killed all their own meat within their house, as sheep, lambs, poultry and such like, and they turn their faces eastward when they kill any thing; they use beads, and pray to Saints.[13]

Having scorned the Moroccans' religious practices, Stow went on to doubt the sincerity of their commercial activity:

> whereas the chief pretence of their embassy was to require continuance of her majesty's special favour towards their king, with like entreaty of her naval aid, for sundry especial uses, chiefly to secure his

treasure from the parts of Guinea, yet the English merchants held it otherwise, by reason that during their half year's abode in London they have used all subtlety and diligence to know the prices, weights, measures and all kinds of differences of such commodities, as either their country sent hither, or England transported thither.[14]

After nearly six months the diplomatic, religious and commercial tensions that arose from the Moorish embassy's presence finally brought it to an end. With no military or diplomatic agreement in sight, and London's Barbary and Levant merchants increasingly unhappy about the commercially sensitive intelligence they believed al-Annuri was gathering, it was clearly time for them to leave.

As they began to plan their departure, events conspired to hasten it. In January 1601 Elizabeth issued a proclamation with a direct bearing on al-Annuri's retinue. It read:

> Whereas the Queen's majesty, tendering the good and welfare of her own natural subjects, greatly distressed in these hard times of dearth, is highly discontented to understand the great number of negroes and blackamoors which (as she is informed) are carried into this realm since the troubles between her highness and the King of Spain; who are fostered and powered here, to the great annoyance of her own liege people that which covet the relief which these people consume, as also for that the most of them are infidels having no understanding of Christ or his Gospel: hath given a special commandment that the said kind of people shall be with all speed avoided and discharged out of this her majesty's realms.[15]

The proclamation was a sign of the deteriorating political situation in England. The country was in a state of famine due to poor harvests, depopulation and the devastating impact of enclosures. Elizabeth's grip on power was slipping, and her immediate response was that of political leaders since time immemorial when faced with a crisis: attack economic immigrants, refugees fleeing religious persecution and 'aliens', even though in this case it made little sense considering the commercial benefits of her long-standing alliance with Morocco. Nor were the proclamation's proposed deportations of blacks and Moors quite what they seemed. Elizabeth had 'appointed Casper van

Zenden, merchant of Lubeck, for their speedy transportation'. Van Zenden was a particularly unscrupulous character who four years earlier had hit on the idea of deporting black slaves and selling them in Spain. It was the fraudulent bankrupt Sir Thomas Sherley the elder who, spotting a lucrative business opportunity, petitioned Cecil successfully to grant van Zenden the licence in 1601, presumably in return for a percentage of the unsavoury profits.[16]

Whether or not such hypocrisy had any bearing on al-Annuri's decision to go, other even more dramatic events on London's streets probably hastened it. In early February Essex launched his unsuccessful rebellion, and by the end of the month he had been tried and executed. Essex represented the Privy Council's bellicose pro-war party: if anyone could have pursued the kind of reckless Anglo-Moroccan attack proposed by al-Mansur, it was Essex. But his death left Cecil's more cautious faction in the ascendancy. War with Spain was off the political agenda, regardless of Elizabeth's eager allies.

With London in turmoil following the failed rebellion, al-Annuri and his surviving retinue slipped quietly away. By 27 February 1601 they were back in Morocco. Al-Mansur's subsequent letters to Elizabeth reveal that al-Annuri's loyalty to him remained unshakeable. He wrote to her in May, explaining that 'the Andalusian came before our high Porte and relayed to us all your intentions and plans which you had discussed with him and conveyed to him. We listened with attentive ears until we understood them all, and became alert to all you had plotted.' Confirming that al-Annuri was a Morisco (or 'Andalusian'), al-Mansur explained with obvious satisfaction that he knew all about Elizabeth's covert scheme to recruit the Spanish-born Muslims in the ambassadorial party. He would not countenance any Anglo-Morisco alliance because, as he explained to Elizabeth, he feared that the Moriscos might revert back to Christianity, or as he put it, 'we fear that they may be swayed [against us] by the enemy', the Spanish.[17]

Nevertheless, al-Mansur hoped Elizabeth might still agree to a joint venture against the Spanish in the Americas. He reminded her that 'you say the fleet to be employed in that action shall need treasure for the charge to the value of £100,000, and that we should assist you therewith in secret, that the Spaniard may not come to the

knowledge thereof'. He told her that the money 'is ready and provided'; all she needed to do was send 'a strong and tall ship, and some
person of account' to collect it. His other concern was the Muslim
colonization of the Americas. 'For our intent', he wrote blithely, 'is
not only to enter upon the land to sack it and leave it, but to possess
it and that it remain under our dominion for ever and – by the help of
God – to join it to our estate and yours.' He concluded grandly, 'if
your power and command shall be seen there with our army, all the
Moors will join and confederate themselves – by the help of God –
with us and you.'[18] It was the first and last time a Protestant–Muslim
confederation was proposed to rule Latin America, *insha'Allah.*

Elizabeth was sufficiently interested in using al-Mansur's forces
in some way to threaten Spain that she praised al-Annuri for his
'utmost discretion', and sent her agent Henry Prannell to continue
negotiations in Morocco.[19] But the bellicose demands for an attack
on Spain had died with Essex: the political will and much of the
queen's personal strength were gone. The court's interest in a Moroccan alliance for political and commercial reasons seemed to have
come to an end.

Despite the receding enthusiasm for an Anglo-Moroccan alliance
at the highest political levels, interest in the Moroccan delegation
beyond Elizabeth's innermost circle remained intense. Even as
al-Annuri arrived in London, the city's writers continued to publish
histories and translations of Christianity's fraught relationship with
Islam, while dramatists wrote plays that exploited the combustible
mix of politics, religion and espionage generated by the Elizabethan
alliances with the Sa'adian and Ottoman dynasties. In the spring of
1600 the English lawyer Ralph Carr had published *The Mahumetane
or Turkish Historie*, a translation of various French and Italian
accounts of the origins and rise to power of the Ottomans. It ranged
across Islamic history, beginning with the Prophet Muhammad –
described as 'a gentile and very idolater' – and culminating in lengthy
descriptions of the recent conflict in Malta and 'the war of Cyprus,
held betwixt the Turk and Venetians, some thirty years ago'.[20] Carr
also reflected on the religious schism within Islam, describing how
Muhammad's cousin 'Ali ibn Abi Talib, whom he called 'Haly',

'changed, or rather annulled' Muhammad's religious edicts, 'and made new of his own invention, through which innovation of religion, or rather superstition, the Saracens became marvellously divided' between Sunni and Shi'a. Carr concluded that 'albeit the Turks and Persians also are in effect very Mahometists, yet differ they so in ceremonies, & other contraries of opinion, that the one do account the other very heretics.'[21] Carr's account was typical of the equivocal Elizabethan responses to the rise of the Ottomans. At one moment he argued 'you shall find them in my conceit not inferior but superior far in every thing which hath given estimation to former ages'; at another he warned his audience in terms reminiscent of Erasmus that it was a story 'telling of ensuing danger, not much divided from our own doors, when daily we lamentably see our neighbours' houses not far off flaming'.[22]

The excitement and danger created by English relations with the Moroccans as well as those with the Ottomans continued to inspire plays that revelled in the audience's compulsive fascination with them. Within months of the publication of Carr's book, some time in late 1600 or early 1601, a play appeared entitled *Lust's Dominion; or The Lascivious Queen* (also known as *The Spanish Moor's Tragedy*) and probably written by Shakespeare's associate Thomas Dekker, though it has proved difficult to attribute the play to one hand as it involved the collaboration at various points of several other playwrights.[23] It is a nasty, bloody drama, a throwback to the 'Turk' and 'Moor' plays of Peele, Greene, Kyd and Marlowe (to whom it was attributed until the early nineteenth century), but it also added a new and topical twist: in the light of the continued interest in Elizabeth's and al-Mansur's plans to attack Spain, it blends Catholics and Muslims, showing the Moors literally in bed with the Spanish.

At the centre of the dramatic action is Eleazer, a Moor and Prince of Fez and Barbary, who is married to Maria, a Spanish noblewoman. Although admired for his military prowess, Eleazer lives as a royal prisoner in a Spanish court based on King Philip II's, after his father's defeat at the Spaniard's hands left him 'captive to a Spanish tyrant'. Although he is described variously as a 'devil', a 'slave of Barbary', a 'dog' and a 'black fiend'[24] ('black' appears in the play twenty-eight times), Eleazer boasts that his blood is 'as red and royal as the best |

And proudest in Spain'.[25] Unlike previous Moors on stage, Eleazer is a noble character accepted as part of a Christian community.

The play's opening is reminiscent of Shakespeare's *Titus Andronicus*, with Eleazer revealed as the 'minion' and lover of the 'lascivious queen' and wife of the cuckolded and dying Spanish king Philip. The king's subsequent death splits his court into rival factions; one tries to expel Eleazer, but he sidesteps banishment and vows to avenge his humiliating captivity and his father's defeat at the hands of the Spanish. The uncontrollable passion and 'lust' of both Spaniards and Moors leads inevitably to civil war as Eleazer plots the murder of his rivals and sacrifices the queen and his wife in a spree of gleeful villainy and Machiavellian duplicity that culminates in him usurping 'the imperial chair of Spain'.[26] Eleazer's brief reign of terror is ended only when the king's son Philip (modelled loosely on the Spanish king Philip III) disguises himself as a Moor by painting his face 'with the oil of hell' and stabs the Moor. Like Aaron and Barabas, Eleazer dies unrepentant, shouting at the devils that come to claim him that he will 'Out-act you all in perfect villainy'.[27] As Philip assumes the throne he closes the play by announcing:

> And for this Barbarous Moor, and his black train,
> Let all the Moors be banished from Spain![28]

The play was performed as Elizabeth's proclamation demanding the expulsion of 'blackamoors' from England was being circulated, and by 1609 Philip III had formally decreed that all Moriscos should be expelled from Spain.[29] The play could be seen as offering a solemn comment on the Moorish policies of Elizabeth I and Philip III. Yet Dekker's play was more ambiguous than this. It ends with a Spanish king still dressed and painted as a Moor, with his 'lascivious' mother half-heartedly forgiven for her affair with Eleazer. Rather than aiming to offer solemn diplomatic advice about the dangers of England's prospective alliance with a Moorish ruler, *Lust's Dominion* revels in a dramatic fantasy where Spanish Catholics and Moorish Muslims were shown as two facets of the same apostasy. The English Protestant audience could gape and laugh at all of the ensuing violence, passion, tyranny and blood, appalled and delighted in equal measure by the play's anti-hero Eleazer, a Moor who could be admired when causing chaos in the Spanish court, but was probably not to be trusted by the English.

Plays like *Lust's Dominion* remained popular on the late Elizabethan stage during the time of the Moroccan embassy – as well as having his portrait painted and visiting Whitehall's festivities, perhaps al-Annuri also went to the theatre – but the interest in Moors, Turks and even the Prophet Muhammad was so pervasive that other plays dealing with such plots and characters were dreamt up but had hardly more existence than in the fertile imaginations of their unorthodox creators. One such play was William Percy's tragicomedy *Mahomet and his Heaven*, dated 1601.[30] Percy was the third son of Henry Percy, 8th Earl of Northumberland (c. 1532–85), an eccentric minor poet who proved more able to live off his substantial inheritance than off his writing. He was a suspected Catholic recusant, a serial debtor, a skilled duellist and an unsuccessful playwright whose family were implicated in several plots to overthrow Elizabeth. In the 1590s Percy was living in London and writing plays for the Children of Paul's, a theatre troupe of boy actors, for whom he seems to have written *Mahomet and his Heaven*, although the play was never performed publicly (and even a private performance seems unlikely).

There are good reasons why the play never reached the stage. It is a tedious, verbose, poorly plotted piece of work, lacking in both tragedy and comedy. It is hardly a distinguished addition to the canon of Elizabethan plays on Muslim stories and characters, and its manuscript would have remained largely forgotten in the library at the Northumberland family seat of Alnwick Castle were it not for two remarkable facts: it is the first English play that claims to use the Qur'an as its source, with the Prologue announcing 'A text out of the Alcoran we bring you'; it is also the first to feature Muhammad as a dramatic character, naming him 'Mahomet' and describing him as 'the false Prophet in green, and green his turban. He the vicegerent of Heaven.'[31] The opening scenes are rich in details (though many are mistaken) of Islamic history and geography. One character is described as 'A Mahometan friar with gown green of colour and hood of the same', while the opening setting is described as 'HEAVEN, at one door, MEDINA TALNABI, next MELCHIT, with a tomb hanging over the door without, covered with green velvet'.[32] This is a confused description of the mosque, or 'Melchit', in 'Medina', or Madinat al-Nabi ('City of the Prophet'), Islam's second holiest city and the final resting place of the Prophet.

With the scene set, Mahomet makes his entrance with 'an Alcoran and silver crescent on his turban'. He announces his disgust with 'the sins of Araby', swearing 'by the holy Alcoran' to end the world through drought.[33] Two of his angels called Haroth and Maroth plead for mercy on mankind's behalf and ask to be 'sent into the world' of Arabia and its people, to see 'if their sins be less than be report'.[34] The play then introduces a series of farcical characters in Arabia with names like Tubal, Dervis and Chiause, based on stock English dramatic vice characters as much as Muslim ones. They are clumsy vehicles for Percy's ponderous satire of very English concerns with religious and legal hypocrisy, adultery and the abuses of magic and drink. The angels meet and fall in love with the virginal Epimenide, Empress of the Deserts, and offer her a distorted vision of Islamic 'Paradise'.[35] She tricks them into sending her to heaven, where she demands wine, abuses Mahomet and gives him 'a cuff on the ear'.[36] Despite her unruly behaviour Mahomet falls in love with her and in one of the play's most outrageous scenes he swears 'by the Alcoran' to abase himself by cleaning her shoes, only for her to humiliate him further by asking him to 'kiss my cul [backside] and doe [breast]'.[37] As Mahomet prepares to banish Epimenide, a ghost appears named 'Haly', who is Muhammad's cousin, 'Ali ibn Abi Talib, the founding father of the Shi'a Muslim sect. Haly enters surrounded by members 'of both the sects Turks and Persians' and 'with an Alcoran under his arm'.[38] He offers to reconcile his followers with those of Mahomet's Sunni persuasion, telling him 'I have subscribed to your book . . . And all these souls, that died in the Schism'.[39] Appeased, Mahomet lifts his curse on Arabia and banishes Epimenide, Haroth and Maroth to the moon. At the play's conclusion he dispenses divine judgement in a parody of the Book of Revelation and is compared in a stage direction to Antichrist, acting 'contrary to Christ in judgement'.[40]

Despite his claim to have read the Qur'an, Percy seems to have drawn instead on Theodore Bibliander's 1543 garbled Latin version of the Islamic holy book, the *Life and Teachings of Muhammad*, with its naming and description of the earthly descent of the two angels 'Arot and Marot', alongside various other medieval Christian apologetics falsely describing Islam as apostasy and Muhammad as Antichrist. And yet the play appears at the apogee of Anglo-Islamic relations, and seems to acknowledge the divisions plaguing Muslims and Christians by ending with a vision of the resolution of the schism between the Shi'a and Sunni sects. Haly takes Mahomet's hand and describes the dreadful consequences of religious schism in terms that any Catholic or Protestant would have immediately recognized:

> Bootless it is to rehearse with large flow
> Of eloquence, what have been the broils, wars,
> The thefts and massacres, that have been practised
> In world below (whilst yet, alas, we differed
> About one silly quirk, but the only
> Difference but of our contrary sects).[41]

For all its clumsiness and ignorance, Percy's play makes some gesture towards religious reconciliation, even if its concerns are ultimately more Christian than Muslim. It is doubtful that anyone outside of Percy's immediate circle ever even read it, and the Islamic prohibition against representing the Prophet Muhammad means there is little chance of it being seen on a stage anywhere any time soon.

Dekker and Percy were not the only writers interested in Moors, Turks and Muhammad during al-Annuri's time in London. In late 1601 or early 1602 Shakespeare began work on yet another play drawing on such characters, although closer in outlook to Dekker's play (which he may have read or seen) than Percy's (which he certainly did not). It would be set in the Mediterranean world of Ottomans, Venetians and Moors that was so familiar to a generation of Levant and Barbary Company employees and London theatregoers. Its tragic hero would contain elements of the exotic, bombastic characters in Marlowe's and Peele's plays from the 1580s and the more recent black Moors associated with Spain in plays like *Lust's Dominion*. It would rewrite *Henry V* by offering another version of the story of an ambivalent heroic warrior with suspect allegiances required to combat a powerful enemy, who is pushed to his phys-ical and emotional limits and marries outside his community. It would also return to Venice to explore what might have happened if the valiant Prince of Morocco had guessed correctly in the choice of caskets and married the noble Portia. It would be called *The Tragedy of Othello*.

Othello is generally regarded as one of Shakespeare's greatest trag-edies, ranking alongside *Hamlet*, *Macbeth* and *King Lear*, all written in a remarkable six-year burst of creativity between 1600 and 1606. It returns to Venice again, but we are no longer in the company of merchants or Jews; instead we meet the eponymous Moor, Othello, living in a Christian world at the centre of a political, romantic and military story in which he becomes both the master and the captive. It is a play in which nothing is quite what it seems. Black and white, race and sex, seeing and believing, good and evil are all subject to pitiless examination in some of Shakespeare's most intense language and dramatic action. It has been called a 'tragedy of probability', which tests the limits of what the audience is prepared to believe is true, or even likely.[42] Even its date is subject to intense speculation. The play was first performed before James I in November 1604. Recent editors have argued that Shakespeare probably began writing it within months of *Lust's Dominion* and *Mahomet and his Heaven*, during the winter of 1601–2, based on similarities with *Hamlet* (c. 1600) and *Twelfth Night* (c. 1601).

The problem of its date is complicated by its publication history. The first printed edition, entitled *The Tragedy of Othello, The Moor of Venice*, was published in 1622 in a small, pocket-sized quarto for-mat (hence its abbreviation as 'Q'). Just a year later a second edition was published in the celebrated First Folio collection ('F') in the sec-tion 'Tragedies', under the same title. However, this second edition (F) contained 3,685 lines, 160 more than the first edition (Q). At some point more than thirty passages were added to F (or alterna-tively were cut from Q then subsequently reinstated). To add to the confusion, both editions were published after Shakespeare's death in 1616, making it almost impossible to ascertain which version is clos-est to Shakespeare's original intentions, whatever they might have been. Editors are at a loss to provide conclusive evidence as to how and why these changes occurred. Some argue that Q represents Shakespeare's first version of the play, probably intended for a short-ened performance, and that F represents his revised 'second thoughts'. Others claim that the changes are the result of the inevitable corrup-tion that took place once the handwritten play-text passed through the diverse hands of compositors, proof-readers and printers in the chaotic atmosphere of printing shops, and that Q may have been a reduced version of F.[43]

The problem of the play's two versions is compounded by the per-ennial question of race. For over 300 years most Shakespeareans in the English-speaking world fixated with horror on Othello's black-ness and his seemingly 'unnatural' union with the 'fair' Desdemona, while the later twentieth century reacted with equal abhorrence to the play's apparently blatant racial slurs. As early as 1694 the histor-ian Thomas Rymer wondered why Shakespeare would write a play in which the Venetians 'will set a negro to be their general, or trust a Moor to defend them', concluding with the sneering condescension of someone used to seeing black men as servants that 'with us a black-amoor might rise to be a trumpeter; but Shakespeare would not have him less than a Lieutenant-General'.[44] Samuel Taylor Coleridge denied Othello's ethnicity altogether, claiming he 'must not be con-ceived of as a negro' because 'it would be something monstrous to conceive this beautiful Venetian girl falling in love with a veritable negro'.[45] It was only with the advent of decolonization and the rise of the African-American Civil Rights Movement that a profound reas-sessment of the play's racial politics began. Writing in 1997 the novelist Ben Okri voiced a commonly held feeling among black writ-ers that it 'hurts to watch Othello'.[46] 'If it did not begin as a play about race,' Okri argues, 'then its history has made it one.'[47]

Okri is right that Othello did not begin life as a play about race in our modern understanding of it, if the noun is defined strictly as a grouping of mankind determined by physical features (such as skin colour) or shared ethnic characteristics. This sense of the word enters the English language only in the eighteenth century. Its etymology draws on the Middle French rasse, meaning a group of people con-nected by common descent, and the Spanish raza and the Portuguese raça, both referring to lineage and genealogy.[48] This is how

Shakespeare used the word, such as when Mark Antony speaks of the 'lawful race' of Rome in *Antony and Cleopatra* (1608).[49] The crux is Shakespeare's use of 'Moor'. In *Othello*, Shakespeare exploited its dual meaning of 'Mahometan' or Muslim, and 'Maurus' or blackness. The play uses both meanings but blackness as a sign of racial difference has come to predominate for an overwhelmingly secular western audience increasingly indifferent to the word's religious associations.

Shakespeare did not invent the high-ranking Moor: like most playwrights of this period he took his stories and ideas from other writers, and however he read and learned from contemporaries like Ralph Carr, Thomas Dekker and (the least likely) William Percy, he was certainly aware that in 1601–2 Turks, Moors and Muhammads were firmly back on the Elizabethan's diplomatic, commercial and theatrical agenda. In the case of *Othello*, he drew inspiration directly from a source he had used before. The Italian Giovanni Battista Giraldi, popularly known as 'Cinthio', wrote a series of short stories known as the *Hecatommithi* (1565), which, like Boccaccio's *Decameron* (1349–52), revolve around morality tales. In Cinthio's story the character on which Shakespeare based Othello is called simply 'a Moor, a very gallant man'; his blackness is mentioned only once, there are no Turks and the tragedy is primarily domestic. The inspiration for Shakespeare's Iago is also unnamed: he is referred to simply as 'the Ensign', and only Othello's wife is given a proper name: 'Disdemona'. In Cinthio's story although the two men collude in questioning Disdemona's virtue it is the Ensign who beats her to death. Both men's deaths are only reported in the story as happening much later, Othello's following his banishment for his part in the affair, and Iago's after being tortured. Cinthio's story was a standard example of moralized tales castigating the infidelity of husbands and wives that stretched back through Boccaccio as far as Socrates. What Shakespeare brought to the story was a generation of Elizabethan England's horror and fascination with the figure of the Moor, culminating in al-Annuri's embassy.

The play's opening lines immediately set the tone of profound ambiguity towards the Moor. Iago appears, describing himself as 'his Moorship's ancient', or standard-bearer, who has been passed over for promotion by his superior, Othello. He meets the wealthy and foolish Roderigo who is in love with Desdemona, and convinces him to defame her for marrying Othello. He tells the bemused Roderigo, 'Were I the Moor, I would not be Iago. | In following him I follow but myself,' concluding, 'I am not what I am.'[50] Iago's elliptical reference to both himself and Othello begins one of Shakespeare's most troubling presentations of psychological manipulation. Iago is going to penetrate Othello's psyche in order to destroy it. He is 'not what I am', and certainly the end of the play leaves hardly any characters with an unequivocal sense of who and what they are. In a play so often now seen as being about race, Iago's line has a powerful religious dimension that none of its contemporary audience could have missed. He is the opposite of the Old Testament God, who says, 'I am that I am' (Exodus 3: 14). At this stage, although the Moor has yet to appear, the audience has already met a version of him in Iago, who is behaving rather like the 'irreligious' blackamoor, Aaron. When Shakespeare wrote *Titus Andronicus* ten years earlier he followed fashion by showing the Moor as a villainous outsider who destroys the virtuous warrior Titus. His first disturbing innovation in *Othello* was to invert these roles (perhaps in reworking aspects of Morocco in *Merchant of Venice* and Eleazer in a more recent play like *Lust's Dominion*), giving the villain's part to the Italian lieutenant and making the virtuous warrior a Moor.

Within twenty lines Iago is standing in the shadows outside the house of Desdemona's father, Brabantio, taunting him:

> Zounds, sir, you are robbed, for shame put on your gown!
> Your heart is burst, you have lost half your soul,
> Even now, very now, an old black ram
> Is tupping your white ewe! Arise, arise,
> Awake the snorting citizens with the bell
> Or else the devil will make a grandsire of you.[51]

Iago accuses the Moor – who has still not been named nor even appeared – of everything from stealing Desdemona from the paternal household to bestial sexual behaviour and representing the devil. When Brabantio demands Iago and Roderigo explain themselves, Iago imagines once more Othello and Desdemona having sex, warning of the 'monstrous' offspring that could ensue. He goads Brabantio, 'you'll have your daughter covered with a Barbary horse; you'll have your nephews neigh to you, you'll have coursers for cousins and jennets for germans!'[52] Iago uses the image of a Barbary horse to identify Othello as North African. He extends his prurient vision of miscegenation, or crossbreeding, through the animal world by drawing together popular equestrian terms to denigrate the Moor. Iago's insults are rather opaque today – 'jennets' are Spanish horses and 'coursers' were also chargers, noted for their speed and stamina – but by drawing on the aristocratic language of horse-breeding Iago attempts to appeal to Brabantio's sense of propriety. He infers that, by allowing such animals into his world, Brabantio disrupts the natural order of decorum and lineage. It is precisely this kind of insidious racism that makes Shakespeare's play so uncomfortable to watch: today this is the language of white Christian superiority that delights in mocking the black man. Driving home his point with what is by now characteristically voyeuristic pleasure, Iago says, 'your daughter and the Moor are now making the beast with two backs.'[53]

Roderigo's speech that follows (only in the 1623 Folio text and not the 1622 Quarto edition) reiterates Iago's slander and claims that Desdemona is in 'the gross clasps of a lascivious Moor'. She has:

> made a gross revolt,
> Tying her duty, beauty, wit and fortunes
> In an extravagant and wheeling stranger
> Of here and everywhere.[54]

This accusation of the Moor's 'extravagant' strangeness rather than his blackness finally stirs Brabantio into action. Without Roderigo's extra speech the audience sees Iago as a spiteful lone voice; with it, a group voice attacking the Moor begins to emerge. Despite the contradictory claims and reports being made about Othello, at this point the audience haven't even seen him. Shakespeare appears to be wrestling with how he wants it to think about the Moor before he appears, paralleling the disagreement between various factions in London about al-Annuri's presence less than a year before the play was written.

When Othello finally enters in the following scene, Iago, who intimates that Brabantio will try to discredit him in front of the Venetian

Senate, follows him. In only his second speech in the play, Othello responds grandly:

> Let him do his spite;
> My services, which I have done the signiory,
> Shall out-tongue his complaints. 'Tis yet to know –
> Which, when I know that boasting is an honour,
> I shall promulgate – I fetch my life and being
> From men of royal siege.[55]

Just like al-Annuri, Othello possesses a 'sharpness of wit and gift of pen' alongside a barely suppressed boastfulness about his royal lineage. It is a confident, almost arrogant response that proves him to be anything but a 'Barbary horse' and quite ready to 'out-tongue' and refute any charges Brabantio makes against him.

The chances are that Shakespeare had seen al-Annuri on one of his many widely reported London appearances, or during his company the Lord Chamberlain's Men's performances at Elizabeth's court during the winter of 1600–1601 when the Moroccan was locked in negotiations with Elizabeth and her advisers. When Othello is called before the Venetian Senate in the play's third scene it resembles al-Annuri's royal audiences rather than anything to be found in Cinthio. Just as Elizabeth's counsellors discussed the Moor in relation to Turkish affairs, so the duke and senators gather to respond to a serious threat to Venice's security: 'A Turkish fleet, and bearing up to Cyprus'.[56] Cinthio mentions Cyprus – the *Hecatommithi* was written before the island fell to Sultan Selim in 1573 – but not Turks. Shakespeare introduces them here as a shadowy, emblematic menace to Venetian interests in the eastern Mediterranean. As the Venetians discuss how to combat the Turkish threat, Brabantio and Othello enter. The duke then addresses Othello using his proper name for the first time in the entire play:

> Valiant Othello, we must straight employ you
> Against the general enemy Ottoman.
> [*to Brabantio*]
> I did not see you; welcome, gentle signior;
> We lack'd your counsel and your help tonight.[57]

While Othello is welcomed as 'valiant', Brabantio is initially over-looked, then reproached for his absence from important decisions of state. All talk of Othello's skin colour recedes: he is a 'valiant' and 'brave' military leader that the Venetians need to defend themselves against the Turks. At this moment Othello looks and sounds like the Prince of Morocco, a noble Moor who has successfully wooed and married his equivalent of Portia and is now waving his scimitar and promising to go into battle once more against the Turks. Shakespeare now had versions of both kinds of Moor on stage: the diabolical blackamoor Aaron reborn in the guise of Iago, and the chivalric Moroccan prince recast as the exotic mercenary Othello, but whose name sounds uncomfortably close to the Ottomans he must confront in defence of his adopted homeland.

However, the anxieties aroused by Othello are hard to dispel. Bra-bantio accuses him of witchcraft to entrap Desdemona, and when asked to explain himself, Othello delivers what he promised Iago, an orator-ical *tour de force* designed to 'out-tongue' Brabantio's complaints:

> Her father loved me, oft invited me,
> Still questioned me the story of my life
> From year to year – the battles, sieges, fortunes
> That I have passed.
> I ran it through, even from my boyish days
> To the very moment that he bade me tell it,
> Wherein I spake of most disastrous chances,
> Of moving accidents by flood and field,
> Of hair-breadth scapes i' th' imminent deadly breach,
> Of being taken by the insolent foe
> And sold to slavery; of my redemption thence
> And portance in my traveller's history:
> Wherein of antres vast and deserts idle,
> Rough quarries, rocks and hills whose heads touch heaven
> It was my hint to speak – such was my process –
> And of the cannibals that each other eat,
> The Anthropophagi and men whose heads
> Do grow beneath their shoulders. This to hear
> Would Desdemona seriously incline.[58]

The speech has shades of Tamburlaine in its high-flown rhetoric – the young Othello even sounds as though he could have fought for the Scythian emperor – but Shakespeare uses it to tease the audience with an explanation of how Othello came to be in Venice. Othello recounts stories of how he was invited into the household – rather like his dramatic predecessors Aaron and Morocco – to convey his life as a boy-soldier (from the age of seven, as he reminds the senators). He tells exotic tales of his travels, including epic battles and encounters with the monstrous races of anthropophagi (cannibals) and headless monsters that enthral Desdemona. It is precisely these references that editors use to date the play some time after 1601, when Philemon Holland published his English translation of Pliny's *Historie of the World*, with its stories of Ethiopian cannibals and 'Blemmyes', with their mouth and eyes in their chest. But if Shakespeare had read the fantastical tales of Africa in Pliny, then he could also have heard the reports of warfare, slavery and vast wealth being reported by English travellers and diplomats like Jasper Thomson and his stories of gold, unicorns, dwarfs and concubines.

What is particularly striking about Othello's speech is his description of how he ended up in Venice. We assume that as a Moor he grows up in Morocco (or what Shakespeare calls 'Mauretania' later in the play), but his childhood is a blank. He claims to have been captured 'by the insolent foe', to have been sold into slavery and then to have experienced some form of 'redemption'. Intriguingly for the Elizabethans 'redemption' meant both 'delivered from sin' and 'freed from slavery': Othello is bought, set free and offered salvation through the sacrament of baptism to become the first Christian Moor on the Elizabethan stage. This would suggest that the 'insolent foe' is the Turk who captured and sold Othello as a galley slave before Christians rescued and converted him. What he does not say is if he was born a Muslim, or a pagan, like many Berbers in sixteenth-century Mauretania. Whatever the case, the audience is presented with a character who moves with suspicious ease from one religion to another. What is the probability, Shakespeare seems to ask, that having turned away from one religion, Othello might just as easily embrace another?

There were various similarly ambiguous examples of conversion from which Shakespeare could draw his inspiration, the most recent being that of Chinano the Turk's baptism at St Katharine's Church in 1586 (discussed in chapter 6). There was also the case of al-Hasan ibn Muhammad ibn Ahmad al-Wazzan, also known as Leo Africanus. It was al-Wazzan's book *The Geographical Historie of Africa* that had been published in English in November 1600 to coincide with Elizabeth's Accession Day celebrations and the arrival of al-Annuri's Moroccan embassy. If, as many believe, Shakespeare read al-Wazzan's book, he would have discovered that many inhabitants of Mauretania were categorized as 'pagans' as well as Muslims. Like Othello, al-Wazzan had converted to Christianity after being captured by Christian pirates while returning to Fez from Cairo in 1518. Like Othello his birth name was discarded in favour of a Christian name – Leo Africanus – but only al-Wazzan knew how far his baptism in Rome in 1520 was genuine, coerced or a strategic decision that lay somewhere in between the two. Just seven years later he had returned to North Africa where he seems to have reverted to Islam.[59] Then there was al-Annuri, another Moor around whose identity revolved contradictory suppositions, someone who spoke well and thought much of himself, but who was either from Fez, and therefore not a 'true' Sa'adian Moroccan, or a Muslim-born Morisco, forcibly converted to Christianity who had reverted to Islam under al-Mansur and had been invited to fight with English Protestants against Spanish Catholics. Whatever his exact origins, al-Annuri was just another example of how religious conversion was accepted as part of the fabric of imperial and diplomatic business.

Listening to Othello's enigmatic yet captivating tales of romance, monsters and warfare, the duke is forced to admit, 'I think this tale would win my daughter too.' Shakespeare gives his 'extravagant' stranger a history so that he stands before us, unlike Iago, as he is and declares: 'This only is the witchcraft I have used.'[60] With Brabantio defeated, Othello agrees to travel to Cyprus to lead the 'war against the Ottomites'. When Desdemona pleads successfully to travel with her new husband, Brabantio walks out, delivering the valedictory lines:

> Look to her, Moor, if thou hast eyes to see:
> She has deceived her father, and may thee.[61]

By the close of the first act, with Othello bound for Cyprus, the play looks as though it might end as a comedy. Like so many of Shakespeare's early comedies, this play has two apparently mismatched lovers facing the wrath of a father and the machinations of a malcontent character intent on ruining the relationship. By retreating to another world, like a forest or an island, the ensuing conflict and chaos is resolved and everyone is reconciled. But in *Othello*, as soon as the action moves to Cyprus, the play swerves away from comedy and irrevocably towards tragedy.

Upon landing in Cyprus, an advanced party of Venetians discover that a 'desperate tempest hath so banged the Turks | That their designment halts' and their fleet is scattered. Othello arrives and announces with grandiloquent complacency 'our wars are done, the Turks are drowned'.[62] It seems as though the Turkish threat was just an awkward plot device to get the protagonists to Cyprus, but Shakespeare transforms the Turk gradually from a military into a more insidious psychic threat. When Iago engineers a drunken brawl between Roderigo and the lieutenant Michael Cassio, Othello intervenes, horrified at the Christian divisions in contrast to the famed Turkish military discipline:

> Are we turned Turks, and to ourselves do that
> Which heaven hath forbid the Ottomites?
> For Christian shame, put by this barbarous brawl.[63]

The idea was familiar to many who knew Erasmus' warning in his essay 'On the War against the Turks': that if Christians wanted to eradicate the Turk they must first expel from their hearts the 'Turkish' traits of ambition, anger, hatred and envy. Yet these are precisely the vices that Iago has unleashed in Cyprus and which he cultivates in Othello as he tries to persuade him that Desdemona has been unfaithful with Cassio.

As Othello begins to accept this 'monstrous' deception, he and Iago become associated increasingly with the Turks as cruel and deceitful. The audience know from early on in the play that Iago will destroy Othello because his name is the Spanish for James. St James, or Santiago, is the patron saint of Spain, who as we have seen is popularly known as Matamoros – the 'Moor-slayer'.[64] Iago has also flirted with the idea that he too might turn Turk, joking with his wife Emilia and

Desdemona that women are sexually duplicitous 'or else I am a Turk'.[65] Othello also invites the comparison. Once Iago has convinced him of Desdemona's adultery, they make a pact to kill her which Iago fears Othello will renounce. The geographical grandeur of Othello's response is reminiscent of Tamburlaine and returns yet again to the Turks:

> Never, Iago. Like to the Pontic sea
> Whose icy current and compulsive course
> Ne'er feels retiring ebb, but keeps due on
> To the Propontic and the Hellespont,
> Even so my bloody thoughts with violent pace
> Shall ne'er look back, ne'er ebb to humble love
> Till that a capable and wide revenge
> Swallow them up.[66]

Othello's vengeance is as irreversible as the sea flowing into the ocean, but the one he chooses is not accidental. The Pontic or Black Sea flows past Constantinople into the Propontic or Marmara Sea before debouching into the Aegean via the Hellespont or Dardanelles. By associating him with the topography of the Ottoman Empire, Shakespeare adds another layer to Othello's already complex identity: Moor, convert, pagan, revert and finally murderous raging Turk.

Even as Othello starts to behave like an Ottoman Turk, Desdemona travels in the opposite direction, until she makes a final extraordinary identification with Barbary. In the fourth act Othello accuses Desdemona publicly of infidelity and hits her before sending her to her bedchamber with her serving woman Emilia, Iago's wife. In one of the most poignant and intimate scenes in the whole play, known as the 'Willow Song' scene, Desdemona is undressed for bed by Emilia, and they discuss marriage and infidelity. Emilia attacks Othello for slandering Desdemona, but Desdemona defends him, saying 'my love doth so approve him'[67] that she forgives his anger. Suddenly she remembers a song from her childhood, the 'Willow Song', an old Tudor refrain about a spurned, doomed lover:

> My mother had a maid called Barbary:
> She was in love, and he she loved proved mad
> And did forsake her. She had a song of 'willow',

An old thing 'twas, but it expressed her fortune
And she died singing it. That song tonight
Will not go from my mind. I have much to do,
But to go hang my head all at one side,
And sing it like poor Barbary.[68]

She starts to sing the song of Barbary's abandonment by her lover but as she comes to the end of the first verse she misremembers its last line: 'Let nobody blame him, his scorn I approve – | Nay, that's not next.'[69] It is one of the play's most devastating moments: Desdemona admits she loves Othello so much she even approves of his public humiliation of her reputation, even though she has done nothing wrong. She alters the song to fit her own circumstances, not only mistaking the last line but also changing the gender of the spurned lover from male to female.[70] For just a moment she becomes her mother's Barbary maid. 'Barbary' suggests the woman came from Barbary, a loyal servant (or possibly slave) of the Venetian state without her birth name – not unlike Othello, the Moor of Venice, and the Barbary horse of Iago's insults. Desdemona identifies herself as a Barbary maid while Othello, like Henry V, has been tempted to turn Turk. They have both undergone a 'monstrous' and irrevocable metamorphosis, and within hours both will be dead.

Having murdered Desdemona and discovered his terrible mistake, Othello turns on the 'demi-devil' Iago, to ask why he 'ensnared my soul and body'.[71] In one of the most chilling couplets uttered by any of Shakespeare's villains, Iago also turns Turk, describing himself as a mute slave which evokes immediate associations with the Ottomans:

Demand me nothing. What you know, you know.
From this time forth I never will speak word.[72]

He never speaks again and is led off to be tortured; like another 'demi-devil', his predecessor Aaron, death is too good for him.

Having realized the tragedy of his situation, Othello prepares to take his own life, but not before he undergoes one final shocking transformation. As the Venetians try to arrest him, he ends where he began, telling a story:

Soft you; a word or two before you go.
I have done the state some service, and they know't.
No more of that. I pray you, in your letters,
When you shall these unlucky deeds relate,
Speak of me as I am; nothing extenuate,
Nor set down aught in malice. Then must you speak
Of one that loved not wisely but too well;
Of one not easily jealous, but being wrought,
Perplexed in the extreme; of one whose hand,
Like the base Indian, threw a pearl away
Richer than all his tribe; of one whose subdued eyes,
Albeit unused to the melting mood,
Drop tears as fast as the Arabian trees
Their medicinal gum. Set you down this,
And say besides that in Aleppo once,
Where a malignant and a turbaned Turk
Beat a Venetian and traduced the state,
I took by th' throat the circumcised dog
And smote him – thus!
He stabs himself.[73]

Ever the fabulist, Othello asks that the Venetian authorities be told one last story of his exploits as a loyal servant of the state. It includes his naive deception at the hands of Iago, and how he lost the precious 'pearl' Desdemona, and that his loyalty is best remembered by recounting the time he killed a Turk in Aleppo for slandering Venice.

Nowhere in this speech does Othello mention his blackness or his Christianity. Instead, he compares himself first to an Indian, and then to a Turk. Both comparisons are riddled with contradictions. His behaviour towards Desdemona is like that of an Indian who threw away a pearl richer than all his tribe. 'Indian' is the word used in the 1622 Quarto version of the play, but the 1623 Folio version has 'Iudean'. It is a crux that goes to the heart of who Othello is. Pliny spoke of the wealth of India and the supposed ignorance of its inhabitants who discarded pearls, though if Shakespeare meant to use 'Indian' here it could also refer to Native American Indians. Most modern editors choose the Quarto's 'Indian', even though when confronted with such cruxes elsewhere their default position is to choose the Folio's version, as it is seen as the 'better', later and longest text. Racially it seems obvious to align the Moor with an Indian rather than a 'Iudean', or Jew. But, as we have seen, the Elizabethans were convinced that Jews and Muslims (including Moors) were as one in refusing to accept Jesus as the Son of God. The 'Iudean' of the Folio could refer to either Judas Iscariot's betrayal of Christ or Herod's execution of his wife Mariamne, both of which make absolute sense as metaphors for Othello's behaviour.[74] Which was correct? Did Shakespeare change his mind in revising his text, or did someone else quietly amend it? We will probably never know, but it is striking that this irresolvable crux captures Othello's overdetermined character, part Muslim, Christian, Jew and even pagan.

It is a conflation that finds its most extraordinary conclusion in the final lines. Othello takes us to Aleppo, the Syrian city where Anthony Jenkinson first met Sultan Süleyman the Magnificent fifty years before the play was written, where al-Annuri had claimed he was heading just the previous year, and which today has a very different tragic resonance. Othello has travelled a long way eastwards from his homeland in Barbary, via Venice and Cyprus deep into the Ottoman Hellespont, Arabia and its 'medicinal' trees, and finally Syria. The Turk he kills is 'turbaned' and 'circumcised', surely a sign that these are not attributes that Othello shares. If he is not circumcised then surely he cannot have been born or converted into the Muslim faith. Nor is he described as sharing close sartorial affinities with the ostentatiously turbaned al-Annuri. But in acting out his stabbing of the Turk, Othello enacts the most remarkable moment of tragic self-division in all of Shakespeare. He has been interpreted as the loyal Christian soldier, atoning for his sins by defending Venice against the Turk and killing the heresy within himself, or as finally embracing his true barbarism as a demonic, murderous apostate, who becomes the raging, violent Turk, the culmination of a generation of plays depicting the Ottomans. He is of course both simultaneously: a profoundly ambivalent figure who embodies so much of Elizabethan England's contradictory relations with the Islamic world. Here, in the split second of Othello saying 'thus', Othello becomes a Turk. The only one ever to grace a Shakespeare play appears on stage for a moment and then exits with the self-inflicted blow that kills Othello the Moor–Christian–Pagan–Turk–Jew of Venice.

Othello was the culmination of over ten years of the Elizabethan theatre's fascination with Turks and Moors. Just two years earlier Shakespeare had written *Hamlet*, a revenge tragedy that eclipsed all previous examples and redefined the genre. Othello did something similar in combining every facet of the Muslim characters that had appeared on the stage up to that point. It drew on the bombast of Tamburlaine, the evil of Aaron, the melancholic grandeur of the Prince of Morocco and the raging Turk buried deep within Henry V. The audience, then as now, are not asked to sympathize with Othello, but instead to delight guiltily in the dreadful prejudices, stereotypes and violent fantasies unleashed by this most ambivalent of characters and his nemesis Iago, safe in the knowledge that it was, after all, just a performance.

Although he could not have known it, Shakespeare had written *Othello* at the zenith of Elizabethan England's relationship with the Muslim world, which was about to come to an abrupt end. Queen Elizabeth never saw the play. She died on 24 March 1603 aged sixty-nine, and was succeeded by the Stuart king James I. James, guided by Robert Cecil, opened negotiations for peace with Catholic Spain almost immediately to bring England back into the economic and political life of Europe after half a century of self-imposed exile. In the summer of 1604 another embassy arrived from the south, but this time it was Spanish, and Catholic. In August Spanish and English diplomats signed the Treaty of London, ending nineteen years of war between the two kingdoms. It was a tacit acknowledgement – albeit with grave circumspection – of Protestant England's right to exist within Christian Europe. King James had ended England's diplomatic isolation from the rest of Europe and the need for English alliances with Muslim kingdoms to act as a bulwark against Spain's religious and imperial menace. In the same month the Moroccan ruler Mulay Ahmed al-Mansur died of the plague, and his kingdom descended into a bloody civil war between his three sons that temporarily put an end to all diplomatic and commercial relations with England. Elizabeth's other great Muslim ally Sultan Mehmed III had died of a sudden heart attack in December 1603. As the Spanish and English sat down at Somerset House to agree the Treaty of London, the only visible sign that remained of the Anglo-Ottoman alliance was the Turkey carpet that covered the table between them.

On 1 November 1604 James and his new royal court watched the first recorded production of *Othello* at the Banqueting House in Whitehall. It is one of the play's many paradoxes that a king called James saw his villainous namesake destroying a Moor, but perhaps James took comfort from watching Othello kill the circumcised and turbaned Turk. Nine years earlier, while king of Scotland, James had written a rather indifferent poem called 'Lepanto'. It celebrated the Holy League victory in 1571:

> Which fought was in Lepanto's gulf,
> Betwixt the baptized race
> And circumcised turban'd Turks.[75]

The new king had no interest in pursuing alliances with the Moors or what he elsewhere called the 'faithless Turks'. The Elizabethan age was over, and with it England's alliance with the Islamic world.

Epilogue

By the time Shakespeare prepared to say farewell to the London stage and retire to Stratford in 1611, the English were leading figures in the eastern Mediterranean trade even though King James had turned away from military and diplomatic alliances with Islamic rulers. The Levant Company was exporting English goods worth £250,000 per annum to Turkey, prompting one of its merchants, Sir Lewis Roberts, to write that the company had 'grown to that height that (without comparison) it is the most flourishing and beneficial company to the commonwealth of any in England'.[1] The company was beginning to face competition from a newer joint-stock initiative. The East India Company had been awarded its royal charter in December 1600 – during al-Annuri's time in London – with the aim of trading throughout the vast emporium of the Indian and Pacific oceans, stretching eastwards from the Cape of Good Hope to the Magellan Straits. By the 1630s the company was exporting over £100,000 of bullion and importing more than £1 million's worth of pepper and spices with a variety of trading communities of different religions throughout India and the Indonesian archipelago.

Like the Levant Company, the East India Company did not involve itself in its early years in the kind of diplomatic or military state policy that had led the Elizabethans into such close alliances with Muslim rulers. James's rapprochement with Spain brought him into closer alignment with the rest of Europe in opposing Ottoman expansion, just at the time the Turks disengaged from Europe as they became more preoccupied with Persian threats to their eastern borders. The new Stuart king's delusions of grandeur led him to believe that his destiny was to unify Christendom, which resulted in peace with Spain and correspondence with leading figures in the Greek Orthodox Church after 1615 to propose a Christian union with the Church of England. It can have done little to ingratiate him with the new Ottoman sultan Ahmed I.[2] In direct contrast to Elizabeth's attempts to draw the Ottomans into war with Spain in the 1580s, James had no interest in appealing to them for military assistance during the central European conflict of the Thirty Years' War (1618–48) that dogged the later years of his reign thanks to his decision in 1613 to marry his eldest daughter Elizabeth Stuart to Frederick V, Elector Palatine and a claimant to the Bohemian crown. Besides, James's interests had been drawn westwards to the New World of the Americas. In 1606 he had sanctioned the creation of the Virginia Company, a new joint-stock initiative aimed at settling English colonies on the north-east coast of America. The company could hardly compete with the Spanish domination of the Americas, but it represented the beginnings of a global dimension to English foreign and commercial policy, one that was no longer centred on the Mediterranean and Muslim world.

This geopolitical shift can be discerned in the drama of the period. Shakespeare never again portrayed Moors and Turks with the detail and intensity of the plays from *Henry VI* to *Othello*. However, he still had something to say about the growing scale and plight of migrants and refugees in early seventeenth-century London. Some time around 1603–4 he was involved in drafting revisions to a play written by several other playwrights (including Thomas Dekker) called *Sir Thomas More*, which dramatized the life and times of Henry VIII's famous councillor.[3] Scene 6 is now believed to have been drafted by Shakespeare, and is the only surviving example of the author's handwriting the text of a play. It is a response to the infamous 'May Day' riots that took place in 1517, when English artisans attacked foreign residents – or in the language of the time 'strangers' or 'aliens' – residents they blamed for monopolizing trade and taking 'local' jobs. Such riots had taken place throughout London in the sixteenth century, some as recently as the early 1590s, so it was a highly sensitive and topical subject (as it has become once more today). In scene 6 Shakespeare recreates the moment More tries to calm the rioters, who demand 'the removing of the strangers', to which he responds:

> Grant them removed, and grant that this your noise
> Hath chid down all the majesty of England.
> Imagine that you see the wretched strangers,
> Their babies at their backs, with their poor luggage,
> Plodding to th' ports and coasts for transportation,
> And that you sit as kings in your desires,
> Authority quite silenced by your brawl,
> And you in ruff of your opinions clothed;
> What had you got? I'll tell you: you had taught
> How insolence and strong hand should prevail,
> How order should be quelled. And by this pattern
> Not one of you should live an aged man;
> For other ruffians, as their fancies wrought,
> With self same hand, self reasons, and self right,
> Would shark on you, and men like ravenous fishes,
> Would feed on one another.[4]

It is a powerful and emotive rejection of xenophobia, arguing that if mob rule triumphs over the dispossessed and the rule of law, it will unleash a vicious and anarchic individualism where everyone will 'feed' on one another. To clinch his point, More asks the rioters what might happen if their roles were reversed with those of the strangers, and they found themselves seeking asylum:

> Say now the king,
> As he is clement if th' offender mourn,
> Should so much come too short of your great trespass
> As but to banish you: whither would you go?
> What country, by the nature of your error,
> Should give you harbour? Go you to France or Flanders,
> To any German province, Spain or Portugal,
> Nay, anywhere that not adheres to England:
> Why, you must needs be strangers. Would you be pleased
> To find a nation of such barbarous temper
> That, breaking out in hideous violence,
> Would not afford you an abode on earth,
> Whet their detested knives against your throats,
> Spurn you like dogs, and like as if that God

Owed not nor made not you, nor that the elements
Were not all appropriate to your comforts
But chartered unto them? What would you think
To be thus used? This is the strangers' case,
And this your mountainish inhumanity.[5]

More's speech works and the rioters disperse. His compassionate plea for toleration of aliens and strangers might seem inconsistent coming from a playwright who seemed to relish identifying and then expelling outsiders from his plays, including many of those discussed in the course of this book, from Aaron and the Prince of Morocco to Shylock and Othello. But perhaps buried within their dramas is an abiding sympathy for toleration and reconciliation that finds its clearest expression in this fragment from another play.[6] It is surely one of the reasons why they continue to hold our attention 400 years later.

The desire for reconciliation can be found in a play Shakespeare wrote towards the end of his career. Around 1611 he returned to the Mediterranean a final time for the setting of one of his last plays: *The Tempest*. The play opens on board a storm-tossed ship carrying Alonso, King of Naples, and Antonio, Duke of Milan, with other members of a wedding party; they are returning to Italy after marrying Alonso's daughter Claribel to the unnamed African King of Tunis. They are shipwrecked on an island somewhere between Tunis and Naples, where Antonio's deposed brother Prospero had been exiled with his daughter Miranda. Having escaped from his usurping brother, Prospero is washed up on the island with his young daughter and all the books he could salvage from his library. Tutored in the arts of magic, Prospero establishes a way of life on the island with his 'spirit' Ariel[7] and his one-time companion, now slave, Caliban. But the island has a longer history: Ariel has been imprisoned in a cloven pine by the island's previous resident, the 'damn'd witch'[8] Sycorax, mother of Caliban. With the witch gone and Ariel released, the 'bare isle' is governed by Prospero and inhabited by his daughter, his slave and his ethereal assistant.

For centuries, critics have debated the location of Prospero's island, some placing it in what Ariel calls 'the Mediterranean float [sea]', others noting that in the same speech he speaks of 'the still vexed Bermudas'.[9] This, alongside Caliban's apparent similarity to Native Americans has led many scholars (mostly Americans) to assume that the play is set in the 'brave new world' (5.1.186) of the Americas. Such interpretations point to the reports from the recently established Jamestown colony in Virginia where in 1609 a fleet of English ships had been sent to reinforce the beleaguered English settlement. The fleet was struck by storms and was shipwrecked in the Bermudas, but miraculously everyone survived and managed to reach Jamestown.

Even if Shakespeare had read such reports, his play remained rooted in the myths and histories of the Mediterranean world, past and present. He reminds his audience that Caliban's mother was born 'in Algiers',[10] an Ottoman stronghold throughout the late sixteenth and seventeenth centuries. One of Shakespeare's sources for the story was the Roman poet Virgil's classical epic of the foundation of Rome, the *Aeneid*, in which its hero, Aeneas, travels from Troy to Rome via Carthage where he meets its queen, Dido. The play's courtiers even quibble over Dido's and classical Carthage's location in relation to sixteenth-century Tunis. One of them insists, 'This Tunis, sir, was Carthage,'[11] a dispute that also serves to remind the audience of the transitory nature of empire. As in Virgil's poem, Shakespeare imagines the gulf between North Africa and Europe as vast. The seaborne crossing between Tunis and Naples is less than 370 miles, but Claribel, the 'Queen of Tunis', is described as 'she that dwells | Ten leagues beyond man's life',[12] in Muslim North Africa. One of Alonso's courtiers accuses him of failing to marry his daughter off to a European prince, 'But rather lose her to an African'.[13] Once again, Shakespeare returns to a story of Christian women – first Portia, then Desdemona, finally Claribel – being offered in marriage to North African men – the Prince of Morocco, Othello, now the King of Tunis. In *The Tempest*, the far away becomes near at hand as the various dreams of colonization, interracial marriage, republicanism and revolution are rehearsed through the characters as they arrive or reflect on this 'desolate isle'.

But in this play Claribel, the King of Tunis and the Algerian witch Sycorax remain far away, and never appear on stage. Yet the rich potential of the island's location and history remain buried in its many layers of meaning. The stories of trade, and the threats of privateering, piracy, enslavement and conversion that affected thousands of English men, women and even children throughout the Mediterranean as it was being performed in London are almost completely silenced. Only a whisper can be heard in the implied geographies and histories of Ariel, Algiers, Caliban, Tunis, Naples and Bermuda. The geography of *The Tempest* is only relevant insofar as it is labelled self-consciously as irrelevant: the island is nowhere and anywhere, a utopia in the Greek sense of the terms *eu-topos* and *ou-topos*, meaning both 'good place' and 'nowhere'. Shakespeare understood that by 1611 King James's foreign and economic policy left Jacobean England looking east *and* west, gazing backwards to the Mediterranean 'Old World' of Greece, Rome, Spain and the Ottoman Empire, and forward to the Atlantic 'New World' of the Americas. His play uses this new global awareness to tell a story of uncertain habitation and conflicted identity, filtered through the layered geographical history of the Mediterranean.

The Tempest provides a fitting conclusion to the history of Elizabethan England's relations with the Islamic world. Shakespeare had grown up under a regime that, for the political and religious reasons described in the course of this book, found that its isolation from much of Catholic Europe propelled it into alliances with Muslim rulers from places as diverse as Marrakesh, Algiers, Tunis, Constantinople, Qazvin and Isfahan. With the accession of King James, this policy came to an abrupt end, and with it a tradition of representing formidable, eloquent Turks, Moors and Persians on the Elizabethan stage. They would be reinvented in a different key by a new generation of Jacobean playwrights. As we have seen, the Sherleys had already been given their own play, *The Travailes of the Three English Brothers*, first performed at the Curtain Theatre in 1607. Robert Daborne was at work on *A Christian Turned Turk* (1612), the story of the English pirate and Muslim convert John Ward who took the name Yusuf Reis and lived out his life in Tunis in opulent luxury. In 1623 Philip Massinger premiered his tragicomedy *The Renegado*, also set in the privateering capital of Tunis, where Christian and renegade Italians flee the temptations of the Muslim court to return to Italy. Such plays responded to what were by this time reports of thousands of Englishmen and women living and working in the Mediterranean, some captives, others converts (willing or forced) to Islam. But the preoccupations of their authors were not those of Marlowe, Peele and Shakespeare; instead their interests were primarily historical, their tone comical, and their aim pure entertainment, lacking the urgent topicality of the 1590s and the fear that Protestant England could at any moment be invaded – and more likely by Catholic than by Muslim forces. The Islamic world was just one of many within the emerging global economy with which the Jacobeans found themselves entangled, with now the threat – or hope – of a religious and political rapprochement between Protestants and Muslims a thing of the past.

As if to emphasize this shift, in 1632 the London draper Thomas Adams endowed the first English professorship in Arabic at Cambridge University for 'the good service of the King and State in our commerce with those Eastern nations, and in God's good time to the enlarging of the borders of the Church, and propagation of Christian religion to them who now sit in darkness'.[14] In 1636 Oxford followed suit when Archbishop William Laud, then Chancellor of the University, appointed Edward Pococke, an English chaplain working in Aleppo, as the first Laudian Professor of Arabic (it is a post that still exists, and was recently filled by a woman for the first time in its history).[15] In 1649 the first English translation of the Qur'an was published, entitled *The Alcoran of Mahomet*, based on André du Ryer's French edition, *L'Alcoran de Mahomet translaté d'arabe en françois*.[16] The Arabic-speaking Islamic world became the subject of scholarly study that promised (though did not always manage) to dispel the fantasies, misconceptions and prejudices which had driven English perceptions of the subject for centuries and which were so rich a resource for Shakespeare and his contemporaries. England would now try to contain the Islamic world through orientalist scholarship and the painstaking study of philology, archaeology and comparative religion.

Scholarly endeavour was aided by political disengagement. The long, slow decline of the Ottoman Empire and its withdrawal from western Europe's borders from the end of the seventeenth century enabled European scholars to recreate the 'orient' anew; it became an exotic, sensuous world that was also regarded as despotic and backward, where Europeans, including the English, needed to impose order, rationality and enlightenment (though only on their own terms). The orient isle of Elizabethan England, for so long almost a confederate of the Islamic world, became an island of orientalism, replacing one set of myths and misconceptions of Islam with another, obscured by the veneer of western intellectual enquiry. Over time, England's early relations with Islam were quietly forgotten as the grander, more memorable fables of imperialism and orientalism prevailed. But that is part of another era's history.

The story told in this book is one of a much longer connection between England and the Islamic world, one that emerged out of a very specific set of circumstances during the European Reformation. English history still tends to view the Elizabethan period as defined by the timeless rhythms of agrarian Anglo-Saxon traditions, ethnically pure and exclusively white. But, as I hope this book has shown, there are other aspects to this island's national story that involve other cultures, and in the Elizabethan period one of them was Islam; to occlude the role Islam played in this past only diminishes its history. Now, when much is made of the 'clash of civilizations' between Islam and Christianity, it is also timely to remember that the roots of the connections between the two faiths are much deeper and more entangled than many contemporary commentators (liberal or otherwise) seem to appreciate, and that in the sixteenth century Islamic empires like those of the Ottomans far surpassed the power and influence of a small and relatively insignificant state like Elizabethan England in their military power, political organization and commercial reach. It turns out that Islam in all its manifestations – imperial, military, cultural, theological and commercial – is part of the national story of England. One way of encouraging tolerance and inclusiveness at a time when both are in short supply is to show both Muslim and Christian communities how, over four centuries ago, absolute theological belief often yielded to strategic considerations, political pressures and the pursuit of wealth. In a period of volatile and shifting political and religious allegiances, Muslims and Christians were forced to find a common language of messy and uneasy coexistence, regardless of the official injunctions of their faith. Despite the sometimes intemperate religious rhetoric, the conflict between Christian Europe and the Islamic world was then, as now, defined as much by the struggle for power and precedence as by theology. This story is part of the heritage of Christians, Muslims and any others who call themselves English.

Today England is a multicultural society, with a significant community of Muslim believers. Developments over the past half-century, intensified by recent international events, require the country to confront once more the question of its relations with Islam, although they are very different to those experienced by the Elizabethans, when mass migration and the concept of multiculturalism were almost non-existent. The impetus towards cultural integration that (mostly) followed the mass immigration of various communities into Britain as its empire collapsed in the mid-twentieth century, including Muslim communities from South Asia, is now being questioned as politicians and the media of various persuasions accuse British Muslims of failure to assimilate into the national culture. Born in Bradford in the late 1960s, I went to school in Leeds with Muslims, Hindus and Sikhs and we hardly ever spoke about religious belief and sectarian divisions as we played and learned together. It was not a multicultural idyll, but neither was it defined by theological absolutes. This was my experience of Englishness, and I realize now that it partly explains why I wrote this book. If what I have written makes a small contribution to understanding the long and often difficult history of connections between Islam and England, then it will have been worth the while.

Notes

ABBEVIATIONS USED IN THE NOTES

APC	*Acts of the Privy Council*
Castries	Henri de Castries et al. (eds.), *Sources inédites pour l'histoire du Maroc* (Paris, 1905–65), 26 vols.
CP	Cecil Papers at Hatfield House, Hertfordshire
CSPD	*Calendar of State Papers, Domestic*
CSPF	*Calendar of State Papers, Foreign*
CSPS	*Calendar of State Papers, Spain*
CSPV	*Calendar of State Papers, Venice*
Hakluyt	Richard Hakluyt, *The Principal Navigations, Voyages, Traffiques and Discoveries of the English Nation* (Everyman's Library, J. M. Dent, London, 1907), 7 vols.
LP	*Letters and Papers, Foreign and Domestic, Henry VIII*
ODNB	*Oxford Dictionary of National Biography*
OED Online	*Oxford English Dictionary*
TNA	The National Archives of the UK

All the official government records and reference books listed above are available online.

All references to Shakespeare's plays (with the exception of *Othello*) are taken from Stephen Greenblatt et al. (eds.), *The Norton Shakespeare* (W. W. Norton, New York, 1997, 1st edn).

INTRODUCTION: THE AMBASSADOR ARRIVES

1. John Stow, *Annales, or a Generale Chronicle of England* (John Windet, London, 1603), p. 1405.

2. Paul Hentzner, *Paul Hentzner's Travels in England, During the Reign of Queen Elizabeth*, trans. Horace Walpole (Edward Jeffery, London, 1797), p. 34.

3. Castries, vol. 2, p. 187.

4. Sir Henry Sydney, *Letters and Memorials of State*, 2 vols. (Arthur Collins, London, 1746), vol. 2, p. 211.

5. Quoted in Bernard Harris, 'A Portrait of a Moor', in Catherine M. S. Alexander and Stanley Wells (eds.), *Shakespeare and Race* (Cambridge University Press, Cambridge, 2000), pp. 23–36: p. 28.

6. Sydney, *Letters and Memorials*, vol. 2, p. 212.

7. Ibid.

8. Quoted in Harris, 'Portrait', p. 29.

9. Sydney, *Letters and Memorials*, p. 212.

10. Ibid., p. 214.

11. Castries, vol. 2, p. 178.

12. Ibid., pp. 178–9.

13. Edward Hall, *Hall's Chronicle: Containing the History of England during the reign of Henry the Fourth, and the succeeding Monarchs, to the end of the reign of Henry the Eighth* (British Museum, London, 1809), p. 513.

14. Miriam Jacobson, *Barbarous Antiquity: Reorienting the Past in the Poetry of Early Modern England* (University of Pennsylvania Press, Philadelphia, 2014), pp. 2–4.

15. See 'Muslim, n. and adj.', OED Online.

16. See 'Islam, n.', OED Online.

17. *A Geographical Historie of Africa, written in Arabicke and Italian by Iohn Leo a More, borne in Granada, and brought vp in Barbarie* (London, 1600), sig. A2.

18. Richard Knolles, *The General Historie of the Turkes, from the first beginning of that Nation to the rising of the Othoman Familie* (London, 1603), sig. B47.

19. John Wright (ed.), *The Works of Lord Byron ... and his Life* (by Thomas Moore), 14 vols. (John Murray, London, 1832), vol. 2, p. 7.

20. Samuel Johnson, 'A criticism on the English historians', *Rambler*, no. 122, 18 May 1751.

21. Stow, *Annales*, p. 791.

22. For varying estimates and definitions see Mark Hutchings, 'The "Turk Phenomenon" and the Repertory of the Late Elizabethan Playhouse', *Early Modern Literary* Studies, 16 (2007), pp. 1–39. Jonathan Burton has identified over sixty dramatic works with Islamic themes, charac-

ters or locations. Burton, *Traffic and Turning: Islam and English Drama, 1579–1624* (University of Delaware Press, Newark, DE, 2005), pp. 257–8.

23. *Othello*, 1.1.135. This and all subsequent references to the play are taken from E. A. J. Honigmann (ed.), *Othello* (Arden, Thomas Nelson, Walton-on-Thames, 1997).
24. Ibid., 1.3.140.
25. Ibid., 1.3.133–4.
26. John Ayre (ed.), *The Early Works of Thomas Becon* (Cambridge University Press, Cambridge, 1843), p. 239.
27. Quoted in Noel Malcolm, 'Positive Views of Islam and of Ottoman Rule in the Sixteenth Century: The Case of Jean Bodin', in Anna Contadini and Claire Norton (eds.), *The Renaissance and the Ottoman World* (Ashgate, Farnham, 2013), pp. 197–220: p. 212.
28. *Richard II*, 2.1.40.

CHAPTER I: CONQUERING TUNIS

1. CSPS, vol. 13: 1554–1558, no. 60, p. 49.
2. John Elder, 'The Copy of a Letter Sent into Scotland, of the Arrival and Landing, and Most Notable Marriage of the Most Illustrious Prince, Philip of Spain', in J. G. Nichols (ed.), *The Chronicle of Queen Jane* (Camden Society, London, 1850), Appendix x, pp. 139–40.
3. Ibid.
4. Ibid.
5. Quoted in Henry Kamen, *Philip II* (Yale University Press, New Haven, 1997), p. 59.
6. Elder, 'Letter', pp. 139–40.
7. Quoted in Alexander Samson, 'Changing Places: The Marriage and Royal Entry of Philip, Prince of Austria, and Mary Tudor, July–August 1554', *Sixteenth Century Journal*, 36, 3 (2005), pp. 761–84: p. 767.
8. CSPV, vol. 5: 1534–1554, no. 898, p. 511. I am grateful to Alexander Samson for drawing this reference to my attention and allowing me to read his forthcoming work on the subject.
9. Quoted in James D. Tracy, *Emperor Charles V, Impresario of War: Campaign Strategy, International Finance, and Domestic Politics* (Cambridge University Press, Cambridge, 2002), pp. 155–6.
10. On the campaign see Hendrik J. Horn, *Jan Cornelisz Vermeyen, Painter of Charles V and his Conquest of Tunis: Paintings, Etchings, Drawings, Cartoons and Tapestries*), 2 vols. (Davaco, The Hague, 1989).

11. CSPS, vol. 13: 1554–1558, no. 227, p. 236.

12. LP, vol. 9: August–December 1535, no. 596, p. 200.

13. Thomas Burman, *Reading the Qur'ān in Latin Christendom, 1140–1560* (University of Pennsylvania Press, Philadelphia, 2009).

14. For the classic account of these prejudices, see Norman Daniel, *Islam and the West: The Making of an Image* (Edinburgh University Press, Edinburgh, 1960).

15. Margaret Meserve, *Empires of Islam in Renaissance Historical Thought* (Harvard University Press, Cambridge, MA, 2008); Nancy Bisaha, *Creating East and West: Renaissance Humanists and the Ottoman Turks* (University of Pennsylvania Press, Philadelphia, 2004).

16. Dorothée Metlitzki, *The Matter of Araby in Medieval England* (Yale University Press, New Haven, 1977).

17. See Suzanne Conklin Akbari, 'The Non-Christians of *Piers Plowman*', in Andrew Cole and Andrew Galloway (eds.), *The Cambridge Companion to Piers Plowman* (Cambridge University Press, Cambridge, 2014), pp. 160–78: p. 170.

18. Quoted in Michael J. Heath, *Crusading Commonplaces: La Noue, Lucinge and Rhetoric against the Turks* (Droz, Geneva, 1986), p. 15.

19. Burman, *Reading the Qur'ān*, pp. 110–16.

20. Quoted in Ina Baghdiantz McCabe, *Orientalism in Early Modern France: Eurasian Trade, Exoticism and the Ancien Régime* (Berg, Oxford, 2008), pp. 33–4.

21. Adam S. Francisco, *Martin Luther: A Study in Sixteenth-Century Polemics and Apologetics* (Brill, Leiden, 2007), pp. 69–70.

22. Luther, 'On the War against the Turk', in *Luther's Works*, vol. 46, trans. Robert C. Schultz (Concordia Press, Philadelphia, 1962–71), pp. 157–205.

23. CSPV, vol. 3: 1520–1526, no. 616, p. 297.

24. Sir Thomas More, 'A Dialogue Concerning Heresies', in Thomas Lawler et al. (eds.), *The Yale Edition of The Complete Works of St. Thomas More. Volume 6, Parts I & II, A Dialogue Concerning Heresies* (Yale University Press, New Haven, 1981), pp. 1–435: p. 236.

25. 'Instruction Given to the Emperor by the Most Reverend Cardinal Campeggio at the Diet of Augsburg, 1530', in Leopold von Ranke, *The History of the Popes during the Last Four Centuries*, 3 vols. (Bell & Sons, London, 1913), vol. 3, p. 40.

26. Gülru Necipoğlu, 'Süleyman the Magnificent and the Representation of Power in the Context of Ottoman–Hapsburg–Papal Rivalry', *Art Bulletin*, 71, 3 (September 1989), pp. 401–27.

27. Dorothy Vaughan, *Europe and the Turk: A Pattern of Alliances* (Liverpool University Press, Liverpool, 1954).

28. Desiderius Erasmus, 'A Most Useful Discussion Concerning Proposals for War against the Turks, Including an Exposition of Psalm 28', trans. Michael J. Heath, in *The Collected Works of Erasmus*, vol. 64: *Expositions of the Psalms*, ed. Dominic Baker-Smith (Toronto University Press, Toronto, 2005), pp. 201–66: pp. 218, 231, 258–9.

29. Ibid., p. 242.

30. J. R. Tanner, *Tudor Constitutional Documents, 1485–1603* (Cambridge University Press, Cambridge, 1922), p. 124.

31. John Foxe, *The Unabridged Acts and Monuments Online or TAMO* (1573 edn) (HRI Online Publications, Sheffield, 2011). Available from: http//www.johnfoxe.org, 1563 edn, Book 5, p. 957.

32. Eamon Duffy, *Fires of Faith: Catholic England under Mary Tudor* (Yale University Press, New Haven, 2009).

33. Samson, 'Changing Places'.

34. Ian Lancashire, *Dramatic Texts and Records of Britain: A Chronological Topography to 1558* (Cambridge University Press, Cambridge, 1984), p. 213.

35. Hakluyt, vol. 2, p. 227–8.

36. Ibid., p. 267.

37. Ibid., p. 253.

38. Ibid., pp. 318–29.

39. Robert Batchelor, *London: The Selden Map and the Making of a Global City, 1549–1689* (University of Chicago Press, Chicago, 2014), p. 40.

40. Peter Barber, *The Queen Mary Atlas* (Folio Society, London, 2005), pp. 3–81.

CHAPTER 2: THE SULTAN,
THE TSAR AND THE SHAH

1. David Loades, *Elizabeth I: A Life* (Hambledon Press, London, 2003), p. 138.

2. E. Delmar Morgan and C. H. Coote (eds.), *Early Voyages and Travels to Russia and Persia by Anthony Jenkinson and Other Englishmen*, 2 vols. (Hakluyt Society, London, 1886), vol. 2, p. 341.

3. Anthony Jenkinson, 'The Manner of the Entering of Süleyman the Great Turk with his Army into Aleppo', in ibid., vol. 1, pp. 1–5.

4. Quoted in Palmira Brummett, 'The Myth of Shah Ismail Safavi: Political Rhetoric and "Divine" Kingship', in John Tolan (ed.), *Medieval*

Christian Perceptions of Islam (Routledge, New York, 2000), pp. 331–59: p. 343.

5. Quoted in Max Scherberger, 'The Confrontation between Sunni and Shi'i Empires: Ottoman–Safavid Relations between the Fifteenth and the Seventeenth Century', in Ofra Bengio and Meir Litvak (eds.), *The Sunna and Shi'a in History* (Palgrave, New York, 2011), pp. 51–68: p. 55.

6. Quoted in Palmira Brummett, *Ottoman Seapower and Levantine Diplomacy* (State University of New York Press, Albany, NY, 1994), p. 36.

7. Quoted in ibid., p. 29.

8. Ibid.

9. Morgan and Coote (eds.), *Travels to Russia*, vol. 1, pp. 5–6.

10. Hakluyt, vol. 1, p. 390.

11. Morgan and Coote (eds.), *Travels to Russia*, vol. 1, p. 30.

12. Ibid., p. 58, 97.

13. Ibid., pp. 84–5.

14. Ibid., pp. 87–8.

15. Ibid., p. 93.

16. Ibid., p. 97.

17. Ibid., pp. 108–9.

18. Ibid., p. 58.

19. Daryl Palmer, *Writing Russia in the Age of Shakespeare* (Ashgate, Aldershot, 2004), p. 54.

20. Morgan and Coote (eds.), *Travels to Russia*, vol. 1, pp. 112–13.

21. Ibid., pp. 113–14.

22. Ibid., p. 125.

23. Ibid., p. 126.

24. Ibid., pp. 143, 133.

25. Ibid., p. 140.

26. Kathryn Babayan, *Mystics, Monarchs, and Messiahs: Cultural Landscapes of Early Modern Iran* (Harvard University Press, Cambridge, MA, 2002), pp. 295–348.

27. Jean-Do Brignoli, 'Princely Safavid Gardens: Stage for Rituals and of Imperial Display and Political Legitimacy', in Michael Conan (ed.), *Middle East Garden Traditions: Unity and Diversity* (Dumbarton Oaks, Washington, DC, 2007), pp. 113–39.

28. Morgan and Coote (eds.), *Travels to Russia*, vol. 1, pp. 153–4.

29. Ibid., pp. 145–7.

30. Colin P. Mitchell, 'Am I My Brother's Keeper? Negotiating Corporate Sovereignty and Divine Absolutism in Sixteenth-Century Turco-Iranian

Politics', in Mitchell (ed.), *New Perspectives on Safavid Iran* (Routledge, London, 2011), pp. 33–58.

31. Morgan and Coote (eds.), *Travels to Russia*, vol. 1, pp. 144, 148.

32. Ibid., pp. 149–50.

33. Ibid., pp.155–6.

34. Kenneth Andrews, *Trade, Plunder and Settlement: Maritime Enterprise and the Genesis of the British Empire, 1480–1630* (Cambridge University Press, Cambridge, 1984), pp. 76–86; Jane Grogan, *The Persian Empire in English Renaissance Writing, 1549–1622* (Palgrave, Basingstoke, 2014), pp. 20–21.

35. Bernadette Andrea, 'Elizabeth I and Persian Exchanges', in Charles Beem (ed.), *The Foreign Relations of Elizabeth I* (Palgrave, Basingstoke, 2011), pp. 169–99: pp. 184–5. Ippolyta appears to have had an important influence upon female portraiture of the time, including Marcus Gheeraerts's mysterious painting known as *The Persian Lady*, c. 1590.

36. Quoted in Morgan and Coote (eds.), *Travels to Russia*, vol. 1, p. cxlix.

CHAPTER 3: THE BATTLE FOR BARBARY

1. Hakluyt, vol. 4, p. 32.

2. Ibid., p. 34.

3. T. S. Willan, *Studies in Elizabethan Foreign Trade* (Manchester University Press, Manchester, 1959), pp. 98–9.

4. Ibid., pp. 113, 314.

5. CSPF, vol. 5: 1562, no. 103, p. 54.

6. 'Garrard, Sir William (c.1510–1571)', ODNB.

7. Quoted in Gustav Ungerer, 'Portia and the Prince of Morocco', *Shakespeare Studies*, 31 (2003), pp. 89–126: p. 100.

8. Quoted in Willan, *Foreign Trade*, p. 127.

9. 'Felton, John (d. 1570), Roman Catholic martyr', ODNB.

10. 'The Bull of Excommunication, 1570', in Tanner (ed.), *Tudor Constitutional Documents*, pp. 143–6.

11. 'Felton, John', ODNB.

12. Robert Horne, Bishop of Winchester, *An Answeare Made by Rob. Bishoppe of Wynchester, to a Booke entituled, The Declaration of svche Scruples, and staies of Conscience, touchinge the Othe of the Supremacy, as M. Iohn Fekenham, by wrytinge did deliuer vnto the L. Bishop of Winchester, with his Resolutions made thereunto . . .* (London, 1566), p. 102v.

13. Nate Probasco, 'Queen Elizabeth's Reaction to the St. Bartholomew's Day Massacre', in Beem (ed.), *Foreign Relations*, pp. 77–100.

14. Quoted in Sophia Menache, *Clement V* (Cambridge University Press, Cambridge, 1998), p. 106.

15. Jerry Brotton and Lisa Jardine, *Global Interests: Renaissance Art between East and West* (Reaktion, London, 2000); Christine Isom-Verhaaren, *Allies with the Infidel: The Ottoman and French Alliance in the Sixteenth Century* (I. B. Tauris, London, 2011).

16. Andrew C. Hess, 'The Moriscos: An Ottoman Fifth Column in Sixteenth-Century Spain', *American Historical Journal*, 74, 1 (1968), pp. 1–25.

17. Andrew C. Hess, *The Forgotten Frontier: A History of the Ibero-African Frontier* (University of Chicago Press, Chicago, 1978), pp. 85–90.

18. For the best recent account of the battle placed in the context of Christian–Islamic exchanges, see Noel Malcolm, *Agents of Empire: Knights, Corsairs, Jesuits and Spies in the Sixteenth-Century Mediterranean World* (Allen Lane, London, 2015), pp. 151–74.

19. Quoted in Benjamin Paul, ' "And the moon has started to bleed": Apocalyptism and Religious Reform in Venetian Art at the Time of the Battle of Lepanto', in James G. Harper (ed.), *The Turk and Islam in the Western Eye, 1450–1750* (Ashgate, Farnham, 2011), pp. 67–94: p. 69.

20. Raphael Holinshed, *The Third Volume of Chronicles* (London, 1587), pp. 1226–7.

21. Kervyn de Lettenhove, *Relations politiques des Pays Bas et de l'Angleterre sous le règne de Philippe II*, 11 vols. (Louvain, 1882–1900), vol. 6, p. 225.

22. Letters of William Herle Project, Centre for Editing Lives and Letters, www.livesandletters.ac.uk. Transcript ID: HRL/002/HTML/022.

23. Andrews, *Trade, Plunder and Settlement*, p. 111.

24. Castries, vol. 1, p. 201.

25. Ibid.

26. Ibid., p. 202.

27. Ibid., pp. 204–5.

28. Ibid., pp. 212–13.

29. Ibid., pp. 226–7.

30. CSPF, vol. 12: 1577–78, 9 August 1577, no. 94, p. 68.

31. Quoted in Andrew C. Hess, 'The Battle of Lepanto and its Place in Mediterranean History, *Past and Present*, 57 (1972), pp. 53–73: p. 54.

32. Leslie Peirce, *The Imperial Harem: Women and Sovereignty in the Ottoman Empire* (Oxford University Press, Oxford, 1993).

33. Quoted in Susan Skilliter (ed.), *William Harborne and the Trade with Turkey, 1578–1582: A Documentary Study of the First Anglo-Ottoman Relations* (Oxford University Press, Oxford, 1977), p. 37.

34. Hakluyt, vol. 3, p. 51.

35. Skilliter, *Harborne*, pp. 1–2.

36. 'Stucley, Thomas (*c*.1520–1578)', ODNB.

37. Charles Edelman (ed.), *Three Stukeley Plays* (Manchester University Press, Manchester, 2005), p. 7.

38. Quoted in Susan Iwanisziw, 'England, Morocco, and Global Geopolitical Upheaval', in Robert Applebaum and John Sweet (eds.), *Envisioning an English Empire* (University of Pennsylvania Press, Philadelphia), pp. 152–71: p. 163.

39. John Polemon, *The Second Part of the Booke of Battailes, Fought in Our Age Taken out of the Best Authors and Writers in Sundrie Languages* (London, 1587), p. 79.

40. E. W. Bovill, *The Battle of Alcazar: An Account of the Defeat of Don Sebastian of Portugal at El-Ksar El-Kebir* (Batchworth, London, 1952), p. 97.

41. Edelman (ed.), *Stukeley Plays*, p. 15.

42. Polemon, *Booke of Battailes*, p. 86.

43. Bovil, *Alcazar*, p. 145.

CHAPTER 4: AN APT MAN IN CONSTANTINOPLE

1. Quoted in Skilliter, *Harborne*, pp. 28–30.

2. On Harborne's life see 'Harborne, William (*c*.1542–1617)', ODNB.

3. Zeynep Çelik, *The Remaking of Istanbul: Portrait of an Ottoman City in the Nineteenth Century* (University of California Press, Berkeley, 1993), pp. 22–9.

4. Skilliter, *Harborne*, p. 45.

5. Quoted in ibid.

6. Hakluyt, vol. 3, p. 51.

7. Skilliter, *Harborne*, pp. 62–4.

8. Ibid., p. 63.

9. Ibid., p. 49.

10. Hakluyt, vol. 3, p. 52.

11. Ibid., pp. 52–3.

12. Skilliter, *Harborne*, p. 54

13. Ibid., p. 59.

14. CSPF, vol. 14: 1579–1580, no. 71, p. 77.

15. Rayne Allinson, *A Monarchy of Letters: Royal Correspondence and English Diplomacy in the Reign of Elizabeth I* (Palgrave, Basingstoke, 2012), pp. 131–50.
16. Skilliter, *Harborne*, p. 51.
17. CSPS, vol. 2: 1568–1579, no. 609, pp. 705–6.
18. Ibid., p. 706.
19. Ibid., p. 710.
20. Hakluyt, vol. 3, p. 54.
21. Cornell H. Fleischer, *Bureaucrat and Intellectual in the Ottoman Empire: The Historian Mustafa Ali (1541–1600)* (Princeton University Press, Princeton, 1986), pp. 72–3.
22. Skilliter, *Harborne*, pp. 79–80.
23. Hakluyt, vol. 3, p. 58.
24. Ibid., p. 61.
25. Skilliter, *Harborne*, p. 120.
26. Ibid., p. 151.
27. Quoted in Andrew P. Vella, *An Elizabethan–Ottoman Conspiracy* (Royal University of Malta Press, Valletta, 1972), pp. 41–2.
28. Skilliter, *Harborne*, p. 159.
29. Vella, *Conspiracy*, p. 46.
30. Ibid., pp. 46–7.
31. Skilliter, *Harborne*, pp. 155–7.
32. De Lamar Jensen, 'The Ottoman Turks in Sixteenth Century French Diplomacy', *Sixteenth Century Journal*, 16, 4 (1985), pp. 451–70.
33. Vella, *Conspiracy*, pp. 64–5.
34. Skilliter, *Harborne*, p. 166.

CHAPTER 5: UNHOLY ALLIANCES

1. Quoted in Willan, *Foreign Trade*, p. 155.
2. John Wheeler, *A Treatise of Commerce* (London, 1601), p. 13.
3. Hakluyt, vol. 3, p. 65.
4. Stephen Gosson, *The School of Abuse* (London, 1579), sig. D3r.
5. Stephen Gosson, *Playes Confuted in Five Actions* (London, 1582), sig. G8r.
6. Peter Thomson, *Shakespeare's Professional Career* (Cambridge University Press, Cambridge, 1992), p. 69.
7. Andreas Höfele, *Stage, Stake and Scaffold: Humans and Animals in Shakespeare's Theatre* (Oxford University Press, Oxford, 2011).
8. Robert Wilson, *The Three Ladies of London*, 1.11–17. This and all subsequent references to the play are taken from Lloyd Edward Ker-

mode (ed.), *Three Renaissance Usury Plays* (Manchester University Press, Manchester, 2009), pp. 79–163.

9. Ibid., 2.222.

10. Ibid., 2.228, 241.

11. Ibid., 3.32.

12. Ibid., 3.42–6.

13. Ibid., 3.53–7.

14. Jonathan Gil Harris, *Sick Economies: Drama, Mercantilism and Disease in Shakespeare's England* (University of Pennsylvania Press, Philadelphia, 2003).

15. Lloyd Edward Kermode, 'Money, Gender and Conscience in Robert Wilson's *The Three Ladies of London*', *Studies in English Literature 1500–1900*, 52, 2 (2012), pp. 265–91.

16. Wilson, *Three Ladies*, 9.3–9.

17. Ibid., 9.26–7.

18. Ibid., 9.34.

19. Ibid., 14.13.

20. Ibid., 14.15–16.

21. Ibid., 14.20.

22. Ibid., 14.49.

23. Ibid., 14.58–9.

24. Alan Stewart, ' "Come from Turkey": Mediterranean Trade in Late Elizabethan London', in Goran Stanivukovic (ed.), *Remapping the Mediterranean World in Early Modern English Writings* (Palgrave, Basingstoke, 2007), pp. 157–78.

25. Wilson, *Three Ladies*, 17.103.

26. Norman Jones, *God and the Moneylenders: Usury and the Law in Early Modern England* (Blackwell, Oxford, 1989); Craig Muldrew, *The Economy of Obligation: The Culture of Credit and Social Relations in Early Modern England* (Palgrave, Basingstoke, 1998).

27. John Aylmer, Letter to Lord Mayor of London (23 September 1582), London Metropolitan Archive (LMA) COL/RMD/PA/01 f. 199r. For a discussion of the letter's significance see Matthew Dimmock, 'Early Modern Travel, Conversion, and Languages of "Difference"', *Journeys*, 14, 2 (2013), pp. 10–26. I am grateful to Professor Dimmock for bringing this letter to my attention.

28. CSPS, vol. 3: 1580–1586, no. 265, pp. 366–7.

29. Alfred C. Wood, *A History of the Levant Company* (Oxford University Press, London, 1935), pp. 12–13.

30. Skilliter, *Harborne*, p. 183.

31. Hakluyt, vol. 3, pp. 85–8.
32. Quoted in Nabil Matar, 'Elizabeth through Moroccan Eyes', in Beem (ed.), *Foreign Relations*, pp. 145–67: p. 147.
33. Castries, vol. 1, p. 391.
34. CSPS, vol. 3: 1580–1586, no. 150, p. 199.
35. Quoted in Willan, *Foreign Trade*, p. 167.
36. Castries, vol. 1, pp. 413–16.
37. Ibid., pp. 418–19.
38. Ibid., p. 419.
39. 'Barton, Edward (1562/3–1598)', ODNB.
40. Hakluyt, vol. 3, p. 109.
41. CSPV, vol. 8: 1581–1591, no. 131, pp. 55–6.
42. Bodleian Library MS Lansdowne 57, f. 66r.
43. Hakluyt, vol. 3, p. 114.
44. Quoted in H. G. Rawlinson, 'The Embassy of William Harborne to Constantinople, 1583–88', *Transactions of the Royal Historical Society*, Fourth Series, vol. 5 (1922), pp. 1–27: p. 8.
45. CSPV, vol. 8: 1581–1591, nos. 126, 130, pp. 50–53.
46. Ibid., no. 131, p. 56.
47. CSPF, vol. 17: January–June 1583, Addenda, 12 and 23 May 1583, no. 738.
48. J. Horton Ryley, *Ralph Fitch: England's Pioneer to India and Burma* (Unwin, London, 1899).
49. *Macbeth*, 1.3.17.
50. Castries, vol. 1, p. 459.
51. Ibid., p. 460.
52. Hakluyt, vol. 4, pp. 268–73.
53. Ibid., vol. 3, pp. 146–7, 150.
54. Ibid., p. 159.
55. Colin Martin and Geoffrey Parker, *The Spanish Armada* (Hamish Hamilton, London, 1989), pp. 89–90.
56. Letters of William Herle Project, Centre for Editing Lives and Letters, www.livesandletters.ac.uk. Transcript ID: HRL/002/PDF/325.
57. Conyers Read, *Mr. Secretary Walsingham and the Policy of Queen Elizabeth*, 3 vols. (Clarendon Press, Oxford, 1925), vol. 3, p. 226.
58. Ibid., p. 228.
59. Quoted in Arthur Leon Horniker, 'William Harborne and the Beginning of Anglo-Turkish Diplomatic and Commercial Relations', *Journal of Modern History*, 14, 3 (1942), pp. 289–316: p. 315.
60. Castries, vol. 1, p. 545.

61. Hakluyt, vol. 4, p. 274.
62. Quoted in Mercedes García-Arenal, *Ahmad al-Mansur: The Beginnings of Modern Morocco* (Oneworld, Oxford, 2009), p. 115.
63. Hakluyt, vol. 4, p. 274.
64. Emily Gottreich, *The Mellah of Marrakesh: Jewish and Muslim Space in Morocco's Red City* (Indiana University Press, Bloomington, 2007).
65. Nabil Matar, *Islam in Britain 1558–1685* (Cambridge University Press, Cambridge, 1998), pp. 22–3.
66. Carsten L. Wilke, *The Marrakesh Dialogues: A Gospel Critique and Jewish Apology from the Spanish Renaissance* (Brill, Leiden, 2014).
67. Hakluyt, vol. 4, p. 274.
68. Castries, vol. 1, pp. 480–83.
69. Willan, *Foreign Trade*, pp. 253–5.
70. Wood, *Levant Company*, p. 17.
71. CSPV, vol. 8: 1581–1591, no. 336, p. 154.

CHAPTER 6: SULTANA ISABEL

1. Meredith Hanmer, *The Baptizing of a Turke: a sermon preached at the Hospitall of Saint Katherin, adioyning vnto her Maiesties Towre the 2. of October 1586. at the baptizing of one Chinano a Turke, borne at Nigropontus: by Meredith Hanmer, D. of Diuinitie* (Robert Waldegrave, London, 1586).
2. D. B. Quinn, *Explorers and Colonies: America, 1500–1625* (Hambledon Press, London, 1990), pp. 198–204.
3. APC, England, vol. 14: 1586–1587, p. 205.
4. Bodleian Library MS Tanner 77, f. 3v.
5. Hakluyt, vol. 3, p. 150.
6. Nabil Matar, *British Captives from the Mediterranean to the Atlantic, 1563–1760* (Brill, Leiden, 2014), pp. 71–5; and Daniel Vitkus (ed.) and Nabil Matar (intro.), *Piracy, Slavery, and Redemption: Barbary Captivity Narratives from Early Modern England* (Columbia University Press, New York, 2001).
7. C. E. Bosworth, *An Intrepid Scot: William Lithgow of Lanark's Travels in the Ottoman Lands, North Africa and Central Europe, 1609–21* (Ashgate, Basingstoke, 2006), p. 115.
8. Quoted in Gerald MacLean, *Looking East: English Writing and the Ottoman Empire before 1800* (Palgrave, Basingstoke, 2007), chapter 3, n. 15.
9. Hakluyt, vol. 3, p. 131.

10. Edward Webbe, *The Rare and most wonderfull things which Edward Webbe an Englishman borne, hath seene and passed in his troublesome travailes, in the cities of Jerusalem, Damasko, Bethlehem and Galely: and in the landes of Jewrie, Egypt, Grecia, Russia, and Prester John* (William Wright, London, 1590).
11. 'Webbe, Edward (*b.* 1553/4)', ODNB.
12. Bodleian Library MS Tanner 77, f. 4r.
13. Ibid.
14. Quoted in Skilliter, *Harborne*, p. 36.
15. Bodleian Library MS Tanner 77, f. 4r.
16. Roger M. Savory, *Iran under the Safavids* (Cambridge University Press, Cambridge, 1980), pp. 72–5.
17. Read, *Walsingham*, vol. 3, pp. 329–30.
18. Ibid., p. 330.
19. Quoted in Horniker, 'William Harborne', pp. 309–10.
20. Bodleian Library MS Tanner 77, ff. 4r–5r.
21. Ibid., f. 4r.
22. Quoted in Rawlinson, 'Harborne', p. 15.
23. CSPF, vol. 22: July–December 1588, pp. 97–110.
24. Hakluyt, vol. 3, p. 368.
25. Castries, vol. 1, p. 502.
26. The description of these events is based on Gustav Ungerer, 'Portia and the Prince of Morocco', *Shakespeare Studies*, 31 (2003), pp. 89–126: pp. 97–8.
27. Quoted in Matar, 'Elizabeth through Moroccan Eyes', p. 150.
28. Ibid., pp. 150–51.
29. Loades, *Elizabeth I*, p. 253.
30. Matar, 'Elizabeth through Moroccan Eyes', p. 150.
31. Hakluyt, vol. 4, p. 275.
32. Ibid.
33. Quoted in Matar, 'Elizabeth through Moroccan Eyes', p. 152.
34. Hakluyt, vol. 4, p. 275.

CHAPTER 7: LONDON TURNS TURK

1. Castries, vol. 1, pp. 513–14.
2. R. B. Wernham, 'Elizabeth and the Portugal Expedition of 1589', *English Historical Review*, 66, 258 (1951), pp. 1–26.
3. Castries, vol. 1, pp. 516–17.
4. Willan, *Foreign Trade*, pp. 229–32.
5. Wilson, *Three Ladies*, Prologue, 1–2.

6. Christopher Marlowe, *Tamburlaine the Great, Part 1*, Prologue, 1–8. All references to both parts of *Tamburlaine the Great* are taken from David Bevington and Eric Rasmussen (eds.), *Christopher Marlowe: Doctor Faustus and Other Plays* (Oxford University Press, Oxford, 1995), pp. 1–68.

7. C. H. Herford, Percy Simpson and Evelyn Simpson (eds.), *Ben Jonson: The Complete Works*, 11 vols. (Clarendon Press, Oxford, 1925–63), vol. 8, p. 587.

8. Thomas Nashe, 'To the Gentlemen Students of Both Universities', in Robert Greene, *Greene's Arcadia or Menaphon* (London, 1589), sig. A2.

9. Robert Greene, *Perimedes the Black-Smith* (London, 1588), sig. A3r.

10. Marlowe, *Tamburlaine, Part 1*, 3.3.40–47.

11. Ibid., 4.2.2.

12. Ibid., 4.2.31–2.

13. John Michael Archer, 'Islam and Tamburlaine's World Picture', in Jyotsna Singh (ed.), *A Companion to the Global Renaissance: English Literature and Culture in the Era of Expansion* (Blackwell, Oxford, 2009), pp. 67–81: pp. 76–7.

14. Marlowe, *Tamburlaine, Part 2*, 1.1.137–42.

15. Ibid., 5.1.171–4.

16. Ibid., 5.1.185–9.

17. Ibid., 5.1.190–95.

18. Ibid., 5.1.196, 198.

19. Ibid., 5.3.42–53.

20. David Riggs, 'Marlowe's Life', in Patrick Cheney (ed.), *The Cambridge Companion to Christopher Marlowe* (Cambridge University Press, Cambridge, 2004), pp. 24–40.

21. Title page of the first edition of the two parts of Christopher Marlowe, *Tamburlaine the Great* (London, 1590).

22. George Peele, *The Battle of Alcazar*, 1. Prologue, 6–7, 16. All references to Peele's play are taken from Edelman (ed.), *The Stukeley Plays*, pp. 59–128.

23. See 'moor, n.2', OED Online.

24. Leo Africanus, quoted in Jerry Brotton, 'Moors', in Michael Dobson and Stanley Wells (eds.), *The Oxford Companion to Shakespeare* (Oxford University Press, Oxford, 2011), p. 304.

25. Peele, *Battle of Alcazar*, 1.1.64–5.

26. Ibid., 1.1.10–11.

27. Ibid., 2.2.15–16.

28. Ibid., 2.2.69–82.

29. Emily C. Bartels, *Speaking of the Moor: From Alcazar to Othello* (University of Pennsylvania Press, Philadelphia, 2008), pp. 21–44.

30. George Peele, 'A Farewell: To the Most Famous Generals of our English Forces by Land and Sea, Sir John Norris and Sir Francis Drake Knights', in David Horne (ed.), *The Life and Minor Works of George Peele* (Yale University Press, New Haven, 1952), pp. 220–23.

31. Wernham, 'Portugal Expedition of 1589', pp. 19–23.

32. Quoted in R. B. Wernham, 'Elizabeth and the Portugal Expedition of 1589 (Continued)', *English Historical Review*, 66, 259 (1951), pp. 194–218: p. 207.

33. Nabil Matar, *Britain and Barbary, 1589–1689* (University Press of Florida, Gainesville, 2005), pp. 18–19. García-Arenal, *Ahmad al-Mansur*, pp. 84–5.

34. Castries, vol. 1, pp. 532–4.

35. Ibid., pp. 537–8.

36. Ibid., pp. 536–7.

37. Matar, *Britain and Barbary*, p. 19.

38. Quoted in Matar, 'Elizabeth through Moroccan Eyes', p. 152.

39. *The Fugger Newsletter, Second Series: Being a Further Selection from the Fugger Papers Specially Referring to Queen Elizabeth and Matters Relating to England during the Years 1568–1605* (John Lane, London, 1926), p. 217.

40. Quoted in García-Arenal, *Ahmad al-Mansur*, p. 105.

41. Matar, 'Elizabeth through Moroccan Eyes', p. 154.

42. Peter Berek, 'Tamburlaine's Weak Sons: Imitation as Interpretation before 1593', *Renaissance Drama*, 13 (1982), pp. 55–82: p. 58.

43. All references to Greene's play are taken from Daniel Vitkus (ed.), *Three Turk Plays from Early Modern England* (Columbia University Press, New York, 2000), pp. 55–148.

44. Greene, *Selimus*, 10.16, 12.20, 2.98, 2.102, 105.

45. Ibid., Conclusion, 5–6.

46. Robert Greene, *Alphonsus King of Aragon*, 3.3.1248, s.d. All references to the play are taken from W. W. Greg (ed.), *Alphonsus King of Aragon, 1599* (Malone Society, Oxford, 1926).

47. Greene, *Alphonsus*, 5.1.2077.

48. Jonathan Gil Harris, *Untimely Matter in the Time of Shakespeare* (University of Pennsylvania Press, Philadelphia, 2009), pp. 77–81.

49. Marlowe, *The Jew of Malta*, 1.1.37, 127. This and all subsequent references to the play are from Bevington and Rasmussen (eds.), *Christopher Marlowe*, pp. 247–322.

50. Marlowe, *The Jew of Malta*, 2.3.216.
51. Ibid., 5.5. 83–5.
52. Ibid., 2.3.175–99.
53. James Shapiro, *Shakespeare and the Jews* (Columbia University Press, New York, 1996).
54. Marlowe, *The Jew of Malta*, 1.1.19–24.
55. Ibid., 1.1.37.
56. Charles Nicholl, *The Reckoning: The Murder of Christopher Marlowe* (Jonathan Cape, London, 1992).

CHAPTER 8: MAHOMET'S DOVE

1. R. A. Foakes (ed.), *Henslowe's Diary*, 2nd edn (Cambridge University Press, Cambridge, 2002), pp. 16–18. On the exact sequence in which the three parts of *Henry VI* were written and with whom, see Gary Taylor, 'Shakespeare and Others: The Authorship of *Henry the Sixth*, Part One', *Medieval and Renaissance Drama*, 7 (1995), pp. 145–205.
2. *Henry VI, Part 1*, 1.1.28.
3. James Bednarz, 'Marlowe and the English Literary Scene', in Cheney (ed.), *Cambridge Companion*, pp. 90–105; and Jonathan Bate, *The Genius of Shakespeare* (Picador, London, 1997), p. 108.
4. Quoted in *Henry VI, Part 1*, ed. Michael Taylor, The Oxford Shakespeare (Oxford University Press, Oxford, 2003), p. 2.
5. Ibid., 1.2.7, 1.3.18–19.
6. Ibid., 1.3.31–3.
7. Ibid., 1.3.51, 63.
8. Ibid., 1.3.119–24.
9. Hanmer, *Baptizing of a Turke*, p. 9.
10. Sir Walter Raleigh, *The History of the World*, 6 vols., vol. 2 (Edinburgh, 1820), p. 170.
11. Thomas Nashe, 'The Terrors of the Night, or a Discourse of Apparitions', in *The Unfortunate Traveller and Other Works*, ed. J. B. Steane (Penguin, London, 1972), p. 214.
12. Wallace T. MacCaffery, *Elizabeth I: War and Politics 1558–1603* (Princeton University Press, Princeton, 1992), pp. 137–83; Chris Fitter, 'Emergent Shakespeare and the Politics of Protest: 2 *Henry VI* in Historical Contexts', *English Literary History*, 72, 1 (2005), pp. 129–58.
13. Quoted in Matthew Dimmock, *New Turkes: Dramatizing Islam and the Ottoman Empire in Early Modern England* (Ashgate, Basingstoke, 2005), p. 163.

14. 'Barton, Edward (1562/3–1598)', ODNB; Jensen, 'The Ottoman Turks', p. 468.

15. Quoted in Nancy Lyman Roelker, *One King, One Faith: The Parlement of Paris and the Religious Reformations of the Sixteenth Century* (University of California Press, Berkeley, 1996), p. 412.

16. Quoted in MacCaffery, *Elizabeth I*, p. 178.

17. Robert Verstegen, *A Declaration of the True Causes of the Great Troubles, Presupposed to be Intended against the Realm of England* (Antwerp, 1592), p. 48.

18. Ibid., pp. 48–9.

19. Francis Bacon, 'Certain Observations made upon a Libel Published this Present Year, 1592', in James Spedding (ed.), *The Letters and the Life of Francis Bacon*, 7 vols. (London, 1861–74), vol. 1, pp. 146–208: p. 204.

20. CSPD, vol. 3: 1591–1594, no. 79, 27 April 1594.

21. Hakluyt, vol. 4, p. 8.

22. Peirce, *Imperial Harem*, pp. 224–8; Susan Skilliter, 'Three Letters from the Ottoman "Sultana" Safiye to Queen Elizabeth I', in S. M. Stern (ed.), *Documents from Islamic Chanceries* (Harvard University Press, Cambridge, MA, 1965), pp. 119–57.

23. Quoted in Skilliter, 'Three Letters', pp. 131–2.

24. Arthur Golding (trans.), *The xv bookes of P. Ovidius Naso, entytuled Metamorphosis* (London, 1567), sig. B1.

25. *Titus Andronicus*, 3.1. s.d.

26. Ibid., 2.4.12.

27. Ibid., 3.1.184.

28. T. S. Eliot, 'Seneca in Elizabethan Translation', in *Selected Essays, 1917–1932* (Faber & Faber, London, 1932), pp. 65–105.

29. Quoted in Dominic Shellard, *Kenneth Tynan: A Life* (Yale University Press, New Haven, 2003), p. 137.

30. http://www.theguardian.com/commentisfree/2014/may/12/theatre-blood-gore-titus-andronicus.

31. *Titus Andronicus*, 4.2.65.

32. Ibid., 5.1.63–4.

33. Ibid., 4.2.91.

34. Ibid., 5.3.178.

35. For the case that Peele wrote much of the play's first act and three other scenes see Brian Vickers, *Shakespeare, Co-Author: A Historical Study of Five Collaborative Plays* (Oxford University Press, Oxford, 2002), pp. 148–243. Vickers argues that the preponderance of alliteration and

polysyllabic words suggests Peele had a hand in writing the first act and some of the later scenes.

36. *Titus Andronicus*, 5.3.120.
37. Ibid., 2.3.34–6.
38. Ibid., 3.1.203–4.
39. Ibid., 5.1.124–44.
40. Ibid., 5.3.184–9.
41. Ibid., 5.1.21.
42. Ibid., 5.1.68, 71.
43. Ibid., 5.1.73–83.
44. Castries, vol. 2, pp. 89–90.
45. R. B. Wernham, *The Return of the Armadas: The Last Years of the Elizabethan War against Spain, 1595–1603* (Oxford University Press, Oxford, 1994), pp. 91–113; Edward Tenace, 'A Strategy of Reaction: The Armadas of 1596 and 1597 and the Spanish Struggle for European Hegemony', *English Historical Review*, 118, 478 (2003), pp. 855–82; Paul E. J. Hammer, 'Myth-making: Politics, Propaganda and the Capture of Cadiz in 1596', *Historical Journal*, 40, 3 (1997), pp. 621–42.
46. Castries, vol. 2, pp. 93–4.
47. Quoted in Wernham, *Return of the Armadas*, p. 107.
48. Quoted in Matar, 'Elizabeth through Moroccan Eyes', p. 156.
49. See Matar, *Britain and Barbary*, which characterizes this moment as a 'jihad', p. 21.
50. Wernham, *Return of the Armadas*, pp. 130–69.
51. *The Merchant of Venice*, 4.1.304–5.
52. Ibid., 4.1.382.
53. Quoted in Shapiro, *Shakespeare and the Jews*, p. 73.
54. *The Merchant of Venice*, 3.1.49–54.
55. Ibid., 3.1.54–61.
56. Ibid., 4.1.169.
57. Ibid., 1.2.109–10.
58. Ibid., 2.1.1–7.
59. Ibid., 2.1.8–12.
60. Ibid., 2.1.4–6.
61. Ibid., 2.7.78–9.
62. Willan, *Foreign Trade*, p. 296.

CHAPTER 9: ESCAPE FROM THE SERAGLIO

1. Quoted in H. G. Rosedale, *Queen Elizabeth and the Levant Company* (London, 1904), p. 18.
2. Quoted in ibid., p. 27.
3. Quoted in ibid., pp. 27–8, 39.
4. Quoted in Gerald MacLean, *The Rise of Oriental Travel: English Visitors to the Ottoman Empire, 1580–1720* (Palgrave, Basingstoke, 2004), p. 40.
5. 'Barton, Edward (1562/3–1598)', ODNB.
6. Quoted in Franklin L. Baumer, 'England, the Turk and the Common Corps of Christendom', *American Historical Review*, 50, 1 (1944), pp. 26–48: p. 35.
7. Wood, *Levant Company*, pp. 22–4.
8. Anders Ingram, 'English Literature on the Ottoman Turks in the Sixteenth and Seventeenth Centuries', PhD thesis, University of Durham, 2009, pp. 388–95. Available at Durham E-Theses Online: http://etheses.dur.ac.uk/86/. See also his book, *Writing the Ottomans: Turkish History in Early Modern England* (Macmillan, Basingstoke, 2015).
9. On carpets, rugs and other material imports through the Ottoman territories see MacLean, *Looking East*, pp. 27–62.
10. Karen Hearn, *Dynasties: Painting in Tudor and Jacobean England, 1530–1630* (Tate Publishing, London, 1996), p. 64.
11. Jean Lobbet to Sidney, Strasburg, 5 July 1575, in Roger Kuin (ed.), *The Correspondence of Sir Philip Sidney*, 2 vols. (Oxford University Press, Oxford, 2012), vol. 1, p. 483.
12. *Astrophil and Stella*, 30.1–2. This and all subsequent references to the work are taken from William A. Ringler (ed.), *The Poems of Sir Philip Sidney* (Clarendon Press, Oxford, 1962), pp. 163–239.
13. Ibid., 8.1–4.
14. R. W. Maslen (ed.), *An Apology for Poetry (or The Defence of Poesy): Philip Sidney* (Manchester University Press, Manchester, 2002), p. 105.
15. Charles Lethbridge Kingsford, 'Essex House, formerly Leicester House and Exeter Inn', *Archaeologia, or Miscellaneous Tracts Relating to Antiquity*, 73 (1923), pp. 1–51.
16. Lionel Cust, 'The Lumley Inventories', *Walpole Society*, 6 (1918), pp. 15–35.
17. Robert Brenner, *Merchants and Revolution: Commercial Change, Political Conflict, and London's Overseas Traders, 1550–1653* (Cambridge University Press, Cambridge, 1993), pp. 25, 42.

18. *The Taming of the Shrew*, 2.1.345.
19. *The Comedy of Errors*, 4.1.104.
20. Santina M. Levey, *The Embroideries at Hardwick Hall: A Catalogue* (National Trust Books, London, 2007), pp. 380–85. Hakluyt, vol. 2, pp. 201–3.
21. Wood, *Levant Company*, p. 24; T. S. Willan, 'Some Aspects of English Trade with the Levant in the Sixteenth Century', *English Historical Review*, 70, 276 (1955), pp. 399–410.
22. Sir William Foster (ed.), *The Travels of John Sanderson in the Levant, 1584–1602* (Hakluyt Society, London, 1931), pp. 32, 33.
23. Gillian White, ' "that whyche ys nedefoulle and nesesary": The Nature and Purpose of the Original Furnishings and Decoration of Hardwick Hall, Derbyshire', PhD thesis, University of Warwick, 2 vols., 2005, vol. 1, p. 99.
24. Levey, *The Embroideries at Hardwick Hall*, pp. 99–109.
25. Dimmock, *New Turkes*, pp. 167–8.
26. *Richard II*, 4.1.125–32.
27. *Henry IV, Part 1*, 1.1.12–13.
28. Ibid., 1.1.24–7.
29. Ibid., 5.2.85.
30. Ibid., 2.5.94–7.
31. *Henry IV, Part 2*, 2.4.136, 141, 155.
32. Ibid., 5.2.46–9.
33. William Hazlitt, *Characters of Shakespeare's Plays* (London, 1817), p. 192.
34. Norman Rabkin, 'Rabbits, Ducks and *Henry V*', *Shakespeare Quarterly*, 28, 3 (1977), pp. 279–96.
35. *Henry V*, 3.3.115–18.
36. Nabil Matar and Gerald MacLean, *Britain and the Islamic World, 1558–1713* (Oxford University Press, Oxford, 2011), p. 28; Burton, *Traffic and Turning*, p. 163; Deanne Williams, *The French Fetish from Chaucer to Shakespeare* (Cambridge University Press, Cambridge, 2004), pp. 51–2.
37. *Henry V*, 3.1.34.
38. John Calvin, *Institutes of the Christian Religion*, ed. John Allen, 2 vols. (Thomas Regg, London, 1844), vol. 2, pp. 94–5.
39. Foxe, *The Unabridged Acts and Monuments Online or TAMO* (1573 edn). Available from: http//www.johnfoxe.org, 1570 edn, Book 6, p. 893.
40. Ronald Lightbown, *Carlo Crivelli* (Yale University Press, New Haven, 2004), p. 117.

41. Edward Seymour Forster (ed.), *The Turkish Letters of Ogier Ghiselin de Busbecq* (1927; reprinted Oxford University Press, Oxford, 1968), pp. 54–5.
42. Ibid., pp. 56, 131.
43. Edmund Spenser, *The Faerie Queene*, Book 1.1.2. This and all references to Spenser's poem are taken from Edmund Spenser, *The Faerie Queene*, ed. Thomas P. Roche (Penguin, London, 1978).
44. Ibid., Book 1.2.12.
45. Ibid., Book 1.10.40.
46. Ibid., Book 1.10.61.
47. Brotton and Jardine, *Global Interests*, pp. 13–23.
48. Spenser, *Faerie Queene*, Book 5.8.51.
49. Ibid., Book 5.8.28.
50. Ibid., Book 5.8.41.
51. Benedict Robinson, *Islam and Early Modern English Literature* (Palgrave, Basingstoke, 2007), pp. 33–56.
52. Richard Johnson, *The Famous History of the Seven Champions of Christendom* (London, 1596), pp. 16, 21.
53. Ibid., p. 23.
54. Ibid., p. 101.
55. *Henry V*, 5.2.193–6.
56. Ibid., Epilogue, 9-13.
57. Foster (ed.), *John Sanderson*, p. 242.
58. Hakluyt, vol. 1, p. 43.
59. CSPD, vol. 6: 1598–1601, 31 January 1599, p. 156.
60. CSPV, vol. 9: 1592–1603, no. 814, p. 375.
61. Ibid., 2 October 1599, no. 817, p. 377.
62. Thomas Dallam, 'The Diary of Master Thomas Dallam, 1599–1600', in J. Theodore Bent (ed.), *Early Voyages and Travels in the Levant* (Hakluyt Society, London, 1893) pp. 1–99: pp. 67–8.
63. Ibid., pp. 74–5.
64. Ibid., p. 84.
65. Quoted in Pierce, *Imperial Harem*, p. 228. This amends the version translated in Skilliter, 'Three Letters', p. 139.
66. Skilliter, 'Three Letters', p. 139 n. 57.
67. Ibid., p. 143.
68. Alison Games, *The Web of Empire: English Cosmopolitans in an Age of Expansion, 1560–1660* (Oxford University Press, Oxford, 2008), p. 171.
69. Quoted in Skilliter, 'Three Letters', p. 153.
70. 'Dallam, Thomas (*bap.* 1575, *d.* in or after 1630)', ODNB.

CHAPTER 10: SHERLEY FEVER

1. *Twelfth Night*, 1.2.52.
2. Ibid., 5.1.365.
3. Ibid., 3.2.67–8.
4. Patricia Parker, '*Twelfth Night*: Editing Puzzles and Eunuchs of all Kinds', in James Schiffer (ed.), *Twelfth Night: New Critical Essays* (Routledge, London, 2011), pp. 45–64: p. 47. On Wright's map see Helen Wallis, 'Edward Wright and the 1599 World Map', in D. B. Quinn (ed.), *The Hakluyt Handbook*, 2 vols. (Hakluyt Society, Cambridge, 1974), vol. 1, pp. 69–73.
5. *Twelfth Night*, 2.5.156–7.
6. Ibid., 3.4.243–8.
7. See Richard Wilson, ' "When Golden Time Convents": *Twelfth Night* and Shakespeare's Eastern Promise', *Shakespeare*, 6, 2 (2010), pp. 209–26.
8. Samuel Purchas, *Hakluytus Posthumus, or Purchas His Pilgrimes*, 20 vols. (James MacLehose, Glasgow, 1905), vol. 1, p. 374.
9. Quoted in R. M. Savory, 'The Sherley Myth', *Iran*, 5 (1967), pp. 73–81.
10. *Gentleman's Magazine*, new series, vol. 22 (1844), p. 474.
11. See Sir Edward Denison Ross, *Sir Anthony Sherley and his Persian Adventure* (Routledge, London, 1933); Boies Penrose, *The Sherleian Odyssey: Being a Record of the Travels and Adventures of Three Famous Brothers during the Reigns of Elizabeth, James I, and Charles I* (Simpkin Marshall, London, 1938); D. W. Davies, *Elizabethans Errant: The Strange Fortunes of Sir Thomas Sherley and his Three Sons, as well in the Dutch Wars as in Muscovy, Morocco, Persia, Spain, and the Indies* (Cornell University Press, Ithaca, NY, 1967); Kurosh Meshkat, 'Sir Anthony Sherley's Journey to Persia, 1598–1599', PhD thesis, Queen Mary University of London, 2013.
12. Ross, *Sherley*, pp. 86–7.
13. Penrose, *Sherleian Odyssey*, p. 245.
14. CP, Part 4, 2 May 1594, p. 522.
15. CP, Part 8, 30 December 1597, p. 526.
16. CP, Part 8, March 1598, pp. 116–17. See Sanjay Subrahmanyam, *Three Ways to be an Alien: Travails and Encounters in the Early Modern World* (Brandeis University Press, Waltham, MA, 2011), pp. 91–2. A different translation appears in Davies, *Elizabethans Errant*, pp. 80–81.

17. Subrahmanyam, *Three Ways*, pp. 93–5; Davies, *Elizabethans Errant*, pp. 81–3.

18. George Mainwaring, 'A True Discourse of Sir Anthony Sherley's Travel into Persia', in *The Three Brothers; or, The Travels and Adventures of Sir Anthony, Sir Robert and Sir Thomas Sherley, in Persia, Russia, Turkey, and Spain* (Hurst, Robinson, London, 1825), pp. 23–96: p. 26.

19. CSPD, vol. 7: 1601–1603, 27 June 1602, p. 209.

20. CSPD, vol. 6: 1598–1601, no. 6, p. 130.

21. Mainwaring, 'A True Discourse', pp. 34–5.

22. Ibid., p. 55.

23. William Parry, *A New and Large Discourse of the Travels of Sir Anthony Sherley Knight, by Sea and over Land to the Persian Empire* (Felix Norton, London, 1601), pp. 15, 18.

24. On Shah Abbas and Isfahan see Savory, *Iran under the Safavids*, pp. 76–103, 154–76.

25. Mainwaring, 'A True Discourse', p. 60.

26. Ibid., pp. 60–61.

27. Quoted in Ross, *Sherley*, p. 121.

28. Quoted in ibid., p. 154.

29. Quoted in ibid., p. 158.

30. Mainwaring, 'A True Discourse', p. 68.

31. Sir Anthony Sherley, *Sir Anthony Sherley his Relation of his Travels into Persia* (Nathaniel Butter, London, 1613), p. 64.

32. *A True Report of Sir Anthony Sherley's Journey* (London, 1600), sig. A4r.

33. Mainwaring, 'A True Discourse', p. 69.

34. Parry, *Discourse*, p. 21.

35. Sherley, *Relation*, p. 29.

36. Parry, *Discourse*, p. 23.

37. Ibid., p. 24.

38. Quoted in Ross, *Sherley*, pp. 159, 162, 163.

39. Sherley, *Relation*, p. 29.

40. Ibid., p. 74.

41. Ibid., pp. 79–82.

42. Ibid., pp. 83–5, 96, 106.

43. Ibid., pp. 113, 115–17.

44. Manwaring, 'A True Discourse', p. 92.

45. *True Report*, sig. B1.

46. 'Two Letters from Anthony Sherley from Russia', in Ross, *Sherley*, p. 239.

47. Quoted in Ross, *Sherley*, p. 167.
48. Parry, *Discourse*, pp. 33–4.
49. Ibid., p. 35.
50. CP, Part 10, 8 July 1600, p. 227.
51. Quoted in Ross, *Sherley*, pp. 244–6.
52. Quoted in ibid., p. 37.
53. CSPV, vol. 9: 1592–1603, no. 925, p. 431.
54. Quoted in Ross, *Sherley*, p. 41.
55. CSPV, vol. 9: 1592–1603: no. 943, p. 438.
56. Ibid., no. 940, p. 437.
57. Quoted in Davies, *Elizabethans Errant*, p. 132.
58. Quoted in ibid., p. 133.
59. Quoted in Ross, *Sherley*, p. 47.
60. Quoted in Penrose, *Sherleian Odyssey*, pp. 107–8; and Davies, *Elizabethans Errant*, pp. 134–5.
61. 'Devereux, Robert, second earl of Essex (1565–1601)', ODNB.
62. Quoted in Ross, *Sherley*, pp. 49–50.
63. Quoted in Evelyn Philip Shirley, *The Sherley Brothers: An Historical Memoir of the Lives of Sir Thomas Sherley, Sir Anthony Sherley and Sir Robert Sherley, Knights* (London, 1848), p. 33.
64. Quoted in Penrose, *Sherleian Odyssey*, p. 125.
65. Quoted in ibid., pp. 127–8.
66. Quoted in ibid., p. 256.
67. TNA, SP 94/23/258, Cottington to Naunton, 12 December 1619.
68. Scott Surtees, *William Shakespeare, of Stratford-on-Avon, His Epitaph Unearthed, and the Author of the Plays run to Ground* (Henry Grey, London, 1888), pp. 21–2. On Sherley and Surtees see Subrahmanyam, *Three Ways*, pp. 79–80. See also Jonathan Sell, *Rhetoric and Wonder in English Travel Writing, 1560–1613* (Ashgate, Aldershot, 2006), pp. 105–11.

CHAPTER 11: MORE THAN A MOOR

1. Castries, vol. 2, pp. 143–5.
2. Ibid., p. 146.
3. Ibid., p. 160.
4. Ibid., pp. 161–2.
5. Ibid., pp. 165–7.
6. Willan, *Foreign Trade*, pp. 302–3.

7. Matar, *Britain and Barbary*, pp. 26–7. I am grateful to Professor Matar for personal correspondence on the portrait and al-Annuri's Morisco heritage.

8. Castries, vol. 2, p. 192.

9. Ibid., p. 199.

10. Stow, *Annales*, p. 791. See also Castries, vol. 2, p. 203.

11. Castries, vol. 2, pp. 194–5.

12. Ibid., p. 200.

13. Stow, *Annales*, p. 791.

14. Ibid., p. 791.

15. P. L. Hughes and J. F. Larkin (eds.), *Tudor Royal Proclamations*, 3 vols. (Yale University Press, New Haven, 1964), vol. 3, pp. 221–2.

16. CP, Part 10, p. 399; Davies, *Elizabeths Errant*, pp. 187–8.

17. Quoted in Matar, *Britain and Barbary*, p. 27.

18. Castries, vol. 2, pp. 208–9.

19. Ibid., p. 196.

20. Ralph Carr, *The Mahumetane or Turkish Historie Containing Three Books* (Thomas Este, London, 1600), unpaginated 'Preface', and p. 103.

21. Ibid., p. 5.

22. Ibid., p. 1.

23. All references to the play are from Fredson Bowers (ed.), *The Dramatic Works of Thomas Dekker*, 4 vols. (Cambridge University Press, Cambridge, 1961), vol. 4, pp. 115–230. On the question of the play's complicated authorship and date see Charles Cathcart, 'Lusts's Dominion; or, The Lascivious Queen: Authorship, Date, and Revision', *Review of English Studies*, 52, 207 (2001), pp. 360–75.

24. Dekker, *Lust's Dominion*, 1.1.151–2.

25. Ibid., 1.2.158.

26. Ibid., 1.2.156.

27. Ibid., 5.3.166.

28. Ibid., 5.3.182–3.

29. Bartels, *Speaking of the Moor*, pp. 118–37.

30. All references to the play are from Matthew Dimmock (ed.), *William Percy's Mahomet and His Heaven: A Critical Edition* (Ashgate, Aldershot, 2006). Dimmock discusses the difficulties of the play's date and its various titles, including *Arabia Sitiens, or A Dream of a Dry Year, Epimenide Grand Empress of the Deserts of Arabia* and *The Weather-Woman*.

31. These names are listed in the play's 'Names of the Persons', in ibid., pp. 60–61.

32. Percy, *Mahomet*, 'The Properties'.

33. Ibid., 1.1.26.

34. Ibid., 1.1.31, 49.

35. Ibid., 4.3.347.

36. Ibid., 4.6.37.

37. Ibid., 5.4.6.

38. Ibid., 5.13, s.d.

39. Ibid., 5.13.3–4.

40. Ibid., 5.13.129, s.d.

41. Ibid., 5.13.9–14.

42. Joel B. Altman, *The Improbability of Othello: Rhetorical Anthropology and Shakespearean Selfhood* (University of Chicago Press, Chicago, 2010).

43. For the most comprehensive and up-to-date account of the play's dating and textual history see E. A. J. Honigmann, *The Texts of 'Othello' and Shakespearian Revision* (Arden, London, 1996) and his Arden Shakespeare edition of *Othello*, pp. 344–67.

44. Thomas Rymer, 'A Short View of Tragedy' [1693], in Curt Zimansky (ed.), *The Critical Works of Thomas Rymer* (Yale University Press, New Haven, 1956), pp. 132–64: p. 133.

45. Thomas Middleton Raysor (ed.), *Coleridge's Shakespeare Criticism*, 2 vols. (Harvard University Press, Cambridge, MA, 1930), vol. 1, p. 47.

46. Ben Okri, 'Leaping out of Shakespeare's Terror: Five Meditations on *Othello*', in *A Way of Being Free* (Phoenix, London, 1997), pp. 71–87: p. 80.

47. Ibid., p. 72.

48. See 'race, n.6', OED Online.

49. *Antony and Cleopatra*, 3.13.107.

50. *Othello*, 1.1.56–7, 64.

51. Ibid., 1.1.85–90.

52. Ibid., 1.1.109–12.

53. Ibid., 1.1.114–15.

54. Ibid., 1.1.132–5.

55. Ibid., 1.2.17–22.

56. Ibid., 1.3.8.

57. Ibid., 1.3.49–52.

58. Ibid., 1.3.129–47.

59. Natalie Zemon Davis, *Trickster Travels: In Search of Leo Africanus, a Sixteenth-Century Muslim between Worlds* (Hill & Wang, New York, 2006).

60. *Othello*, 3.1.172, 170.
61. Ibid., 3.1.293–4.
62. Ibid., 2.1.21–2, 201.
63. Ibid., 2.3.166–8.
64. Barbara Everett, '"Spanish" *Othello*: The Making of Shakespeare's Moor', *Shakespeare Survey*, 35 (1982), pp. 101–12; and Eric Griffin 'Unsainting James: or, *Othello* and the "Spanish Spirits" of Shakespeare's Globe', *Representations*, 62 (1998), pp. 58–99.
65. *Othello*, 2.1.114.
66. Ibid., 3.3.456–63.
67. Ibid., 4.3.17.
68. Ibid., 4.3.24–31.
69. Ibid., 4.3.51–2.
70. Ernest Brennecke, '"Nay, That's Not Next!": The Significance of Desdemona's "Willow Song"', *Shakespeare Quarterly*, 4, 1 (1953), pp. 35–8.
71. *Othello*, 5.2.298–9.
72. Ibid., 5.2.300–301.
73. Ibid., 5.2.336–54.
74. Honigmann (ed.), *Othello*, pp. 342–43; Richard Levin, 'The Indian/ Iudean Crux in *Othello*', *Shakespeare Quarterly*, 33, 1 (1982), pp. 60–67.
75. Quoted in James Craigie (ed.), *The Poems of James VI of Scotland* (Blackwood, Edinburgh, 1955), p. 202.

EPILOGUE

1. Bruce McGowan, *Economic Life in Ottoman Europe: Taxation, Trade and the Struggle for Land, 1600–1800* (Cambridge University Press, Cambridge, 1981), p. 21; Wood, *Levant Company*, p. 42; Lewis Roberts, *A Merchant's Mappe of Commerce* (London, 1638), pp. 79–80.
2. W. B. Patterson, *King James VI and I and the Reunion of Christendom* (Cambridge University Press, Cambridge, 1997), pp. 196–219.
3. John Jowett (ed.), *Sir Thomas More: Original Text by Anthony Munday and George Chettle* (Arden, London, 2011). All references to the play are from this edition. Jowett dates the original text to c. 1600, in contrast to earlier critics who dated it to c. 1593–5, during the period of anti-alien insurrections. Jowett dates Shakespeare's revised additions to c. 1603–4.
4. Ibid., 6.83–98.

5. Ibid., 6.138–56. In his essay 'On "Montanish Inhumanyty" in *Sir Thomas More*', *Studies in Philology*, 103, 2 (2006), pp. 178–85, Karl P. Wentersdorf argues that 'mountainish' should be read as 'Mohammetanish', an intriguing possibility that would make it Shakespeare's second direct reference to the Prophet Muhammad after the example discussed above in *Henry VI*.

6. The point is made in Charles Nicholl, *The Lodger: Shakespeare on Silver Street* (Penguin, London, 2007), pp. 175–88.

7. *The Tempest*, 1.2.194.

8. Ibid., 1.2.259.

9. Ibid., 2.1.230, 235.

10. Ibid., 1.2.263.

11. Ibid., 2.1.82.

12. Ibid., 2.1.242–3.

13. Ibid., 2.1.125.

14. Quoted in Christopher Brook, Roger Highfield and Wim Swaan, *Oxford and Cambridge* (Cambridge University Press, Cambridge, 1988), p. 180.

15. G. J. Toomer, *Eastern Wisedome and Learning: The Study of Arabic in Seventeenth-Century England* (Oxford University Press, Oxford, 1996), pp. 111–26.

16. Authorship of the 1649 translation remains contested, with arguments for and against a variety of candidates: Alexander Ross, Thomas Ross or Hugh Ross. See Noel Malcolm, 'The 1649 English Translation of the Koran: Its Origins and Significance', *Journal of the Warburg and Courtauld Institutes*, 75 (2012), pp. 261–95; Mordechai Feingold, ' "The Turkish Alcoran": New Light on the 1649 English Translation of the Koran', *Huntington Library Quarterly*, 75, 4 (2012), pp. 475–501.

Acknowledgements

Writing acknowledgements brings with it the realization that the origins of a book often go back much further than its author has appreciated. In my case they reach all the way to my inspirational English teacher at secondary school, Maggie Sheen, who first interested me in Shakespeare. She started me on a path that eventually led to this book, and another important figure in my life, my great mentor, collaborator and friend Lisa Jardine. In the 1990s Lisa and I worked together on exchanges between western and eastern cultures in the Renaissance. Lisa's untimely death in the autumn of 2015 robbed the country of one of its great public intellectuals, and left me bereft of a dear friend and confidante who made me believe anything was possible. I wish she were still with us for many reasons, not least to see the publication of a book that, like its subject, is haunted by her absent presence.

Family and friends provided practical support, shrewd guidance and less tangible but equally crucial care and encouragement as I have tussled with this book. For that I would like to thank Peter Barber, Shaul Bassi, Jonathan Burton, Miles and Ranj Carter, Jonathan and Rachel Christie, Rebecca Chamberlain, Nick Crane, Kath Diamond, Simon Curtis, Dave and Sarah Griffiths, Lucy Hannington and Bence Hegedus, Helen Leblique, Ita MacCarthy, Lucy and Al Myers, Nick Millea, Patricia Parker, Mark Rickards, Richard Scholar, Vik Sivalingam, Guy Richards Smit, Mike Spink, Tim Supple, Ben and Katherine Turney, Dave and Emily Vest and Dan Vitkus. Emma and James Lambe provided their characteristically unwavering calm and unhesitating domestic help. Nabil Matar advised me on matters of dating and al-Annuri (and his peerless work in the field continues

ACKNOWLEDGEMENTS

to be an inspiration), Alexander Samson kindly shared unpublished research with me, Mia Hewitt and Alice Agossini helped translate documents from the Spanish, Ton Hoenselaars read related articles and encouraged me to continue writing when I thought the project had defeated me, as did my dear old friend Maurizio Calbi. I am grateful to Patrick Spottiswoode, Director of Education at the Globe Theatre, for inviting me to hold the International Shakespeare Globe Fellowship in 2004 on the topic of 'Shakespeare and Islam', which allowed me to develop some of this book's ideas; William Dalrymple for allowing me a memorable opportunity to present the work in Jaipur; and to Peter Florence, who generously allows me to say and do wonderful things at his remarkable festivals in Hay and beyond. The dream team of my editor Stuart Proffitt at Allen Lane – supported by Ben Sinyor, Pen Vogler and Richard Duguid – and my agent Peter Straus at Rogers, Coleridge and White rose to the occasion yet again, and once more Cecilia Mackay proved herself to be the best picture researcher in the business. Peter James did a marvellous and unexpectedly poignant job copy-editing the text.

Every book I have ever written has celebrated the unique environment provided by Queen Mary University of London, where I have studied and worked for over twenty years. A dedicated team of people within the School of English and Drama make my working environment a real pleasure, and for that I want to thank Jonathan Boffey, Richard Coulton, Rob Ellis, Jenny Gault, Patricia Hamilton, Suzi Lewis, Huw Marsh, Matthew Mauger, Kate Russell and Bev Stewart. I am also proud to be an associate of the People's Palace Projects at Queen Mary, led by the inspirational Paul Heritage, and thank him and his team, especially Rosie Hunter and Thiago Jesus, for allowing me to work with them in Brazil on Shakespeare and many other exciting initiatives. Among my colleagues I am lucky enough to have the support and friendship of Ruth Ahnert, John Barrell (who goes back even further), Michèle Barrett, Julia Boffey, Mark Currie, Markman Ellis, Katie Fleming, Paul Hamilton, Alfred Hiatt, Pete Mitchell, Claire Preston, Yossef Rapoport, Kirsty Rolfe, Morag Shiach, Bill Schwarz and Andrew van der Vlies. Acting as Associate Director on my old friend David Schalkwyk's 'Global Shakespeare' project has also given me fantastic opportunities to explore Shakespeare beyond this sceptred isle. It would embarrass David Colclough were I to tell him how much I cherish our enduring friendship, so I will stop here. I seem to have a weakness for Miltonists, because Joad Raymond has become a great friend since his arrival at Queen Mary, and I hope our alliance will generate more than one Penguin.

Several people were kind enough to read the whole manuscript and pointed out various omissions and infelicities. Matthew Dimmock and Gerald 'Mac' MacLean gave me the benefit of their unrivalled expertise in the field, while the masterly Timothy Brook and his wife Fay offered sage advice on tone and structure. I am extremely grateful to them for taking time out of their busy schedules: friends indeed. Adam Lowe watched it all unfold from faraway, but is always near at hand, and I am very luck to have him. My father, Alan Brotton, has not read the book, nor should he: all he needs to know is the love and admiration I feel for him sticking by me long enough for us to understand how much we care for each other.

The book is dedicated to my wife Charlotte, not to settle a debt, but to honour a meeting of minds. A distinguished Shakespeare scholar in her own right, she read and commented on every line of this book, improving it immeasurably while also writing her own, bringing our daughter Honey into the world, and holding everyone in our family together with an effortlessness borne of supreme endeavour. She will understand if I leave it to Shakespeare to tell her that my bounty is as boundless as the sea, my love as deep; the more I give to her, the more I have, for both are infinite.

Index